The Good War That Wasn't—and Why It Matters

The Good War That Wasn't— and Why It Matters

World War II's Moral Legacy

TED GRIMSRUD

CASCADE *Books* · Eugene, Oregon

THE GOOD WAR THAT WASN'T—AND WHY IT MATTERS
World War II's Moral Legacy

Copyright © 2014 Ted Grimsrud. All rights reserved. Except for brief quotations in critical publications or reviews, no part of this book may be reproduced in any manner without prior written permission from the publisher. Write: Permissions, Wipf and Stock Publishers, 199 W. 8th Ave., Suite 3, Eugene, OR 97401.

Cascade Books
An Imprint of Wipf and Stock Publishers
199 W. 8th Ave., Suite 3
Eugene, OR 97401

www.wipfandstock.com

ISBN 13: 978-1-62564-102-1

Cataloging-in-Publication data:

Grimsrud, Ted, 1954–

    The good war that wasn't—and why it matters : World War II's moral legacy / Ted Grimsrud.

    x + 286 p. ; 23 cm. —Includes bibliographical references and indexes.

    ISBN 13: 978-1-62564-102-1

    1. World War, 1939–1945—Moral and ethical aspects. I. Title.

D743 .G75 2014

Manufactured in the U.S.A.

For all the warriors for peace who have challenged and inspired me, including, among many others:

The World War II conscientious objectors

Vietnam War–era prophets such as Earl and Pat Hostetter Martin

My teachers of blessed memory, John Howard Yoder, Walter Wink, and Gordon Kaufman

My life partner, Kathleen Temple, and my sister, Sally Grimsrud

And, maybe most of all, Johan Grimsrud and Jill Humphrey, who (with Elias and Marja) remind me why the fight must continue

Contents

Preface ix

1. Introduction: The United States and the Myth of Redemptive Violence 1

PART ONE: Total War

2. Why Did America Go to War? 27
3. Was America's Conduct in World War II Just? 54
4. What Did the War Cost? 78

PART TWO: Aftermath

5. Pax Americana 103
6. The Cold War 126
7. Full Spectrum Dominance 149

PART THREE: Alternatives

8. No to the War 175
9. Social Transformation 198
10. Servanthood 221
11. Conclusion: World War II's Moral Legacy 244

Bibliography 267
Name Index 277
Subject Index 283

Preface

I have lived with World War II all my life. I remember, now with shame, playing "bombs over Tokyo" as a child in the late 1950s and early 1960s in western Oregon. It was "the War," a defining event for both of my parents—for one thing, it brought them together. I grew up believing this indeed was a "good war."

My views long ago changed, and I came to believe that no war could possibly be good. However, the beliefs I grew up with about the "good war" are widespread. They have been expressed by countless conversation partners I have had over many years. Since these conversations are always too short to give the beliefs about World War II adequate scrutiny, I decided to write this book as an extended version of my side of the ongoing conversation.

I am grateful for the many people and institutions that have encouraged me to keep talking and thinking and writing about World War II and about war and peace more generally. I am able to mention only a few in this short space.

Eastern Mennonite University has provided a place for many conversations about peace issues and much encouragement for the work of peace theology. I deeply appreciate the friendships and academic stimulation—and, most practically in relation to this book, the yearlong sabbatical during the 2010–11 school year when I completed the first draft of the book.

Ever since I studied the phenomenon of conscientious objection to World War II for my doctoral dissertation in the mid-1980s, I have drawn inspiration from the experiences of those few who, at great cost, said no and testified to the reality that the embrace of war was not unanimous in their society. Not many survive now, but their witness lives on. I offer this book in gratitude to them.

In the years since the 1970s, I have come to know many people who actively opposed one of the most terrible wars in modern times, the U.S. war in Southeast Asia. Some of the first were vets I met in college who spoke against the war after returning home. Others were antiwar activists. Maybe the most inspirational have been a few I have become friends with who put their own lives on the line to live in Vietnam during the war years and seek to help repair at least a little of the damage the war caused, including especially Earl and Pat Hostetter Martin.

Though I am comfortable with the label "theologian," in this book I do little overt theological reflection. But I would not want to suggest that my theological sensibilities are absent—they are probably present in ways I can't even see myself. In any writing I do, my main theological mentors are always present, even if subconsciously. Two of the three most important, Gordon Kaufman (himself a World War II CO) and Walter Wink, have passed on in recent years. I miss their presence—as I still miss the presence of my third mentor, John Howard Yoder.

I am certain that this book would never have seen the light of day apart from the steady encouragement of my wife, Kathleen Temple. Her most recent, deeply appreciated, contribution was to join me on a wonderful weeklong road trip along the Blue Ridge Parkway and Natchez Trace Parkway—and to read the entire penultimate draft of this book aloud. My sister, Sally Grimsrud, also graciously read earlier drafts of almost all the chapters. Both made many helpful suggestions.

Though our son Johan and his wife Jill didn't contribute directly to this book, by living their own integrity-filled lives and by bringing Elias and Marja into the world, they inspire and motivate me more than I can ever say.

1

Introduction: The United States and the Myth of Redemptive Violence

TAKING THE MEASURE OF *THE* WAR

World War II was big, maybe the biggest event in human history. During the six years of what became an immense global conflict, as many as eighty million people lost their lives. That's more than the entire population of most countries. Many times more people had their lives profoundly traumatized. Uncounted millions were displaced. The earth itself suffered immense damage. The War's[1] impact remains present and alive throughout the world. It has shaped the morality of all subsequent generations. For many, especially in the world's "one superpower," the United States of America, World War II remains the historical and moral touchstone for understanding the necessity and even moral "goodness" of military force.[2]

My own life, in ways typical for Americans of my generation, has been shaped by the War. Both of my parents served in the U.S. Army. My father, Carl Grimsrud, enlisted in the National Guard in 1941. After Japan's attack on Pearl Harbor (December 7, 1941), he was pressed into active duty. The Army placed him in eastern Oregon to guard against a feared Japanese

---

1. I grew up with World War II being referred to as "the War." Throughout this book, I will use the uppercase "War" to refer to World War II.

2. Two widely influential expressions of this cultural embrace of the "goodness" of the War in the United States were Tom Brokaw's bestselling book *The Greatest Generation* and the popular PBS documentary *The War* (2007), directed and produced by Ken Burns and Lynn Novick.

invasion; there he met my mother, Betty Wagner. In time, Carl was shipped to the South Pacific, where he spent three intense years—he was wounded, he killed, he contracted malaria, but he managed to survive, even to thrive. He received a battlefield commission and reached the rank of captain. As the Army later demobilized, he was asked to stay in and make a career of the military, with the promise of further advancement. He said no, not because of any negative feelings about "the Service," but because he had made a commitment to Betty to return to Oregon and establish a life together. While Carl served in combat, Betty worked as a military recruiter, gaining the rank of sergeant prior to her discharge.

My father never talked with me about his experience. (Actually, there was *one* conversation. When I was seventeen, he told me how meaningful his experience was in the context of encouraging me to consider applying to one of the military academies for college. When I showed no interest, he dropped the subject.) He did share one important part of his experience, though. He had a close friend in the Army who died in combat. His name was Ted.

There was another way the War impacted my life. I was born in 1954, my parents' fourth child. Their mixture of blood types made me an "Rh factor" baby. For the mother, this condition gets worse with each pregnancy. By the time I came along, it was bad enough that if left to my own devices as a newborn, I would not have been able to create my own blood and I would have perished. Medicine was learning how to combat this condition, and one type of intervention that met with success was total blood transfusions for the baby. Few pediatricians had yet mastered the procedure—mainly those who had served in the War and learned about blood transfusions through working on severely wounded soldiers. It happened that in our small hospital in Eugene, Oregon, we did have one such doctor, who saved my life with this new procedure.

So, World War II brought my parents together, it provided my name, and it made the medical intervention that saved my life possible. But the War also shaped me as an American in other ways. It provided a mythology of the redemptive possibilities of violence. It was a "good war" that defended the American way of life and defeated forces that were clearly evil. As such, it set the tone for belief that America was a force for good in the world, that America's ongoing military actions were in continuity with the Good War, and that just as my parents served this good in the world with their military service, so should I be ready to do the same.

I'll say more later in this chapter about how I personally came to *disbelieve* in the redemptive possibilities of violence (what I will call "the myth of redemptive violence"). However, I have been unusual in my disbelief.

Introduction: The United States and the Myth of Redemptive Violence

Perhaps in large part because Americans mostly experienced the benefits of being on the winning side of World War II without much of the cost of destructive side of the War,[3] it was easy for young people growing up in the 1950s and 1960s to accept without much dissonance the idea that war can be a good thing, that at times it is necessary, and that Americans in particular almost always fight in good wars.

The U.S. war on Vietnam created significant disillusionment concerning America's wars, and subsequent military actions have also contributed to serious doubt about their goodness by some in our society. Nonetheless, the general orientation I grew up with concerning the positive value of preparing for and when necessary fighting in "good wars" and certainty about America's goodness in her wars has remained widespread. Witness the almost complete unanimity in the U.S. concerning the attacks on Afghanistan following the trauma of September 11, 2001. Witness also the sacrosanct character of the U.S. military budget that dominates federal spending even in times of budget crises and spiraling national debt (and that nearly matches the total military spending of all the rest of the world combined).[4]

I encounter this positive orientation toward America's war fighting preparations and history of good wars regularly—and I usually see it overtly linked with U.S. involvement in World War II. As a convinced pacifist who teaches college classes in ethics, I make a point to introduce students to the ideals of principled nonviolence. The most instructive encounters with students generally come in my introductory ethics course, which is required for a cross section of the students at our college. Many of these students have never heard of pacifism before. Quite a few of them come from families with long histories of participation in the military.

Time after time, year after year, students are taken aback by my principled opposition to war. They quickly evoke World War II, the need to defeat Hitler and the Nazis, and the lack of any other viable alternatives to stop such overwhelming evil. One student spoke for many others in class in the immediate aftermath of the attacks of September 11, 2001: "Why would they be attacking us? We've never done anyone wrong. The U.S. stands for freedom, democracy, and against tyranny. Look what we did to stop Hitler."

Not only conservatives and strong believers in the virtues of the American military evoke the battle against Hitler and the Good War as

---

3. See Sheehan, *Where Have All the Soldiers Gone?* Sheehan shows how direct experience of the destructiveness of the two world wars has led even the European nations who were victorious in those wars to move away from militarism in recent years.

4. In December 2010, *New York Times* columnist Nicolas Kristof wrote a succinct essay titled "The Big (Military) Taboo" that summarized these points. Sadly, this column serves as the exception that proves the rule—a voice crying in the wilderness.

the definitive refutation of pacifism. Even progressive do it. Katha Pollitt, a decidedly leftist columnist for the politically progressive and antimilitarist magazine *The Nation*,[5] attacks pacifism in her sharply critical column on Nicholson Baker's book on World War II, *Human Smoke*. Pollitt begins her column by stating that after reading Baker's book she "felt fury at pacifists" and concludes that Franklin Roosevelt and Winston Churchill "got it right" when they realized that only massive violence could stop the Nazis.[6]

Such evocations of World War II seem to make war in general seem more acceptable. If we have a clear case of a necessary and, to some extent, redemptive war in history, we more easily imagine war being necessary in the future. And because war may be necessary in the future (as it was in the past), it is necessary now to prepare for war by devoting massive resources to the military. That is, when we sustain the myth of redemptive violence in relation to World War II, we will find it much more difficult not to accept that myth in relation to our current cultural context.

So, my concern in this book ultimately is with our current cultural context, the ways that wars and preparation for wars are tolerated, even embraced. I want to examine one key element of America's toleration of present-day militarism—the belief that America's military involvement in the greatest event of human history (World War II) was necessary, good, and even redemptive.

In this book, I offer an essay in moral philosophy with historical illustrations. I do not make any claims to originality in my use of the historical cases. I will rely on the work of historians, political thinkers, and moral philosophers. Perhaps my synthesis of their ideas and application to my own agenda will be distinctive, but my main goal is to raise questions, not to provide new information. I will raise questions that are not often asked. And I will offer responses to those questions that I believe could help free Americans from the spiral of violence heightened by acceptance of the myth of redemptive violence.

I have three sets of questions and issues I will engage. First, I will look at the War itself through moral eyes and ask whether it had just causes and employed just means. Second, I will consider the aftermath of World War II, especially as the American experience of the War has shaped U.S. foreign policy in the years since. The sum of my examination of these first two sets of questions and issues will be a sharp critique of the mythology that World War II *and its legacy* have had a redemptive impact on the world. This

---

5. For example, *The Nation* provided one of the rare venues for writing that consistently opposed the Bush administration's attacks on Afghanistan after 9/11.

6. Pollitt, "Blowing Smoke," 9.

Introduction: The United States and the Myth of Redemptive Violence

critique will lead to the third set of questions and issues: are there viable nonviolent alternatives to seeking human well-being in the face of tyranny and aggression?

Looking at World War II "through moral eyes" puts the ethical criteria that make up "the just war theory" on the table. As a pacifist, I do not see the just war theory to be an adequate moral response to the question of support for war. However, in ways that pacifism can't (since it does not reason about war's bases and conduct so much as simply deny the moral validity of all wars), the just war tradition offers us a framework for evaluating the morality of particular wars. So I will have in mind various just war criteria as they apply to the actual war we call World War II. Along with the more abstract traditional just war criteria, I will also seek to use as bases for moral evaluation the stated ideals that American leaders and their allies used to justify involvement in this war. I will summarize these in the next section of this Introduction.

I will reflect on the legacy of the War using moral criteria that can help us discern whether it was a "good" or "just" war. I do this in order to ask our moral reasoning to "have teeth."[7] I challenge those who think of World War II as a "good war" (with the recognition that the notion of "good" here is a moral notion that implies not all wars are "good" and we have some bases for determining what is "good" and what is not "good") to think more carefully about that assignation. Further, I hope to show that if "goodness" is our fundamental criterion, we in fact should rethink our affirmation of World War II. And if World War II does not actually serve as an example of a "good war," then it also should not serve as a basis for our acceptance of contemporary American military policies, practices, and claims.

I will test two main theses in the pages to come: (1) *For the United States, World War II was morally problematic, not morally good.* American leaders addressed authentic concerns when they made the moral case for entering World War II: the German threat in Europe and the military aggression of the Japanese in the Pacific. However, if we think of the War as a "tool" that served some morally valid goals, when we consider the actual execution of the War itself we will see that this "tool" broke free from the moral sensibilities that justified its use. In the course of the War, the linkage between the stated moral values and the actual practices became

---

7. This demand that moral reasoning, specifically the just war philosophy, "have teeth" is inspired by John Howard Yoder's challenging book *When War Is Unjust*. Yoder, himself a widely influential pacifist, seeks to take just war philosophy seriously. He asks its adherents to think about how to apply their convictions when faced with wars that do not meet their criteria for a just war.

increasingly tenuous. Thus, by August 1945, the moral legacy of World War II in terms of its immediate justification had already become ambiguous.

When we follow the story through the postwar years, the War's legacy becomes even more problematic. World War II transformed the United States. This transformation has resulted in a series of military interventions that share none of the possible moral defensibility of the initial entry into World War II. The "tool" came to dominate American foreign policy, leading to one violation after another of the criteria for just war.

So, if we look at World War II in its immediate context, we do see the U.S. responding to immoral actions by the Germans and the Japanese. However, the U.S. fought in ways that contradicted the moral values that had justified the nation's involvement. When we consider the overall impact of World War II on America, we may be led to conclude that it was not a "good" war at all. It was a war that in the long term undermined the very moral values that had led to its support by millions of Americans.

(2) When we conclude that World War II was not a "good" or justifiable or even necessary war even as it was fought to support important moral values, we need not conclude that those moral values could not be (and were not) furthered. So, this is my second thesis: *There are alternatives to war that address authentic moral concerns raised by injustice and tyranny.*

Part One of this book will examine the events of World War II. Part Two will look at the War's aftermath, focusing especially on its impact on American foreign policy. And Part Three will provide examples of how the moral ideals that stood at the center of the Allied rationale for going to war actually were furthered by committed people generally operating outside the auspices of nation-states and practice of warfare.

WHY MORALITY IS NOT A PERIPHERAL ISSUE

To insist that the issue of warfare is inherently a *moral* issue is not simply to take a naïve, idealistic stance of trying to impose values on a situation that is inherently amoral. From start to finish, from the ground to the planning room, for all actors, warfare is infused with moral choices, moral convictions, and moral priorities.

I suspect if we looked at every war that societies have fought we would see that the rationale for the war and, especially, the appeals that were made to gain people's support and participation in the war were overtly couched in moral terms. Certainly, this would be the case for World War II, probably on all fronts but without a doubt in the United States.

Introduction: The United States and the Myth of Redemptive Violence

The Atlantic Charter was the foundational statement of war aims stated by American president Franklin Roosevelt and British prime minister Winston Churchill in August 1941.[8] The American government used the Charter as a central appeal to gain support for involvement in the War. The Atlantic Charter served as the core content in the January 1, 1942, Declaration of Shared Commitment by the twenty-six nations that made up the first "United Nations" who joined together to defeat the "Tripartite Pact" (Germany, Italy, and Japan).[9]

The Charter emphasized a couple of main points: the centrality of self-determination for the world's people and the need to disarm first the aggressor nations (the Axis powers) and ultimately all other nations. These two key moral appeals—that all people have the right of self-determination and that the world needs to be disarmed—indeed did stand at the center of the meaning the War had for many. The Atlantic Charter also provided the basis for a statement formulated by the American Federal Council of Churches in the midst of the War, "The Six Pillars of Peace"; released in 1943, and widely circulated, the "Six Pillars" supplied bases for a moral appeal to support and participate in the War.[10] The Six Pillars also centered on self-determination ("autonomy for subject peoples") and disarmament ("controlling military establishments everywhere").

Americans supported the War, risked their lives and their children's lives, and made other sacrifices mostly without complaint because they believed in the moral importance of this war. They understood this war to be fought in opposition to tyranny, in support of democracy, and in the hope of establishing an enduring peace that would make future wars obsolete.

Another reason for recognizing the centrality of moral convictions to the American experience of World War II (as would be the case with any other war) is that the decision intentionally to kill another human being is always a moral decision. The decision to kill is based on a sense that there are values, commitments, convictions that have enough moral weight to justify this ultimate sanction against other human beings. There are greater goods that must be furthered even when that involves overriding the general moral assumption that human life should not intentionally be taken.

---

8. For the text of the Atlantic Charter, see http://www.nato.int/cps/en/natolive/official_texts_16912.htm.

9. For the text of the Declaration, see Avalon.law.yale.edu/20th_century/decade03.asp.

10. For the text of "The Six Pillars of Peace," see http://www.stanleyfoundation.org/courier/1998summer3.html#6pillars.

The psychic cost of killing other human beings, the cost in material resources that preparation for killing in warfare requires of a society, the cost in risking one's own life to engage in warfare, the cost in war's destruction of human life and nature—all these costs can only be justified on moral grounds. There is some moral good that is seen to make the cost worthwhile, even if in part this "good" is simply resisting moral evil.

When a society makes the commitment to go to war, it makes a commitment to devote its "blood and treasure" for some purpose of high import. This purpose almost by definition must be expressed in moral terms: right versus wrong, good versus evil.

For those who fight in war, the ability to sustain the willingness to pay the extreme costs such engagement requires depends upon belief that one's cause is in the right. We have learned in recent years—in relation to America's war on Vietnam, for example—that soldiers who lose this sense of being in the right are much more prone to sustained emotional and psychological trauma after their participation in battle ends.[11]

Ultimately, warfare has to do with our convictions concerning the value of human life. This is probably the most fundamental moral issue we all face. Warfare involves making choices to end human lives. These choices are made based on moral criteria (even if not always self-consciously understood in this way). We take life because we affirm some value that must be sustained by the killing and that takes priority over the particular human lives that are ended.

Because warfare is inherently a moral issue, in trying to understand any war we have to take into account the moral convictions that justified that particular war. What values (directly or implicitly) did the arguments in favor of that war draw upon? What moral principles or assumptions drew people into the war, gained their support and undergirded their willingness to participate?

In trying to assess the moral legitimacy of any war, then, we look at the rationales that were given in favor of the war at its beginning. We then evaluate how the war itself served those rationales. Certainly, philosophers and theologians, not to mention nonacademics, have always struggled to provide clear definitions for the term *morality*. However, there is a sense that we all have some kind of awareness of morality; it seems to be in our bones as human beings and infuses our experience of life. We do find it difficult to put into words what morality precisely is. I want to suggest that part of any solid definition of morality is the notion of stability. Human morality in some sense applies over time and across communities.

11. Brock and Lettini, *Soul Repair*.

Introduction: The United States and the Myth of Redemptive Violence

The point that is crucial for our purposes here is that in making moral appeals for certain actions and responses, we make ourselves accountable to the values and convictions we base those appeals upon.

So, in relation to World War II, we may say, first of all, that Americans' involvement in the War followed from certain moral convictions. The War was understood to serve the rights of peoples to self-determination and the goal of the ultimate disarmament of all major nations in the world. Other purposes that were popularly supported included the need to defend the existence of our democratic institutions and to resist the expansionist tyrannies of Germany and Japan.

The popular moral appeals provide us with criteria for evaluating both the execution of the war during the years 1941–45 and the longer-term consequences of the War. Our reasons for making such evaluations may be simply to evaluate the moral authenticity of the War itself: was it truly a just war? Was it worth all that it cost? Was it consistent with the stated purposes for engaging in it? More importantly, though, we undertake this evaluation in order to consider how the legacy of this war might shape our current and future attitudes toward war and preparation for war.

In what follows we will engage in a moral evaluation of World War II. How do we think morally about this War that dwarfed all other wars? One way to answer this question, unfortunately often the default answer, is to *assume* that this was a necessary war, one that was fought honorably enough and was ultimately successful in defeating the evil Axis powers and furthering the cause of democracy in the world.[12] Even if not overtly couched in moral terms, this answer indeed makes a profoundly moral evaluation of the War. The operative word here, though, is *assume*. Such an answer—that American participation in World War II was self-evidently just and morally good—follows from assumptions more than from careful evaluation of the evidence.

Such a conclusion about the moral goodness (all things considered) of America's War could, however, indeed follow from careful consideration of the evidence. Certainly much evidence can be interpreted to point in this direction. However, a careful evaluation of the evidence is rarely undertaken. We may thus use the term *myth* here. We have a myth of a good war—meaning not that belief in the moral goodness of the War is a lie or

---

12. Michael Walzer, one of the more influential and careful of recent just war philosophers, nonetheless simply assumes that World War II was necessary (and, hence, just) when he dismisses as a possible criticism of that war that it was too terrible to be just. "There are acts of aggression and acts of cruelty that we ought to resist, by force if necessary. I would have thought that our experience with Nazism ended this particular argument, but the argument goes on" (*Arguing About War*, xi).

clearly wrong, but that the belief is more on the realm of acceptance by faith than of consideration of evidence.

Historian Harry Stout provides a template for a moral evaluation of a major war in his "moral history" of the American Civil War.[13] Stout uses the basic tenets of the just war theory, both those concerning just causes for going to war and just conduct in war, to provide his bases for evaluating how the Civil War began and unfolded. His analysis concludes that while the Civil War may have been justifiable from the Union side in terms of just causes, both sides egregiously violated the just conduct criteria. Unfortunately, Stout does not add what I believe is a necessary component to this kind of analysis: a moral accounting of the aftermath of the Civil War. It is impossible to evaluate the moral legacy of any war without including as a central element of the evaluation a sense of what the war actually accomplished and what consequences resulted from the war.

British historian Norman Davies discusses the importance of a moral evaluation in his one-volume history of the War. He outlines five central factors that must be part of coming to terms with the War: geographical, military, ideological, political, and moral.[14]

Under the "moral" rubric, Davies provides helpful guidelines for thinking morally about the War: "All sound moral judgments operate on the basis that the standards applied to one side in a relationship must be applied to all sides.... Secondly,... 'Patriotism is not enough.' 'My country, right or wrong' is an amoral slogan.... Lastly, it is essential that all moral judgments, all attempts to assess whether something be 'Good' or 'Evil,' be made by reference to universal principles and not to partisan feelings of hatred or contempt." To illustrate this last point, Davies cites the Nuremberg Tribunal after the War in which judges from the Allies determined the guilt or innocence of alleged Nazi war criminals. Nuremberg established categories of conduct that were asserted to apply to everyone as a basis for convicting people judged to have committed crimes against humanity.[15] Davies provides a good framework for a moral accounting of World War II—supporting my earlier comment about the importance of "stability" in moral reasoning. His book does not make the moral factor central, but he does seek more than many historians to be self-conscious about how the moral dimension does factor in.

We do have two recent books that more explicitly focus throughout on a moral evaluation of the War: Michael Bess's *Choices Under Fire: Moral*

13. Stout, *Upon the Altar*.
14. Davies, *No Simple Victory*, 9–72.
15. Ibid., 63–64.

Introduction: The United States and the Myth of Redemptive Violence

Dimensions of World War II[16] and Michael Burleigh's *Moral Combat: A History of World War II*.[17]

Bess takes a questioning approach. How did World War II stack up in relation to moral criteria? He seeks objectively to evaluate various aspects of the War on moral grounds.[18] Bess shies away from strong conclusions. The general sense he gives is that for Americans the war was necessary, and Americans fought it for just reasons. They did cross the line numerous times in the use of unjust or disproportionate means, but overall, the War was morally "good" enough, says Bess.

Burleigh, on the other hand, is more directive and certain in his conclusions. He essentially argues that the Allied cause was just; war is a nasty business that unfortunately requires actions that in normal life would be considered immoral, but the good that was served by the Allied war effort justified the at times morally ambiguous means. The big question with Burleigh's book, for our purposes, is whether he follows Davies' criteria for moral evaluation. Does he apply his moral criteria equally to all sides? Does he cross the line to make the amoral slogan "my country right or wrong" into a moral justification for otherwise morally problematic actions? Furthermore, Burleigh clearly understands the aftermath of World War II quite differently than I do. So in some ways, his book stands as an alternative interpretation of the moral legacy of World War II to mine.

In the chapters to follow I will take the moral appeals that shaped Americans' initial entry into World War II seriously. What were the criteria for a morally appropriate war that we may extrapolate from the Atlantic Charter, the Six Pillars of Peace, and other public statements (such as Franklin Roosevelt's appeal to the "Four Freedoms")? Also, I will consider the moral content of the arguments made by religious leaders such as the prominent theologian Reinhold Niebuhr in favor of intervention.

From these moral appeals, I will establish a set of values we may use to evaluate the War and its aftermath. How consistent was the execution of the War with those stated values? How well did the outcome of the War and its aftermath further the moral aspirations that provided the rationale for involvement in the War?

I will give evidence to support my argument that the execution of the War, when evaluated in light of the moral framework that justified entering

16. Bess, *Choices Under Fire*.
17. Burleigh, *Moral Combat*.
18. Bess's success in maintaining a genuinely objective stance may be seen in the hostile response he received in one forum from a historian who denies the need to ask moral questions of the Allies in the War because America's cause was so clearly just. Bergerud, "Critique of *Choices Under Fire*," 41.

it, leaves us with numerous questions. The strongest case for a positive moral evaluation is that the moral justification for entering the War was so strong that even if some of the conduct criteria were violated, the War could still be seen as justifiable. However, this case must be evaluated in relation to the sheer cost of the War. Using the criterion of proportionality, it remains a challenging question whether (thinking mainly within the chronological parameters of the War itself) the good that was achieved outweighed the enormous cost in blood and treasure.

As the war proceeded, the Allies moved further and further from the moral framework that was used to justify entering the war. For example, by the end of the War, the intentional bombing of civilian populations became a direct part of the War effort, culminating in the use of atomic bombs twice on targets that were largely nonmilitary. The "tool" of warfare increasingly took on its own logic of ever-increasing and indiscriminate violence. Hence, the War slipped ever further from the logic articulated in the Atlantic Charter that centered on democracy and demilitarization.

My central argument in Part Two of this book will be that the War's *aftermath* sheds crucial light on the War's moral legacy for the United States. As a direct consequence of World War II, America was transformed into the world's one superpower, with a permanent war economy, that in its foreign policy tended to disregard the moral logic of the rationales for entering the War.

The ongoing role World War II plays for Americans, I will suggest, makes it much easier for policymakers to pursue what has now come to be called "full spectrum dominance." Americans have by and large supported all post-World War II wars (the military engagements they have known about; there have been many hidden from the public as well). They have believed stated governmental rationales justifying those wars. In large part, such uncritical acceptance of military actions has followed from an acceptance of the myth of redemptive violence. This myth has generally been grounded in the memory of America's "good" war that saved the world from Hitler and prepared the way for the American brand of democracy.

THE MYTH OF REDEMPTIVE VIOLENCE

I mean by "the myth of redemptive violence," in a nutshell, the quasi-religious belief that we may gain "salvation" through violence. People in the modern world (as in the ancient world), and not least people in the United States, put tremendous faith in instruments of violence to provide security and the possibility of victory over their enemies. The amount of trust people

Introduction: The Myth of the United States and the Myth of Redemptive Violence

put in such instruments may be seen perhaps most clearly in the amount of resources they devote to preparation for war.

American theologian and social critic Walter Wink helps us understand how this myth of redemptive violence works to achieve "salvation."[19] Wink asserts, "Violence is the ethos of our times. It is the spirituality of the modern world. It has been accorded the status of a religion, demanding from its devotees an absolute obedience to death" (13).

Part of the effectiveness of this myth stems from its invisibility as a myth. We tend to assume that violence is simply part of the nature of things; we see acceptance of violence to be factual, not based on belief. So we are not self-aware about the faith-dimension of our acceptance of violence. We think we *know* as a simple fact that violence works, that violence is necessary, that violence is inevitable. We don't realize that, instead, we operate in the realm of belief, of mythology, of religion, in relation to the acceptance of violence.

Wink proposes that our present-day belief in redemptive violence actually echoes ancient Babylonian mythology. This Babylonian mythology has at its heart the belief that creation itself stems from the violence of the gods and that violence is simply inherent in the fabric of the universe.[20] "The religion of Babylon—one of the world's oldest, continuously surviving religions—is thriving as never before in every sector of contemporary American life, even in our synagogues and churches. It, not Christianity, is the real religion of America" (13).

The Babylonian creation myth, according to Wink, teaches that subduing chaos and establishing order requires violence. To have human life at all, such order must be enforced; that is, violence is necessary for social life. Violence is the foundational requirement for human beings to sustain life on earth. Those who recognize violence as the core operating dynamic in human culture understand that those who most successfully practice chaos-subduing violence have the gods on their side. Victory through violence better than anything else indicates the blessing of the gods.

In this myth, religion serves people in power. Human life always exists on the edge of chaos. We need strong (and violent) leaders to keep the chaos at bay. Such leaders are blessed by the gods and deserve our obeisance. We should not hope for perfection in this life but recognize the reality of

---

19. What follows summarizes the chapter titled "The Myth of the Domination System," in Wink, *Engaging the Powers*, 12–31. Page numbers will be given in parentheses in the main text.

20. Wink's analysis of Babylonian mythology draws heavily on Paul Ricoeur's chapter "The Drama of Creation and the 'Ritual' Vision of the World," in Ricoeur, *Symbolism of Evil*, 175–210.

never-ending conflict. We must trust in violence and the wielders of violence for our survival, for the limited security that we might hope for—and we must recognize that the gods are blessing those who wield this legitimate violence.

The myth of redemptive violence operates on all levels of our society. Certainly on the level of our recognizing the need for state power, based on violence, to keep chaos at bay and our appropriate subordination to this state power. Also, we continually encounter the myth on the level of popular culture. The books we read, the movies we watch, television, sports, reiterate that the basic story of creation is grounded in violence and chaos. Hence, we need violence to subdue chaos and defeat our enemies. We must subordinate ourselves to the human beings in authority who exercise this necessary and redemptive violence. It is appropriate for us to join in the exercise of violence against our nation's enemies when called upon.

Wink points out that the myth shapes our children from early on. "No other religious system has ever remotely rivaled the myth of redemptive violence in its ability to catechize the young so totally. From the earliest age children are awash in depictions of violence as the ultimate solution in human conflicts" (23). Children hear a simple story in cartoons, video games, movies, and books: we are good, our enemies are evil, the only way to deal with evil is to defeat it with violence, let's roll.

The myth of redemptive violence links directly with the centrality of the nation-state. The welfare of the nation, as defined by its leaders, stands as the highest value for life here on earth.

> There can be no other gods before the nation. This myth not only establishes a patriotic religion at the heart of the state but also gives the nation's imperialistic imperative divine sanction. All war is metaphysical; one can only go to war religiously. The myth of redemptive violence is thus the spirituality of militarism. By divine right, the state has the power to order its citizens to sacrifice their lives to maintain the privileges enjoyed by the few. By divine decree, it utilizes violence to cleanse the world of evil opponents who resist the nation's sway. The name of God—any god, the Christian God included—can be invoked as having specially blessed and favored the supremacy of the chosen nation and its ruling caste. (26)

The belief in the redemptive necessity of violence in America goes way back. I will discuss the history of trusting in violence in America in the final section of the introduction. Part of my argument in this book, though, is that World War II and its direct aftermath greatly accelerated the evolution of

Introduction: The United States and the Myth of Redemptive Violence

the United States into a militarized society and that this militarization relies on the myth of redemptive violence for its sustenance. Americans continue to embrace the myth of redemptive violence even in face of mounting evidence that its resulting militarization has corrupted American democracy and is destroying the country's economy and physical environment.

Wink suggests that the name for what has emerged as the operating framework for American militarism is "the ideology of the national security state." He sets the date for this emergence as 1947, when the American government created two new political institutions that came to embody this ideology: the National Security Council and the Central Intelligence Agency. Then, "to propagate national security doctrine, the National War College was established in Washington in 1948. . . . These institutions were but the outer form of a new Power being spawned: the national security system. . . . The spirituality of the national security system is the ideology of the national security state" (26–27).[21]

Wink does not discuss the role World War II played in the emergence of this ideology and its attendant structures. I will argue in this book that the War was absolutely crucial. Certainly, American history is full of various expressions of the national security ideology. However, this ideology was limited in its influence. As recently as the late 1930s, American military spending was minimal and powerful political forces opposed involvement in "foreign entanglements." President Franklin Roosevelt, a supporter of the global expression of American military force going back to his days as Assistant Secretary of the Navy during World War I, was greatly constrained in his ability to pursue interventionist policies in the years leading up to World War II. In fact, his efforts to get the U.S. to enter the War succeeded only after Japan's attack and Germany's declaration of war on America.

The "shock"[22] of the War opened many new possibilities for the advocates of the American national security ideology. In addition to the institutions mentioned by Wink (the National Security Council, CIA, and War College), if we go back a few years earlier we can find two more key institutions that did not exist until the War and that exerted great power in the years afterward in support of the national security state: the Pentagon and the nuclear weapons program.

---

21. See also Wills, *Bomb Power*.

22. See Klein, *Shock Doctrine*, for an analysis of more recent examples in which social upheaval and severe trauma (war, economic collapse, natural disasters) have provided occasion for social transformation to enhance the power of economic and military elites. She does not go back to World War II, but her analysis has obvious application to how the dynamics of power in the United States were transformed following the trauma of the War.

Wink characterizes the doctrine of the national security state as follows:

> The survival of the nation is the absolute goal. National strategy intends to incorporate the whole nation into the national survival plan, to make it the total and unconditional object of each citizen's life. In this view, all times are times of war. Peace is nothing more than the conventional name given to the continuation of war by other means. All politics is a politics of war. (27)

I will suggest that one way to look at American history is to see a continual struggle between what we could call a "democracy story" and an "empire story."[23] World War II brought a decisive turn in this struggle. We may mark this turn by noting that prior to the War, when America engaged in military conflict (and tended more toward the empire story), at the end of the conflict the nation demobilized (tending back toward the democracy story). Since World War II, there has been no full demobilization because we have moved directly from World War II to the Cold War to the War on Terrorism. That is, we have moved into a situation where "all times are times of war."

The national security ideology links inextricably with the myth of redemptive violence (remember Wink's insistence that this myth is America's central *religion*). The purveyors of this ideology use the language, rituals, and symbols of already existing religions. They justify their use of violence in the name of God and Christian faith. As Wink concludes, though, "the real faith of these National Securocrats is redemptive violence" (27).[24]

One element of the national security state that most clearly reveals its religious dimension is surfaced by the question, Why would non-elites, who bear terrible costs by living in a permanent war society, submit to this arrangement, even in many cases offering intense support? For Wink,

> The answer is quite simple: the promise of salvation. The myth of redemptive violence offers salvation through identification with Marduk (the Babylonian god) and his earthly regent. . . . Salvation through identification . . . is tied inextricably with the fortunes of the hero-leader. Right and wrong scarcely enter the picture. Everything depends on victory, success, the thrill of

---

23. Grimsrud, "Anabaptist Faith."

24. For example, see Inboden, *Religion and American Foreign Policy*, for an examination of the way President Harry Truman utilized Christian language to garner support for the newly engaged Cold War against "godless communism." Inboden himself is in sympathy with Truman's efforts, but he's a good enough reporter to make it clear that Truman meant Christian motifs to serve a militarized response to the Soviet Union.

belonging to a nation capable of imposing its will in the heavenly council and among the nations. (28–29)

FOR WHOM AM I WRITING ETHICS?

In assessing the moral legacy of World War II, we tend to start with a question such as this: What would you do if you were Roosevelt or Churchill? We focus on the choices of the very few people in power and assume that those choices should be the locus for our ethical reflection.

My concerns are significantly different. I am not uninterested in the choices made by policymakers; in fact, those choices will play a major role in the discussion throughout this book. However, more than with the elites, I am concerned with the regular person as a moral actor. How do I, as a citizen, a member of a faith community, a person in committed family relationships, act morally in the world of which I find myself a part?

In reflecting on the moral significance of World War II, I seek to focus on the actual events. My concern is how someone like me would implement my ethical stance in view of the concrete choices I would have faced. What can/should *we* do as regular people in the face of these big issues of war and peace? In the "real world," I am not in a policymaking position; few of the people who will read this book are in a policymaking position in relation to the military practices of the United States. So I am not going to write from the point of view of a policymaker or imagine myself as a policymaker.

In reflecting on moral choices that were made during World War II and in the years following, I have two goals. First, I hope to provide a critical perspective on those choices. Let's try to understand better the choices that were made and evaluate them in terms of moral criteria. The main moral criteria I will refer to are the stated moral values explicit and implicit in the rationales given for supporting the War, especially in the United States—such as the Allies' Atlantic Charter, the Federal Council of Churches' "Six Pillars of Peace," and Franklin Roosevelt's "Four Freedoms."

The second hoped-for outcome will be greater clarity about our convictions, commitments, and choices concerning our *present* context. How should we respond to America's present-day wars in light of America's past wars (especially since 1941)? I am interested in the story of World War II and in the story of the legacy of that war in the second half of the twentieth century and early years of the twenty-first. A big part of this interest, though, is on how this story relates to our present choices and commitments.

As I have stated already, World War II as America's "good war" casts an enormous shadow that still shapes how we see our world, and especially how we view war and peace. We will have to come to terms with the moral legacy of the War in order to escape that shadow and to evaluate the morality of our present choices. Too often, World War II serves as a trump card in discussions of the present appropriateness of violence (or pacifism). The War clearly was morally good (Americans assume); hence, these other wars might well be too.

I will shine a critical light on the mythology of World War II as a "good war" in order to remove that trump card. If we realize that even World War II turns out *not* to be a good war, perhaps we will thereby be freed to be much more critical of present-day claims about the appropriateness of current military action.

Though I write this book as a committed pacifist, I will evaluate World War II on pragmatic grounds. I will draw on accepted just war criteria and the moral values that advocates for the War themselves established as the grounds for American participation. When I come to negative conclusions about the War, I will do so in terms of how it fell short of the moral criteria war proponents themselves articulated—and not only in relation to the years 1941–45 but also for the years since.

At the same time, a non-pacifist may not be as troubled by the unquestioned assumptions so many Americans have about World War II as I am. I tend to assume that all wars are deeply morally problematic rather than to assume that, of course, some wars are appropriate. In starting with the assumption (to be tested) that even World War II was morally problematic, I am inclined to scrutinize it more critically than if I didn't start with that assumption. However, even though I raise questions because of my pacifist assumptions, I will pursue those questions pragmatically, not ideologically. The bases for my negative portrayal of World War II and its moral legacy will be the actual events of history, open for evaluation by everyone, pacifist or not.

Still, I am a pacifist. I mentioned above that my sense of connection to World War II stems in part from my parents' participation in it along with the origins of my name and the medical technology that saved my life. I have several reasons to be positively disposed toward the War, no direct personal reasons not to be (in contrast to friends of mine whose fathers were deeply traumatized by their participation in the War in life-shaping ways and in contrast to people throughout the world who grew up with the direct destruction of the War).

My disbelief in the moral legitimacy of war has been shaped by three sources. (1) My parents were proud veterans, but they were also kind, gentle people who raised their five children with deep respect. I grew up without violence, and I was always encouraged to think for myself, to exercise my

Introduction: The United States and the Myth of Redemptive Violence

own moral responsibility, to make my own decisions. My parents' values of kindness and respect ran deeper than their values of patriotism. When as a young adult I came to the point of being able to perceive a contradiction between kindness and respect, on the one hand, and support for the wars of America, on the other, I naturally chose the former.

(2) I came of age at the tail end of the American war on Vietnam. Through my high school years, we watched that war on television. I expected to be called into the military. I was not exposed to dissent and opposition to that war. Had I been drafted when I turned nineteen, I would have without serious question gone into the military. As it turned out, the year I did turn nineteen (1973), the Nixon administration abolished the draft so I did not go. But by 1973 I had become more interested in war issues. In time, I came to feel relieved to have missed participation in what I learned was an extraordinarily unjust war. One bit of exposure I gained to this war came through learning to know returning vets, almost all of whom had stories of horror and trauma, of doing things they were ashamed of, and of developing a profound disrespect toward the political and military leaders who had placed them in such terrible situations.

(3) The final catalyst for my pacifist convictions came through theological reflection—realizing that, in the words of a popular song of the time, "Jesus don't like killing, no matter what the reason for."[25] As my Christian faith deepened during my college years, I spent more time thinking about the relationship between the message of Jesus and warfare, especially the war I was most familiar with, the one in Vietnam. More or less on my own, I came to the conviction that as a follower of Jesus, I could not support war in any form.

Shortly after that point of clarity in my convictions, I discovered a long-standing Christian pacifist tradition, the Mennonites. I began to read Mennonite writings on pacifism and sought to converse with actual Mennonites. My wife Kathleen Temple and I attended Associated Mennonite Biblical Seminary for a year and then joined a Mennonite congregation in Eugene, Oregon.

My sojourn among Mennonites has been an opportunity to develop my theoretical position concerning pacifism, to learn to know many other pacifists of all ages and many nationalities, and to learn about ongoing alternatives to acceptance of and participation in warfare. As it turns out, Mennonites will not play a major role in this book, but my experience in and

---

25. John Prine, "Your Flag Decal Won't Get You into Heaven Anymore." From the album *John Prine* (Atlantic Records, 1970).

appreciation of Mennonite communities stand behind what I have written here.

THE MYTH OF REDEMPTIVE VIOLENCE IN AMERICAN HISTORY

We must take a moment before turning to the War and its aftermath to think about the longer sweep of American history. Americans have always believed in the redemptive possibilities of violence; America has always had violence as a major part of its ethos. While World War II added new dimensions to the place of militarism in American society, we cannot say that America has ever been free from deep-seated acceptance of the myth of redemptive violence.

As historian Alan Taylor has shown in his volume in the Penguin History of the United States, *American Colonies*,[26] establishing and expanding the European presence in North America relied on extraordinary amounts of violence. He traces especially the violence done to native peoples and to forcibly imported slaves. Both forms of violence contributed greatly to the "success" of the Europeans in creating new societies that ultimately dominated most of the North American continent. Long prior to the nation's official birth (itself grounded in warfare), violence played quite a "redemptive" role in the formation of the United States of America beginning with the first colonists. Taylor writes,

> The traditional story of American uplift excludes too many people. Many English colonists failed to prosper, finding only intense labor and early graves in a strange and stressful land.... And those who succeeded bought their good fortune by taking lands from Indians and by exploiting the labor of others—at first indentured servants, later African slaves. The abundant land for free colonists kept wage labor scarce and expensive, which promoted the importation of unfree laborers by the thousands. Between 1492 and 1776, North America lost population, as diseases and wars killed Indians faster than colonists could replace them. And during the eighteenth century, most colonial arrivals were Africans forcibly carried to a land of slavery, rather than European volunteers seeking a domain of freedom. More than minor aberrations, Indian deaths and African slaves were fundamental to colonization.[27]

---

26. Taylor, *American Colonies*.
27. Ibid., x–xi.

Introduction: The United States and the Myth of Redemptive Violence

We could consider any number of specific examples in the years between 1492 and 1939 when America's belief in the efficacy of violence found expression.[28] I will mention only a few.

Jill Lepore's account of the 1675–76 war between Algonquian Indians and Puritan colonists in New England, *The Name of War: King Philip's War and the Origins of American Identity*, suggests that this early colonial war exerted a profound influence on the character of the emerging American society. Beginning with the murder of an Indian informer, followed by the execution of two of the murderers, the conflict quickly grew. "When the English and Algonquian peoples of seventeenth-century New England went to war in 1675, they devastated one another. In proportion to population, their short, vicious war inflicted greater casualties than any other war in American history."[29] Though the Algonquian inflicted severe casualties on the colonists, in the end they were crushed—ruthlessly. And with this victory in battle, the European-Americans learned a crucial lesson: sometimes one simply has to fight, and when one fights hold nothing back. They had a calling, they had been placed here for a purpose—and this purpose was important enough to justify massive violence in its furtherance.

Most Americans with some historical awareness would tend to point to the Civil War, nearly two centuries after "King Philip's War," as the paradigmatic expression (prior to World War II) of massive violence for the sake of America's vocation—that is, the paradigmatic expression of redemptive violence.

Harry Stout's "moral history of the American Civil War," *Upon the Altar of the Nation*, provides a perceptive analysis of the religious underpinnings of the Civil War on both the Confederate and Union sides. Stout shows how these religious underpinnings lent a sense of divine approval of ruthless tactics of total war, especially as practiced by the Union. And in the American memory, these tactics have been seen as fully justified because they served the greater goods of the preservation of the Union and the abolition of slavery.

Virtually all of the military leaders for both North and South had received their education at the United States Military Academy in West Point, New York. Part of this education included learning the West Point Code.

> West Point cadets and officers were taught . . . to be "gentlemen." The term "gentleman" carried with it powerful moral imperatives of "honor" and justness in the conduct of war. Through

---

28. For a survey of the role of warfare in American history, see Anderson and Cayton, *Dominion of War*.

29. Lepore, *Name of War*, xi.

intensive training and indoctrination, cadets imbibed a code that stressed the ideal of a "limited war." The tactics, such as they were, ... stressed the reserved use of interior lines of operations and campaigns of position and maneuver against armies rather than crushing overland campaigns across civilian populations. This West Point Code demanded that real gentlemen protect the innocents and minimize destruction to achieve desired results.[30]

One way to think of the history of the Civil War is to see it as a process wherein President Abraham Lincoln sifted through various top commanders until he found one unhindered by adherence to the West Point Code. Lincoln found his general in Ulysses S. Grant, complemented by Generals William Tecumseh Sherman and Philip Sheridan. And with this team in place, the Union overwhelmed the Confederacy. This success stemmed in large part from tactics that *did* center on "crushing overland campaigns across civilian populations."

The Civil War validated the use of total war for the sake of the "greater good." Lincoln's powerful and thoughtful speeches and writings reflect admirable humility. He always resisted the tendency to label the Civil War a holy war in which God directly supported whatever tactics were necessary. However, in practice, Lincoln supported whatever tactics were necessary. His humility was joined with religious-tinged language that did hint at divine support for the massive "redemptive violence" the Union utilized to defeat the enemy. In many ways, the Union cause in the Civil War remains the template for American trust in the efficacy of military force—and in the presumed "goodness" of the American cause.

At the close of the nineteenth century, a third dimension of the "redemptive" exercise of American military power emerged (the first being military power against Native Americans for the sake of the European vocation of settling North America; the second being military power against internal movements that threatened the vocation of the American nation-state). This third dimension was the use of military power outside of North America to bring foreign peoples under America's umbrella. The Spanish-American War of 1898 ushered in a new century that would be marked by the commitment of the U.S. to a global presence, culminating by the end of the twentieth century in the U.S. becoming the world's one superpower.

Walter Karp, in *The Politics of War*, argues that the war of 1898 set off a twenty-year struggle for the soul of the United States. The struggle was between two visions for what America could be: America as an empire and America as a republic. He suggests that two American wars, the

---

30. Stout, *Upon the Altar*, 21.

Introduction: The United States and the Myth of Redemptive Violence 23

Spanish-American War and World War I, "altered forever the political life of the American Republic." In looking at these two wars, "a single dramatic story emerges . . . , the story of the last great popular struggle in America to maintain a genuinely free republic—a republic free of oligarchy, monopoly, and private power—and the defeat and final obliteration of that struggle in two foreign wars."[31]

I think Karp may overstate the significance of these wars in "obliterating" the struggle against the transformation of the United States into a military-centered world empire. The struggle certainly preceded 1898, but also has continued. The roots of America's imperial tendencies go back to its beginnings.[32] Those tendencies have always been, and continue to be, resisted.[33]

Still, Karp's account of the "two wars" points to a set of key moments in which America entered the "modern world" and in a qualitatively new way turned its focus beyond its own continent. And this move toward "world citizenship" centered on the efficacy of military force to spread the American way, to "redeem" people worldwide.

With "evangelists" such as William McKinley, Theodore Roosevelt, and Woodrow Wilson, the United States moved to a point where Americans would advocate using war to make the world "safe for democracy." Americans would use war to end war, violence to defeat violence—all part of their special vocation to spread their way of life to the ends of the earth.

Nonetheless, even after America's intense mobilization to join the "Great War" in 1917–18, and the concomitant devastation of many of the hopes and values of genuine democracy that Karp documents, the United States did step back after that war ended. The military was demobilized. Strong antiwar sentiment emerged.

Franklin Roosevelt, elected president in 1932, had from his time as Assistant Secretary of the Navy during World War I shared Wilson's vision for the American vocation in the world and the centrality of military force in that vocation. However, Roosevelt took office in a United States of America deep in the throes of the Great Depression. Roosevelt's focus up until nearly the end of his second term by necessity centered on the domestic economy. So, as late at 1937, the United States military remained quite small (smaller even than the military of Portugal[34]). And, as events in Europe and East

---

31. Karp, *Politics of War*, xvi.
32. See Williams, *Empire*.
33. See Nichols, *Against the Beast*.
34. Zelizer, *Arsenal of Democracy*, 42.

Asia cast a dark cloud over the entire world and wars and rumors of war abounded, noninvolvement sentiment stood strong in the United States.

It is truly difficult for those of us today who are concerned by American militarism to put ourselves back in history to the 1930s, to imagine the peripheral role the military played in American life, the lack of political power militarists had, and the constraints Congress and public opinion placed on those in power (including the president himself) who did desire a more interventionist and militarized foreign policy.

American society, even with the historical legacy of the various outpourings of major violence and the long-inculcated belief in redemptive violence that I have sketched above, truly has been transformed since 1937. Throughout American history, we can trace expansions followed by contractions of militarism. That is, up until World War II. Roosevelt did manage greatly to increase military spending and preparation in the late 1930s, but only with Pearl Harbor did the tide truly change. The notable truth, for our purposes in this book, is that the tide has never turned back.

World War II unleashed the "tool" of military force (not necessarily all that different than in King Philip's War, the Civil War, the Spanish-American War, and World War I). But this time the "tool" broke loose from its constraints. The United States after World War II has remained a militarized state, a mobilized society, a permanent war economy—and this is the main moral legacy of World War II.

PART ONE: Total War

2

Why Did America Go to War?

In moral evaluation of warfare, traditional just war thought has typically divided analysis into two general categories. Political philosopher Michael Walzer describes these categories as follows:

> War is always judged twice, first with reference to the reasons states have for fighting, secondly with reference to the means they adopt. The first kind of judgment is adjectival in character: we say that a particular war is just or unjust. The second is adverbial: we say that the war is being fought justly or unjustly.[1]

The first category is often called "just cause" (or *jus ad bellum*, justice in going to war) and the second category "just conduct" (or *jus in bello*, justice in fighting war). Chapters 2 and 3 will look at World War II in light of these two just war categories, especially in relation to the United States. Did the U.S. approach its entry into the War consistently with just cause criteria, and was the conduct of the U.S. military coherent with just conduct criteria?

THE STORM CLOUDS GATHER

My father, Carl Grimsrud, graduated from high school in the tiny western Minnesota town of Hitterdal in 1934. Those were challenging times. On a personal level, just before high school graduation, Carl's mother, Dora, died of cancer. This was the height of the Depression. Carl's father, Carl Sr., served as a Lutheran pastor in congregations made up of farmers whose

1. Walzer, *Just and Unjust Wars*, 21.

economic depression dated back to the early 1920s and had only gotten worse and worse. Western Minnesota was at the northeastern edge of the Dust Bowl, environmental devastation that gave dramatic visual expression to the economic devastation shaking the Great Plains.

Lurking in the background, but surely present in the consciousness of a socially aware person such as young Carl, deeply problematic global political dynamics foreshadowed profound crises to come. In 1934, Adolf Hitler was in his second year of power in Germany, consolidating his National Socialist dictatorship. Joseph Stalin's Soviet Union was in the midst of government-imposed famine meant to consolidate its power over the Ukraine. Japan's effort to expand its power in China was building into a full-scale attempt at military conquest.[2]

In 1934, though the likelihood of major international conflicts became more apparent, the U.S. as a whole remained focused on internal concerns. The philosophy stated in various ways by American founding fathers to "avoid foreign entanglements" retained a great deal of force.

While certainly the focus on finding a way through the Depression provided the main impetus for Americans paying limited attention to world problems, other factors also played important roles. The Wilson administration had whipped up widespread support for America joining in the Great War—and American engagement actually played a decisive role in the Allied victory. However, this support, while widespread, had not run very deep.

When World War I ended without obvious benefit to the U.S. and at the cost of thousands of lives, anti-interventionist forces gained ascendency. They defeated the proposed membership in the League of Nations and elected Republican Warren Harding to the presidency by a wide margin. Harding's successors as president, Republicans Calvin Coolidge and Herbert Hoover, shared his reluctance to push America into a global leadership role. Roosevelt, the first Democratic Party president since Wilson, did not share that reluctance, but his election—popular as it was—did not include a mandate to make significant changes in America's foreign policies.[3]

Reinhold Niebuhr, the child of German immigrants who was to become America's most influential public theologian, had supported U.S. involvement in the Great War—in part, at least, as a means of establishing his identity as a full-fledged *American*.[4] He began to become disillusioned as

2. For an account of these developments, see Maialo, *Cry Havoc.*

3. In his inaugural address in 1933, Roosevelt devoted only one sentence to foreign policy, blandly stating that "in the field of world policy I would dedicate this nation to the policy of the good neighbor." Quoted in Herring, *From Colony to Superpower*, 497.

4. Fox, *Reinhold Niebuhr*, 43–58.

the postwar peace conference unfolded and Wilson's ideals failed to impact the proceedings. Within a couple of years, Niebuhr came to be totally negative about the Great War, and all other wars. Upon visiting Germany in 1923, he wrote, "This is as good a time as any to make up my mind that I am done with the war business."[5] Though, in time, Niebuhr came to change his mind decisively, his sentiment in 1923 reflected that of a great many others. In the following decade, this sense of being "done with the war business" only grew in the U.S.

However, maybe not so much in 1934, but by 1937, many internationally aware Americans felt the outside world closing in on them. At this point, though, the U.S. remained relatively disarmed. The American military in 1937 was roughly one-tenth the size of Germany's. It was the sixteenth largest in the world, between Portugal's and Romania's.[6] This was soon to change, because the global trajectory moved ominously toward new wars. Some had already begun.

Japan in China

In the fall of 1931, Japan sought control of Manchuria, a large, semiautonomous area between China and the Soviet Union, and succeeded in February 1932. This area provided a base of operations for Japan's expanding aggression toward China. The U.S. protested Japan's takeover of Manchuria, as did the League of Nations—but with little effect. In 1936, China's government, led by Chiang Kai-shek, formally declared war on Japan.

Italy in Ethiopia

In the mid-1930s, Benito Mussolini's fascist Italian state took on the northern African nation of Ethiopia, one of the few African countries that had not been colonized. The Italians invaded Ethiopia in October 1935, completing their conquest by May 1936. Again, the League of Nations (in which both Ethiopia and Italy held membership) protested ineffectually. The world saw pictures of the terrible military mismatch that resulted in the slaughter of thousands of Ethiopians, heightening the sense that the fascists were on the move.

---

5. Ibid., 78–79.
6. Zelizer, *Arsenal of Democracy*, 42.

Germany in the Saarland, Rhineland, Austria

Adolf Hitler led the German Nazi Party to the highest vote total in the 1932 national elections (though less than a majority). He refused President von Hindenburg's offer of the position of vice chancellor, then within a year was offered the position of chancellor; he accepted and moved quickly to consolidate his power as Germany's leader. Many in the West, while dubious of Hitler's abilities and character, welcomed the Nazi ascent as an alternative to the growth in popularity of the German Communist Party.

From the start, Hitler appealed to Germany's need to strengthen its military and break free from the constraints of the post-World War I peace treaties. In 1935, Germany repudiated the Versailles Treaty and reinstituted compulsory military service. The Germans took over the Saarland, a state in western Germany that since World War I had been under French administration. The German area near Holland called the Rhineland was also occupied by the French following World War I. That occupation ended in 1930 with the understanding that the area would remain demilitarized. In 1936, the Nazi government repudiated that understanding and expanded Germany's militarization into the Rhineland.

Hitler himself was born and grew up in Austria. He only became a German citizen formally in 1932. He understood Austria to be part of greater Germany and moved to absorb Austria into Germany in 1938. He also wanted the traditionally German city of Danzig—established as a "free city" under League of Nations oversight after World War I—returned to Germany. For Danzig to be part of Germany, the area between Danzig and the German border would also have to become part of Germany. The Polish government refused (though the political leadership of Danzig had fallen into the hands of Nazi sympathizers and many residents of Danzig wanted to be part of Germany), setting the stage for violence to come.

The Spanish Civil War

In 1936, a number of Spanish generals attempted a military takeover of their country, setting off a civil war that lasted until 1939. The leader of the generals, Francisco Franco, had strong fascist sympathies and his Nationalist Party eventually prevailed. They were aided in the war by the Germans, who took the opportunity to test their military weaponry and tactics. The Soviet Union offered some assistance to the Republicans who opposed Franco, but the Western democracies remained on the sidelines—again content to see the anti-communists prevail.

Soviet Union in Finland

In the years following World War I and the Russian Revolution that ended with the Communist Party in absolute power in what became the Soviet Union, relations between the Soviets and their neighbors to the northwest, Finland, remained tense. By 1937, it was clear that a major conflict was impending. It was not until after the European war started with Germany's invasion of Poland in September 1939 that the Soviets finally took action, invading and with difficulty finally conquering Finland.

Many American pacifists, like their British and other European counterparts, followed news of these conflicts. In fact, they spoke directly about them, worked at possible responses, and sought to have an impact on American policymakers with far greater urgency than probably any other segment of the American population.[7]

We may recognize with great respect the insights, the commitment, and the creativity of the pacifist internationalists. However, we also must recognize that for members of the general population in the United States in the late 1930s, this time was indeed tremendously frightening. While political leaders failed to seek creative responses to the conflicts that did not follow the simple violence-responding-to-violence paradigm, they certainly did face genuine crises. Profoundly violent men—Adolf Hitler, Joseph Stalin, the Japanese generals, Benito Mussolini—exercised tremendous power, with hearts set on dominance.

In reflecting on the moral legacy of World War II, we will not be aided by trying to minimize the threat to human wholeness posed by these authoritarian leaders and their nations in the lead-up to World War II. Our question, rather, is what kind of lessons we should learn from how the U.S. and its allies responded to the extreme violence of the authoritarians. Was the total war that ensued a victory for humane values over tyrannical values? Or did the means used to defeat the tyrants in fact transform those who used them? What emerged victorious after World War II—democracy and human rights, or the myth of redemptive violence?

THE ARGUMENTS FOR "INTERVENTION"

In face of Germany, Italy, and Japan acting so aggressively during the 1930s, strong arguments emerged in the U.S. that pushed for American

---

7. See Baker, *Human Smoke*. Scattered throughout Baker's book are examples of pacifists' actions and arguments.

intervention in opposition to those aggressive moves. President Roosevelt, though inclined toward intervention, moved cautiously.

Roosevelt recognized that the American people remained resistant to America's becoming "entangled" in others' wars. The U.S. was not under direct threat from anyone. Reluctance to jeopardize American lives and devote American resources to conflicts that did not involve national defense characterized the nation as a whole. While Roosevelt's Democratic Party would have been more open to intervention than Republicans, many within the party opposed intervention. Roosevelt remembered the fate of Woodrow Wilson's Democratic Party in the aftermath of World War I when Wilson's push for American internationalism bumped disastrously against the nation's inclination to avoid "foreign entanglements."[8]

Nonetheless, Roosevelt did build the case for increasing intervention. He did not wait for a national consensus but began taking greater and greater steps to oppose Germany and Japan. These steps first took the form of increasing the size of the American military and strengthening ties with the Nationalist government of Chiang Kai-shek in East Asia and with Great Britain in Europe.

When the Japanese moves toward China reached the point of overt war in 1936, Roosevelt supported military action against the Japanese, in principle. However, he believed he could not actually pursue that path for the time being. He did not believe that the American navy had achieved the strength that would make such action effective, and he recognized that such action would meet with sharp opposition in Congress.[9]

These years did see a sharp increase in the public rhetoric supporting the need for Americans to face the threats that were arising throughout the world. Americans watched more and more newsreels filled with frightening images and a sense of foreboding. They received the message of "darkness' spread" across parts of the world in an ever-widening path—and clearly heading even toward isolated North America.[10]

On the one hand, the interventionists stopped short of overtly calling for the U.S. to go to war. To go "officially" would involve extensive troop deployment. But on the other hand, all of the rhetoric in favor of increased intervention assumed that the only way to deal effectively with the crises would be direct military action. There were internationalists who advocated activity in global affairs of a nonviolent sort, but by and large in the broader societal debate, the only type of intervention on offer was military centered.

---

8. Brands, *Traitor to His Class*, 357.
9. Ibid., 370.
10. Kennedy, *Freedom from Fear*, 381–515.

Most of those opposed to interventionist policies took what was often called an "isolationist stance." They argued in the name of nationalism that America should avoid intervention. As the events proved, when Japan attacked the U.S. military base at Pearl Harbor in the Hawaiian colony, most isolationists rallied to the flag and supported the American war effort against both the Japanese and the Germans.

A much smaller element of the anti-interventionist side of the debate were internationalists who did indeed support American involvement in the world's conflicts, but advocated for this involvement to be nonmilitary. In this view, the U.S. should seek to prevent and resolve conflicts, rather than focus on military violence.[11] These anti-interventionists tended toward principled opposition to warfare (i.e., pacifism). They based much of their argument on moral principles and ideals. However, they also warned of severe damage to democratic principles should the U.S. pursue a more militarized response. Part Two below ("Aftermath") will make the case that those concerns were indeed prescient, though the damage was more subtle than the most dire warnings predicted.

At the heart of interventionists' views[12] lay a concern for "civilization."[13] "Civilization" included "justice and freedom," religious freedom, "civilized decency," liberties, "universal principles of justice," willingness to resist the "gangsters and bandits" who threaten democracy, and self-determination.[14] Interestingly, these advocates did not see "civilization" as incompatible with the colonialism of the "great democracies" such as Britain and France.

From June 1940, when France surrendered to the Nazis, until Germany attacked the Soviet Union just about one year later, the focus for American pro-interventionist arguments was on Great Britain and the Battle of

---

11. For a representative collection of writings from these internationalist non-interventionists, see Loconte, *End of Illusions*, 33–121. Though Loconte's agenda is to present these anti-interventionists as a foil to the pro-interventionist arguments that constitute the second half of his book, to his credit he does let "The Peacemakers" (Loconte's section heading) speak for themselves.

12. It is fascinating to note that none of the interventionists, including President Roosevelt in his public statements, overtly advocated direct military engagement for the United States. "We should support those fighting against the Axis with every means short of committing our own troops" was the common refrain. It seems clear that most (probably all, certainly Roosevelt himself) did expect and desire the U.S. to go to war. It is testimony to the political strength of the anti-interventionists that the arguments in favor of intervention could not openly articulate that expectation and desire.

13. Reinhold Niebuhr made the defense of civilization central to his case for intervention. For example, see Niebuhr, "End to Illusions," 129.

14. For the common use of the quoted terms, see Part Two of Loconte, *End of Illusions*, "The Prophets: Resisting the Evils of Nazism," 123–249.

Britain. Pro-interventionists argued that Britain's ability to repel the German attack was all that stood in the way of a complete German victory.[15]

For the pro-interventionists, British resistance to German attacks loomed as decisive. Britain stood for civilization; Germany stood for barbarism. We should, of course, be honest about the failures of American society and British society, the pro-interventionists admitted, but these failures pale against the accomplishments of the British ("The British Navy has been the protector of the liberties of the world; it has not been a menace to the freedom of man—on the whole, what a splendid achievement in freedom and law is represented by the British flag!"[16]).

The pro-interventionist argument went like this: Britain is the bulwark in Europe of democracy and the best of civilization. The British stand alone against some of the greatest barbaric forces the world has ever seen. Should they fall, the world will face an unimaginable catastrophe. The United States will find itself standing alone, an island of democracy and justice in a world of the darkest political tyranny. So we must support Britain in its dire need. Still, interventionists did *not* advocate officially going to war. We should offer generous military aid to Britain, thus clearly taking a side. But even though the crisis could not be more dire (in the rhetoric of the pro-interventionists) it still did not necessarily require American soldiers to enter combat.

The pro-intervention arguments, thus, had a limited purview. They focused on the emotional level—challenging Americans to accept the call to support Britain and to overcome their inclination toward noninvolvement. They mainly focused on preparing Americans for further involvement—without naming the shape that involvement would take.

Relatively little was said, before December 1941, about intervention against Japan's military actions. And lurking in the background prior to Hitler's June 1941 turn against the Soviets, but rarely named, was the challenge of how the fundamental incompatibility of Nazism with communism (and the certainty that this incompatibility would lead to war in central and eastern Europe) entered into the discernment process of American intervention.

At the heart of pro-interventionist concern was a belief in Western civilization, especially as embodied in the British traditions of democracy,

---

15. Such a perception was fundamentally flawed. There was never a chance that Germany would not turn to its true enemy and attack the Soviet Union (see Kershaw, *Hitler: 1936–1945*). A German victory in the Battle of Britain quite likely would have meant Britain accommodating itself to German domination of western Europe but otherwise remaining fairly intact—at least until the German/Soviet struggle found resolution.

16. Hough, "Defending Justice," 219.

religious liberty, and rule of law. This is a war to protect those traditions, they said, the basic institutions of free societies. Of course, we know today that these ideals were embodied in Britain to a much greater degree than in Britain's colonies (especially the "colored" colonies such as India and Kenya).

THE "PURPOSE STATEMENTS"

Germany blitzkrieged Poland in September 1939. After this, though the British and French were officially at war with the Germans, western Europe settled into a time of uneasy stasis that lasted into the spring of 1940—what was called the "phony war." The conflict flared up initially in the far north, where both the British and Germans coveted neutral Norway.

After a disastrously brief campaign in which British intervention to oppose German efforts in Norway ended in their defeat and the Germans' conquest of Norway, British Prime Minister Neville Chamberlain was forced out of office in early May. Ironically, the main instigator of that failed campaign, Winston Churchill, escaped blame and ended up succeeding Chamberlain.[17]

Chamberlain's own choice as successor was E. L. F. Wood (Lord Halifax). Chances are high that had Halifax been willing to become prime minister, the office would have been his. Chances are also high that with Halifax as prime minister, Britain would have reached a peace settlement with the Germans.[18] Hitler took initiative after initiative toward the British in hopes of ending the war in the west, with the intention of turning Germany's full attention to the east and the impending showdown with the Soviet Union.

Hitler offered that the British would retain a large amount of domestic autonomy and retain its empire and the Germans would be given a free hand on the continent, especially in central and eastern Europe. Halifax was a part of the more conservative element of the Conservative Party and throughout the 1930s had been favorably inclined toward the emerging Nazi power in Germany as a bulwark against communism. He had himself been active in proposing peace initiatives toward Germany. As events unfolded, it seems believable that Halifax would have taken German peace initiatives quite seriously—certainly more than Churchill, who consistently responded negatively toward such initiatives.

---

17. Baker, *Human Smoke*, 168–69; Beevor, *Second World War*, 70–75.
18. Kershaw, *Fateful Choices*, 47–53.

Halifax's decision to stand aside and leave the prime minister's position to Churchill[19] set the British path. Churchill, like most other British Conservatives, opposed communism and had been somewhat favorably inclined toward the Nazis when they came into power. However, by 1940 he was unalterably committed to war against the Nazis and refused to consider capitulation.

The same day on which Chamberlain resigned and Churchill stepped in, the Germans ended the "phony war" and began their attack on the Low Countries and France. Shockingly, that conflict ended only six weeks later with France's surrender. With their main European ally out of commission, the Britons faced the onslaught of Germany's air force in the Battle of Britain.

Churchill, whose mother was from the United States, had always been committed to a strong alliance with the Americans. As prime minister, Churchill moved quickly to deepen his relationship with Roosevelt. He "asked Roosevelt to modify the American position from neutrality to 'nonbelligerency.'" That is, Churchill wanted the United States to become a close ally in terms of support and commitment, everything short of sending American troops to fight. Churchill asked for military hardware—destroyers to resist German submarines and as many fighter planes as possible—and raw materials. Roosevelt welcomed the close connection with Churchill and affirmed the British-American alliance, but for domestic political reasons responded with caution. Churchill continued to push for more American support.[20]

By August 1940, Roosevelt was ready to commit the U.S. to this "co-belligerent" relationship with Britain, though he insisted on waiting until after the November 1940 presidential election to be open publicly about this commitment. Roosevelt's ability to move toward such a role for the U.S. was greatly improved when the Republican Party, home for much of the American non-interventionist sentiment, surprised the country by nominating Wendell Willkie as its candidate for president. Willkie represented the fairly small pro-interventionist wing of the Republican Party, and his focus in the campaign would be on issues of difference with Roosevelt *other*

---

19. With Chamberlain's loss of status (and his fall from power was extraordinary—he had been acclaimed for his role in the Munich accord in 1938 that had averted war with Germany over Czechoslovakia; after Germany continued its expansionary tactics, Munich looked more problematic and Chamberlain's standing took a big hit; as it turned out his health disintegrated dramatically after his resignation and he died of cancer six months after leaving office) and Halifax's reluctance to step up, Churchill more or less came into power by default. Alone among Britain's major leaders, Churchill relished the chance to exercise power during this time of profound crisis (Herman, *Gandhi and Churchill*, 457–65).

20. Brands, *Traitor to His Class*, 405–6.

than policies toward the European war (or the growing conflict in East Asia). Willkie's pro-interventionist stance freed Roosevelt from having to run against his own interventionist tendencies in his reelection. The large anti-interventionist population was left without a candidate.

Then, with his reelection safely and comfortably in hand, Roosevelt more actively pursued the policy of being Britain's "ally in all but actual fighting." As well, the U.S. pursued ever more hostile policies toward Japan, including increasing direct military aid to China in the Chinese-Japanese War.

Between November 1940 and the formal entry of the U.S. into the War in December 1941, Roosevelt took several opportunities to lay out what we could call the philosophical groundwork for American participation in the War. The American people required persuasion, and Roosevelt presented his case in large part on moral grounds.

Roosevelt's statements of purpose during the months before Pearl Harbor established the values that many American people understood themselves to be fighting for. They also provide us today with important guides for our moral evaluation of American participation in World War II. The two most important statements came in January 1941 and August 1941, respectively, the first being Roosevelt's "Four Freedoms" speech, and the second the agreement established by Roosevelt and Churchill that became known as the Atlantic Charter. These two statements are full of moral content that help us establish our criteria for evaluating the moral legacy of World War II.

During the 1940 presidential campaign, Roosevelt continually reiterated that the United States would not be going to war, that his advocacy of support for Great Britain was intended to keep America *out of* the War. In an October campaign speech, Roosevelt asserted that it was an outrageously false charge that he wanted to push America toward war. "To Republicans and Democrats, to every man, woman, and child in the nation I say this: Your President and your Secretary of State are following the road to peace. We are arming ourselves not for any foreign war." He pledged that the U.S. would send troops into war only in the case of a direct attack. "It is for peace that I have labored, and it is for peace that I shall labor all the days of my life."[21]

The public stance Roosevelt took in the months after his reelection continued to emphasize that the U.S. would be an "arsenal of democracy," not a combatant, in the War. The focus of debate concerning America's role in the War centered by the beginning of 1941 on the policy of supplying

---

21. Quoted in Baker, *Human Smoke*, 242.

Britain with armaments "without reference to the dollar sign," a policy known as "Lend-Lease." This policy required congressional authorization, which meant that a debate would indeed happen.[22]

Roosevelt got the debate going with his State of the Union address in which he announced that he would be sending the Lend-Lease bill to Congress on January 6, 1941. He concluded his speech by introducing what became an enduring statement of key values, what he called "the four essential human freedoms" that he sought to further with his policies: freedom of speech, freedom of religion, freedom from want, and freedom from fear:

> In the future days, which we seek to make secure, we look forward to a world founded upon four essential human freedoms. The first is freedom of speech and expression—everywhere in the world. The second is freedom of every person to worship God in his own way—everywhere in the world. The third is freedom from want—which, translated into world terms, means economic understandings which will secure to every nation a healthy peacetime life for its inhabitants—everywhere in the world. The fourth is freedom from fear—which, translated into world terms, means a world-wide reduction of armaments to such a point and in such a thorough fashion that no nation will be in a position to commit an act of physical aggression against any neighbor—anywhere in the world. That is no vision of a distant millennium. It is a definite basis for a kind of world attainable in our own time and generation. That kind of world is the very antithesis of the so-called new order of tyranny which the dictators seek to create with the crash of a bomb.[23]

In the words of historian David Kennedy, "These Four Freedoms, promulgated in every then-known medium, including a sentimental painting and poster by the popular artist Norman Rockwell, soon became a sort of shorthand for America's war aims."[24] Rockwell published his paintings early in 1943, and they quickly became iconic. The government utilized them in the campaign for selling war bonds; they helped raise over $130 million. Many Americans saw the pictorial vision of the American way of life that Rockwell captured as portraying well the ideals of the nation and the principles for which they fought[25]—both to protect these ideals domestically and, as Roosevelt stated, to protect them "anywhere in the world."

22. Kennedy, *Freedom from Fear*, 469.
23. Quoted in Brands, *Traitor to His Class*, 433–34.
24. Kennedy, *Freedom from Fear*, 469–70.
25. Westbrook, *Why We Fought*, 49–50.

In August 1941, the U.S. inched ever closer to direct combat. Still the support in Congress was not clear and Roosevelt held back from the final step. For the last time in American history, a president assumed he must defer to the Constitutional requirement for a formal declaration of war by Congress. Roosevelt acted to solidify the connection with Great Britain even more and, on August 14, held a secret summit meeting with Churchill off the coast of Newfoundland. Anticipating that the U.S. would as soon as possible formally enter the War, Roosevelt and Churchill produced a document known as the Atlantic Charter.

The Atlantic Charter outlined the Allies' war aims—though Roosevelt insisted they be called "common principles in the national policies of the their respective countries on which they base their hopes for a better future for the world" in recognition that it would not be politic at this point publicly for the U.S., officially still "neutral," to use language that would imply that the U.S. was a belligerent. This statement shaped virtually everything that the Allies were later to say about their purposes for fighting and also played a major role in the political organization of the postwar world (at least on the level of formal statements).[26]

Historian H. W. Brands summarizes the eight points thus:

> The first point eschewed aggrandizement, territorial or otherwise. The second forswore changes not in accord with the "freely expressed wishes of the peoples concerned." The third affirmed "the right of all peoples to choose the form of government under which they will live." The fourth promised equal terms of trade to all nations, with "due respect" for the "existing obligations" of the United States and Britain. The fifth endorsed improved labor and living standards in all countries. The sixth looked forward, "after the final destruction of the Nazi tyranny," to a peace "which will afford to all nations the means of dwelling in safety within their own boundaries, and which will afford assurance that all the men in all the lands may live out their lives in freedom from fear and want." The seventh supported free travel and commerce across the world's oceans. The eighth called on the nations of the world to disarm, "pending the establishment of a wider and permanent system of general security."[27]

---

26. A little more than four months later, on January 1, 1942, twenty-six allied countries who called themselves "the United Nations" (including, most notably, the U.S., Britain, and the Soviet Union) issued a declaration of alliance that included pledges to uphold the Atlantic Charter—as well as to go all out to defeat the Axis militarily and to promise not to seek a separate peace from the rest of the signatories.

27. Brands, *Traitor to His Class*, 454.

Together, the Four Freedoms and the Atlantic Charter delineate the outcomes that, American leaders would claim, the country's participation in the War would seek to achieve. As such, they played a central role in the moral appeal made to American people to support and prosecute the War. This vision gives us bases for evaluating the moral legacy of the War. These statements provided moral legitimacy for the War at the time and decisively shape the mythology of World War II as a "good" war.

In assessing the moral legacy of World War II, I will use the values articulated in these two statements—both to consider the tactics used to prosecute the War and, more importantly, to consider the aftermath of the War. What kind of world did follow from World War II? Most especially, how did the United States participate in this world? In our moral assessment, we will seek honestly to examine the evidence. We will hold up the stated ideals as our bases for evaluation. The "success" of the War will be measured in relation to these stated purposes.

OTHER FACTORS

In their collective memory of World War II, Americans tend to take the pro-interventionist arguments from the late 1930s and early 1940s as objective portrayals of the conflicts. However, as is to be expected with wartime propaganda, these arguments did not tell the entire story. They were statements of persuasion and advocacy, not nuanced accounts of the situation in all its complexity.

By the mid-1930s many people acknowledged the Nazi's claims that Germany had been treated poorly by the peace treaties that ended World War I. These treaties were almost guaranteed to foster bitter resentment among the Germans, and they also made the economic and social health of the German nation difficult to sustain. During the 1920s and early 1930s, the World War I victors rejected numerous opportunities to make the conditions placed on Germany less onerous. Especially during the difficulties of the Great Depression, the fragile democracy of the German Weimar Republic struggled to retain its legitimacy in the face of the growth of extremist movements on both the right (the Nazis) and the left (the communists).

As the Nazis grew in strength, other western Europeans and Americans looked on with mixed reactions.[28] Many perceived the rise of the Nazis as a mixed blessing. Hitler seemed a bit cartoonish and some of his rhetoric was alarming, and in the background always lurked the specter of a revival of traditional German/Prussian militarism. On the other hand, the

28. Kershaw, *Hitler: 1889–1936*, 542–58.

Nazis countered the growing influence of communists in Germany—and elsewhere.

By and large, conservatives in Britain such as Neville Chamberlain and in France such as Philippe Pétain believed the benefits of the anti-communist counterweight superseded the risks in Nazi extremism. Even Winston Churchill, later portrayed as one who opposed Nazism from early on, as late as 1937 published a book that described Hitler in mostly positive terms: "Those who have met Herr Hitler face to face in public business or on social terms have found a highly competent, cool, well-informed functionary with an agreeable manner, a disarming smile, and few have been unaffected by a subtle personal magnetism."[29]

As the Nazis gained power and expanded the German military, they deepened the economic ties between Germany and American corporations. In fact, as late as February 1936, Germany bought more arms from American companies than did any other country in the world except China and Chile.[30]

Then came the showdown between Britain and Germany in 1939. This was preceded by several aggressive moves by the Germans that met with only token opposition from Britain and France—culminating in Germany taking over Czechoslovakia. At this point, somewhat paradoxically, Britain (with the reluctant cooperation of France) made a pact with Poland. Though Britain had no close ties with Poland and the British leadership tended to agree that the formerly German areas of northwestern Poland, especially the port city of Danzig, should probably be returned to Germany (given that the vast majority of the people of Danzig desired this return), Britain felt it was worth going to war should Germany use military force rather than diplomacy to regain Danzig.[31]

Certainly it was not Britain's commitment to democracy that fueled this war commitment. Poland, like Germany, was ruled by a militaristic, right-wing dictatorship. Probably the most likely rationale behind Britain's decision was concern for Britain's "prestige" and the need to bolster Britain's imperial standing.[32] Regardless, the British commitment to Poland was the final step leading to the outbreak of the greatest of all wars.

German aggression and militarism clearly were the main factors that led to the European war. The "democracies" had helped enable the growth of that militarism due to both the opportunity it gave their arms dealers to

29. Quoted in Baker, *Human Smoke*, 70.
30. *New York Times*, March 15, 1936; cited in Baker, *Human Smoke*, 60.
31. Hastings, *Inferno*, 3–25.
32. For one argument along these lines, see Buchanan, *Churchill*.

make money from Germany and the Nazis' hostility to communism. Imperial powers such as Britain and France likely cared little about the principle of self-determination for the peoples of central Europe given their decidedly antidemocratic treatment of so many of their colonies. By 1939, though, British leaders understood that their Nazi "anticommunist bulwark" had become a terrible problem.

We cannot say, of course, how events would have played out had Britain not made their war commitment to Poland. Quite likely, without that agreement, the Polish government would have given in to Hitler's demands rather than reject them and go to war. With terrible irony, when the war on Poland came, Britain and France left the Poles pretty much to their own devices. Poland's resistance was stiff but short-lived. Any imaginable alternative to what actually happened would have been better for Poland. As things turned out, the war that followed devastated Poland, more by far than any other country. And the War's outcome left Poland on the wrong side of the Iron Curtain, subject to a Stalinist dictatorship for nearly another half-century. Ironically, Czechoslovakia, which capitulated to the Germans, came through the War relatively unscathed.

Hitler did not seek war with Great Britain,[33] and when the war nonetheless came, Germany never poured its full energy into defeating the British. Concerning Britain, Hitler mainly wanted the British not to resist the German expansion on the European continent. Quite possibly, as well, apart from Britain and France declaring war on Germany, the Germans would not have conquered the Low Countries and France right away in the spring of 1940.

The further we proceed in our speculations, the more uncertain they become, but it is imaginable that without the British war guarantee to Poland, Hitler would not have entered the "devil's alliance" with Stalin (the nonaggression pact that secretly included an agreement to divvy up Poland). Even had the German-Soviet agreement been reached, in light of Hitler's quick decision to abandon the Battle of Britain and turn the attack toward the Soviets (a decision made in September 1940, though not implemented until June 1941), it is quite possible that the War in western Europe would not have happened, that the only full-bore fight against the Nazis would have come from the Soviet Union.

Despite beliefs in the West about the important roles the U.S. and Britain played in defeating the Nazis, we must admit as possible that the Soviet Union would have defeated Germany even without much involvement from

---

33. "Since the mid-1920s Hitler had wanted Great Britain as a friend and ally, not an enemy, in the war envisaged, and desired, against 'Jewish-Bolshevism'" (Kershaw, *Fateful Choices*, 62).

the U.S. and Britain. Historian Norman Davies, for one, argues that by far the biggest force that defeated Germany was the Soviet Union.[34] The war in the east, for example, led to three times more German casualties than the war in the west. Had Germany first turned to their doom in the east, the democracies in western Europe (e.g., France, Holland, and Belgium) would probably not have been directly overthrown. And had the Soviets indeed defeated the Germans, the postwar fate of central and eastern Europe likely would have been much the same—forty-plus years of communist dictatorships.

These points do not change the fact that by 1940–41 Britain was at war with Germany and the Roosevelt administration felt that the best policy for the U.S. was direct support of Britain, a "co-belligerency" just short of full-fledged war. And that Roosevelt actually welcomed Hitler's declaration of war on the U.S. shortly after Pearl Harbor. But they do complicate the story a bit.

I note one other issue related to the European war. I have not had anything to say up to now about the moral imperative humane people faced to resist Nazi treatment of Jews. In the mythology of the "good war," the saving-Jews factor looms large. However, identifying that motivation came after the fact. As the War drew to a close, and Westerners learned of the evils that we now call the Holocaust, the story about why we were fighting the Nazis came to include saving Jews. However, one looks in vain for evidence that this genocide motivated either the British or the Americans in the run-up to the War or even in the decisions about how the War would be pursued. It's a simple fact that America's involvement in World War II had virtually nothing to do with "saving Jews."[35]

The actual reasons for the Far East war are even more complicated than for the European war. This part of the story could go back to the 1850s when American warships visited Japan with the demand that the Japanese isolation from the Western world end. The relationship between the U.S. and Japan from the 1850s to 1941 was filled with tension.[36]

Japan had sided with the Allies during World War I, forging especially close ties with Britain. However, as Japan emerged as a world power in the early years of the twentieth century, the U.S. perceived this emergence more as a threat to American power in the Far East than as something to

---

34. Davies, *No Simple Victory*.

35. Wyman, *Abandonment of the Jews*, and Hamerow, *Why We Watched*. Hamerow is much more sympathetic concerning the rationales for the western Allies not working harder to rescue Jews than Wyman. Nonetheless, his book reinforces Wyman's point that the United States did *not* enter or fight in the War for the purpose of saving Jews.

36. Bradley, *Imperial Cruise*.

be welcomed. In a crucial move after World War I, the U.S. insisted that the British terminate their alliance with Japan; the British did so in 1922.

Stung by American hostility, Japan's military grew increasingly motivated to establish Japan as a genuine power in the world, imitating the imperial practices of the Western powers. This led to heightened tensions between two imperialistic states—Japan and the United States—over spheres of influence and domination in the Far East.

As Japan became more militaristic and expansionist, the U.S. responded with increased hostility. These tensions found their locus in China, the largest nation in the world and one that both the British and Americans long exploited. As Japan sought to join in that exploitation, relationships got more tense.

Yet these points of tension did not limit the role American corporations played in providing Japan with crucial natural resources, many of which Japan turned into military hardware to empower the expansionist policies. When Japan annexed Manchuria in 1932, and used that satellite state as a base for incursions into China proper, the U.S. increased its support for the Chinese government. As with Britain's "concern" for Poland, the Americans were not supporting democracy in China. The leader of the Chinese government, Chiang Kai-shek, was far from a supporter of democracy. The basis for support for Chiang had mostly to do with his acceptance of the American and British presence in China.[37]

A couple of key moments prior to the Pearl Harbor attack in December 1941 pushed the tensions near to the breaking point. The U.S. imposed an economic embargo on Japan that led to panic on the part of the Japanese regarding their access to vital materials. Roosevelt ordered the American Pacific Fleet greatly to expand its presence in the Pearl Harbor base that was located in the American colony of Hawaii—an expansion perceived by the Japanese as highly provocative.

Finally, Japanese Prime Minister Fumimaro Konoe, who had resisted extremist elements in the military and desired to avoid war with the U.S., desperately sought a meeting with Roosevelt in the summer and fall of 1941 to seek to find ways to resolve the differences. Roosevelt put these meetings off.[38] It may well be that Roosevelt actually desired a confrontation with the Japanese, at least in part as a way to make full-scale war on Germany more acceptable to Americans. With this failure, Konoe resigned as prime minister in October 1941. He was succeeded by General Tojo, one of the strongest of the hardliners. Less than two months later the Japanese attacked.

37. Chomsky, *American Power*, 159–220.
38. Brands, *Traitor to His Class*, 461.

As in Europe, the eastern war was primarily a consequence of the aggression and extreme militarism of one of the Axis powers. Japan cannot be excused for its acts of aggression. Certainly, once the American navy was directly and viciously devastated, no one could have stopped the U.S. from declaring war and pouring immense resources into defeating those responsible for the attack.

However, when we take seriously the historical background and the immediate lead-up to the Far East war, we can't avoid the possibility that Pearl Harbor is best seen as more a quantitative than a qualitative step of escalation following a mutual process of alienation for which the U.S. bears responsibility along with the Japanese.

THE HAMMER FALLS—AND THE MYTH BEGINS

After the U.S. Congress approved the Lend-Lease program with Great Britain in March 1941, the Americans joined the European war as almost full-scale participants. The U.S. had not yet committed soldiers to direct participation and had not yet formally declared war. Likewise, in the Pacific, conflict with Japan continued to escalate, but still remained short of all-out war. When the Roosevelt administration ordered an economic boycott of Japan, including especially the suspension of deliveries of oil, the conflict ratcheted up and full-scale war seemed inevitable.

Yet American political forces in opposition to all-out war remained strong even into the fall of 1941. In October, an American destroyer, the *Reuben James*, leading a convoy of supply ships on their way to Great Britain, was attacked and sunk by German submarines—the most serious direct encounter between Germany and the U.S. to that point.

Rather than immediately using this incident, which resulted in the deaths of more than one hundred American sailors, as a trigger for further movement toward all-in war, Roosevelt waited to gauge the response of the American public. As it turned out, the sinking of the *Reuben James* didn't change much; interventionists pushed for war, and anti-interventionists remained unconvinced—and powerful. As Roosevelt biographer H. W. Brands reports,

> The isolationists contended that the attack revealed why the neutrality law should *not* be revised. "If the losses are going to be this heavy in convoying in our defensive waters," [Ohio Republican Senator] Robert Taft said, "they may be so heavy convoying the rest of the way into British ports that we won't have anything left to defend ourselves with." [Republican Senator] Gerald Nye

[of North Dakota] said bluntly, "You can't expect to walk into a barroom brawl and hope to stay out of the fight."[39]

Brands then adds: "The opposition stopped Roosevelt in his tracks. He refused to take even the symbolic step of suspending relations with Berlin."[40] Roosevelt believed that more direct involvement by the U.S. in the conflicts in Europe and Asia had become ever more necessary, but he still found the resistance of the anti-interventionists a severe constraint. Roosevelt did apparently sense that he had just enough congressional support to overturn the neutrality legislation that formally limited American partisan acts in the conflicts. But, ever the careful politician, he knew that even as he got the revisions of the neutrality rules narrowly passed, he had nothing close to the support needed for a war declaration. Something more extreme than the sinking of the *Reuben James* would be necessary to turn the tide.

In the fall of 1941, tensions with Japan reached the breaking point after Roosevelt rebuffed Konoe's initiative to meet—leading directly to Konoe's resignation. The new Japanese leader, General Hideki Tojo, had commanded the Japanese army that occupied Manchuria and had directed the negotiations that led to Japan's alliance with Germany and Italy. Tojo became prime minister in October 1941.

As prime minister, Tojo spoke of America's policies in early November:

> Two years from now we will have no petroleum for military use. Ships will stop moving. When I think about the strengthening of American defenses in the southwest Pacific, the expansion of the American fleet, the unfinished China Incident, and so on, I see no end to difficulties. We can talk about austerity and suffering, but can our people endure such a life for a long time?[41]

It seems likely that Roosevelt looked for opportunities to escalate the conflict to the point of undermining opposition from anti-interventionists. He probably did expect some dramatic provocation from the Japanese or Germans, but expected this provocation not severely to damage the American war capabilities. That is, he likely did not anticipate that the American fleet harbored in the American Hawaiian colony would be devastated by a sudden attack.

Of course, this sudden attack did happen. Though the damage to the American navy was more severe than may have been expected, the Pearl Harbor incident more than fulfilled Roosevelt's hopes for a transformation

---

39. Ibid., 460. Brands' italics.
40. Ibid.
41. Quoted in Kershaw, *Fateful Choices*, 331.

of American public opinion. The reluctance in Congress to go to war ended. December 7, 1941, became one of the most famous dates in all American history.

The next day, Roosevelt addressed the nation with his brilliant "Day of Infamy" speech to Congress. His speech led to a unanimous vote in the Senate and nearly unanimous vote in the House to declare war on Japan. Only Jeanette Rankin, Montana Republican House member, voted against the War (as she had in 1917, in response to Wilson's request for a war declaration).

The situation with Germany was still uncertain at the time of the war declaration on Japan. Germany remained a much greater concern, but the U.S. had no overt provocation to justify declaring war on Germany. Roosevelt began to push for a declaration nonetheless. He addressed the country on December 9 with the claim that the Japanese attack had been pushed by Hitler. Roosevelt, in the words of biographer Brands, aimed to convince America that "the Germans and Japanese conducted their military and naval operations according to a single global plan, one that treated any victory for an Axis nation as a victory for all. Japan had struck the United States more openly than Germany and Italy had thus far, but the danger from those countries was no less."[42]

As it turned out, before Roosevelt could test Congress in this new situation with a request for a war declaration on Germany, Hitler solved the problem. Germany, somewhat surprisingly,[43] declared war on the United States on December 11. With this declaration, soon matched by the U.S. in response, the *world* war truly began. Roosevelt pushed full speed ahead: "The forces endeavoring to enslave the entire world now are moving toward this hemisphere," he said. "Never before has there been a greater challenge to life, liberty, and civilization. I therefore request the Congress to recognize a state of war between the United States and Germany."[44]

Roosevelt's December 8 "Day of Infamy" speech established the basic framework for the American understanding of the war with Japan.

---

42. Quoted in Brands, *Traitor to His Class*, 473. Actually, according to British historian Ian Kershaw, the Japanese attack came as a (welcome) surprise to Hitler (*Fateful Choices*, 384).

43. Kershaw suggests that Hitler's decision to declare war on the U.S. was not necessitated by Germany's treaty obligations toward Japan. Rather, the most likely motivation for Hitler was a strong desire to seize the initiative again in his campaign for world power in the context of the bogged-down attack on the Soviet Union. Hitler was enormously impressed with the decisiveness of Japan's attack and likely overestimated the impact of that attack in damaging the U.S. (ibid., 382–430).

44. Quoted in Brands, *Traitor to His Class*, 474.

> Yesterday, December 7th, 1941—a date which will live in infamy—the United States of America was suddenly and deliberately attacked by naval and air forces of the empire of Japan. The United States was at peace with that nation and, at the solicitation of Japan, was still in conversation with the government and its emperor looking toward the maintenance of peace in the Pacific. . . .
>
> This morning, the Japanese attacked Midway Island. Japan has, therefore, undertaken a surprise offensive extending throughout the Pacific area. The facts of yesterday speak for themselves. . . .
>
> Always will we remember the character of the onslaught against us. No matter how long it may take us to overcome this premeditated invasion, the American people in their righteous might will win through to absolute victory. I believe I interpret the will of the Congress and of the people when I assert that we will not only defend ourselves to the uttermost, but will make very certain that this form of treachery shall never endanger us again. Hostilities exist. There is no blinking at the fact that our people, our territory and our interests are in grave danger. With confidence in our armed forces—with the unbounding determination of our people—we will gain the inevitable triumph, so help us God.
>
> I ask that the Congress declare that since the unprovoked and dastardly attack by Japan on Sunday, December 7th, 1941, a state of war has existed between the United States and the Japanese empire.[45]

Roosevelt's basic message asserted: this attack was totally unprovoked ("and dastardly"). The U.S. was committed to peace until the fundamentally aggressive Japanese acted so treacherously to violate this peace. America's "might" is "righteous." Our response to this attack will be an act of national "defense," even as we are now committed to "absolute victory." The seeds were sown in this speech both for a strong sense of American innocence and pure intentions in responding to Japanese aggression and for what would become a highly potent basis for motivation: revenge for the unprovoked and devastating violence of the Japanese.[46]

45. Excerpted from the text of Roosevelt's speech; see http://en.wikisource.org/wiki/Pearl_Harbor_speech.

46. The potency of this motivation may be seen, in just one example, in the words of President Harry Truman after the U.S. use of nuclear weapons on Hiroshima and Nagasaki: he asserted that one of the reasons he had no qualms whatsoever about using these weapons of mass destruction was the lack of qualms the Japanese had had in their unprovoked attack on Pearl Harbor—implying that the killing of tens of thousands of

An awareness of the relationships between the U.S. and Japan in the years and months prior to December 7, 1941, make it clear that Pearl Harbor was not an "unprovoked" act by the Japanese. Roosevelt had expressed desire for the Japanese to act in such a way that would make a military escalation by the Americans possible. Also, to state that the U.S. had been actively seeking peace with Japan flies in the face of many aspects of America's actual behavior, most obviously Roosevelt's rebuffs of former Prime Minister Konoe that seem to have led to the prime minister's resignation and opened the door for the extreme militarist Tojo to move directly into power.

A more accurate reading of Pearl Harbor, I suggest, would be that it was simply another step in a long-running dynamic of escalation between two competing imperial powers.[47] The U.S. resisted Japanese expansionism in antagonistic ways that empowered the more extreme elements of the Japanese leadership. It does not seem that Japan actually was motivated by a desire to move into the western hemisphere nearly so much as a desire to end the U.S. resistance to Japan's efforts in the East. Japan still remained dependent upon the U.S. as a major source of natural resources, especially oil.

The attack on Pearl Harbor was a terrible tactical miscalculation by the Japanese.[48] They likely hoped that after receiving such a severe blow, the U.S. would pull back and withdraw more deeply into its isolationist shell, allowing Japan a freer rein. Surely no leader in Japan contemplated actual acts of conquest aimed at the U.S. In actuality, the response of the Americans was exactly the opposite from what the Japanese expected. Pearl Harbor turned the U.S. toward an even more aggressive policy in relation to Japan, one that ended only with immense destruction visited upon the Japanese mainland and (nearly) unconditional surrender (Roosevelt's "absolute victory").

The revenge dynamic unleashed by the Pearl Harbor attack had a tremendous impact on American sensibilities in the war that followed—and in the years since.[49] I believe that we need to take seriously the moral grounding for the call for Americans to support the War—what I call the "purpose statements" above, especially Roosevelt's "Four Freedoms" speech and the Atlantic Charter. However, we must also remember the role the powerful

---

Japanese (mostly civilians of all ages) was morally equivalent to the killing of roughly twenty-four hundred American soldiers.

47. Chomsky, *American Power*, 357.

48. Dower, *Cultures of War*, 3–147.

49. Consider the controversies over the proposed fifty-year recognition of the Hiroshima/Nagasaki nuclear attacks at the Smithsonian Institution in 1995. See Linenthal and Engelhardt, *History Wars*.

desire for revenge against the Japanese played in fostering support for the war.

We will need to reflect, though, on the moral significance of revenge motives. If indeed one key element of the moral legacy of World War II was the actual empowering of desires for revenge, how did that empowerment play out—both in the War that followed Pearl Harbor and in the living memory of that war in the years since? One question is why a strictly military action on a colonial military base thousands of miles from the continental United States would have played such a potent role in the moral justifications of massive attacks on civilian populations in Japan that resulted in thousands upon thousands of deaths.

The immediate effect of the quest for revenge against the Japanese centered on a target significantly different from the Japanese themselves. Ever since Winston Churchill's ascent to the role of prime minister of Great Britain, the Roosevelt administration had faced ever-mounting pressures to intervene in the war versus Germany. Roosevelt supported moving in that direction but, as we have noted, had great difficulty given the democratic constraints of U.S. governmental processes.

That the attack on Pearl Harbor served Roosevelt's interests in joining the European war may be seen in the commitment made at the very beginning of U.S. involvement and maintained for the duration of the War: for the U.S. to devote its energies primarily to the war with Germany, not Japan.[50] Roosevelt's actions gave this message: certainly, the Japanese attack will live forever in infamy, being unprovoked and dastardly. And that attack has profoundly damaged and endangered the United States. Nonetheless, the war that we must turn our focus toward and devote the bulk of our resources to is not the war with our attacker, but the war in Europe with Germany. The revenge spirit against Japan that transformed "America first" isolationists (many of whom had German sympathies—e.g., Charles Lindbergh) into strong war supporters most of all served the purpose of ending just about all opposition to American participation in the war against Germany.

When Roosevelt took to the air on December 8, 1941, and established the template for America's commitment to total war (the "unprovoked," "dastardly" attack of a war-mongering tyranny against a totally "peace-oriented" democracy), he actually established a template for deeply problematic militarism and wars in the United States from the immediate postwar years down to the present.

The question, in the end, of whether the U.S. was morally justified in becoming a full participant in World War II turns out to be a bit complicated.

---

50. Brands, *Traitor to His Class*, 473–83.

In terms of the immediate formal entry of the Americans into the war, it is true that the initiative was taken by U.S. enemies. Japan attacked the U.S. Navy in its colonial outpost at Pearl Harbor. Only then did the U.S. declare war on Japan. Germany formally joined as a Japanese ally, saving President Roosevelt the difficult task of persuading Congress to pass a war declaration to join the European war.

However, the U.S. had clearly initiated actions on both fronts that made full-scale involvement inevitable at some point. Did American leaders have legitimate "just cause" grounds to do so? The mythology about the War that now holds sway in American popular consciousness seems to see three key factors as central to the justifiability of engaging this war as an active belligerent. All three factors, if present, would have persuasive just cause support. However, none of these three seem actually to have played major roles in America's movement toward war. These three factors are (1) to defend against a literal invasion of the U.S. with the intent to take it over, (2) to further the cause of democracy vis-à-vis aggressive tyranny, and (3) to save Europe's imperiled Jews.

In fact, the United States' national borders were never under threat. Japan attacked Pearl Harbor *not* as a first step in a campaign to conquer the U.S.—the Japanese war-makers never imagined that would be possible. They hoped to deal the U.S. a severe blow in order to strengthen their hand in the Far East. They believed—mistakenly—that the U.S. would pull back from support of China and of British colonial outposts.

Likewise, Germany did not have invading the U.S. as part of its agenda.[51] Conceivably, had the Germans succeeded quickly in defeating the Soviet Union and over the next several years consolidated their dominance over all of Europe, they may have turned West. But such a possibility was at best in the distant future—and the most likely German hope would have been to find ways to coexist with the U.S. (a not unimaginable prospect given the large investments of American corporations in Germany in the 1930s).

While American leaders, and even more the broader American public, did in some general sense support democratic practices and the principle of self-determination around the world, such support *never* determined American foreign policy. Various anticolonial movements would learn this to their great chagrin in the years immediately after World War II.[52]

Put simply, when the U.S. aligned itself with the Soviet Union and Nationalist China, American leaders made it clear that their war effort simply

---

51. Kershaw, *Fateful Choices*, 382–430.
52. See Bills, *Empire and Cold War*.

was not animated by principled opposition to tyranny—no matter what the purpose statements declared.

I will take up Germany's destruction of European Jewry in chapter 4 below. Here I will simply reiterate the statement I made earlier in this chapter: we have no bases for saying that either the U.S. entry into the War or the U.S. prosecution of the War was shaped in any appreciable way by an effort to intervene on behalf of the Jews.[53]

Why, then, *did* American leaders involve their nation in the War to an ever-increasing degree prior to the final (all but inevitable) step in December 1941?

These seem to be some of the factors:

(1) Japan's expansionistic policies in the Far East came to a point of threatening America's own imperialistic interests in that region—especially in China and the Philippines. Political theorist Michael Walzer, in his widely cited book *Just and Unjust Wars*, argues in favor of the U.S. war with Germany as a just war, but he sees the Pacific War as essentially a conflict between rival imperialistic powers.[54]

(2) The U.S. had a close alliance with Great Britain and was bound by this alliance to support Britain in its war effort. However, the U.S. certainly went beyond the treaty obligations with Britain in effect in September 1939. And why was Britain at war? Most immediately, Britain entered into war with Germany due to a dubious mutual defense treaty with Poland that emerged mostly because of Britain's imperial concerns, not because of a threat to the viability of the British nation itself. And Britain's conflict with Japan stemmed from Japan's threat to Britain's colonial possessions in the Far East.

(3) American leaders certainly came to have deep concerns with regard to Germany's atrocities. However, these concerns likely were not mainly concerns about violations of democratic values such as self-determination and disarmament. Major American corporations profited quite handsomely from their investments in Nazi Germany after 1933. However, by the late 1930s, it was becoming clear that German nationalism placed the American corporate presence in jeopardy. Germany was proving to be unanswerable to outside economic interests and becoming too much of a free agent.

---

53. As mentioned above, see Wyman, *Abandonment of the Jews*, and Hamerow, *Why We Watched*. Hamerow's book is especially pertinent to my point here because he is quite sympathetic toward the dilemmas faced by Amercian and British leaders, but he acknowledges that saving Jews did *not* play a major role in war aims—even if he thinks there are good reasons why it did not.

54. Walzer, *Just and Unjust Wars*, 113.

(4) A more general, and perhaps central, dynamic that gradually emerged was the opportunity this conflict provided for powerful forces in the U.S. to benefit from a rearrangement of global power dynamics. Certainly, in terms of the *results* of the U.S. investment in the War, the payoff for these powerful forces far exceeded what may have seemed possible in 1939. The U.S. became *the* world's economic superpower—and, to a somewhat lesser extent, the world's military superpower.[55]

In light of these four dynamics, the just cause question becomes more complicated in relation to America's participation in the War. For now, let us simply note that none of these four factors would pass muster in traditional just war reasoning.

---

55. "In 1945, the United States had two-thirds of the world's gold reserves, three-fourths of its invested capital, half of its shipping vessels, and half of its manufacturing capacity. Its gross national product was three times that of the Soviet Union and more than five times that of Great Britain. It was also nearing completion of the atomic bomb" (Leffler, *For the Soul of Mankind*, 41).

3

Was America's Conduct in World War II Just?

CRITERIA FOR "JUST MEANS"

In chapter 2, I looked at the rationale for the United States entering the War: was the *cause* just? In the European war, the violence of Nazi Germany provided several bases for warfare being the appropriate response: "an injustice demanding reparation," "offense committed against innocent third parties," and "moral guilt demanding punishment," among others. In the Pacific War, Japan provided the key basis for the response of war, "an aggression demanding reparation."[1]

However, the American mythology of World War II, established at the very beginning of the U.S. formal entry into the War with Franklin Roosevelt's "day of infamy" speech, masks numerous complicating factors that made the "just cause" bases for America joining the War a bit more complicated than the mythology of the "good war" would admit. As we saw, none of the three standard reasons for war (i.e., resist invasion, further democracy, and save Jews) actually played a major role in America's initiative to enter the conflict between September 1939 and December 1941.

The mythology asserts (not necessarily inaccurately) that the U. S. had more legitimate causes for entering World War II than probably any other war. However, this assertion may actually be making more a statement

---

1. The criteria that are quoted here come from Yoder, *When War Is Unjust*, 151.

about the lack of justifiability in going to war in the other cases than the clear justness of entering this particular war.

In the "good war" mythology, the initial affirmation that entering this war was justifiable seems to end the process of discernment. Of course, in the mythology, *justifiable* is a weak term. The Nazis are seen to be the embodiment of evil in the modern world. So of course it was "justifiable" to go to war to end their tyranny and to save the world from their aggression and remorseless racism. More than "justifiable," going to war with them was a moral imperative; it was a *necessity*.[2] The mythology sees the Japanese almost as negatively due to their aggression at Pearl Harbor and the general viciousness with which they attacked China and other countries.

Michael Bess's useful book *Choices Under Fire* rejects the notion that the "justness" of American involvement in World War II (a notion he in the end affirms) should lead to an end of moral evaluation of the tactics the U.S. used. Some of his critics disagree. According to historian Eric Bergerud, the key adjective to describe America's participation in World War II is "necessary." It was necessary for the U.S. to go to war in order to resist effectively the evils of Nazism and Japanese militarism. This "necessity" provides all the moral justification needed; to nitpick the details of how Americans actually conducted themselves in this war threatens to negate the morally exemplary character of American involvement.

Bergerud concludes his sharp critique of Bess's work this way:

> I find it almost incomprehensible that anyone would claim to discover moral ambiguity in World War II. . . . The general public in the West does not seem to suffer any major ethical quandary concerning the war. The gut-wrenching argument that Bess sees inside the West concerning the conduct of World War II exists, in my view, between a small number of people in academia against the vast bulk of the population who may regret the violence of the war but do not question for a minute its necessity. Machiavelli, criticized by Bess, was quite right when describing a necessary war as a just war. If World War II was not necessary, no war has been.[3]

These comments direct us to several key points in relation to my intentions with the present book. That actions that result in the violent deaths of millions of people (perhaps three-fourths of whom were noncombatants[4]) could be anything but *at best* "morally ambiguous" seems obvious if the

2. Walzer, "World War II."
3. Bergerud, "Critique of *Choices Under Fire*," 41.
4. Judt, *Postwar*, 18–19.

term *morality* is to have meaning (and I add the reminder again that the main appeal to Americans to go to war was fundamentally a *moral* appeal). Bess's analysis seems like the minimum a morally responsible person could undertake in response to the mass paroxysm of death-dealing violence we call World War II. Of course, the danger in Bess's enterprise arises when we realize, as Bergerud does at least implicitly, that once we *honestly* raise more questions we have to be open to the possibility that the actions we are considering were in fact *immoral*.[5]

With his rejection of the validity of critical moral discernment in relation to Allied conduct in the War, Bergerud helpfully illustrates the power of the myth of redemptive violence. In light of this myth, it would of course not be surprising that "the general public in the West does not suffer any major ethical quandary concerning the war." This lack of "ethical quandaries" even though the American military directly destroyed so much human life is not evidence that this obviously was a "necessary and therefore just war" nearly so much as it is evidence of a powerful moral blind spot.

This moral blind spot, I will argue in Part Two, has resulted in a devastating legacy of American violence throughout the world over the past sixty-five years. If Americans have no ethical qualms about what they did in World War II, and refuse even to consider the possibility of careful reflection on the way they conducted themselves in that war, how could they not but be vulnerable to multiple largely unquestioned military excursions in the years since?

The consideration of conduct in war is, certainly, a difficult endeavor. One of the basic issues points to the heart of the entire question about the relationship between morality and war. Moral rationales are necessary to mobilize support for and participation in war—certainly for democracies but also for most other states. People go to war for moral reasons; they justify past wars for moral reasons, using moral criteria to determine where a "cause" is just. Also, the Western moral tradition has established criteria for what is understood to be just conduct in war—some elements of which have become part of international law and the laws of most countries. Underlying these criteria are moral principles that would require combatant nations to hold back, to limit in some sense their tactics to stay within the parameters of the moral just war criteria.

5. Burleigh's *Moral Combat* purports to be working on the level of moral analysis, but in reality its approach echoes Bergerud's. Burleigh's agenda is apologetics—to show that the Allies were "moral"—not genuine moral reflection that treats moral values as stable notions that we seek to apply equally to all sides (in contrast to Davies, *No Simple Victory*, 63–64).

PART ONE: Total War   *Was America's Conduct in World War II Just?*   57

This is the issue: how much is a nation that has made the commitment to war going to weaken its chances of winning the war in order to operate within the just conduct criteria? And, if it does not operate within those criteria, does that then mean that the nation is fighting an *unjust* war? And if the nation *is* fighting an unjust war, what becomes the moral responsibility of its citizens?

Another way of stating this issue is to ask, how much evidence do we have that the war leaders in our most democratic nations (i.e., the United States and Great Britain) self-consciously considered moral concerns as they formulated and put into practice their strategies for fighting World War II? It does seem, from accounts of how the two nations developed their theories and practices for military bombing and, specifically, the American run-up to the use of nuclear weapons on Japan, that moral considerations played virtually *no* role.[6]

The two central elements for considering just conduct are proportionality (that the damage the war creates not be out of proportion with the good to be achieved by successful prosecution of the war) and noncombatant immunity (that war is to be focused on soldiers fighting soldiers; those not fighting in the war should not be targets of military aggression).[7]

As we reflect morally on the tactics used in World War II, these two elements provide our basic framework. How do the various tactics cohere (or not) with these two general criteria? We may recognize that states at war do not let proportionality and noncombatant immunity, as moral criteria, shape their policy decisions. Given the centrality of these elements in the Western moral tradition, however, such recognition should be part of our questioning the "goodness" of this war. Again, the Western moral tradition provided most of the content for the moral appeal that Allied leaders used to gather support from their citizens for fighting World War II. Was such support appropriate given the failure to operate within the moral tradition in actually fighting the war people were asked to support?

My main interests in this book are not to make definitive judgments about whether World War II actually meets the criteria of the proverbial "just war" as one defined by just cause and just conduct. I do think that

6. On the general philosophy of air war as it shaped policies for Great Britain and the United States, see especially Grayling, *Among the Dead Cities*. For the American run up to bombing Hiroshima and Nagaski, see Carroll, *House of War*. On the past century as a whole, see Tanaka and Young, *Bombing Civilians*. See also Markusen and Kopf, *Holocaust and Strategic Bombing*, which draws unsettling parallels between the Holocaust and Allied World War II bombing practices.

7. "Just war theorists talk about the *jus ad bellum* question of going to war in response to a [just cause]. In the midst of war they focus on questions of *jus in bello*, which includes prohibitions on [unjust] actions" (Fiala, *Just War Myth*, 9–10).

working at such an evaluation *is* worthwhile. Contrary to the assumptions of those who would say the only issue for drawing conclusions is whether the war was "necessary" or not,[8] our evaluation must take into account *both* just cause *and* just conduct themes, that we may more wisely evaluate choices in our present world.

My *main* concern, therefore, is with our *present* in the twenty-first century. We must consider conduct questions in order to assess the moral legacy of World War II and our evaluation of the role it has played in American society in the years since. If we conclude that the conduct of the War so violates the standards of justice that it renders the War's moral legacy highly problematic, we must then struggle with the question of whether we need to find other means to address problems like what the War allegedly sought to address (problems of Nazi tyranny and Japanese militarism). And we would need to think about means other than war that may achieve the legitimate goals articulated in the "Four Freedoms" speech and Atlantic Charter (especially the principles of self-determination and disarmament).

I will suggest that total war, the war America actually fought, and maybe the institution of war in general, simply did not have the capability of achieving good ends without creating, in balance, more problems. The War itself provides at best mixed evidence—its execution and immediate impact did overwhelmingly violate the criteria of proportionality and noncombatant immunity. At the same time, the War achieved some good things—most centrally the defeat of German and Japanese imperialism. However, the aftermath of the War in the United States, and in the United States' role on the postwar world, make it clear that the moral legacy of World War II is a problem to overcome, not an accomplishment to celebrate (or so I will argue in Part Two below).

AREA BOMBING IN THE EUROPEAN WAR

Probably only the debate over the American use of atomic weapons on Japan in August 1945 (to be discussed below) has been more intense in the years since World War II than the debate about the morality (and tactical value) of the bombing strategy followed by the Allies in the European war. Did the intentional targeting of major civilian populations in Germany for bombing raids violate the core just conduct criterion regarding noncombatant immunity? And, then, how much should that matter? Do the self-apparent

---

8. I should note here, though, that I don't think the issue of "necessary" is open-and-shut. See chapter 2 above. For an interesting argument that indeed World War II was *not* necessary, see Buchanan, *Churchill*.

PART ONE: Total War   Was America's Conduct in World War II Just?   59

evils of Nazi Germany justify whatever tactics were deemed necessary to subdue the beasts?

Clearly, this question is not simply a post-World War II armchair moralist's after-the-fact debate. It was stated explicitly as the war began. The precise day on which Germany invaded Poland and the European war began, September 1, 1939, President Roosevelt took to the airwaves with an internationally broadcast speech that called upon the belligerents *not* to target civilians. He feared that "hundreds of thousands of innocent human beings who have no responsibility for, and who are not even remotely participating in, the hostilities" would be killed. Let the belligerents "affirm [a] determination that [their] armed forces shall in no event, and under no circumstances, undertake the bombardment from the air of civilian populations or of unfortified cities."[9]

Almost certainly Roosevelt directed his words in 1939 toward the Nazis as they invaded Poland. He most likely sought to establish a base from which to condemn Nazi atrocities when they inevitably occurred. Still, this direct statement by the president of the United States, widely broadcast and stated without qualification, made it clear that in the minds of the leaders of the Allies the taboo against directly targeting "innocent human beings" remained powerful in their consciousness—and that "bombardment from the air of civilian populations" was seen as a clear example of such a forbidden act.

When Roosevelt gave this call to respect noncombatant immunity, the Royal Air Force (RAF) of Great Britain had been planning ever since World War I to make such "bombardments" a central part of their strategy.[10] Nonetheless, Neville Chamberlain, Britain's prime minister in September 1939, did seem to agree with Roosevelt's exhortation. Chamberlain stated to the House of Commons on September 14, "His Majesty's Government will never resort to the deliberate attack on women and children and other civilians for the purpose of mere terrorism."[11] However, Chamberlain's successor, Winston Churchill, had few such scruples—as would be reflected in the policies and practices of the RAF throughout the War.

The RAF had been established as an autonomous part of Britain's military in 1918, near the end of World War I. The leader of the RAF's bombers

9. Quoted in Grayling, *Among the Dead Cities*, 148–49.
10. This is a statement from British air force leader Hugh Trenchard in 1928: "Whatever we may wish or hope, there is not the slightest doubt that in the next war both sides will send their aircraft out without scruple to bomb those objectives which they consider the most suitable. I would, therefore, urge most strongly that we accept this fact and face it." Quoted in Lindqvist, *History of Bombing*, 59.
11. Quoted in Grayling, *Among the Dead Cities*, 149.

at that time and for years following, Hugh Trenchard, affirmed bombing civilian targets and sought to implement that policy during World War I. He stated, "The effect of bombing civilian targets would be that the German government would be forced to face very considerable and constantly increasing civil pressure which might result in political disintegration."[12] The war ended before this policy could be implemented, but the pursuit of such a policy based on Trenchard's convictions about its likely effectiveness became central for the RAF.

The British had opportunity to test Trenchard's doctrines in several places in their empire in the interwar years. For example, the RAF bombed Iraqi and Afghani tribespeople on several occasions—and met with success in repressing uprisings in those colonies. Significantly, a commander of a bomber force in one of those bombing episodes, Arthur Harris, became the person in charge of RAF bombing of Germany during World War II.[13]

In his discussion of the history of the development of doctrines for the use of air power in warfare for the United States and for Britain during the interwar years, philosopher A. J. Grayling demonstrates that the moral considerations central to just war philosophy simply were not part of the picture. The differences between the air war philosophies of the Britons and the Americans lay much more in understandings of effectiveness than in moral scruples.

The British focused more on civilian bombardment as a tactic because they believed the demoralization of the enemy's general population would lead to military success. The American doctrine placed priority on causing enemy collapse by bombing military targets, especially those having most to do with supplying the enemy's armies.

The American priority had *the same goal* as Britain's civilian bombing: "to destroy the will of the people at home." But the best way to "destroy the will of the people" is indirect—disrupting the economy that feeds the war machine. The American strategists argued that to bomb "carefully selected targets," requiring relatively few bombs, "would snap vital threads in the enemy's 'industrial web,' and as a result secure a quick victory." These targets would include networks for electricity, transport, and oil.[14]

The main weapons Britain had that could be used effectively in war with Germany were its navy and its air force. In the months between the declaration of war in September 1939 and the fighting between British and

12. Quoted in Grayling, *Among the Dead Cities*, 131.

13. Ibid., 132, and Lindqvist, *History of Bombing*, 41–55. See also Tanaka, "British 'Humane Bombing,'" 8–29.

14. Grayling, *Among the Dead Cities*, 136.

German forces that began when the Germans invaded Britain's ally France in May 1940, the British military chiefs of staff drew up a strategy for how to defeat Germany. This strategy would focus on three central elements: (1) a naval blockade and other tactics that would greatly reduce access to food in Germany and the occupied countries (as well as other raw materials), leading to massive starvation in the general population and hence to demoralization and resistance to their government; (2) use of the bombing of civilian populations to demoralize the population further; and (3) working to encourage subversion against the German government wherever possible.[15] So, from the very start, the British strategy for defeating Germany relied at its core on directly targeting noncombatants in search of victory through killing, terrorizing, and dispossessing countless millions.

After France surrendered to Germany in June 1940, the central arena of the war became the air battle between the German Luftwaffe and the RAF, known as the Battle of Britain. In what was called its "finest hour," the RAF staved off the German attack. By September 1940, Hitler decided to turn his focus eastward. Germany abandoned its quest to invade Britain and instead took on what Hitler had from the start seen as his ultimate agenda: to crush the Soviet Union. Nobody else knew this at the time, of course, until the Germans sprang their surprise attack on their supposed ally in June 1941.[16] But the air struggle between September 1940 and June 1941 was essentially a holding action. After June 1941, the Luftwaffe turned its main focus eastward.

At this point, the British faced a dilemma. Though they could stop the Germans from invading them, they did not have the ability to invade the continent in force. Their naval blockade could do some damage (though the people who suffered directly were non-Germans in occupied territories[17]), and the Battle of the Atlantic—the naval conflict involving mainly Britain, Germany, and eventually the U.S.—raged on but was not central to

15. Baker, *Human Smoke*, 188.
16. Kershaw, *Fateful Choices*, 54–90.
17. Former President Herbert Hoover led relief efforts to save the lives of starving people in Europe. He harshly condemned the blockade in October 1941 in a radio address: "There were about forty million children in the German-invaded democracies, he said, and the blockade was killing them. 'Their pleas for food ascend hourly to the free democracies of the west' . . . America was now, by failing to compel England to change its policy, a moral participant in the blockade. 'Is the Allied cause any further advanced today as a consequence of this starvation of children? Are Hitler's armies any less victorious than if these children had been saved? Are Britain's children better fed today because these millions of former allied children have been hungry or died? Can you point to one benefit that has been gained from this holocaust?'" (Baker, *Human Smoke*, 411).

the viability of the Nazi state and its war-making capabilities. The only real direct way Britain could hit Germany itself was through the air.

Two major factors limited what the RAF was able to do. One was the inefficacy of bombing technology at that point in the war. The planes simply were unable to hit their targets with any accuracy. Already in the summer of 1941, Britain's military studied the efficiency of the bombing. The report, published in August, concluded:

> The bombing campaign was a massively wasteful and futile effort. . . . Many bomber aircraft never found their targets at all; even in good weather on moonlit nights, only two-fifths of bombers found their targets, but in hazy or raining weather only one in ten did so. On moonless nights the proportion fell to a helpless one in fifteen. In all circumstances, of those that reached their designated target only a third of them place their bombs within five miles of it.[18]

The second problem, made more clear during the course of the war, was the RAF's ideology that hindered its leaders from clear-eyed cost-benefit analysis. RAF *doctrine* focused on the demoralization of enemy civilian populations over attacks against specific targets that would undermine the military capabilities of the enemy. Britain's efforts at demoralization through terror largely failed, especially when considered in light of the costs to the RAF in aircraft shot down and in the expense of making the flights. On the other hand, with greatly improved targeting capabilities by 1944–45, U.S. efforts that focused on military targets met with significant success. American precision bombing actually played a major role in severely undermining German fighting capability in the final months of the War.[19]

Up until the summer of 1941, though most of Britain's air attacks had hit largely civilian targets (as had Germany's), the stated policy was not to *target* civilian populations. This officially changed on July 9. On that day, Britain's War Cabinet approved a directive to Bomber Command that switched its focus from oil and naval targets to "destroying the morale of the civil population as a whole and of the industrial workers in particular." At this point, intentional bombing of civilians became official British practice.[20]

---

18. Quoted in Grayling, *Among the Dead Cities*, 46.

19. "Before bombing attacks on the oil infrastructure began in May 1944, Germany was producing an average of 316,000 tons a month. Bombing caused production to fall to 107,000 tons in June 1944, and 17,000 tons in the following September. Aviation fuel from synthetic-oil plants fell from 175,000 tons in April 1944 to 30,000 in June and then to 5,000 tons in September" (ibid., 109).

20. Quoted in ibid., 47.

For the next several years, especially after Arthur Harris (a true believer in the doctrine of victory through the demoralization of civilians[21]) became the head of Bomber Command, the RAF bombed as many German cities as they could. Harris developed a list of German cities to be destroyed and set about systematically doing so. This is the text of a leaflet dropped on Germany in 1942, as approved by Harris:

> We are bombing Germany, city by city, and ever more terribly, in order to make it impossible for you to go on in the war. That is our object. We shall pursue it remorselessly. City by city; Lubeck, Rostock, Cologne, Emden, Bremen, Wilhelmshaven, Duisberg, Hamburg—and the list will grow longer and longer. Let the Nazis drag you down to disaster with them if you will. That is for you to decide. We are coming by day and by night. No part of the Reich is safe.[22]

The most notorious example of destruction was the devastating attack on the defenseless city of Dresden in February 1945. Dresden had become a magnet for refugees because of its presumed safety (it had little military significance). As reported by an American prisoner of war, William Spanos, who witnessed the bombing, two sets of British bombers descended on Dresden, dropping an immense tonnage of incendiary bombs during the night, followed in the morning by American planes dropping explosive devices.[23] No reliable account of direct deaths caused by the bombing has been universally accepted; some estimates put the total at more than one hundred thousand.

The War finally ended in May 1945, and the bombing stopped. Interestingly, the British government, in the immediate aftermath of the War and in the years to come, did not honor the RAF or Bomber Command for its campaign. When Churchill went on the BBC on May 13, 1945, six days after the German surrender, to address the nation and the world with his victory speech and to name those to whom Britain owed gratitude for the successful war effort, he did not mention Bomber Command—probably intentionally. When campaign medals were passed out to leaders in the war effort, Bomber Command was passed over. Arthur Harris was denied permission to publish his final report that summarized Bomber Command's war work.[24]

---

21. Markusen and Kopf, *Holocaust and Strategic Bombing*, 156–57.
22. Quoted in Grayling, *Among the Dead Cities*, 50.
23. Spanos, *Neighborhood of Zero*, 90–125.
24. Grayling, *Among the Dead Cities*, 176.

THE ALLIANCE WITH THE SOVIET UNION

One element of taking the Allies' stated justifications for the War seriously is to ask how the conduct of the war itself served (or violated) those justifications. Part of this question has to relate to a major element of the Allied war effort: the alliance the United States established with the Soviet Union. Because of this alliance with the Soviets, when we consider the conduct that was associated with defeating Germany, we must also keep in mind the conduct of the Soviets—and the values that were served by playing a major role in what turned out to be a victory for the Soviet Union.

This is how historian Michael Bess summarizes the issue in his book that examines the "moral dimensions of World War II":

> Great Britain and the United States only succeeded in beating down the evils of Nazism through an alliance, shoulder to shoulder, with a regime that was in many ways equally as vicious as Hitler's. This simple fact often gets lost, somehow, amid the celebration of the great triumph over the Germans and Japanese. Here, for example, is the way the historian Stephen Ambrose closes his best-selling book *Citizen Soldiers*: "At the core, the American citizen soldiers knew the difference between right and wrong, and they didn't want to live in a world in which the wrong prevailed. So they fought, and won, and we all of us, living and yet to be born, must be forever profoundly grateful." The impression one gets here is that *because* the citizen soldiers (good guys) beat the bad guys (Nazis), then wrong (general badness) did *not* prevail.
>
> This is misleading in two ways. First, the overwhelming bulk of the killing of Nazis was not done by citizen soldiers at all, but rather by the soldiers of the Red Army: the ratio is about four German soldiers killed by the Russians for every one killed by the British and Americans. And second, the triumphant powers at the end of World War II included one of the most ruthless, pathologically murderous regimes in the history of humankind: our Soviet allies. Badness was actually having a very good day on May 8, 1945.[25]

---

25. Bess, *Choices Under Fire*, 167–68. Another popular example of the lack of attention to the Soviet role in defeating the Nazis and the glorifying of the victory as a vindication of the American way of life is Ken Burns' film series *The War*. An important virtue of Norman Davies' one-volume history of the defeat of the Nazis, *No Simple Victory*, is that he seeks to give the Soviet role its proper weight. See also Glantz and House, *When Titans Clashed*.

Bess concludes his treatment of the moral conundrum with this comment:

> The great victory on the Eastern Front presents an awe-inspiring, and simultaneously horrifying, spectacle: a complex picture rather far from the straightforward ticker-tape jubilation that we usually associate with V-E Day. Soviet bravery, Soviet resourcefulness, Soviet ruthlessness, Soviet mass murder; the suffering of the Russian people, a suffering unlike anything else in this war except perhaps that of the Chinese and the Jews;[26] a will to survive, a will to revenge; a war machine that absorbed the frightful impact of German power and then struck back, smashing its enemy; a nightmare state, led by a cunning and remorseless man, looming over world politics in 1945, casting shadow where there might have been hope.[27]

That it was morally problematic for the Allies to have entered into an alliance with the Soviet Union seems clear on several levels. The Soviet leadership shared virtually none of the stated values of the United States and Great Britain. Roosevelt clearly meant his "Four Freedoms" speech to establish an absolute contrast between American values and those affirmed by Nazi Germany, and to bolster support for furthering the struggle against Germany. Likewise with the stated values that lay at the heart of the Atlantic Charter. Yet, the Soviet Union stood as an antithesis to those stated values just as much as did the Nazis.

Many of the details of the mass killings in the Soviet Union—the forced starvation of millions of Ukrainians in the 1930s, for example, and the terrible purges that led to the deaths of thousands upon thousands[28]—were not widely known in 1941. However, Allied leaders surely knew enough to be aware that Joseph Stalin and his police state embodied an utter disregard for human life. If the true enemy in the War was the *spirit* of Nazism—the tyranny, the threatened obliteration of Western civilization, the implacable threat to democracy—how would this "enemy" be defeated should, through alliance, the U.S. actually serve to empower a parallel spirit, the spirit of Stalinism?

---

26. Bess should have included the Poles here as well, especially in light of a number of references he has to the several atrocities Poles suffered at the hands of the Soviets (and Nazis) during the War. Fully 20 percent of the Polish population of 1939 was killed by 1945 (Judt, *Postwar*, 18). Timothy Snyder gives a grim account of the devastation of Poland in *Bloodlands*, especially in the chapter titled "Molotov-Ribbentrap Europe," 119–54.

27. Bess, *Choices Under Fire*, 178.

28. See Snyder, *Bloodlands*.

We saw in the previous section that the tactics used by America's British allies at times crossed the line and overtly violated the criteria for the just conduct of war. Much, much worse were the tactics of the Soviets. Certainly, in some senses, the Soviet war against the Germans satisfied "just cause" criteria. The Germans attacked the Soviet Union, viciously and unjustifiably, in an overt war of conquest. The Soviets had a far stronger case for "just cause" than the British and the Americans. And whereas Hitler expressed an element of respect for Anglo-American culture and a desire to coexist, he made it clear that he viewed the Russians and other Slavic peoples as lesser humans, that he had utter hatred for communism, and that he went to war to conquer and dominate the Soviet Union. The people of the Soviet Union were literally fighting for their very existence (which made the German task much more difficult—enough Soviet people hated Stalin that with an approach more accommodating to the people of the Soviet Union the Nazis surely would have had many of those people join their efforts).

Nonetheless, the *tactics* of the Soviets violated just conduct criteria—partly, of course, because the tone set by the Nazi invaders was one of brutality. However, even before the Nazis turned on the Soviets, in the early months following the defeat of Poland, Stalin had ordered the cold-blooded murder of roughly four thousand Polish military officers and ten thousand Polish intellectuals and societal leaders.[29]

After the Soviets turned back the Nazi onslaught (an incredible feat of perseverance), they began an inexorable march toward Berlin. This campaign was carried out without restraint or moral compunction.[30] Rape and pillage, terror and retribution were the order of the day. Those of us who recoil with horror at the atrocities of the Nazis may find a bit of grim pleasure in learning about the payback. However, the Soviet conduct in the campaign to drive the Nazis back to Berlin in defeat could hardly have more egregiously violated just conduct criteria.

The U.S. and Britain do not bear responsibility for the Soviets' conduct. That this conduct was reprehensible and thus undermines any claims that the Soviets fought a "just war" is not necessarily a direct indictment of all those in alliance with the Soviets. Nonetheless, we might still ask if Americans were stained by the Soviets' behavior, as the United States did directly benefit from the Soviets defeating Germany.

More importantly for the purposes of my overall argument in this book, the fact that the *major* (by far) element of defeating Germany involved egregious violations of the values for which Americans claimed to

---

29. Bess, *Choices Under Fire*, 175.
30. For a concise account, see Hitchcock, *Bitter Road to Freedom*, 131–69.

PART ONE: Total War   *Was America's Conduct in World War II Just?*   67

fight leaves us with questions about the "goodness" of this war. The role of the Soviets in the "American" victory gives us more cause to question whether the moral legacy of this war might be as positive as America's mythology portrays it (and, again, let's note the near invisibility of the Soviet role in defeating the Nazis in many popular American and British accounts of the War).[31]

We should note another important point that underscores the problematic element of the American alliance with the Soviets. The Allies' stated agenda for the War was to defeat tyranny and further democracy ("self-determination" in the Atlantic Charter) and disarmament. However, the victory by the tyrannical Soviet Union and the resultant dominance gained by the Soviets over hundreds of millions in central and eastern Europe hardly furthered that agenda.

We may use Poland as an example. The Poles were under threat from the Nazis in 1939. Britain and France committed themselves to go to war with Germany should Poland be violently aggressed upon. Germany attacked and war was declared—and Britain and France then did little to stop Germany's conquest. Over the next several years, Poland became a major scene of battle after battle and its people, both ethnic Poles and millions of Polish Jews, the victims of incredible atrocities. When the War ended, six years later, Poland's population was decimated twice over—one-fifth of the people in Poland had been killed, countless others wounded, dispossessed, and deprived of their livelihoods.[32] *Then*, in the end, even though the powers who had gone to war on Poland's behalf defeated the Nazis, Poland ended up being forcibly annexed into the Soviet Empire.

So, if we were to take Poland's fate as our basis for evaluating this war, we would have to say that the War was a failure. It was not a "good war," but a *bad* war. In the name of "self-determination," tens of millions of Poles were killed, the country was devastated—and Poland found itself in 1946 with anything but "self-determination."

The war versus tyrannical Germany was mostly won by the tyrannical Soviet Union (remember Bess's point above that for every German soldier killed by the British and American forces, *four* German soldiers were killed by the Soviets). A major beneficiary of this victory versus the tyrannical

---

31. The well-produced and comprehensive twenty-six-part documentary by the BBC, *The World at War*, has several episodes devoted to the war in eastern Europe (with some extraordinary film footage), but nonetheless gives the clear impression that the war on western fronts was the decisive element.

32. Another terrible irony of this series of events is that while the Poles lost one in five of their population, the imperial power that had "guaranteed" their security versus the Nazis, Great Britain, lost only one in 125 of its population. Judt, *Postwar*, 18.

Nazis was the tyrannical Soviets. In contrast, we would find it difficult to see any benefit Great Britain gained from the War—the Britons basically bankrupted themselves, set themselves up to lose their empire, and became essentially a junior partner to the American empire.[33]

A terrible irony of this outcome may be seen in the way the Soviet-American alliance evolved into the Soviet-American Cold War. After the War American policymakers mistakenly interpreted the Soviet Union more in terms of their reading of Marxist ideology than in terms of Russian czarist history and in terms of an understanding of actual Soviet intentions and practices.[34] As a consequence, American leaders portrayed the Soviets as bent on world conquest (a direct projection of Nazi characteristics onto the Soviets). This projection by American policymakers then underwrote the disastrous Cold War.

UNCONDITIONAL SURRENDER

Given the reluctance of the American people and many congressional representatives to get behind Franklin Roosevelt in his push for military intervention in the conflicts with Germany and Japan, perhaps it was inevitable that the supporters of intervention would be vigorous in their efforts to gain public support. So, the rhetoric emphasized the extreme evils of the Axis powers and powerfully shaped the perceptions of the policymakers, the warriors, and the general public.

Even with the intense propaganda campaign, Roosevelt felt free to pursue war policies only after the Japanese attack on Pearl Harbor. Roosevelt's "day of infamy" speech on December 8, 1941, set the tone for the prosecution of the War:

> Always will we remember the character of the onslaught against us. No matter how long it may take us to overcome this premeditated invasion, the American people in their righteous might will win through to absolute victory. I believe I interpret the will of the Congress and of the people when I assert that we will not only defend ourselves to the uttermost, but will make very certain that this form of treachery shall never endanger us again.[35]

---

33. Moss, *Picking Up the Reins*.

34. For an account of the failure of American intelligence to gather reliable information about the actual Soviet Union—a failure that left American policy based upon its leaders' paranoid fantasies—see Weiner, *Legacy of Ashes*.

35. Quoted in Brands, *Traitor to His Class*, 472.

We are in the right, Roosevelt states. Our enemy's attack was unprovoked and dastardly. We are committed to absolute victory and to making certain that such treachery shall never again threaten us. These sentiments characterized American rhetoric in relation to the war in Europe, as well, from the moment the Germans declared war a few days later.

The American people thus received a powerful message, insistently argued and continually reinforced, that their enemies needed to be crushed. Interspersed with the calls to work for absolute victory that would "forever eliminate" the Nazi and imperial Japanese threats, though, Americans also continually were reminded of the righteousness of their own nation, often linked with America's moral and spiritual values. This was the message: Americans are engaged in a battle to the death; it is not simply a battle for power and domination. Americans are fighting on behalf of values, moral imperatives—the types of ideals expressed in the "Four Freedoms" and Atlantic Charter.

American leaders moved quickly from the rhetoric calling for Americans to join the battle to save Western civilization, to the need to fight all out for an absolute victory, and finally to the insistence that this war must conclude with the unconditional surrender of American enemies. However, at the heart of the insistence on unconditional surrender—and the means that would be required to achieve that outcome—lay serious tensions with the general sensibility of the just war tradition and, specifically, the just conduct criteria.

In fact, traditional just war thought opposes the insistence on unconditional surrender. It assumes the requirement to wage war in ways that limit the damage as much as possible, that always make the outcome of peace possible, and that allow the belligerents to stop their fighting as soon as they can after they achieve their purposes—and those purposes cannot be the complete annihilation of the enemy.[36] The just conduct criteria assume that the goal of a just war is to achieve peace with as little damage as possible, not to crush the enemy.

To achieve unconditional surrender requires inflicting immense damage on the enemy. To bring the enemy to the point of utter obeisance requires a level of damage that inevitably violates the criterion of proportionality and the criterion of noncombatant immunity. Also, should the requirement for unconditional surrender be communicated to the enemy (as it would have to be in order to influence the situation), such a demand would diminish the enemy's incentive to find ways to accommodate and establish a peace

---

36. "Destruction of enemy regimes [is] not in [itself a] valid end" (Yoder, *When War Is Unjust*, 152). See also Bell, *Just War*, 198–99.

prior to their obliteration. If they would have no voice in the terms to be established should they surrender, what motivation would they have to find ways to end the fighting sooner?

Roosevelt made his insistence on unconditional surrender official early in 1943 when British and American leaders held a summit conference in Casablanca, Morocco. This was how Roosevelt stated it in the press conference at the end of the meeting:

> Peace can come to the world only by the total elimination of German and Japanese war power. Some of you Britishers know the old story—we had a general called U.S. Grant. His name was Ulysses Simpson Grant, but in my, and Prime Minister Churchill's, early days he was called "Unconditional Surrender" Grant. The elimination of German, Japanese, and Italian war power means the unconditional surrender by Germany, Italy, and Japan. That means a reasonable assurance of future world peace. It does not mean the destruction of the population of Germany, Italy, or Japan, but it does mean the destruction of the philosophies in those countries which are based on conquest and the subjugation of other peoples.[37]

As it turned out, the insistence on unconditional surrender, especially in the war with Japan, *did*, to a large extent, "mean the destruction of the population" of that country—as it did with Germany to only a somewhat lesser degree. By the end of 1944, Allied victory over the two Axis powers had become certain. Both Germany and Japan had by then lost the ability to defend their countries from Allied aerial attacks. Yet both Germany and Japan fought on—surely in part because they had no incentive to surrender at that point in order to seek better terms. The "unconditional surrender" commitment precluded that possibility.

The British RAF in Europe greatly intensified its air attacks on German cities during the final few months of the war—with virtually no resistance from the German Luftwaffe.[38] The USAF only began bombing Japan's cities at the end of 1944. In the nine months prior to the War's end, the Americans dropped roughly the same number of tons on Japan as the Britons and the Americans combined dropped on Germany during the entire course of the War.

---

37. Quoted in Brands, *Traitor to His Class*, 526.

38. In 1943, Britain dropped 180,000 tons of bombs on Germany; in 1944 it was 474,000 tons; in the first several months of 1945, the bombs fell at a rate that would have totalled 724,000 over the course of a year. Grayling, *Among the Dead Cities*, 104.

The main rationale for the destruction visited on defenseless civilian populations after the War's outcome had been decided stemmed from the "need" for unconditional surrender. This was the argument: we must bomb them, kill their people, show their utter helplessness before our onslaught so they will finally simply stop and surrender, without conditions.

Roosevelt's announcement of the "unconditional surrender" policy early in 1943 at the Casablanca Conference actually went against the instincts of Churchill and caught the latter by surprise.[39] Roosevelt harkened back to the ending of World War I. That war ended without a decisive crushing of Germany's ability to recover its war-making capacities. So when Roosevelt insisted on unconditional surrender as the Allies' policy, he intended to make sure that history would not repeat itself. If Germany was utterly defeated (and likewise Japan), that would leave no bases whatsoever for a new version of the stab-in-the-back claims that sustained Germans in their beliefs that they had not truly lost World War I.[40]

Roosevelt's statement about unconditional surrender also preempted controversy in Congress over the goals of the War. He settled that debate before it ever started. Roosevelt also seemingly hoped to use this statement as a means of giving Stalin some satisfaction in light of Stalin's constant requests for the western Allies to open a second front against the Germans and thereby take some of the pressure off the eastern front.[41]

Roosevelt's declaration had a major impact on the direction of the War. Churchill's reluctance to agree with Roosevelt's position did not come from differences concerning the desire to avoid a new stab-in-the-back myth among the Axis or the value in mollifying Stalin—and certainly not because Churchill was more reluctant than Roosevelt to countenance brutality. Rather, Churchill seemed to recognize, more than Roosevelt, that by insisting on unconditional surrender, the Allies would increase the likelihood of the Axis fighting to the bitter end. Such fighting would have enormous costs for everyone and result in a level of devastation that would lead to future conflicts.

Churchill feared that the Axis would interpret Roosevelt's statement as a commitment by the Allies not only to destroy the Axis armies but also their very societies. In fact, Nazi propaganda chief Joseph Goebbels did seek to exploit Roosevelt's statement in warning Germans of the Allies' intent to conquer and then enslave them. The pursuit of "unconditional surrender" would likely reduce the enemy's incentive to lessen the intensity of its

---

39. Brands, *Traitor to His Class*, 526.
40. Carroll, *House of War*, 7–8.
41. Brands, *Traitor to His Class*, 527–28.

fighting to the bitter end. Evan as the defeat of the Germans and Japanese neared, they would be more likely to fight without restraint, "preferring to take their chances even with the brutally immoral tactics of a last stand rather than to accept defeat at the hands of an enemy refusing to offer any terms whatsoever."[42]

Roosevelt's demand for unconditional surrender also undermined Hitler's internal opponents who had schemed for some time how to overthrow their Führer. They could no longer hope for concessions from the Allies should they take such a step. A number of these opponents proceeded anyhow with an ill-fated attempt to assassinate Hitler. But the potential of their movement to gain wider support was severely weakened. In Carroll's words, "The Casablanca declaration helped protect the Führer from the rational and pragmatic element among his own staff. It reinforced the fanatics."[43] As part of this reinforcement, the forces within Germany who were committed to the Final Solution with regard to the mass murder of Jews probably were empowered.

Churchill and Roosevelt may not have been aware of the depths to which the Germans were sinking with the genocide, but they did know it was well underway. "For the remainder of the war, Roosevelt and other leaders insisted that the best rescue of Jews would be the quick and complete defeat of the German military, but from 'unconditional surrender' forward, that was, in fact, the only real option the Allies had."[44] That is, Roosevelt's policy made any attempt to negotiate a cessation of the mass murder much less possible.

Even if we may agree that it was unlikely that the Germans would have been willing to negotiate such a cessation, we still should note that certainly the unconditional surrender policy did serve to extend the War several months. "The extremities of the war's denouement and the delay of the war's end enabled the Nazi death machine to do its worst. The policy of unconditional surrender, that is, guaranteed that the war would last long enough for the genocide nearly to succeed. The last savage months of war in Europe saw the deaths of millions of people, not merely the defeat of the Nazi war machine."[45]

As it turned out, one motivation Roosevelt had in making this declaration was ill-founded. Stalin had been unable to attend the Casablanca Conference. Stalin told Roosevelt ten months later at the summit meeting

42. Carroll, *House of War*, 8.
43. Ibid., 9.
44. Ibid., 10.
45. Ibid., 11.

in Tehran that it would have been better to allow for some conditions. Even the harshest conditions would have made shortening the war more possible. Tragically, by working under the constraints of Roosevelt's policy, the Soviet Union lost about one million soldiers in the final months of their conquest of Germany.[46]

THE DESTRUCTION OF JAPAN

Japan's surprise attack on the American naval base at Pearl Harbor, Hawaii (an American colony at the time; Hawaii did not become a state until 1959), was a remarkable success, at least momentarily. The attack took Americans by surprise and inflicted extraordinary damage on their Pacific Fleet, which they had relocated to Pearl Harbor in the late 1930s (a move many Japanese felt was intentionally provocative).

The Japanese matched the attack on Pearl Harbor with several other aggressive acts that indeed staggered American and British forces in the Pacific. Japanese leaders knew their only hope in military conflict with the massively more powerful forces of the United States lay in an early and decisive strike. They hoped to hurt the Americans badly enough that the Americans would quickly choose to make a peace suitable for Japan's interests.

As it turned out, brilliant as this first strike was, it ended up being a disaster and led to the worst of possible outcomes for Japan. The Japanese war leaders badly misread the Americans. Instead of a collapse in the face of the horrendous blow of Pearl Harbor, that act of aggression galvanized American sentiment and focused American energies on retaliation. Once the United States gained its equilibrium and unleashed its overwhelming war industry, the defeat of Japan became inevitable.

It took a while, though, for the tide to turn. The first several months following the December 7, 1941, attacks saw the Japanese push the Americans ever further out of the Pacific combat arena. Most notably, Japan drove American troops led by General Douglas MacArthur out of their occupation of the Philippines. Partly the American setbacks were the result of the extreme damage the Japanese had done to the American naval forces. However, it was also the case that the Roosevelt administration all along had its sights more focused on the war in Europe. The Japanese attack on Pearl Harbor had done Roosevelt the favor of transforming American public opinion and the sentiment of Congress. However, the administration

---

46. Ibid., 12. These Soviet losses in this short time were two and a half times more deaths than suffered by the American military in the entire War, both with Germany and Japan (Kennedy, *Freedom from Fear*, 856).

focused on the war in Europe. While the naval forces were being rebuilt, the American military effort versus the Japanese only gradually turned the tide.

The American strategy to defeat the Japanese centered on a quest to drive the Japanese forces back toward Japan, island by island. This plan would culminate in attacks on the Japanese homeland. Roosevelt made clear with his "unconditional surrender" doctrine that these attacks had as their goal the complete defeat of the Japanese war effort and the removal of war advocates from their role in leading the country.

Though the Japanese fought tenaciously, they simply did not have the firepower and resources to resist the ever-expanding American war machine. It took about three years of struggle, though, before the Americans were ready to begin a serious assault on the Japanese homeland itself. Long-range attacks commenced in November 1944, but they did not reach full operation until March 1945—by which point the Japanese ability to resist air attacks was virtually nil.

With the commitment to unconditional surrender, coupled with a strong emotional conviction about avenging the Japanese attack on Pearl Harbor, American forces engaged in heavy air attacks. The American military's goal in bombing Japanese cities was stated after the War by the U.S. Strategic Bombing Survey: "Either to bring overwhelming pressure on her to surrender, or to reduce her capacity of resisting surrender by destroying the basic economic and social fabric of the country."[47]

With this commitment to the full-scale bombing of Japan, the 1939 comments of Roosevelt opposing the targeting of civilian populations were long forgotten. Roosevelt had stated, in a radio address broadcast in Europe, that he was afraid "hundreds of thousands of innocent human beings who have no responsibility for, and who are not even remotely participating in, the hostilities would be killed. [The world's nations should determine] that their armed forces shall in no event, and under no circumstances, undertake the bombardment from the air of civilian populations or of unfortified cities."[48]

A more accurate public statement reflecting Roosevelt's true sentiments came early in 1944 (after several years of RAF bombing of civilian targets in Germany and with the American bombing of civilian targets in Japan being planned). A small furor had erupted in the United States with the publication of British pacifist Vera Brittain's sharp condemnation of RAF practices. Numerous American political leaders rebuked Brittain's essay. Undersecretary of State for War Robert Patterson condemned her for

---

47. Quoted in Seldon, "Forgotten Holocaust," 83.
48. Quoted in Grayling, *Among the Dead Cities*, 148–49.

"giving encouragement to the enemy." Eleanor Roosevelt, the president's wife, labeled Brittain a purveyor of "sentimental nonsense." Then a statement from Roosevelt himself acknowledged his "distress and horror" at the "destruction of life," but insisted that only by compelling the enemy to back down through the bombing could lives truly be saved.[49]

The centerpiece in the American strategy once the way was cleared to begin an aerial assault on Japan was precisely the tactic Roosevelt had spoken *against* in 1939: "bombardment from the air of civilian populations [and] unfortified cities." The actual orders given to the USAF commanders stated that their mission was "disruption of railroad and transportation systems by daylight attacks, coupled with destruction of cities by night and bad-weather attacks." In the event, the focus from the start was on attacking the civilian population. The bombing of railroads had only just begun when the Japanese surrendered in August 1945.[50]

The campaign that began in March focused on cities. The first major step came with nighttime bombing of four major Japanese cities—Tokyo, Nagoya, Osaka, and Kobe. Each of these cities was made up mainly of wooden structures, and the bombings had the express purpose of creating overwhelming firestorms with incendiary bombs. The defenselessness of these cities may be seen in the American ability to fly at extraordinarily low altitudes and the decision to strip the planes of their guns in order to allow them to carry more bombs—they had nothing to fear from counterattacks.

On March 9, 1945, the first of these attacks was unleashed on Tokyo. The Japanese capital had 1,667 tons of incendiary bombs dropped on its most densely populated areas. The bombs created a ferocious firestorm that left more than one hundred thousand people dead. On the other three major cities rained a total of more than nine thousand tons of incendiary bombs, resulting in death and destruction parallel to Tokyo's.[51]

This campaign continued from March until the end of the War in August. Even after several months of the Americans' massive bombing of essentially defenseless cities, the Japanese leaders still had not acquiesced to the demands for unconditional surrender. Probably the main factor preventing surrender was that many in Japan did strongly desire one condition—that their emperor, Hirohito, not be removed from his position. As events proved, when Japan did finally offer their unconditional surrender, the Americans actually allowed Hirohito to remain emperor (and avoid punishment as a war criminal)—but only after the war ended; the

49. Ibid., 203.
50. Ibid., 76.
51. Lindqvist, *History of Bombing*, 109.

Americans were not willing to relent on their principled demand for *unconditional* surrender.[52]

The tactic that the United States war leaders settled on finally to crush Japanese resistance was to use their new mega-weapon: two atomic bombs, dropped without warning on the cities of Hiroshima (August 6) and Nagasaki (August 8). Some people around the world, including presumably Japan's military leaders, were aware of rumors that some kind of superweapon may have been in the works. However, those involved in the Manhattan Project, the effort to create these new weapons, had managed to a remarkable degree to keep their work secret. No one else knew for sure that the bombs had been created and were ready for deployment. President Harry Truman, who had come into office upon the death of Franklin Roosevelt in April 1945, himself did not know about the impending usability of these bombs until after he became president.[53]

The first bomb, on Hiroshima, shocked the world in its instant and massive destruction. Unlike with previous bomb attacks that destroyed so many Japanese cities, incredibly deadly and destructive though they were, this time there was no warning for the population of Hiroshima until the bomb hit. It came from just one small plane, not the legions of bombers that delivered the massive bombings of conventional incendiaries and explosives. Hiroshima did, arguably, have military significance. It was the location of various arms manufacturers. The second bomb, on Nagasaki, came as a bigger shock in some ways, because Nagasaki had no military significance. With this attack, clearly, the bombing had the direct intent of killing tens of thousands of noncombatants and destroying a major and beautiful Japanese city.

When the Japanese leadership did accept the American demands for unconditional surrender on August 10, 1945, many Americans and other supporters of the Allied war effort rejoiced at the use of these new weapons. The nuclear weapons effectively brought Japanese resistance to an end, short of a ground invasion that seemed like the next step to gain the required unconditional surrender.

American dissenters voiced concern right from the beginning, however. Those who had opposed crossing the line into overt, direct mass killing of noncombatants in the RAF's area bombing of Germany and USAF's area bombing of Japan, saw the bombing of Hiroshima and especially Nagasaki as simply carrying an inherently immoral tactic to an ever greater extreme.[54]

52. Dower, *Cultures of War*, 237–41.
53. Rhodes, *Making of the Atomic Bomb*, 617–26.
54. Wittner, *One World or None*, 55–59.

There were some as well who recognized that even if these bombs immediately killed about the same number of people as the firebombing of Tokyo, they opened the door to an entirely new set of problems. I will reflect more on that set of problems and the long-term impact of entering and militarizing the atomic age in Part Two of this book. For now, it is enough simply to note the direct connection between the American participation in World War II and the opening of the nuclear Pandora's box. Moral reflection on the nuclear age over the past sixty-five years must acknowledge that the ongoing presence of atomic weaponry in the world is part of the moral legacy of World War II.

If the question of whether the United States satisfied the "just cause" criteria in relation to World War II is complicated (as I concluded at the end of chapter 2), the second "just war" question—did the United States satisfy "just conduct" criteria—has a more obvious answer.

If we assume these criteria should be stable (that is, our moral evaluation looks at American war conduct in relation to the criteria, not in relation to the behavior of other nations), we have little choice but to conclude that U.S. war conduct was *unjust*—especially when we factor in the conduct of the major American allies.

The two most commonly cited just war criteria, proportionality and noncombatant immunity, both witness to the moral parameters shattered by the American war effort. The post-World War II evolution of American military practices make clear the insignificance of the just war conduct criteria for U.S. policymakers (as I will note in Part Two of this book below when I consider the American wars on Korea and Vietnam and America's nuclear weapons program).

4

What Did the War Cost?

In the popular story in the United States about World War II, we hear almost exclusively about the supposed positive elements of the War—how America defeated the Nazi and Japanese threats, how the United States finally became a committed member of the international community, how the American economy kicked into full gear and led the way to this decisive victory for democracy and the American way of life.

I will question this story on three levels. First, directly in relation to the popular story—did the War actually accomplish positive things in such an unambiguous way? To reiterate one fact: the United States and Britain actually played a relatively small role in defeating Nazi Germany. At least three-quarters of all German casualties came at the hands of the Soviet Union. The Nazi defeat was, if anything, a victory for totalitarian communism not democracy.

Second, what about the aftermath of the War? Have the fruits of the American victory in World War II been as positive as the popular story would have us think? Actually, victory pushed the U.S. in the direction of embracing its role as the world's greatest superpower. That embrace has clearly contradicted the stated purposes of American involvement in World War II—self-determination and disarmament everywhere in the world.

Third, I will consider a kind of cost-benefit analysis. World War II did accomplish the positive outcome of defeating these powerful aggressor states, Japan and Germany. The War's outcome expanded the role of the world's pioneer democratic society, the United States. This expansion of America's role could have been beneficial to the world had it actually

PART ONE: Total War   What Did the War Cost?   79

enhanced the cause of genuine democratic self-determination for the world's people.

DEATH AND DESTRUCTION

For Americans, the War was mostly a positive experience. The U.S. economy expanded tremendously, bringing the Great Depression to an end. Masses of people were put to work, many of whom were able to enhance their social and economic status immensely. The war effort fed directly into the expansion of higher education, of membership in labor unions, and of church membership.

However, even for Americans, the War brought with it many costs. And for people in other parts of the world, especially Europe and East Asia, these costs were extraordinary. Of all the major belligerents in the War, the United States suffered by far the fewest casualties. Even so, more than 400,000 Americans died. By contrast, of the major Allied powers, Great Britain lost about 450,000 (a per capita rate about three times higher than the U.S.) and the Soviet Union perhaps as many as 26,000,000. Of the Axis powers, Germany lost as many as 9,600,000, Japan as many as 2,700,000, and Italy as many as 450,000.[1]

Some of the nations caught in the crossfire sustained casualties greater than most of the belligerents—most notably Poland (5,800,000), China (as many as 20,000,000), Yugoslovia (1,000,000), the Philippines (as many as 1,000,000), French Indochina (Vietnam, Cambodia, Laos; as many as 1,500,000), India (as many as 2,600,000), and the Dutch East Indies (present-day Indonesia; as many as 4,000,000).

We have no way of knowing the total number of deaths caused by the War, especially when we factor in famine and disease, two direct consequences. Estimates now run as high as 80,000,000. On top of the direct deaths, we also should factor in the tens of millions of people (probably hundreds of millions) who were injured, or were driven from their homes, or who suffered disease or severe hunger. On top of the human casualties, we note the death and destruction caused to domestic and wild animals plus the immense damage done to the physical environment. I am aware of no estimates of these costs.[2]

---

1. Statistics concerning World War II casualties are by the nature of the case approximations. Numbers vary widely depending on the source; my numbers come from the Wikipedia article "World War II Casualties" (http://en.wikipedia.org/wiki/World_war_ii_casualties).

2. A book that focuses mostly on more recent wars, Austin and Bruch, *Environmental Consequences of War*, does contain scattered references to World War II.

How do we even approximate a cost-benefit analysis whereby we would try to assess the damage done to the world in relation to the benefits accomplished by the defeat of Japan and Germany? The impossibility of answering this question does not render it irrelevant. For us to avoid the cost-benefit question altogether will too easily hide from our collective memory the reality that this war (like all wars) incalculably damaged the world. We should never imagine preparing for any possible future war or supporting any present war without being acutely aware of these costs. Would Roosevelt or Churchill have made different choices if they had tried to imagine the costs?

One of the most notable facts about the death toll of World War II is the astounding number of non-fighting civilians who lost their lives, directly in the fighting or as a direct consequence of the fighting. Up to 80 percent of the deaths in the War came to non-fighting civilians—that is, for every soldier killed in the War, four noncombatants lost their lives.

A second notable fact about the death toll is the high percentage of deaths that came to people who lived in nations who were not directly engaged in the Allied versus Axis conflict. For example, the number of British, American, and Japanese war deaths *combined* was fewer than the number of war deaths suffered by Indonesians. Great Britain lost about one-sixth the number of people that Britain's Indian colony did.

Again, the United States came through the War relatively unscathed. In one night's bombing raid on Tokyo in March 1945, the United States killed more than fifty times more civilians (in excess of 85,000) than the Americans lost during the entire war (1,700). We cannot accurately say how many deaths the United States was responsible for—certainly many, many times more than it suffered, especially when we note that more than three-quarters of all war dead were civilians, and America lost virtually no civilians.

So, in a strictly numerical sense, the United States came through the War with a pretty good cost-benefit outcome. Americans killed way more than they lost. The U.S. physical environment was essentially untouched. Americans suffered no hunger or disease beyond those encountered by soldiers in foreign postings. The U.S. economy boomed.

However, the War had high costs, even to America. Military deaths for American soldiers during the years of the War totaled 416,000. Of these, 292,000 died in combat. Of the noncombat military deaths, 14,000 were prisoners of war. The number of wounded and injured in the War might total around 1,000,000. Of these, many suffered long-term health consequences.[3] The use of the post-traumatic stress disorder diagnosis for soldiers

---

3. "In 1945, over 10,000 returning veterans a month were diagnosed with a psychiatric disorder" (Rose, *Myth of the Greatest Generation*, 247).

who suffer severe and often debilitating and lingering emotional trauma from their war experiences did not gain recognition until 1980. Historian Thomas Childers suggests that this diagnosis certainly may be applied to many World War II veterans.

> In the aftermath of the Second World War, depression, recurring nightmares, survivor guilt, outbursts of rage (most frequently directed at family members), "exaggerated startle responses," and anxiety reactions—all of which are recognized today as classic symptoms of PTSD—were as common as they were unnerving. With few psychiatrists to treat them and a cultural ethos that hardly encouraged open discussion of emotional problems, especially among men, many veterans simply suffered in private—often with devastating consequences for them and their families.[4]

Childers points out that, contrary to the popular American story about World War II (he cites Tom Brokaw's happy picture of marital bliss and commitment in his paean to America's participation in World War II, *The Greatest Generation*), the trauma of the experience of war for American soldiers was indeed reflected in marital *disharmony*. "Americans did marry in record numbers during the war, but they also divorced in record numbers when it ended. Between 1945 and 1947, the United States experienced a 'divorce boom.' Petitions for divorce skyrocketed, and the country registered the highest divorce rate in the world and the highest in American history. And . . . the divorce rate for veterans was twice as high as that for civilians."[5]

American veterans had to deal, often in silence, with their war traumas and with familial conflicts that, in part at least, seemed directly related to changes in the veterans' emotional and psychological states as a consequence of their war experiences. They also returned to a society not set up to integrate them comfortably back into the social and economic fabric.[6]

---

4. Childers, *Soldier*, 8. This is an important book, though sadly written too late to be of much benefit to World War II veterans themselves. Childers' concerns ring true in my own experience. My father was a combat veteran of the War, having fought for several years in the South Pacific. I cannot identify any evidence of his suffering anything resembling PTSD. But several of my friends growing up also had World War II veteran fathers who, I now see in retrospect, had been damaged in significant ways by their experience. Since I started work on this book, I have discussed this issue with several other friends who are children of World War II veterans. I have been startled at how common it is to hear of major problems in their fathers' lives (and, hence, in the children's lives) that seem linked to World War II traumas.

5. Ibid.

6. "Many veteran's questioning of the war, the home front, American materialism, communal responsibility, and other issues was not compatible with the need for consensus in an unsure postwar world" (Saxe, *Settling Down*, 51).

Jobs were difficult to find. The government did establish programs to ease soldiers' reintegration into the broader society, but even so unemployment was common for vets. The unemployment rate for veterans in 1947 was three times higher than for nonveterans. Many veterans also had trouble finding housing given the lack of building during the Depression and war years. "Returning veterans, many of them married, lived anywhere they could find—barns, trailers, decommissioned streetcars, converted military barracks, and even automobiles. Many moved in with parents or in-laws." Perhaps 1.5 million veterans lived with friends or family in the immediate aftermath of the War.[7]

The negative impact of World War II on the lives of American soldiers was immense. Hundreds of thousands died in combat. Hundreds of thousands more suffered physical wounds—some that took a lifelong toll. And probably many more suffered serious and often long-lasting psychological trauma, including severe cases of post-traumatic stress disorder. Well over one million soldiers suffered from diagnosed psychological damage. The rate of soldiers discharged for psychiatric reasons reached ten thousand per month by July 1943 and increased over the next two years. Twenty thousand psychological casualties resulted from the Battle of Okinawa alone, fought from March to June 1945. By 1947, fully 50 percent of patients in veterans hospitals suffered from "invisible wounds."[8]

I focus on the moral legacy of World War II mostly in relation to the United States in this book. However, I think it important to imagine, at this point, how the picture of immense costs in American society of the traumas of war on U.S. soldiers could be seen as quite *mild* compared to just about every country in the world that directly participated in the War. If American soldiers, their families, and, by extension, the broader society were so damaged by their war experience, imagine what life after the War was like in places where the military casualty list was many times more extensive, where immense numbers of civilians were killed and wounded, and where the physical structures of the society were severely damaged.[9]

THE HOLOCAUST

In considering the losses of World War II, among the most tragic was the systematic destruction of Europe's Jewish population. There were around

7. Childers, *Soldier*, 7.
8. Ibid., 8.
9. One insightful overview for Europe is Judt, *Postwar*, especially "Part One: Postwar 1945–1954," 13–247. For Japan, see Dower, *Embracing Defeat*.

nine million Jews living in Europe in 1939; fully two-thirds of them were killed over the next six years. About 60 percent of the deaths came in Poland, Germany, and immediately surrounding countries (nine out of ten Jews in those countries were killed).[10]

The German perpetrators of these unspeakable evils have justifiably come to be seen as paradigmatic examples of inhumanity. None of the questions I raise in this section are meant to minimize the degree of responsibility we should attribute to the German leaders for the Holocaust. What was done to Europe's Jews (not to mention what was done to other populations considered subhuman by the Nazis, most notably the Roma and Sinti peoples and those labeled "homosexual") must be condemned without qualification.

Nonetheless, we must ask, did the western Allies do what they could have done to prevent what happened—or at least minimize its effects? Was the Allied war effort part of the solution to the problem of the mass extermination of Jews or part of the problem?

Adolf Hitler had explicitly stated early in his public career that his ideology had at its heart a powerful hatred of Jews and a desire to "purify" Germany of its Jewish population. As the Nazis rose in prominence in the 1920s and early 1930s, they made clear their hatred of Jews and their scapegoating techniques in blaming Jews for many of Germany's problems. So when Hitler gained power in 1933, people who had been attentive to the Nazi message began to fear for the safety of Germany's Jewish population. The Nazis wasted little time in beginning to implement anti-Jewish policies. As early as May 1933, Hitler's close colleague Joseph Goebbels led a public burning of Jewish-authored books in Berlin.

Various humanitarian and pacifist groups, including the American Friends Service Committee, tracked the Germans' hostility toward Jews. They worked hard to publicize the growing threat and sought to provide material aid to increasingly persecuted Jews. They advocated for liberalized immigration policies in the United States and Great Britain to accommodate the rapidly increasing number of European Jews who sought to immigrate.[11]

American and British leaders mostly resisted these efforts. In the United States, strict limitations on immigration had been established in light of strong anti-immigration movements in the 1920s. Even with the heightened danger to European Jews, American leaders refused to relent on the strictness of those policies.[12]

---

10 The numbers come from Dawidowicz, *War Against the Jews*, 403.

11. Miller, *Witness for Humanity*, 141–43.

12. Hamerow, *Why We Watched*, 127–48.

By 1938, the situation became ever more dire. A key event that made this clear was the so-called Kristallnacht pogrom on November 9. The Nazis attacked and terrorized Jews, inflicting massive violence against Jewish-owned property and Jewish persons. Afterward, many more Jews sought to leave Germany and the nearby ethnic German areas—with ever-increasing difficulty as the restrictive policies of the British and Americans remained unchanged.

In December, three American Quaker leaders, including well-known theologian Rufus Jones, visited Germany and hoped to relieve some of the problems. They met with Nazi officials and, because of the Quaker history of having saved millions of German lives in the aftermath of World War I with food relief, gained a hearing and were assured that concessions would be made. In their report upon their return, Jones and company emphasized the intense desire of large numbers of Germany's Jews to leave—and the willingness of the Nazis to let them go.[13] Still, the U.S. government refused to relent and accept the Jewish refugees.

The American unwillingness to accept Jewish immigrants was exemplified in the fate of legislation proposed in February 1939 by New York Senator Robert Wagner and Massachusetts Representative Edith Rogers. The Wagner-Rogers bill would have allowed twenty thousand refugees under the age of fourteen to immigrate to the United States. President Roosevelt refused to support this bill. After several months of debate, the bill died.[14]

When the British and French war with Germany began, concern for Jewish people played little role in the Allies' stated motivations. At this point (September 1939), the Nazis apparently had not yet formulated a policy of mass extermination. They did expect to "cleanse" their part of Europe of Jews, but mostly through forced migrations (though they seem to have been open still to voluntary migrations, too—if the migrants could find places in the world that would accept them).[15]

The coming of the War made things immeasurably worse for European Jews. This is how Holocaust historian Doris Bergen states it:

> War—in particular the Nazi war of annihilation to Germany's east—exponentially increased the numbers and kinds of victims, as brutal programs of persecution, expulsion, and murder,

---

13. Baker, *Human Smoke*, 107–9.
14. Ibid., 125.
15. In fact, recent scholarship is pushing the "point of no return" when the Germans were fully committed to extermination further and further back, perhaps even to the early months of 1942 (Snyder, "New Approach," 56).

bloated on carnage, demanded and created even more enemies. Mass killings of non-Jews were also part of the Nazi German war effort, a war launched for the related goals of race and space: so-called racial purification and territorial expansion. War provided killers with both a cover and an excuse for murder; in wartime, killing was normalized, and extreme, even genocidal measures could be justified with familiar arguments about the need to defend the homeland. Without the war, the Holocaust would not—and could not—have happened.[16]

The Allies were aware of the Nazi's extermination efforts nearly from the beginning of the War.[17] Could they have done more had they wanted to? It is impossible for us to say now what kind of difference rescue policies might have made had they been pursued. But the simple fact is that they were not. Historian Theodore S. Hamerow paints a picture sympathetic to the Allied leaders, citing restraints placed on them by domestic and global political dynamics that limited what they perceived they could do on behalf of Europe's Jews. However, Hamerow's argument (which I don't find particularly persuasive) only underscores the reality that the Allies did precious little to save Jews before and during the War. Though *defending* the ineffectiveness of Allied leaders, Hamerow also reinforces my argument that the American World War II effort was *not* about saving Jews.

Likely a major reason the western Allies did not pursue rescue policies was their strategic philosophy. This philosophy required planners to identify their main objectives and then to resist any attempts to divert their focus from those objectives. The core objective was to defeat Germany—not rescue Jews (or Roma or other victims of the genocidal policies).[18] However, this makes my point: stopping the Holocaust simply was not part of the motivation for the Allied war with Germany. And, we must note, the execution of this war itself provided a major impetus for the Germans' genocidal policies.

The Allied indifference to the plight of Nazi victims becomes more troubling as we move closer to the end of the War. We saw above how in the final months of the War the Nazi air defenses were virtually nonexistent. At this point, especially Britain's RAF pursued an overt policy of massive bombing of civilian population centers—with very little resistance from the nearly prostrate German military. If the Allies could bomb with such impunity, why did they not use bombing to hinder the work of the death camps?[19]

16. Bergen, *War and Genocide*, vii.
17. Hamerow, *Why We Watched*, 294–95.
18. Brands, *Traitor to His Class*, 567–70.
19. See Wyman, "The Bombing of Auschwitz," in *Abandonment of the Jews*, 288–307.

Questions about the Allied actions near the end of the War also point back to our discussion in chapter 3 of the Allied policy of "unconditional surrender." As noted there, this policy may actually have exacerbated the genocidal practices of the Nazis. By insisting on unconditional surrender, the Allies cut off the possibility of negotiating with the Nazis concerning their treatment of the Jews.

Even if such a strategy of negotiation may not have been fruitful, certainly the insistence on unconditional surrender prolonged the War by many months. If the end of the War had been moved up six months, many thousands of lives would have been saved—both those who were directly murdered during that final half-year and those who died during that time due to starvation and illness. In James Carroll's words, "the policy of unconditional surrender guaranteed that the war would last long enough for the genocide nearly to succeed."[20]

The final point I will mention in relation to the Holocaust makes especially clear how this was not a war fought to save the Jews. As I have mentioned, the Allied leaders knew the Nazis had begun a terrible campaign of death focused on the Jewish and Roma populations. They may not have quite realized the extent of that campaign, but they knew it was massive.[21]

Yet, when the camps were "liberated," many of their occupants, most suffering terribly from malnutrition and various diseases and most deprived of homes to which to return, were simply left to their own devices.[22] As it turned out, with no resources and no place to go, a scandalously large number of these "liberated" prisoners remained in what we could call "post-concentration camp" camps. They continued to suffer from lack of food and other necessities of life. In a terrible irony, some of these camps were located in Germany and the "liberated" Jews remained more impoverished than many of their defeated German oppressors.

In taking a moral reckoning of this incredibly destructive event, certainly we must focus our blame on the Nazis and their accomplices for the organized massacre of millions of people. However, along with blame, if we are to make progress in a careful assessment of the moral legacy of World War II, we must not make the mistake of assuming that the actions that defeated the morally guilty executioners were then by definition morally good.

In fact, we may conclude most accurately that the Allies did next to nothing to mitigate the horrors of the Holocaust, even when they could have. They did not even have the human decency to put more than minimal

20. Carroll, *House of War*, 9.
21. Novick, *Holocaust in American Life*, 19–29.
22. See Hitchcock, *Bitter Road*, 287–366.

effort into caring for those survivors whose lives had been shattered by the Nazis' actions. The Allies were not guilty of genocide, but they get no credit for trying to stop it. Besides, the tactics they used to win seem to have exacerbated the Nazis' genocidal efforts.

THE SPREAD OF COMMUNISM

One of the major stated reasons for the War was to defend peoples of the world, most specifically in Poland and China, against the aggressions of Japan and Germany. In considering the outcome of World War II, one measure to consider, as I have previously stated, is how the results of the War fit with the purposes given for it—purposes that stood at the center of the appeals in the United States for people to support and participate in the War.

Measuring the outcome of the War in relation to the fate of nations such as Poland and China is complicated by several factors. For one, neither of those nations was a functioning democracy in the 1930s. That is, whatever it was the U.S. defended by going to war for the sake of those countries, it was not a society that functioned according to the democratic ideals expressed in Roosevelt's "Four Freedoms" speech and the Atlantic Charter.

Another complicating factor was that after the U.S. entered the War, Americans found themselves in a close alliance with a major power, the Soviet Union, that did not share the values that lay at the heart of America's purpose statements. So, when the War ended, the U.S. was not in a position to shape the direction of the postwar governments of the nations of central and eastern Europe, nor in eastern Asia.

At the end of the War, therefore, the Americans had limited ability to further their stated purposes for entering the War. The U.S. faced these limitations despite having decisively won the War and imposing unconditional surrender on both major enemies. It's important to note this as we assess the moral legacy of the War. The United States government and its supporters made explicit and far-reaching moral claims to justify devoting the resources and human lives required to enter into a full-scale war. Yet we are left with a big question. Did America's unqualified success in defeating its enemies yield results in line with the purpose statements? Did the U. S. victory lead to "self-determination" and "disarmament everywhere in the world"?

How did the two nations who suffered invasions that served as catalysts for the American entry into the War fare as a consequence of this intervention? For Poland and China, World War II did not have a happy outcome. One of the major costs of the war was the *loss* of self-determination and the possibility of disarmament for the people of Poland and China—not to mention an almost unimaginable loss of life in both countries in this failed struggle for their freedom.

With Germany's attack on the Soviet Union in June 1941, followed a few years later by the Soviets' return invasion of Germany, Poland became a major battleground. As the end of the War approached in 1945, the postwar fate of the Polish nation-state was a major item of discussion among the Allied leaders. Famously, at the February 1945 summit meeting in the Ukrainian resort town of Yalta, Roosevelt, Churchill, and Stalin discussed the fate of the Polish leadership. The Soviets had a pro-Soviet regime on the ground in Poland, though it lacked popular support. The Polish government-in-exile in London strongly opposed cooperation with the communists, remembering very clearly the Soviet treatment of Poland in 1939 and throughout the rest of the War. For their part, the Soviets and their puppet government evinced no openness to working with the government-in-exile. In the end, the Soviets prevailed.[23]

So, Poland ended up with a communist government—certainly not the government the people of Poland would have supported had they been allowed genuine self-determination. The Soviet Union provided strong military support for the communist government. From time to time, popular resistance in Poland surfaced, but it took until the early 1980s and the rise of the Solidarity Movement for Poland to move toward meaningful self-determination.

The Soviet Union also established similar satellite states in the rest of central and eastern Europe. Nations that had been independent, at least during the 1920s and 1930s—such as Czechoslovakia (which had a functioning democracy in the interwar period), Hungary, Romania, Bulgaria, Estonia, Lithuania, and Latvia—became Soviet satellite states.

Symbolizing the lack of "disarmament" in Poland, as well as in these other satellite states, the nuclear weapon–centered military "alliance" the Soviets formed with their satellite states was named the *Warsaw* Pact. When we consider the enormous cost, both in lives lost and material resources, paid by the Soviet Union in the War, as well as the fully justifiable fear the Soviets had of invasions from the West (fear that the United States only exacerbated in the years following World War II), we may understand both the sense of entitlement and the motivation that the Soviets would have had to establish this kind of arrangement. We also must consider the enormous power the Soviets had accumulated in the course of their mobilization to

23. Plokhy, *Yalta*, 152–65; Harbutt, *Yalta 1945*, 174–82.

turn back the Nazi invasion[24]—along with the fact that by the end of the War Soviet forces directly occupied all of these central and eastern European nations.

This is to say, we cannot imagine how the creation of the Warsaw Pact and the Iron Curtain could not have happened given the outcome of the War. In Part Two of this book, we will look more closely at the history of the Cold War and the rivalry between the Soviet Union and the United States. The point to make here, though, is simply to note this one extraordinarily *negative* direct outcome of World War II. The United States went to war for the sake of democracy and disarmament. As far as central and eastern Europe were concerned, in relation to these purposes, the War was an abject failure.

The story of the fate of China as a consequence of World War II is more complicated than that of Europe. The United States allied closely with Chiang Kai-shek's government in the course of the war with Japan. Chiang's was essentially a military dictatorship that never established itself as a popularly supported government. The Chinese communists, led by Mao Zedong, split from Chiang's Nationalist Party in the 1920s, and the two forces engaged in a long-running struggle for dominance. This civil war surely weakened China in face of the Japanese threat as it grew in the 1930s.

The communists entered a truce with the Nationalists, but the struggle with Japan was largely waged by the Nationalists with their American and British allies. Japan won major victories, but the sheer size of China and the Chinese people's unwillingness to acquiesce prevented Japan from gaining full victory. As the war lengthened far beyond the time the Japanese expected it to take, their hold on China gradually weakened. Of course, after December 1941, Japan's attention turned toward the forces of the United States in the Pacific War.

Finally, in August 1945, the War ended with Japan's defeat—and China was left more to its own resources. The communists reemerged from their withdrawal and intensified their confrontation with Chiang's government. The United States continued to side with the Nationalists. However, it soon became clear that the Nationalists did not have the popular support or the competence to prevail.

While the communists had bitterly resisted the Japanese, especially through guerilla warfare (a kind of training for the civil war with the Nationalists), Chiang's forces bore the brunt of the conflict with Japan—and were severely weakened thereby. Certainly in this way, at least, World War

---

24. Glantz and House, *When Titans Clashed*.

II contributed to the ultimate victory of tyrannical communist powers in East Asia.[25]

The civil war essentially ended in 1949 with the retreat of the Nationalist forces to Taiwan. Besides the victory of the communists in mainland China, communist states were also established in several other areas formerly occupied by Japan, including North Korea, North Vietnam, and Manchuria.

As with central and eastern Europe, with China it is difficult to imagine what could have been done to prevent the dominance of communism following the War. My concern here is simply to assess the consequences of World War II in that part of the world in light of American leaders' purpose statements for going to war. The corrupt and tyrannical Nationalists certainly were not forces for democracy in China—and the United States did very little to push them in a more democratic direction.

Nonetheless, it would seem that by pursuing American military objectives against Japan, the U.S. certainly did not achieve anything resembling a democratic outcome in China. When we consider the moral legacy of World War II, one (albeit complicated) outcome we need to remember is that in China the way was paved for the victory of the communist forces—and that as a consequence of that victory the people of China faced extraordinary trauma, violence, famine, and mass death.

AMERICAN DEMOCRACY

In United States history, prior to World War II, the country several times went to war (or, in the 1860s, engaged in a massive civil war). Typically, the pattern would be mobilization, followed by engagement, followed by demobilization. This pattern was repeated earlier in the twentieth century when the U.S. joined in what we now refer to as World War I. President Woodrow Wilson led the U.S. into that war in which the Americans played a decisive role in tipping the balance toward the Allies. Wilson desired that his country stay engaged in international politics in the postwar period (an involvement that presumably would have included continued military preparedness). But Wilson's wishes were thwarted, partly due to principled isolationist sentiment, partly due to (not unrelated) antimilitarist sentiment.[26] The 1920s were a period of demilitarization that followed the engagement in a huge war. In the 1930s, the inclination toward noninvolvement in international conflicts remained strong, bolstered by economic crises that never

25. Keegan, *Second World War*, 588–89.
26. Herring, *From Colony to Superpower*, 436–83.

fully resolved during that decade despite the efforts of Franklin Roosevelt's New Deal.

As the clouds of impending war began to darken in the latter half of the 1930s—potential conflicts with both Germany and Japan—the United States remained far from ready to engage in overt warfare with powerful enemies. The military remained small at roughly 250,000 soldiers—a force that was about the same size as Turkey's (hardly known to be a military power). Numerous congressional leaders consistently expressed strong opposition to "foreign entanglements," offering resistance to just about any initiative by the Roosevelt administration to bring the U.S. toward greater military involvement in these conflicts.[27]

In its opposition, Congress seems accurately to have reflected the broader sentiment of American voters. And most people shared the assumption that Roosevelt would not be able to move ahead without public (and congressional) support. That is, the checks and balances in the American republic still seemed functional and able to limit the potential for unilateral presidential action to engage the nation in armed conflicts.

In the late 1930s, after Britain and France extended their war guarantee to Poland, and even more after September 1939, when the war in Europe began, Roosevelt saw the resistance from Americans to expanded support for the Allied war effort as a *problem*.[28] Setting a precedent for presidential behavior down to the present, Roosevelt did not take his cues from public opinion or congressional perspectives. He did not act as the people's representative given the task of ensuring that the popular will should be enacted. Rather, he acted as if he knew much better than the people or even Congress what was necessary. He acted as if his task was not so much to figure out how to ascertain and embody the will of the people concerning military engagement but rather to figure how to change public opinion to be more compatible with his own wishes or, failing that, how to bypass public opinion.[29]

Part of the vigorous public debate in the United States during the several years prior to Pearl Harbor included a reiteration of strong fears that should the United States move more and more into a war footing, the country would move perilously away from its democratic traditions and

---

27. Kennedy, *Freedom from Fear*, 381–425.
28. Brands, *Traitor to His Class*, 376–80.
29. "The stakes of presidential lies grew immeasurably as the United States began its march toward superpower status. . . . The president present at the creation of this new nation was Franklin Delano Roosevelt, who successfully led America into war to a considerable degree by stealth and deception" (Alterman, *When Presidents Lie*, 16).

ever more toward a type of dictatorship.[30] Reading documents from the debate now, some seven decades later, we are immediately struck with the hyperbolic nature of the warnings. One wonders how literally the debaters meant their warnings about going to war against Germany and Japan being a sure-fire path to dictatorship. However, when we make allowance for the tendency of debaters to overstate their fears and concerns, we can ask whether these anti-interventionists might have nonetheless been more prescient than they have typically been given credit for.

The pro-interventionists won the debate—America did go to war. (Though we may now say that the "debate" actually played little role in the events as they unfolded; the decision-makers were already set on going to war, and once the key catalytic event—Pearl Harbor—occurred, the debate completely ended.) And America did emerge victorious. And did not sink into a dictatorship. Relative to World War I, domestic life in the United States remained open and free. The widespread unity in the country in favor of the War made it much less likely that the government would need overtly to subvert democratic practices in order to sustain social cohesion behind the war effort. But how have we fared in the long run?

In Part Two, I make a case for seeing the War as a key moment in the transformation of American political dynamics *away from* democratic practices. At least in relation to issues of war and peace, the United States would never be the same after World War II. The tendencies of the country throughout its history prior to World War II to enter a war, mobilize, and then demobilize and return to a civilian-centered, more democratic political economy did not return. Something fundamental changed in the United States with this war—and has not changed back. This change has severely undermined American democracy.

Roosevelt's key move was to approach democratic checks and balances on presidential power as a problem to overcome rather than an inherent limit to be respected. Directly linked with Roosevelt's desire for more power we may see the desire of American military leaders likewise to exercise greatly expanded power.[31] These two desires merged in the will to expand American war-making capability and the possibilities of exercising that capability with as few democratic limitations as possible in face of the beginning of World War II. And, as a consequence of the moves—mostly taken by unilateral presidential decisions without passing through the legislative

---

30. For one set of arguments expressing this fear, see the various articles published during this time and collected in Loconte, *End of Illusions*, 33–121.

31. "For generals like [George] Marshall, exasperated at the nation's lack of preparedness in the 1930s, . . . some enlarged, permanent machinery of [military] mobilization seemed necessary" (Sherry, *Shadow of War*, 43–44).

process and without informing the public—the United States, in historian Garry Wills' terms, went from being a democracy to being a "national security state."[32]

Another key step toward the national security state was the construction of what became the largest building in the world, the Pentagon. Work began on September 11, 1941, and the building was dedicated and opened for business in January 1943. Roosevelt intended that this building, built on the Virginia side of the Potomac River, *temporarily* house the leaders of the American armed forces during the time of "emergency." Following this time of emergency, the building was to be turned to civilian purposes and the military offices were to return to closer proximity to the White House and Congress. When he saw the plans, Roosevelt also ordered that the building be cut in half from its proposed size. Colonel Leslie Groves, the director of the building project, ignored Roosevelt's order. By the end of the War (during which the American military grew from 250,000 soldiers under arms to roughly fourteen million) all plans to move the military out of this building had been long forgotten. As traced by James Carroll in his book *House of War*,[33] the Pentagon expanded to become the true center of power in the United States government. And the Pentagon's power had limited accountability to democratic checks and balances.[34]

During the War, Roosevelt initiated the establishment of what emerged after the War as another major, powerful, permanent institution with strong interests in sustaining a militarized national security state—also with little democratic accountability.[35] Originally called the Office of Strategic Services (OSS), this entity was established as a wartime agency to gather intelligence to aid the war effort. The OSS's work turned out to be only marginally useful to the war effort. In any event, Roosevelt intended that the OSS would cease to exist at war's end.

After Roosevelt's death in April 1945, his successor, Harry Truman, expressed the desire to indeed terminate the OSS. However, Truman failed in that effort and the Central Intelligence Agency (CIA) was created in 1947. Truman eventually became persuaded of the CIA's potential utility. Presidents since Truman have come to embrace the work of the CIA as a fundamental resource to circumvent constitutional checks and balances in order

32. Wills, *Bomb Power*.

33. Carroll, *House of War*. For parallel, broader accounts, see Sherry, *Shadow of War*, Zelizer, *Arsenal of Democracy*, and Freeman, *American Empire*.

34. See the section titled "The Pentagon" in chapter 5 below.

35. My main sources on the Central Intelligence Agency are Weiner, *Legacy of Ashes*; Goodman, *Failure of Intelligence*; Prados, *Safe for Democracy*; and Powers, *Intelligence Wars*.

to pursue foreign policy objectives outside of democratic oversight—often with covert use of military violence.[36]

A third key institution, along with the Pentagon and CIA, that emerged as a direct consequence of World War II and that has severely damaged American democratic traditions was the nuclear weapons program.[37] After several nuclear physicists determined in the late 1930s that a superweapon might be possible to construct, Roosevelt ordered the creation of an extraordinarily top secret program to construct this weapon. Called the Manhattan Project, and directed by the same Leslie Groves (now a general) who oversaw the construction of the Pentagon and displayed his disdain for democratic limitations in his disregard for Roosevelt's will that the size of the Pentagon be greatly reduced, this program absorbed a tremendous amount of resources—all hidden from congressional scrutiny. To indicate how top secret this project was, we need only note that Truman himself, the vice president, knew nothing of the Manhattan Project until after Roosevelt's death.[38]

The creation and ongoing development of nuclear weapons has absorbed enormous resources and has profoundly shaped American government and the broader society. As Garry Wills points out in his sketch that traces how the bomb has undermined American democracy, nuclear weapons have played a key role in American government in that they have expanded enormously the unaccountable power of the president.[39] Presidential authority to authorize nuclear war has never been subject to the constitutional requirement that *Congress*, not the president, be the sole authority to send the United States to war.

Truman made his July 1945 decision to drop two nuclear bombs on Japan secretly and independently from Congress.[40] The decisions to expand America's nuclear arsenal, to engage in an "arms race" with the Soviet Union, to share nuclear weapons–making capabilities with various countries (including, notably, Israel) have all been made outside of democratic processes—and have had a profound impact on our nation and the world.[41]

Another way that World War II damaged American democracy was that the United States essentially took the place of Britain as the great

---

36. See the section titled "The Central Intelligence Agency" in chapter 5 below.

37. Among numerous books, see especially the trilogy by Rhodes: *Making of the Atomic Bomb*; *Dark Sun*; and *Arsenals of Folly*.

38. Rhodes, *Making of the Atomic Bomb*, 617–26.

39. Wills, *Bomb Power*.

40. Takaki, *Hiroshima*.

41. See the section titled "The Nuclear Weapons Program" in chapter 5 below.

PART ONE: Total War	What Did the War Cost?	95

imperial power of the world.[42] This move by the U.S. was not the result of an official edict by any American leader or institution. However, from early in the War on, Roosevelt and the U.S. dominated the partnership with Britain. Churchill seems to have been aware of the dynamics. If he did not fully welcome them, he recognized their inevitability and deferred to Roosevelt's superior power.[43]

With the establishment of these power dynamics in the alliance between Britain and the U.S. came implicit shifts in their respective roles in international affairs. British power had been diminished over some years, but this dynamic became starkly clear in the course of the War. Hence, the U.S. made policy decision after policy decision under the assumption that the U.S. of course would be the world's major superpower. As such, the U.S. acted in the years following the end of the War to expand America's network of military bases.[44] One major reason both Japan and (West) Germany could make the transition to active membership in the "Western alliance" in the years following the War was the enormous military presence that the U.S. sustained in those countries.[45]

None of these steps that the United States took to embrace the role of global superpower—a role that involved enormous commitments of military resources and set the U.S. on the path of Cold War with the Soviet Union, followed by the global war on terrorism—involved genuinely democratic processes. The decision to transform the Pax Britannica into a Pax Americana was not a democratic decision—even though it has profoundly affected the American people.

Many of those Americans who argued against military intervention in the years prior to World War II nonetheless supported more international involvement for the country.[46] They envisioned an international structure of the nations of the world that would make peaceful relationships possible. These people, many of whom remained opposed to American participation in the War, believed that the formation of the United Nations would be a silver lining to emerge out of the dark clouds of total war. At the time, many believed that the War might ultimately serve democratic ends should a powerful, effective, and participatory UN be the consequence of the War.

42. On this theme, see Moss, *Picking Up the Reins*, and Clarke, *Last Thousand Days*.
43. Brands, *Traitor to His Class*, 475–83.
44. Johnson, *Sorrows of Empire*, 151–84.
45. Regarding Germany, see Herring, *From Colony to Superpower*, 595–616; regarding Japan, see Dower, *Embracing Defeat*.
46. See Loconte, *End of Illusions*, 33–121. The same debaters who feared a wartime America moving toward a military dictatorship also advocated a peaceable internationalism—they repudiated isolationism.

Many of the foundational statements at the forming of the UN seemed to support those hopes.

However, from the very beginning of the UN, the interests of the leaders of the major powers centered on sustaining their power far more than genuinely internationally shared power. The dominant powers structured the UN in such a way as to protect the interests especially of the United States. The UN for many years reinforced American power.[47] Hence, even in its best outcome (the formation of the UN) World War II had an antidemocratic impact.

To sum up, back in the late 1930s, the U.S. had a relatively small military. The president felt constrained by the Constitution and democratic accountability to rely on a formal declaration of war by Congress before committing American forces to war. In contrast, by the end of the War in 1945, both of these elements of American politics (a small military and effective constitutional constraints on war-making) were gone forever.

Time after time, U.S. presidents have sent American troops into battle strictly based on their own decision without a congressionally approved declaration of war (contrary to the mandate of the U.S. Constitution). America's troop level has remained many times what it was in 1937. Since 1945, the U.S. has generally remained on a level of high readiness for war. And, one more element the War provided that undermined American democracy has been the creation of nuclear weapons and their deployment outside the constraints of the American democratic system of checks and balances.

THE MORAL LEGACY OF WORLD WAR II, PART I: 1941–1945

Our evaluation of the moral legacy of World War II for the United States in this book involves two parts. The first, which we have just completed, is to look at the War itself, the rationales given for the U.S. supporting the Allies and then entering the War as a full belligerent, the conduct of the War, and some of the costs of the War. The second part of this evaluation, to be explored beginning in chapter 5 below, will be to consider the aftermath of the War. What kind of world did World War II lead to? How did the events of World War II and their consequences shape the United States?

47. "The dominant elite view with regard to the UN was well expressed by Francis Fukuyama, who had served in the Reagan-Bush State Department: The UN is 'perfectly serviceable as an instrument of American unilateralism and may indeed be the primary mechanism through which unilateralism will be exercised in the future.' His prediction proved accurate, presumably because it was based on consistent practice going back to the early days of the UN" (Chomsky, *Hegemony or Survival*, 29).

In my discussion of the rationales given for American involvement in World War II in chapter 2 above, I focused on the "purpose statements" given by President Roosevelt and others that articulated the values that the U.S. was seeking to further by their engagement. Most centrally, Roosevelt's "Four Freedoms" speech in January 1941, and the Atlantic Charter, issued in August 1941, established the stated goals that the war effort would serve. For example, the U.S. government used the Four Freedoms and an accompanying set of paintings by Norman Rockwell as the centerpiece of the U.S. War Bond campaign. And the British printed pamphlets by the million of the Atlantic Charter that were spread throughout western Europe.

It is clear, therefore, that the purpose statements had a propagandistic function. They did not stand as official policy directives, and we have no evidence that they played a role in determining military or political decisions. They played an important role in the *moral* appeal made to the American people to support and participate in this war. As such, they provide criteria for evaluating the moral legacy of the War.

The purpose statements and the expression of similar sentiments rarely explicitly evoked traditional just war criteria. However, those criteria have for centuries been embedded in thought about war and, hence, should be seen in the background of the moral appeals made on behalf of the War and in ongoing appeals to the War's "justness." So, it is appropriate that we invoke traditional just war criteria in our reflections here.

The run-up to the War did not necessarily cohere with the expectations of the just war approach. The European war began when the British and French made a war guarantee to one dictator-led nation (Poland) in relation to a different dictator-led nation (Germany). Neither Britain nor France acted in self-defense or in support of self-determination or disarmament for the Polish people. And then, after making this war guarantee, a commitment that surely was decisive in the Polish government defying the Germans, the British and French did virtually nothing to aid the Poles. As a consequence, Poland quickly succumbed to the German invasion. So the beginnings of that war were full of moral ambiguities—ambiguities minimized in most accounts of those beginnings.[48]

In the slightly more than two years between the German invasion of Poland and the formal U.S. entry into the European war, America continually violated standards of "just" behavior for *neutral* countries and provoked Germany's eventual declaration of war.

In the Asian conflict, the United States was far from the innocent, passive, peace-seeking victim of a "dastardly" and totally unprovoked attack

---

48. For an exception, see the provocative analysis in Buchanan, *Churchill*.

characterized by Roosevelt in his "Day of Infamy" speech on December 8, 1941.[49] Certainly, the Japanese attack on Pearl Harbor was a terribly violent and immoral act of aggression. But it was hardly unprovoked.

The decades prior to Japan's attack on Pearl Harbor had seen a succession of hostile acts and policies by the United States toward Japan. These acts included racist anti-Japanese legislation in the U.S. and U.S. pressure on Britain to end its close alliance with Japan in the early 1920s. The background to the American-Japanese conflict and the misleading representation of that conflict in Roosevelt's post-Pearl Harbor speech, however, surely do not justify the Japanese attack.

When we turn to the conduct of the War, however, we cross the lines of ambiguity between just and unjust wars. The two central criteria generally used to evaluate just conduct are proportionality (that the proportion of damage caused in executing the war should not outweigh the good that was achieved by the war) and noncombatant immunity (that tactics should focus on those who are actually doing the fighting and supporting the fighting, seeking to avoid causing harm to those not involved in the conflict).

In relation to both these criteria, we have plenty of evidence that America's war leaders were aware of their existence. It does seem that early in the European war, which began for the U.S. in 1942, American leaders made at least some effort to operate, at least in a loose sense, within the parameters of these two criteria.[50]

When the Americans joined with Britain in the European air war, they initially eschewed the British approach, the intentional bombing of population centers. They focused more on directly attacking military targets. Toward the end of the War, their emphasis paid major dividends as American bombs virtually cut the German military off from its supplies of oil.

Yet, the Americans always did understand their strategy to be a complement to the British strategy of directly and intentionally targeting noncombatants in an attempt to destroy German "morale."[51] Hence, the Americans share responsibility, to some degree, for the Britons' direct violation of the just conduct criteria.

In the war with Japan, the U.S. abandoned both proportionality and noncombatant immunity. The U.S. intentionally targeted Japan's largest city, Tokyo, for the firebombing attack of March 1945 because of its tightly packed wooden housing in hopes of maximizing the deaths of

---

49. See Chomsky, "Revolutionary Pacifism of A. J. Muste."

50. For example, Colonel Richard D. Hughes, a leader in the American air war in London, argued strenuously on moral grounds, with some effect, against terror bombing. Carroll, *House of War*, 81–85.

51. Grayling, *Among the Dead Cities*, 138–42.

noncombatants—hopes that were successfully met (more than eighty-five thousand people died in one night's bombing).

At the time that the U.S. dropped atomic bombs on Hiroshima and Nagasaki, neither of which had major military significance (they were targeted because neither had yet been bombed, thus their destruction would be more visible), the war already was virtually over. The U.S. had ignored efforts by Japanese leaders to call a halt to the fighting, possibly due to American leaders' desire to use this ultimate weapon of mass destruction in full view of the world.[52]

In part, the American abandonment of limits to their destruction followed from President Roosevelt's announcement in January 1943 of the Allied intention to fight until gaining the unconditional surrender of the Axis—that is, to fight in the most destructive way possible for as long as it would take to render the Axis completely powerless.[53]

By 1945, the costs of this war were enormous. It resulted in the deaths of eighty million people, perhaps more. It injured, rendered homeless, and permanently drove from their communities countless millions. After the War's conclusion, all of central and eastern Europe ended up under tyrannical communist governments—as did, in a few years' time, China and several of its neighbors. American democratic governance was transformed with the emergence of military-oriented institutions such as the Pentagon, Central Intelligence Agency, and nuclear weapons programs.

Were the benefits that were gained by these six years of overwhelming death and destruction greater than these (and many other) costs? While most Americans in 1945 would likely have said so, most Europeans would have been less sure. For hundreds of millions around the world, even in 1945, the answer surely would have been no, the War was not worth it—the costs were too high.

As I will argue in the next section of this book, we cannot hope accurately to assess the moral legacy of World War II if we only consider the events up to August 1945. We must also consider how the War shaped the postwar world.

However, even only up to August 1945, it seems clear that we have good reason to conclude that World War II was *not* a just war even for the U.S. Actual American causes for fighting were ambiguously just at best—and the means used by the American military egregiously violated just conduct criteria.

---

52. Dower, *Cultures of War*, 208–20; Hasegawa, "Were the Atomic Bombings Justified?"

53. This is James Carroll's argument in his *House of War*, 5–12.

The purposes given by the American government for policies that made American entry into the War as a full belligerent inevitable did point to admirable moral ideals. And, as events proved, the U.S. was positioned at the end of the war to pursue those purposes with a great deal of potential to fulfill them. Maybe Americans had traditionally been reluctant to engage in international affairs, but in 1945 they were indeed in a position to engage in those affairs on their own terms. The U.S. would be able to shape the world according to how Americans wanted it.

What did the United States do with this incredible opportunity? This question will be the focus of Part Two ("Aftermath") below. One theme we will consider is how the process of fighting World War II affected the way the U.S. handled their opportunity to exercise international power in the aftermath of that war. I will show that though they certainly had the potential to pursue the values expressed in the purpose statements, Americans did *not* do so.

In fact, the history of the impact of the United States on the world since 1945 is a history of the practical (if not theoretical) repudiation of self-determination and disarmament. I will suggest that one central factor in this history is a direct result of the American World War II war effort—the creation of permanent and ever more powerful militaristic institutions at the heart of the American nation-state, with the Pentagon, the CIA, and the nuclear weapons program as the key examples.

PART TWO: Aftermath

5

Pax Americana

WHAT KIND OF PEACE?

After the denouement of the horrible destructiveness of nuclear weapons on civilian populations, the Allies achieved their goal of the unconditional surrender of the Axis powers. When the Japanese gave up the fight in August 1945, the United States stood as the world's one great global power.

The Soviets had the powerful Red Army and the capability to impose their will on nations they occupied. However, the war to the death with Germany had left tens of millions of Soviets dead and countless more wounded and displaced. The main cities had been devastated. You could call the Soviet Union battered but unbowed, but the emphasis would have to be placed on *battered*.

The British Empire remained intact, for the time being. But clearly it was near the end of the line. Though suffering significantly less damage, both in terms of lost lives and devastated infrastructure, than the War's other main belligerents (with the crucial exception of the United States), Britain was exhausted, tremendously weakened, headed for a major decline. The Britons would seek to remain active in international affairs, and for the immediate future intent on sustaining a rapidly disintegrating empire. However, clearly by 1945, Britain was subordinate to the one unambiguously victorious power to emerge from the War, the United States of America.[1]

The U.S. now was an unrivaled economic juggernaut. American military might, now confirmed with its development and use of a weapon

---

1. Clarke, *Last Thousand Days*.

capable of such destruction that it reconfigured the very nature of warfare, stretched throughout the world. The Red Army could probably have matched the U.S. in terms of ability to wage a land war, but certainly not in the air or on the sea. And the Soviet forces were geographically concentrated within the (admittedly huge) boundaries of the Soviet nation-state and its immediate neighbors. The U.S. in 1945 had the Soviets surrounded with its forces in Europe and the Far East.

Perhaps most importantly, at that moment, the U.S. also occupied the moral high ground. It had brought the great tyrannies to their knees; the American way of democracy, free enterprise, anticolonialism, and freedom of thought and expression inspired people everywhere. So, the answer to the world's main question—what kind of peace will follow this terrible war?—lay largely in America's hands. The moral legacy of World War II is to be found most of all in how the United States used its unprecedented global power and prestige.

The world had reason for hope. It did seem that of all the possible outcomes of the War, the United States, the world's pioneering democracy, in the driver's seat was the best one imaginable—and it had come to pass. The purpose statements we have kept in mind throughout our account of the events of the War now came to the place of possible massive implementation.

The Atlantic Charter, especially, could have been meant for just this moment. The western Allies had joined forces, they asserted, in order to shape a new world order. They claimed that this new world order would be characterized by political and economic self-determination throughout the world and by comprehensive disarmament based on an international order founded on rule of law. Franklin Roosevelt popularized the term "united nations" for those fighting the Axis powers, and a few weeks after Pearl Harbor, twenty-six of these Allied countries, calling themselves the "united nations," issued a declaration of common purpose. This designation for war allies morphed into a designation for the rebirth of the old League of Nations.

The new dynamic with the United Nations, in contrast with the post–World War I League of Nations, was that rather than ultimately opting out of participation, the U.S. would be committed to this new attempt at international collaboration. In fact, the key organizing conference was held in San Francisco, California, and the new headquarters for the United Nations were established in New York City.

I will suggest that one of the main elements of our evaluation of the moral legacy of World War II must be the failure to realize the promise of the purpose statements that had fueled support for the War. When we look at the impact of World War II on the United States, we see a major transformation. An essentially nonmilitarized country with a small, marginally powerful military that generally operated in subordination to civilian power and its democratic checks and balances mobilized its military-industrial forces. The structures of the federal government were transformed with the inauguration of a centralized military structure centered in the newly constructed largest building in the world, autonomously located on the other side of the river from the civilian institutions of power.[2] Then, to entrench this new structure even more deeply, the federal government embarked on a massive, top-secret operation to create nuclear weapons, thereby building a structure complementary to the centralized military command—and profoundly reinforced the new regime of militarization.[3]

The War established a powerful momentum that proved strongly resistant to all attempts to make America a leader in moving the world toward Atlantic Charter ideals. The war effort had spread American military power across the globe. The U.S. now had footholds in East Asia, the South Pacific, Western Europe, and elsewhere—and important leaders did not want to retreat. So the country didn't.

The conquered nations of Japan and Germany especially remained crucial as locations for massive permanent American military establishments. In many ways, American support for recovery in those two nations is admirable. However, clearly that support did not have as its main goal self-determination and disarmament. It is true that one purpose was to prevent rearmament in those two traditionally militaristic societies, a purpose successfully fulfilled. However, while the U.S. prevented their return to militarism, Americans also used these countries as key elements in American militarism—not only as home to many thousands of soldiers at various American military bases but also in time as homes to key elements of the American nuclear arsenal. Both Germany and Japan became pawns in the Cold War, with little say on their part.[4]

The War also saw profound growth in the power and wealth of American corporations and helped stimulate expansion of the footprint of many of these corporations around the world. With the heightened power of U.S.-based corporations, possibilities for economic self-determination on the part of the world's peoples were greatly diminished. American corporations stood to gain tremendously from the global expansion of American military power. These corporations both profited greatly from arms contracts and had the coercive might of the American military as an aid to solidifying

---

2. For the story of the creation of the Pentagon, see Carroll, *House of War*, 1–40.

3. The classic study remains Rhodes, *Making of the Atomic Bomb*. For a more recent account, see DeGroot, *Bomb*.

4. Herring, *From Colony to Superpower*, 595–650.

their global presence when it was resisted (for example, see the discussions below of the role of the U.S. in overthrowing governments in Iran and Guatemala in the 1950s, largely in service to corporate interests).

Another important (and complicated) dynamic to emerge from World War II was a hostile stance toward the Soviet Union. From the start, this was an alliance of convenience for the Americans (surely also for the Soviets) based simply on the shared commitment to defeat the Nazis. The U.S. did not take the occasion of this alliance to work at forging longer-term connections with the Soviets for the sake of peaceful postwar coexistence. As soon as it became apparent that the Allied war effort eventually would be successful, the U.S. and Great Britain started to foresee postwar conflicts with the Soviets. Rather than responding to these intimations of future potential conflicts as a challenge to find alternative ways of relating to the Soviets that might minimize the possibilities of conflict, the Americans and British began planning for how to prevail in the impending conflicts.[5]

The dynamics may be seen most clearly in the story of the development and use of nuclear weapons. There were important figures in the American government who advocated sharing at least some information about the development of the bomb with the Soviets and, in time, with the broader international community. They hoped that such sharing, when combined with mutual commitments not to develop and use these weapons in the future, would lead to a time of stability and sustainable peace.

The view that prevailed among governmental leaders took the opposite tack. America kept its development of the bomb secret from the Soviets right up to the dropping of the bombs on Hiroshima and Nagasaki (ironically, this development was not quite as secret as was assumed, since the Soviets had several spies embedded in the Manhattan Project who kept Stalin well informed). The winners in the policy debate hoped that the use of the bomb would intimidate the Soviets and guarantee American world dominance. These American leaders also assumed that the Soviets would not be capable of building their own nuclear weapons for many years, if ever. Of course, after the U.S. struck out on its own with the intent to use the bomb as a basis for domination, the Soviets shocked the Americans and everyone else by successfully creating their own nuclear weapons in a very short period of time. And the arms race was off and running.[6]

Even though the Manhattan Project proved not to be much of a secret, the extraordinary measures taken to ensure its secrecy (most of all from the American people and the structures of American democracy) set the tone

5. Dallek, *Lost Peace*, 20–28.
6. Carroll, *House of War*, 103–60.

for the operations of what we may call the American national security state. From the start, those leading the Manhattan Project kept the development of nuclear weapons hidden. As it turned out, one step of hiddenness followed another, and a profoundly antidemocratic national security regime was established in the United States. This regime was tied not only to the development of nuclear weapons but also to the use of American military forces and other expressions of American power throughout the world.[7]

Policymakers did debate the use of American power in the 1940s. But this debate was mostly kept hidden from the nation at large. The public was not given the opportunity to be part of a national discussion about whether to utilize American power for the sake of creating better possibilities for sustainable peace or for the sake of expanding the wealth and power of American corporations.

The main result (or "product") of World War II for the United States was the transformation of the country from a relatively demilitarized, relatively democratic society into the world's next great empire. The history of the American empire since 1945 has most decidedly not been the history of enhanced freedom everywhere in the world. Political and economic self-determination and disarmament have not followed from the establishment of the Pax Americana. So, was World War II worth this outcome?

THE PENTAGON

By mid-1941, the American military had expanded dramatically in anticipation of full engagement in the War, growing from roughly 250,000 people under arms in 1937 to several million following the establishment of the military draft in 1941—and heading for a high of fourteen million a few years later.

Twice before the United States had undergone a similar mobilization—first the Civil War, and later World War I. In both cases, the rapid growth had been followed by an equally rapid demobilization almost immediately after the war ended. This did not happen following World War II, at least not in as decisive a way. At its peak during the Civil War, the military (Union and Confederacy combined) totaled about 3.2 percent of the American population, before dropping to about 0.1 percent in 1866. In 1918, the military had reached about 2.9 percent of the population, and then dropped to about 0.2 percent, where it stayed until 1940.

During World War II, the percentage of people in the military jumped to about 8.6 percent of the total population. However, while demobilization

7. Wills, *Bomb Power*, 137–83.

decreased the numbers again, they never went lower than 1.0 percent in the years after (that is, until the end of the Vietnam War, when the numbers did slide slightly below 1.0 percent). So the size of the military as a percentage of the population remained five times larger after World War II than it had been between 1919 and 1940. Given the rise in the overall population, the absolute numbers of people in the military was closer to ten times as large in post-World War II "peace time" than prewar.

One of the main differences in the post-World War II era as compared to earlier postwar demobilizations was the existence of a major permanent institution in the federal government that had as its reason for existence the perpetuation of a large military and large military expenditures—the Pentagon.

As noted above in chapter 4, the Pentagon came into existence directly as a consequence of the War. With the sudden growth in the size and importance of the military by 1940, President Roosevelt agreed with leaders of the Army that a new headquarters was needed (in Roosevelt's mind, only until the end of the "emergency"). This new structure would, at least for the time being, also serve as the headquarters of the War Department.

As James Carroll puts it in his history of the Pentagon, "The freshly empowered Army wanted its new building to be set apart from the so-called Federal West Executive Area, apart from entanglements with, and the limits of, the seat of government. In a time of peril, the Army was not about to be treated as just another bureaucratic function, alongside Interior and Commerce and Indian Affairs. The Army would transcend."[8]

The Army settled on a spot on the west side of the Potomac River, in northern Virginia, partly because the size of the building would not be limited by District of Columbia zoning regulations. Army leaders chose Colonel Leslie Groves, known as an effective administrator, to head the building project, and immediately promoted him to brigadier general. When Roosevelt saw the plans, he ordered the size of the building to be reduced by half. General Groves, without Roosevelt's knowledge, retained the original size and, working behind the scenes, had several Virginia Congress members make sure the necessary appropriations were sustained. The Pentagon was built rapidly, leaving Roosevelt no chance to reduce the size.[9]

The groundbreaking ceremony for the Pentagon was held on September 11, 1941. Sixteen months later, the largest building in the United States was ready for occupation. Roosevelt's concerns about problems that might arise with the relocation of the military headquarters away from the civilian

8. Carroll, *House of War*, 2.
9. Ibid., 3.

PART TWO: Aftermath   *Pax Americana*   109

centers of government proved to be prescient. As it turned out, the War Department (renamed the Department of Defense in 1947) stayed in Virginia—along with army and navy headquarters and the headquarters of the third major branch of the military, the air force, established in 1947. And this seat of power in the federal government, symbolically now separate from the rest of the government, grew ever larger and unassailable.

In the immediate aftermath of the War, with victory in hand and the nation's powerful desire to return to "normalcy,"[10] the future of the military in the United States entered a period of uncertainty. During the debates and turf battles to define postwar priorities, the cause of the military was enormously enhanced by the presence now (as had not been the case before in American history) of a central and extraordinarily powerful single institution, the Pentagon, that advocated for retaining a more powerful military than the U.S. had had before in peacetime.

In 1947, the passage of the National Security Act ensured that the role of the military in this postwar period would be markedly different than in earlier postwar eras. This legislation formalized the country's commitment to sustain an unprecedented level of military presence. Something fundamental about the American nation-state had been transformed.[11] We may see this change symbolized by the intent that Roosevelt had for the War Department headquarters to be returned to its previous location near the other federal institutions once the "emergency" had ended. The headquarters remained in the Pentagon, separate from the civilian seats of power—symbolizing that the "emergency" never ended.

The National Security Act formalized the centralization of the military that the building of the Pentagon had created de facto. Instead of having a Department of Navy and a War Department, we would have a single Department of Defense. The head of the Department of Defense, the secretary of defense, would become a full member of the president's cabinet.

The abandonment of the term "War Department" for the new term, "Defense Department," ironically signaled a major change. Before 1947, "War" was seen as an exceptional, rarely encountered event. The "War Department" rose to prominence on those rare occasions when the nation entered into armed conflict. Now, "Defense" is a permanent situation,

---

10. The term "normalcy" was coined during the 1920 presidential campaign by Republican candidate Warren Harding explicitly as a promise to demobilize from World War I and pull back from foreign military entanglements. Harding's victory ensured that such a pulling back would happen. The response of the federal government after World War II proved to be quite different.

11. Wills, *Bomb Power*, 70–85.

always present and demanding resources, always playing a central role in governmental activity and planning.

The National Security Act of 1947 also authorized the creation of two other institutions that would diminish democratic oversight of American foreign policy. One of these was the National Security Council (NSC); the other was the Central Intelligence Agency (CIA).

The National Security Council was commissioned to provide policy advice to the president on national security matters. In practice, the NSC operated independently of the State Department and congressional oversight. It formulated and executed policy (mostly in secret) outside of the normal democratic channels. The formal membership of the NSC would include the president, vice president, secretaries of defense, state and treasury, chairman of the joint chiefs of staff, director of the CIA, and a presidentially appointed national security advisor.

As noted above in chapter 4, the CIA (to be discussed in more detail below) was established as a greatly expanded successor to the Office of Strategic Services (OSS). The National Security Act's authorization of such "covert activities" soon essentially became a blank check that allowed the CIA, often acting on behalf of the president, and sometimes on its own initiative, to engage in a long series of hidden, violent, disruptive acts around the world.[12]

By viewing the world through military-oriented lenses, Pentagon leaders undermined whatever chances the U.S. had to utilize its stature as the world's superpower in 1945 to foster ideals of the Atlantic Charter. A key hope in the Charter was disarmament. However, insofar as the expanded and permanently empowered military establishment in the United States shaped American policies, that hope for disarmament would remain mostly an empty ideal.

Even the idealistic language of Woodrow Wilson during World War I, gathering support for the Great War by insisting that it would be "the war to end all wars," was not often repeated in the run-up to World War II or in the war years. The sentiment behind that language, however, that the best justification for paying the extraordinary price this war demanded was to create a sustainable peace, remained central. Certainly the Atlantic Charter evoked such sentiment.

The very success of the American war effort, however, itself insured that these ideals of disarmament and sustainable peace would be virtually impossible to implement. The War empowered warriors. The dynamics of governance in the United States were transformed, with the result that the

---

12. Weiner, *Legacy of Ashes*; Prados, *Safe for Democracy*; and Blum, *Killing Hope*.

PART TWO: Aftermath   Pax Americana   111

forces that insured Americans would crush their enemies gained and retained their position as the main determinants of the shape of American foreign policy.

THE NUCLEAR WEAPONS PROGRAM

As noted above in chapter 4, another key permanent pillar for the militarization of American society that serves as one of the main moral legacies of World War II is the nuclear weapons program. In 1939, as the actions of Germany terrified people around the world, a prominent nuclear physicist, Leo Szilard,[13] sent a letter (also signed by Albert Einstein) to Franklin Roosevelt that raised the possibility of the creation of a uranium bomb with extraordinary destructive power. Szilard had been the first scientist to conceive of such a weapon and was aware of German scientists who had begun to work on such a project.

Roosevelt took Szilard's 1939 letter seriously. The Manhattan Project, the top-secret program to develop nuclear weapons, was launched on October 9, 1941—four weeks after the groundbreaking of the Pentagon and eight weeks prior to the attack on Pearl Harbor. The project originated, and attracted European physicists such as Szilard, out of fear that the Germans might develop such a weapon first and use it without scruples. As it turned out, unbeknownst to those initially engaged in the Manhattan Project, the German effort to create the bomb never got off the ground. However, the American project once underway generated tremendous momentum on its own.

Leslie Groves, after his success in quickly constructing the Pentagon, was named director of the project. The quest for the mega-weapon became one of the highest priorities in the American government.[14] Roosevelt gave Groves almost unlimited power and resources to complete the project in as little time as possible.

Despite the number of people involved, spread across the United States (and spilling into Canada), word of the work that was being done hardly leaked out at all to the surrounding society—though several Soviet spies did infiltrate the project. The U.S. intended to keep its Soviet allies completely in the dark concerning the project, but Stalin actually knew a great deal of what went on.

---

13. Szilard (1898–1964) grew up in a Jewish family in Hungary, moved to Germany for graduate school and his early professional career, and then moved to England after Hitler's ascent to power in 1933. He lived the last third of his life in the United States.

14. See Rhodes, *Making of the Atomic Bomb*.

Even with the extraordinary success of the project in constructing three usable bombs in slightly more than three years, circumstances changed by the time the bombs were ready. The fear of Germany creating its own bombs had dissipated not long after the project began. Another impetus for the project—as a means of ensuring the unconditional surrender of the Germans—ended by May 1945 when Germany fell.

The decision by the Americans to drop the bomb on Japan has remained one of the most controversial in the history of warfare.[15] James Carroll makes a persuasive case that this decision was *both* the consequence of the simple momentum of the Manhattan Project ("we have invested so much in this process that we need to see it through to the end") *and* the explicit desire in that particular context of a few key decision-makers.[16]

Several factors played into the decision, insofar as it was an actual decision.[17] A central background force was Roosevelt's January 1943 proclamation of the Allied commitment to "unconditional surrender" in the war with the Axis. As the momentum toward conquest of the Japanese built (a key moment in this process was the March 1945 firebombing of Tokyo that resulted in over eighty-five thousand deaths), Japanese leaders sent signals to the Soviets that they would like to negotiate peace with the U.S. They had one condition: Hirohito would remain emperor (if only as a figurehead) and would not be liable for prosecution as a war criminal.

The Japanese peace overtures had little effect as the Americans began to plan for an actual land invasion of Japan. As the story came to be told after the nuclear bombs were used, the U.S. feared losing up to one million soldiers in such an invasion. With the completion of the bomb (successfully, and secretly, tested in New Mexico on July 16, 1945), there was a weapon that would make such an invasion and massive loss of American life unnecessary.

The figure of one million deaths was created as a general estimate some time after the bombings.[18] The military had before the bombing undertaken a formal estimate of possible casualties, but this estimate was not released publicly at the time. Rather than one million deaths, the actual estimate had been about forty thousand. This formal estimate also concluded that Japan

---

15. For just one example of the ongoing intensity of the debate, see the account of the controversy over the Smithsonian Institution's attempt to create a wide-ranging, somewhat critical exhibit marking the fiftieth anniversary of the bombing of Hiroshima and Nagasaki, in Linenthal and Englehardt, *History Wars*.

16. Carroll, *House of War*, 53–58. See also Bess, *Choices Under Fire*, 198–253.

17. Takaki, *Hiroshima*.

18. One such assertion came in an article published under the name of Secretary of War Stimson in *Harper's* in 1948.

surely would have surrendered before the end of 1945 without the bombs being used and without a land invasion—even with the American insistence on unconditional surrender.[19]

A couple of other factors played central roles in the decision to use these bombs on Japanese civilian populations. The bomb's makers desired better to understand the effect of these weapons. They chose Hiroshima and Nagasaki as bomb targets because those cities had not suffered major damage from previous aerial attacks and thus offered the best laboratories for observation of the effects of nuclear bombs in "real life."

More important, surely, was the anticipation on the part of important American leaders (most centrally Secretary of State James F. Byrnes and, of course, President Truman, as well as Leslie Groves) of a struggle in the near future with the Soviet Union for world domination. The Soviets agreed to enter the war with Japan within three months of the end of the European war, and it seemed likely that were they to engage in the Asian war in a major way they would expect to play an important role in the postwar peace settlement (as they certainly did in Europe).[20]

So, part of the urgency in using the bombs as soon as they were available had to do with preventing the Soviets from gaining a stronger foothold in the Far East, and even more so simply to establish a point of dominance over the Soviet Union due to the American monopoly on this weapon of all weapons. As it turned out, the Americans did get the bombs dropped before the Soviet presence in the Asian war became significant (the Soviets declared war on Japan on August 9, and engaged the Japanese in battle in Manchuria). Postwar arrangements with Japan were shaped almost exclusively by the United States.

The Americans showed a willingness to use these weapons they possessed. Tragically, the Americans' monopoly on nuclear technology turned out to have exactly the opposite impact of what they intended. Rather than establishing a position of dominance over the Soviet Union, the American capability spurred the Soviets on to their own development of a comparable capability.

Henry Stimson, who had signed off on the development and deployment of the nuclear bombs, nonetheless recognized that it would not be in

---

19. This is what the report concluded: "It is the Survey's opinion that certainly prior to 31 December 1945, and in all probability prior to 1 November 1945, Japan would have surrendered even if the atomic bombs had not been dropped, even if Russia had not entered the war, and even if no invasion had been planned or contemplated." Quoted in Wills, *Bomb Power*, 28.

20. For a thorough discussion of this argument, see Alperovitz, *Decision to Use the Atomic Bomb*.

the best interests of the U.S. for an arms race to follow from Hiroshima and Nagasaki. He argued in the back rooms of American policymaking for an attempt to control and limit the spread of nuclear weaponry. In a memo to Truman, dated September 11, 1945, he proposed that the U.S. "enter into an arrangement with the Russians, the general purpose of which would be to control and limit the use of the atomic bomb." To so link with the Soviets, we would pledge to "stop work on any further improvement in, or manufacture of, the bomb as a military weapon, provided the Russians and the British would do likewise." As part of the agreement, Americans would "impound what bombs we now have in the United States provided the Russians and the British would agree with us that in no event will they or we use a bomb as an instrument of war unless all three governments agree to that use." Stimson made a radical suggestion here: the U.S. would voluntarily surrender its monopoly on nuclear weaponry and its exclusive control of its existing bombs.[21]

Stimson was nearing the end of his career. In an allusion to Joseph Stalin, he pled with Truman to seek the path of mutual trust rather than mistrust: "The chief lesson I have learned in a long life is that the only way you can make a man trustworthy is to trust him; and the surest way to make him untrustworthy is to distrust him and show him your distrust."[22] Stimson argued for a new approach: "Unless the Soviets are voluntarily invited into the partnership upon a basis of cooperation and trust, we are going to maintain the Anglo-Saxon bloc over against the Soviet in the possession of this weapon. Such a condition will almost certainly stimulate feverish activity on the part of the Soviets toward the development of this bomb in what will in effect be a secret armament race of a rather desperate character."[23]

American leaders made a decision almost as momentous as the actual bombing of the two Japanese cities when they rejected Stimson's proposal. Stimson believed Stalin would resist expansionist tendencies among his advisors and respond favorably to an American initiative for shared control of nuclear capabilities. Despite Americans' "memory" of the Soviets being aggressive from the beginning of the postwar period, Stimson actually was accurate in his belief.

The Soviets withdrew from Iraq and left Western nations in control of that nation on the Soviet's border. They also left Norway and withheld support for communists in Greece, Italy, and Finland as well as offering only limited support for the communists in China. Stalin actually supported

21. Carroll, *House of War*, 113.
22. Quoted in ibid., 114.
23. Quoted in DeGroot, *Bomb*, 115.

"bourgeois elements over Socialists" in Germany, and he grudgingly accepted loss of control over the entrance to the Black Sea and the refusal of the Americans to adhere to the reparations agreements made in the summer of 1945. "If Stimson wanted to approach Stalin in 'trust,' it was obviously because he knew that the Soviet leader faced severe constraints of his own just then, and knew that the atomic bomb had put Washington in a position of superiority, however pontoon-like in its firmness."[24]

Ten days after Stimson circulated his vision for cooperation, Truman made it the focus for the president's cabinet at their September 21 meeting. Carroll writes,

> There is reason to conceive of the meeting as a turning point in the American century. What would remain the basic question of the Cold War was put on the table: Is Soviet foreign policy motivated by an offensive strategy for the sake of an ideologically driven global empire or by normal big-power defensiveness, aiming at security?[25]

Stimson's proposal found support from many cabinet members, including Undersecretary of State Dean Acheson, but was opposed by Secretary of the Navy James Forrestal and, later, by Secretary of State James Byrnes, who was unable to attend the September 21 meeting. The legacy of the attack on Hiroshima hung in the balance during these deliberations. If the cabinet and Truman had affirmed and implemented Stimson's proposal, the outcome of Hiroshima would have been a balance of power rather than a balance of terror. Surely, the consequent Soviet behavior would not have been nearly so adversarial.

At first, the joint chiefs of staff supported Stimson's proposal. However, Secretary of the Navy Forrestal (eventually to succeed Stimson as secretary of war—a position then renamed secretary of defense) persuaded the chiefs to change their stance by emphasizing that their own interests would be furthered by a more hard-line approach to the Soviets.

Truman rejected Stimson's proposal. The U.S. did propose a different kind of international control of the bomb. This approach required internal inspections of each nation's nuclear arsenal and insisted that the U.S. would retain custody of some bombs, forbidding the Soviets to do likewise (since they had not yet built bombs)—elements guaranteed to lead to Soviet rejection.

One way the story of the nuclear arms race has been told has been to assert that with all its scary moments, we must recognize that nuclear

---

24. Carroll, *House of War*, 115.
25. Ibid., 116.

weapons have not been used since Nagasaki (August 10, 1945). However, as Joseph Gerson shows in his book *Empire and the Bomb: How the U.S. Uses Nuclear Weapons to Dominate the World*, nuclear weapons have in a genuine sense actually been used often in American foreign policy ever since. Gerson writes that U.S. use of its nuclear capability to enhance its power in the world accelerated nuclear proliferation.

> On at least 30 occasions since the atomic bombings of Hiroshima and Nagasaki, every US president has prepared and/or threatened to initiate nuclear war during international crises, confrontations, and wars—primarily in the Third World. And, while insisting that nearly all other nations fulfill their Nuclear Nonproliferation Treaty (NPT) obligations (India being one exception, and Israel, which has not signed the NPT, falling into a category of its own), the US government has never been serious about its Article VI obligation to engage in "good faith" negotiations for the complete elimination of nuclear weapons.[26]

As Garry Wills argues, the presence of the bomb has profoundly subverted democracy. The U.S. invented the atomic bomb in a way that led to victory for the forces of official secrecy and military discipline. The president started the process and authorized secret funding to make it possible. The project became the model for further hidden projects and other secretive behavior. What began in the context of a wartime "emergency" became the institutional status quo.

Wills' argument may be summarized thus:

> The Bomb forever changed the institution of the presidency, since only the President controls "the button" and, by extension, the fate of the world, with no constitutional check. This has been a radical break from the division of powers established by our founding fathers, and it has enfeebled Congress and the courts in the postwar period. The Bomb also placed a stronger emphasis on the President's military role, creating a cult around the Commander in Chief that has no precedent in American history. The tendency of modern presidents—and presidential candidates—to flaunt military airs is entirely a post-Bomb phenomenon. As well, the Manhattan Project inspired the vast, secretive apparatus of the National Security State, including intelligence agencies such as the CIA, which remain largely unaccountable to Congress and the American people.[27]

26. Gerson, *Empire and the Bomb*, 2.
27. Wills, *Bomb Power*, dustcover.

PART TWO: Aftermath   *Pax Americana*   117

CENTRAL INTELLIGENCE AGENCY

In some ways, the Central Intelligence Agency is like the proverbial camel who initially manages to get its nose under the edge of the tent, and then in time maneuvers its entire body inside to take over the tent. During World War II, as noted above, Roosevelt agreed to create an ad hoc intelligence-gathering organization, called the Office of Strategic Services (OSS), in part due to the Americans' failure to realize that Pearl Harbor was going to be attacked. Even though the American military had cracked some of Japan's communication codes and had thereby become aware that some attack was imminent, the government had no central coordinating agency to help put various pieces of information together.

The OSS, led by General William J. Donovan, was not carefully planned or well led, and did not contribute much to the war effort. From the start, OSS leaders seem to have been more interested in exotic schemes of subterfuge and covert violence than careful information gathering and analysis.[28] Due to this undistinguished record, Roosevelt became doubtful about the work of the OSS and appointed his chief White House military aide, Colonel Richard Park Jr., to prepare a report on how the OSS had fared during the War. Park completed his report shortly after Roosevelt's death in April 1945 and submitted it to the new president, Harry Truman. Colonel Park was unstinting in his critique. The report concluded that the OSS had done "serious harm to the citizens, business interests, and national interests of the United States." It could not find any examples of how the OSS had contributed to winning the war, only examples of failure.[29]

Some of the negative examples: Chinese strongman Chiang Kai-shek subverted OSS agents to serve his purposes. OSS operations were compromised by German spies throughout their areas of engagement. Japan learned of OSS plans to compromise Japan's codes and thus made changes that "resulted in a complete blackout of vital military information" in the summer of 1943. The OSS provided flawed information that led to thousands of French soldiers falling into a German trap following the fall of Rome in June 1944. The report concluded that the analysis branch of the OSS should be absorbed into the State Department and the rest should be eliminated. "The almost hopeless compromise of OSS personnel makes their use as a secret intelligence agency in the postwar world inconceivable."[30]

---

28. Weiner, *Legacy of Ashes*, 3–8.
29. Quoted in ibid., 7.
30. Quotes from ibid., 8.

This report confirmed for Truman his already deep suspicion of what he saw as an agency too similar to the Nazi's Gestapo. Though General Donovan worked tirelessly during the summer of 1945 to save his agency and give it permanent status, on September 20, Truman made his decision known. Donovan was fired and the OSS was to disband.

Donovan, though, had his supporters who shared his conviction that in order to function as a great power, the United States needed a powerful spying agency. Truman's decision to abolish the OSS set off two years of intense lobbying and resistance. The spy-supporters would not be denied. Stimson, who also opposed a peacetime spying agency, retired at about the same time as Truman's abolition order. OSS supporters used the time of transition as an opportunity to countermand Truman's decision. The assistant secretary of war, John McCloy, believed in the OSS and was able to issue an order that continuing operations of the OSS would be sustained on a temporary basis under a new name, Strategic Services Unit. This bought some time.

As advocates for an adversarial response to the Soviet Union gained ascendency in the federal government, various agencies sought to expand or establish clandestine intelligence departments (e.g., the army, the navy, the FBI). The pro-spy forces persuaded Truman to change his perspective, and in January 1946 he appointed a "director of central intelligence"—an appointment made with no congressional involvement. This person had the task of overseeing the intelligence officers and their support staff remaining from the OSS.

By the next year, advocates for clandestine intelligence work got the establishment of the Central Intelligence Agency (CIA) into 1947's National Security Act.[31] Truman later stated that this new CIA was being created to serve him by delivering daily news bulletins: "It was not intended as a 'Cloak & Dagger Outfit'! It was intended merely as a center for keeping the President informed on what was going on in the world." He never wanted the CIA "to act as a spy organization. That was never the intention when it was organized."[32]

Along with the emphasis on information gathering and analysis, the National Security Act also allowed for "covert action" in order to influence "conditions abroad" in situations in which the involvement of the U.S. should remain secret. As a consequences of this opening, the CIA as it evolved had a twofold mission—to gather and analyze information, and to engage in covert action to further America's foreign policy agendas.

31. Prados, *Safe for Democracy*, 28–41.
32. Quotes from Weiner, *Legacy of Ashes*, 3.

Contrary to Truman's stated wishes, this second mission came to dominate the CIA's work, and gained it its reputation.

The National Security Act attempted to establish parameters for these covert acts. When the CIA sought to engage in a covert activity, it was to gain authorization for each activity from a written presidential "finding" that the action was necessary. The Act continued, "a finding may not authorize any action that would violate the Constitution or any statute of the United States." The Act also required that CIA leaders "shall keep the congressional intelligence committees fully and currently informed of all covert actions which are the responsibility of, are engaged in by, or are carried out on behalf of, any department, agency, or entity of the United States Government including significant failures." The Act also asserted that "nothing in this Act shall be construed as authority to withhold information from the congressional intelligence committees on the grounds that providing the information to the congressional intelligence committees would constitute the unauthorized disclosure of classified information or information relating to intelligence sources and methods."[33]

As it turned out, the CIA from the start would be staffed with many holdovers from the OSS who tended not to be concerned about democratic limitations on their actions.[34] The restrictions—no acts by the CIA that would violate the United States Constitution and the CIA's transparency in relation to Congress—never played a major role in CIA operational philosophy.

The CIA scarcely distinguished itself in its intelligence work. Early on, the agency misread virtually every global crisis. It had no inkling of the Soviet atomic bomb until it was successfully tested. It helped little in gaining insights into the conflict that became the Korean War. And disastrously, several months after that war had begun, in October 1950, as U.S. General Douglas MacArthur aggressively moved toward the Chinese border, the CIA denied that the Chinese military had gathered in force. Even two days before the Chinese attacked and nearly routed the American troops, the CIA still denied that such an attack was likely.[35]

Allen Dulles, an advocate of covert operations, was appointed chief of the CIA's covert operations in 1951. After Dwight Eisenhower was elected president in 1952 and appointed Dulles's brother, John Foster Dulles, as secretary of state, Allen Dulles became the director of central intelligence. His

---

33. Quotes from Wills, *Bomb Power*, 83–84.
34. Weiner, *Legacy of Ashes*, 28.
35. Ibid., 59.

appointment pushed the CIA even harder to emphasize covert operations over information gathering and analysis.[36]

In short order, the CIA involved itself in the overthrow of democratic governments in Iran and Guatemala—in both cases justified by the alleged Soviet sympathies of the governments (though, more telling, in both cases American corporations had direct interests threatened by governmental policies that sought to gain more self-determination). The CIA also engaged, less successfully, in an attempt to overthrow Indonesia's government. All three actions had disastrous long-term consequences for these nations.[37] During this time the U.S. began its self-destructive engagement with the nationalist movement in Vietnam. Throughout most of the 1950s, the American role in Vietnam was primarily a matter of covert CIA activities.[38]

In general, the CIA's work, especially the covert operations championed by Allen Dulles, spurred the evolution of American foreign policy away from any actual efforts toward self-determination of the world's nations and away from disarmament. The CIA's covert operations time after time subverted self-determination and served to militarize conflicts and further the spread of armaments and military violence.[39]

The CIA actually provided little reliable information concerning the Soviet Union. Tim Weiner, in his history of the CIA, summarizes thus:

> The CIA's formal estimates of Soviet military strength were not based on intelligence, but on politics and guesswork. . . . In 1960, the agency projected a mortal threat to the U.S.; it told the president that the Soviets would have five hundred ICBMs ready to strike by 1961. The Strategic Air Command used those estimates as the basis for a secret first-strike plan using more than 3,000 nuclear weapons to destroy every city and every military outpost from Warsaw to Bejing. But Moscow did not have 500 nuclear missiles pointed at the United States at the time. It had four.[40]

It is impossible to calculate the cost of these misperceptions fueled by the CIA—in terms of American wealth devoted to what was throughout the 1950s a one-sided arms "race," in terms of the environment due to the rapid expansion of the American nuclear arsenal, in terms of the continual undermining of democratic processes, and in terms of the destruction of

36. Goodman, *Failure of Intelligence*, 11.
37. Prados, *Safe for Democracy*, 97–123; 167–80.
38. Young, *Vietnam Wars*, 1–88; Logevall, *Embers of War*.
39. See Blum, *Killing Hope*, for a comprehensive chronicle of covert interventions.
40. Weiner, *Legacy of Ashes*, 183.

any chance of working with the Soviet Union toward peaceful coexistence (especially after Stalin's death in March 1953 and the internal changes in the Soviet Union that followed).

PAX AMERICANA REPLACES PAX BRITANNICA

The transition from the "hot war" of 1939–1945 to what came to be known as the "Cold War" of 1947–1991 is a crucial period of time in the modern world. In many ways, these few years determined the moral legacy of World War II for the United States.

The key point that signaled defeat for advocates of peaceful coexistence with the Soviet Union among the American policymaking elite came with a speech by President Truman on March 12, 1947. The explicit focus of his speech was to announce that the United States would offer military aid to interests in Turkey and, especially, Greece that struggled with forces aligned with the Communist Party for control of those countries. Truman asserted that "assistance is imperative if Greece is to survive as a free nation."[41]

The speech was a watershed for several reasons. (1) Truman made clear that he identified Soviet communism as the implacable foe of the United States, the enemy to be resisted at a high cost, if necessary, and no longer the ally of World War II. (2) Beyond simply stating the enmity with which the United States would now regard Soviet communism, Truman committed American military support to this conflict. He indicated that the U.S. would not return to the pre-World War II approach of reluctance to involve itself militarily in other country's conflicts, especially those outside the western hemisphere. (3) To justify intervention on behalf of anticommunist forces in Greece and Turkey, Truman presented a basic principle that became known as the Truman Doctrine. The Truman Doctrine set the tone for the American side of the Cold War that would last until the breakup of the Soviet Union in 1991. "America must oppose any Communist threat to freedom anywhere in the world."[42] (4) Not stated openly in Truman's speech, but implied with the steps he announced, this intervention made clear that as the British Empire diminished and the Britons stepped back from their role as the world's main imperial power, the United States would be "picking up the reins."[43]

From the beginning of the Soviet-American-British alliance in the summer of 1940 following Hitler's surprise attack on the Soviets (in violation

41. Quoted in Dallek, *Lost Peace*, 231.
42. Quoted in Wills, *Bomb Power*, 72.
43. This term comes from one account of this transition: Moss, *Picking Up the Reins*.

of the Nazi-Soviet nonaggression treaty), instability and mistrust characterized the relationship between the Soviets and the Western democracies. Important American leaders, most prominently Secretary of War Stimson, nonetheless hoped to establish nonhostile postwar relationships with the Soviets. Many historians (though not all, of course—this area of study is one of the most controversial in all recent historical studies) argue that the Soviets also hoped to sustain a cordial relationship with the Americans, a style of relating that would involve mutual respect for each nation's legitimate spheres of influence.[44]

Stimson and his allies lost this debate when Truman sided with the more militant members of the policymaking elite and insisted that the U.S. would go it alone on the nuclear weaponry route. Even so, the Soviets still gave indications of a willingness to cooperate with a regime of peaceful coexistence.

As the Americans demobilized (partially) after August 1945, leaders of the army, the navy, and, especially, the newly established independent air force came to see that their own interests (i.e., keeping their forces as strong and well supplied as possible) would be served by increased enmity with the Soviet Union. For example, the air force eagerly sought the development of a new strategic bomber. In making their case, air force advocates placed the darkest possible interpretation on Soviet intentions:

> Legendary bomber commander Carl Spaatz, Air Force chief, stunned his interrogators at a congressional hearing. Flashing the image on a screen, he replaced the traditional . . . projection of the globe, which showed the United States protected by two vast oceans, with a polar projection, which showed a hulking Soviet Union all set to gobble Alaska, and then the rest of the forty-eight states, from across the narrowest of straits. America the vulnerable.[45]

Truman chose alleged Soviet expansionism as a catalyst for (in the words of a supporter, Senator Arthur Vandenberg) "scaring the hell out of the American people."[46] He felt he had to fan flames of fear in order to push the people to accept this move back into a kind of war footing. In fact, the Soviets were not involved in the struggle in the Greek civil war in any appreciable way. Stalin honored the informal agreement he had made with the

---

44. Leffler, *For the Soul of Mankind*, 36–37.
45. Carroll, *House of War*, 108.
46. Ibid., 139.

PART TWO: Aftermath   *Pax Americana*   123

western Allies at the conference in Yalta, acknowledged spheres of influence, and saw Greece as being in the British sphere.[47]

The struggle in Greece was between indigenous communists operating independently of the Soviet Union and a right-wing, nondemocratic monarchy that the British wanted to restore to power. Earlier, during the war years, the Nazis had easily taken control in Greece, helped by a good deal of collaboration from the monarchist forces. The consequent resistance to the Nazis was perhaps the fiercest and most effective in all of Europe. Various leftist and indigenous forces fought the Nazis under the umbrella of the Greek communists. Even without Soviet aid, the leftists, due to their strong support from much of the Greek population, effectively resisted the British attempts to reinstate the monarchy.

Truman's statement essentially promised that the U.S. would now involve itself militarily virtually anywhere in the world. It was not as if the U.S. had never been willing to use military force on foreign lands before.[48] However, as I have noted throughout this book, the general American philosophy of foreign affairs minimized a sense of responsibility for intervening in overseas conflicts—certainly this was the American position in the 1930s. Now, though, Truman changed the tone of American foreign policy and announced that indeed the U.S. would be sending extensive military aid (with the possibility of actual soldiers, if needed[49]) to foreign lands for a cause that did not directly affect American national security.

America's commitment to intervene in Greece opened the door for regular military excursions—mostly covert, but on numerous occasions out in the open. Likely few, if any, of these excursions would have been acceptable to the American people or even to Congress prior to World War II. That war transformed the way Americans thought about American military force being used around the world.

By embracing military aid to the monarchist forces in Greece, the U.S. affirmed the military action taken by the British beginning in 1944.[50] The Britons understood the return of the right-wing Greek government to power vis-à-vis the communist-led resistance forces as a key element of sustaining their imperial status quo.

---

47. Dallek, *Lost Peace*, 234–35.

48. For a short summary of many of these interventions, going back to the beginning of U.S. nationhood, see Williams, *Empire*.

49. I only learned a few years ago, several years after my mother's death, the cause of her brother's death. An Air Force pilot, he lost his life as an American soldier fighting in the Greek civil war.

50. Clarke, *Last Thousand Days*, 110–24.

The British action followed closely after the Yalta summit meeting that essentially divided Europe into spheres of influence. Prime Minister Churchill's use of violence to assert British dominance in Greece (which was combined with Stalin's willing withdrawal of support for the Greek communists) predated any of the military actions the Soviets took likewise to assert their "sphere of influence" over noncooperative nations. So, the first step in the acceptance of the use of violence for subduing populations who sought self-determination was taken not by the Soviets but by the British. For Americans willingly to step in when the British could not continue the fight signaled the American approval of such violence[51] (directly contradicting the Atlantic Charter's commitment to self-determination and disarmament).

This is how historian Robert McMahon summarizes the impact of Truman's speech:

> What is particularly significant about the Truman Doctrine . . . is less that basic fact of power politics than the manner in which the American president chose to present his aid proposal. Using hyperbolic language, Manichean imagery, and deliberate simplification to strengthen his public appeal, Truman was trying to build a public and Congressional consensus not just behind this particular commitment but behind a more activist American foreign policy—a policy that would be at once anti-Soviet and anti-communist. The Truman Doctrine thus amounted to a declaration of ideological Cold War along with a declaration of geopolitical Cold War.[52]

The Truman Doctrine lumped together all expressions of "communism" around the world as part of one phenomenon. This idea, that there was only one communism, underwrote American intervention throughout the Cold War period, leading to mistaking local efforts at self-determination for part of a Soviet effort to establish world domination—hence the tragic American misreading of social dynamics in nations such as Vietnam, Indonesia, and Cuba that led to literally millions of deaths in the several decades following Truman's speech.

In more than a symbolic way, the American replacement of Britain in Greece reflected the transformation of the international order. The Americans would not try to duplicate the British Empire in a literal sense. However, in terms of the projection of military and economic power, the ensuing Pax Americana in many respects would exceed the Pax Britannica.

51. Moss, *Picking Up the Reins*, 66–76.
52. McMahon, *Cold War*, 28–29.

American power projection found expression in the establishment of the North Atlantic Treaty Organization (NATO), a military alliance made up of the U.S., Canada, and most Western European nations. From the start, the ideal of NATO's being made up only of democracies was compromised due to the desire to have dictator-ruled Portugal part of the Alliance for strategic benefits. In 1952, after the communist threat in Greece had been defeated, the Greeks along with Turkey (neither of which remotely functioned as a democracy) were also welcomed into NATO, bringing important strategic benefits with them—not least the ability to serve as hosts for major American military bases.

The implications of the Truman Doctrine—committing the U.S. to an entirely new type of war of choice—did lead to covert military involvement in the Greek civil war. Very shortly, though, the postwar era of permanent military "emergency" would move into a much more costly and widespread military intervention, the Korean War. And the militarization of American foreign policy would proceed apace. The pre-World War II days of avoiding foreign entanglements were gone forever.

6

The Cold War

THE AMERICAN INITIATIVE

A crucial step in the acceleration of the arms race came when American leaders decided to build and deploy hydrogen bombs, a tremendous enhancement of the U.S. nuclear weapons arsenal.[1] As nuclear physicists developed the atomic bombs that devastated Hiroshima and Nagasaki, they soon realized they would be capable of creating much more devastating bombs. However, priorities on speed required a focus on the less powerful bombs. After the Japanese surrendered, the physicists' knowledge presented decision-makers with the question of whether to proceed with further development of this new kind of bomb. Most of the physicists opposed such development. But by now the momentum toward the militarization of American foreign policy moved swiftly, enhanced by the demonization of the Soviet Union.

The Soviets successfully tested their first nuclear bombs in 1949. At this point, the Atomic Energy Commission (AEC), the federal agency charged with overseeing the American nuclear weapons program, recommended that the U.S. step back from the brink of an accelerated arms race. The AEC opposed the development of the hydrogen bomb:

> There is no limit to the explosive power of the bomb except that imposed by the requirements of delivery. The weapon would have an explosive effect some hundreds of times that of present [atomic] bombs. It is clear that the use of this weapon would

1. Rhodes, *Dark Sun*.

bring about the destruction of innumerable lives; it is not a weapon which can be used exclusively for the destruction of material installations of military or semi-military purposes. Its use therefore carries much further than the atomic bomb itself the policy of exterminating civilian populations.[2]

President Truman refused to accept this recommendation by the AEC. He formed a new committee made up of AEC chair David Lilienthal, Secretary of Defense Louis Johnson, and Secretary of State Dean Acheson. Johnson, echoing the commitments of the Pentagon now to unrestricted weapon development, supported proceeding with the hydrogen bomb, while Lilienthal represented the AEC position.

Acheson became the key figure. Several years earlier he had supported Henry Stimson's attempt to get the U.S. to cooperate with the Soviets in avoiding an arms race. By 1950, though, partly spooked by the unleashed anticommunism of American militarists and influenced by new advisors such as Paul Nitze, Acheson had committed himself to the full militarization of American foreign policy. His State Department now placed the priority on military force over diplomacy. He supported the hydrogen bomb.[3]

An already rapid process of creating weapons of mass destruction ratcheted up exponentially. Truman gave the "Super" (the term used for the hydrogen bomb) the official go-ahead on January 31, 1950. The U.S. decision to proceed with the Super accelerated the arms race almost beyond comprehension. For example, during Dwight Eisenhower's eight-year presidency (1953–1961), the American nuclear arsenal grew from roughly one thousand warheads to sixteen thousand.[4]

Paul Nitze, of Acheson's staff, was charged with writing up a "policy review" that would be, in effect, a philosophical rationale for the expansion of American military power.[5] Nitze's report, known as NSC-68, established the basic foundation for American policy for the decades following.[6] NSC-68 echoed the Truman Doctrine, asserting that the Soviets were bent on world domination: "the Soviet Union, unlike previous aspirants to hegemony, is animated by a new fanatic faith, antithetical to our own, and seeks to impose its absolute authority over the rest of the world."[7]

2. Quoted in Carroll, *House of War*, 172–73.
3. Thompson, *Hawk and the Dove*, 101–9.
4. McMahon, *Cold War*, 74–75.
5. Thompson, *Hawk and the Dove*, 105–14.
6. Wills, *Bomb Power*, 92–97.
7. NSC-68, quoted in Carroll, *House of War*, 182–83.

The report committed the government to seeing all threats to "freedom" anywhere as deadly threats to the U.S. NSC-68 stated it this way: "The assault on free institutions is worldwide now, and in the context of the present polarization of world power, a defeat of free institutions anywhere is a defeat everywhere." With its assumption, re-emphasizing the Truman Doctrine, that "free institutions" must be defended with force everywhere in the world, the report committed the U.S. to further expansion of its global system of military bases. Even more fatefully, the report committed the U.S. to continue its course, wherein any perceived "communist" threat anywhere in the world must be resisted, placing an equal priority on the defense of nondemocratic regimes in remote corners of the world as on supporting key allies in Western Europe.[8]

NSC-68 had as its main immediate intention a drastic expansion of American military resources. Such an expansion faced strong opposition from many sources in the broader American society. Truman himself, ideologically sympathetic with this paranoid view of the Soviets and, of course, a major contributor to that view, nonetheless was also committed to keeping budgets down. The eruption of war in Korea, and the decision to commit American troops to that war, was, for the supporters of NSC-68, "a fortuitous turn of events."[9] In September 1950, three months into the Korean War, Truman ordered that NSC-68 become official policy. The direction NSC-68 intended for American foreign policy became entrenched—aided by the aggressive acts of the communist forces of North Korea and a paranoid and distorted reaction to the aggression by the U.S.

Truman's resistance to expanded military spending ended, as the defense budget increased from $13.5 billion in 1951 to more than $50 billion two years later. Between 1950 and 1953, military spending as a percentage of all federal expenditures grew from less than one-third to almost two-thirds.[10] The dominance of the American budget by military spending became a permanent reality.

The war in Korea serves as a paradigmatic example of how the Truman Doctrine would work out in practice. In light of the Truman Doctrine, American leaders would see any advance of communism as a direct threat to American national security and a call for military response. The conflict that emerged in 1950, like so many other later conflicts that were misunderstood by Americans as expressions of Soviet expansionism, actually was most fundamentally a civil war. In the words of Bruce Cumings, "The

8. Carroll, *House of War*, 183.
9. Ibid., 186, quoting a history of America's Strategic Air Command.
10. Ibid., 186, 546.

PART TWO: Aftermath					The Cold War 129

Korean War [is] now widely seen as a civil war that had its origins in the 1930s if not earlier, but was made inevitable by the thoughtless decision, taken the day after the obliteration of Nagasaki, to etch a frontier along a line no one had ever noticed before in Korea's continuous history: the 38th parallel."[11]

At the end of World War II, the U.S. and Soviet Union could not agree on a single government for a unified Korea, so the nation was divided along the 38th parallel—North Korea fell under the rule of a communist dictatorship led by Kim Il-Sung, and South Korea under the rule of a right-wing dictatorship led by Syngman Rhee. Neither side was content with this division; both hoped to gain control of the entire nation.

The victory of communist forces in the Chinese revolution of 1949 complicated American policymakers' perception of Korea. Their victory emboldened the North Koreans to take offensive action against the South. Contrary to American assumptions, Joseph Stalin was not a strong supporter of this action; he greatly feared drawing the Americans into a conflict so near the eastern boundary of his empire. Throughout the Korean conflict, the Soviet Union played only a minor role.[12]

The North Koreans expected that by striking quickly and decisively, they would conquer the South before the Americans could come to their client state's aid. They almost succeeded, but under the command of famous World War II general Douglas MacArthur, the Americans intervened just in time and pushed the northerners back. As the Americans successfully moved north, MacArthur made the fateful decision to continue past the 38th parallel and seek to crush the North Koreans. Then, due to MacArthur's own hubris[13] and the failures of American intelligence,[14] the American forces pressed on. They acted in denial of the possibility that as they approached the Chinese border they ran the risk of drawing Chinese forces into the conflict. In fact, the Chinese did strike, and routed the Americans, rapidly driving them south.

At this point, the conflict came close to triggering an American nuclear bomb attack. Most of Truman's advisors, including even the recently appointed Secretary of Defense George Marshall, a supposed moderate, supported using nuclear weapons—a step that had been prepared for in recent months by the Strategic Air Command.

11. Cumings, *Korean War*, 226.
12. Ibid., 144–45.
13. Halberstam, *Coldest Winter*.
14. Weiner, *Legacy of Ashes*, 55–70.

As it turned out, though Truman blamed the Soviets for the actions of North Korea, Stalin actually had a very different perspective. According to materials uncovered in post-Cold War archives, Stalin actually hoped *against* the U.S. losing in Korea. "Let the United States of America be our neighbors in the Far East," he was quoted as having said in the fall of 1950. He feared that if the Americans neared defeat, they would start a world war. He knew of SAC's plans.[15]

Several factors seem to have played important roles in restraining Truman's hand when he faced the actual decision about whether to go nuclear or not. Perhaps the most significant one was simply Truman's further reflection on the consequences of destroying masses of humanity.[16] Truman stated, "It is a terrible weapon and it should not be used on innocent men, women, and children who have nothing whatever to do with this military aggression."[17] So, Truman made the decision to move the U.S. back from the brink. He thereby reversed the momentum toward nuclear weapons as simply another arrow in the quiver.

When he defied the counsel of his top advisors and chose *not* to use nuclear weapons, Truman set a couple of crucial precedents. First, he stepped back from engulfing the world in another total war. War could be limited and the big powers realize that achieving victory could come at too great a cost. Second, Truman reinforced the sense that the use of nuclear weapons should be taboo. The same person who made the ultimate decision to introduce nuclear bombs into actual battlefields now refused to do it again. Though leaders after this, including Truman himself, threatened the use of nuclear weapons in Korea, they always stopped short. In James Carroll's view, if Truman had ordered the use of nuclear weapons, even in a limited sense, "there is no doubt that subsequent presidents and other leaders of nuclear powers would have followed suit."[18]

As it turned out, the Americans managed through conventional warfare to stem the tide and retain a foothold in South Korea in face of the Chinese onslaught. Truman fired MacArthur and replaced him with a more competent commander, and the war settled into a World War I–style bloody stalemate for a couple more years until, in 1953, an uneasy truce was achieved that restored the 38th parallel as the border between North and South Korea.[19] In the end, roughly three million Koreans lost their lives

15. Carroll, *House of War*, 192.
16. DeGroot, *Bomb*, 186–87.
17. Quoted in Carroll, *House of War*, 192.
18. Ibid., 194–95.
19. Cumings, *Korean War*, 225–43.

in this conflict, 75 percent of them noncombatants. The main legacy of the Korean War was to solidify in most respects the influence of NSC-68 on the American nation. It marked the transformation of the State Department's focus from diplomacy to military action. And it marked a similar transformation of the presidency.

After 1950 and the prosecution of the Korean War, military matters remained *the* central focus of American presidents. The National Security Council became the locus of executive power in the U.S. From now on, "it was not that the Pentagon would be forever in the loop, but that the Pentagon would be the loop."[20]

THE 1950S—OVERTHROW

The Truman Doctrine invoked the "Soviet threat" as the basis for American armed intervention anywhere in the world in response to alleged threats to U.S. national security. Such intervention in fact became common during the 1950s. I will mention just three examples here—none of which, in actuality, had much to do with the Soviet Union. These three occasions of direct American involvement in the quest to overthrow existing governments are paradigmatic, though, of how the Pax Americana actually took shape on the ground.

The nation of Iran was for some time part of the British Empire. In 1901, the Anglo-Iranian Oil Company established a monopoly over Iranian oil, from extraction to refining and marketing, and claimed at least 85 percent of the earnings, leaving precious little in Iran: "Anglo-Iranian made more profit in 1950 alone than it had paid Iran in royalties over the previous half-century."[21]

In the aftermath of World War II, many in Britain's colonial holdings saw the opportunity to move toward independence—including powerful forces in Iran. The Iranian nationalist movement was headed by Mohammad Mossadegh, a committed democrat who became prime minister in 1951. Mossadegh's program, at its center, sought to gain for Iran a fair share of oil revenue as a means of strengthening the nation's civil society.

Shortly after Mossadegh gained power, the Iranian parliament, with strong support across political factions, moved to nationalize the oil industry. "All of Iran's misery, wretchedness, lawlessness, and corruption over the

---

20. Carroll, *House of War*, 193–94.
21. Kinzer, *Overthrow*, 117–18.

last fifty years has been caused by oil and the extortions of the oil company," one radio commentator declared.[22]

These Iranian moves infuriated Britain's elite. They actively resisted Iran's efforts to implement the takeover but without much success. Finally, they decided the only option would be literally to overthrow the democratic government of Iran. Mossadegh learned of the plans, however, and threw the British out of Iran. At this point, the tail end of the Truman presidency, the Americans opposed the British coup effort. But the election of Dwight Eisenhower as president, just weeks after the Britons were expelled, changed the scenery.

Eisenhower's new secretary of state, John Foster Dulles, had more sympathy for the British concerns. So the Britons began making the allegation that Mossadegh was moving Iran in a communist direction—a pure fabrication. Iran did have a small communist party, called Tudeh. Tudeh, like all Iranian political parties, supported the nationalization. But Mossedegh strongly opposed Tudeh's political philosophy and made a point to keep any Tudeh members out of his government. As a believer in democracy, he did allow Tudeh to operate without restrictions. This party, though, had little influence anywhere in the country.[23]

No matter—in the name of the Truman Doctrine and resisting the communist move for world domination, the U.S. government entered the fray. This was an opportunity for the young Central Intelligence Agency to try out its covert operations chops. Mossedegh was removed from power and placed under house arrest, where he would remain for the rest of his life. "A year ago," Eisenhower wrote his brother Edgar in November 1954, "we were in imminent danger of losing Iran, and sixty percent of the known oil reserves in the world. . . . The threat has been largely, if not totally, removed."[24]

Iran's monarch, Mohammad Reza Shah, whose power had been reduced by Iran's democratic transformation, led the new government. In time, the oppressiveness of the Shah's rule, which was strongly backed by the U.S.—the notorious Iranian secret police, SAVAK, received training from the CIA in torture techniques[25]—ended in an Islamic revolution in 1979. Since that revolution, Iran has opposed American intersts in the Middle East. Instead of accepting Mossadegh's desire for a relationship characterized

---

22. Quoted in ibid., 118.
23. Ibid., 121.
24. Quoted in Leffler, *For the Soul of Mankind*, 130.
25. Blum, *Killing Hope*, 72.

by mutual respect, the U.S. helped create and sustain decades of misery for the Iranian people and, ultimately, an intransigent enemy.

For the CIA, the successful 1953 coup in Iran became an inspiration to continue on the path of violently subverting unattractive governments. The next opportunity arose within a few months of the conclusion of the Iranian operation—and was much closer to home. Jacobo Árbenz Guzmán became the second elected president of Guatemala in 1951. Thanks to the CIA, he did not finish his term, and his country entered into a long and terrible nightmare of repression and murder that left hundreds of thousands dead.

Guatemala had emerged from generations of dictatorships in 1944 with a commitment to democracy that seemed solid and fruitful. Árbenz, like Iran's Mossadegh, was a committed democrat who cared deeply about the poverty all too widespread in his country. And also like Mossadegh, Árbenz saw that one important step his government could take to address the needs of civil society would be to nationalize properties held by foreign corporations.

Árbenz, though, made a tragic mistake when he challenged a powerful American corporation at a time when America had a secretary of state, John Foster Dulles, who had himself been a longtime lawyer for that same corporation. The United Fruit Company dominated Guatemala, operating free from governmental interference. "It simply claimed good farmland, arranged for legal title through one-sided deals with dictators, and then operated plantations on its own terms, free of such annoyances as taxes or labor regulations." This system drew Dulles' support; Guatemala was considered a "friendly" and "stable" country—though one ripe for change given its widespread poverty and political disenfranchisement. The changes that did emerge met with Dulles' and United Fruit's disapproval.[26]

After a "people's revolution" in 1944, the election of a democratic government, led by Juan José Arévalo, led to major changes. Arévalo's term lasted six years. During that time, Guatemala's National Assembly took important steps to provide help for the Guatemalan people—and to challenge United Fruit's hegemony. At the end of Arévalo's term, the newly elected Árbenz took office. This transition marked the first peaceful transfer of power in Guatemalan history.

Arbenz saw the need to move things even further toward economic self-determination within Guatemala. A key element of his program was a land reform law to allow the government to buy hoarded, uncultivated land and transfer ownership to small farmers who would work the land. United

---

26. Kinzer, *Overthrow*, 130.

Fruit bore the brunt of this new law, since the company cultivated only about 70,000 of the more than 550,000 acres of workable land it owned.[27]

The lack of actual communist involvement in Guatemala did not deter American leaders who sought to crush this effort at self-determination in their own backyard. The Guatemalan threat lay in its model of self-determination, given its status as the traditional leader in Central America. The problem was not the spread of actual communism, but the spread of self-determination represented in these reforms.[28]

So, supported by Eisenhower and Secretary Dulles, the CIA overthrew President Árbenz, ended Guatemala's democratic era, and set into motion what was probably the worst expression of massive government terrorist violence in the modern history of the western hemisphere. As Kinzer puts it, "by overthrowing [Árbenz], the United States crushed a democratic experiment that held great promise for Latin America. As in Iran a year earlier, it deposed a regime that had embraced fundamental American ideals but that had committed the sin of seeking to retake control of its own natural resources."[29]

The CIA's "winning streak" came to an end when it attempted to overthrow the government of Indonesia, another nation that sought self-determination and freedom from dependence on Western corporations and politics.[30] As the Dutch East Indies, Indonesia had been the scene of terrible fighting during World War II, with millions of casualties. When the Allies' drove the Japanese out, they created an opportunity for the end of Dutch control and Indonesian self-determination. Independence forces, with their leader, Sukarno, declared Indonesia a free nation in 1945. However, the Dutch would not give up their colony and created an armed struggle before they finally relented and allowed the nation its independence in 1949.

Sukarno remained in power. In a complicated and challenging environment, he sought both internally to hold together a wide coalition of Indonesian parties and externally to follow a path in international affairs that would foster Indonesian independence from both sides of the Cold War. Indonesia played a major role along with nations such as India, Yugoslavia, and Egypt in what was called the Non-Aligned Movement.

Three elements of Sukarno's path troubled the U.S. One was his role in the Non-Aligned Movement. Many American leaders accepted this simple dictum: "If you are not with us, you are against us." Second, as part of his

27. Ibid., 133.
28. Ibid.
29. Ibid., 147.
30. Prados, *Safe for Democracy*, 166–80.

balancing act within Indonesia, Sukarno did allow the Indonesian Communist Party (the PKI) to play a role—a relatively minor role given the PKI's small size. Third, Sukarno sought economically to foster Indonesian self-determination and resisted Western corporate influence, including the residue of the Dutch colonial presence.

In light of the CIA's other successes, Eisenhower authorized an attempt to overthrow Sukarno's government in 1957. In this case, though, the CIA could not overcome its ineptness to the degree that it had in Iran and Guatemala.[31] The coup effort was a dismal failure. Nonetheless, the coup attempt had disastrous long-term repercussions for the Indonesians. It enhanced the status of the communist PKI in Indonesia, especially among many of the nation's poorer people. Indonesians recognized the PKI as the opponents of the CIA, which made the PKI more attractive. So the PKI grew in power, though more as an expression of Indonesian nationalism than as a beachhead for the Soviet Union.

By the mid-1960s, another attempt at getting rid of the Sukarno government was launched. This time, unlike in 1957, forces within Indonesia took the initiative rather than relying on an externally generated CIA intervention. The precise events of October 1965 remain shrouded in secrecy, but when the dust cleared after a supposed coup attempt to overthrow Sukarno allegedly undertaken by a small force of junior military officers said to be sponsored by the CIA, General Suharto stood as the "defender" of the Indonesian government.

Within a short time, though, the true outcome of these events became clear. Sukarno was removed from power and Suharto (who had served both the Dutch colonialists and the Japanese invaders) was established as the supreme ruler of Indonesia, a role he remained in until 1998. Under Suharto's direction, the security forces undertook a campaign to eradicate PKI influence. As many as one million Indonesians were killed in this campaign, undertaken with the support of the American government. In fact, American diplomats provided thousands of names of supposed communist operatives to the Indonesian military—directly leading to their murders. Robert Martens, an American diplomat in Jakarta, stated in 1990, "It really was a big help to the army. They probably killed a lot of people, and I probably have a lot of blood on my hands, but that's not all bad. There's a time when you have to strike hard at a decisive moment." Another American diplomat, Howard Federspiel, said, "No one cared, as long as they were Communists, that they were being butchered."[32]

---

31. Weiner, *Legacy of Ashes*, 164–78.
32. Quoted in Blum, *Killing Hope*, 194.

CUBA

If we were to summarize American foreign policy in the era following World War II in light of the "purpose statements" discussed in chapter 2 concerning involvement in the War, we would have good reason to say that those purpose statements were stood on their head.

The failure of post-World War II American foreign policy to seek disarmament and self-determination for the world's peoples became apparent in a tragic and costly way in relation to the small Caribbean island nation of Cuba. After centuries as a Spanish colony, Cuba gained its "independence" following the brief Spanish-American War of 1898. However, for the first half of the twentieth century, Cuban political life was dominated by the Americans. This domination included support for dictators who served U.S. economic and organized crime interests.

During the 1950s, Cuban dictator Fulgencio Batista faced increasing unrest due to his corrupt and exploitative style. His hold on power relied on support from the Eisenhower administration. Finally, congressional actions forced the U.S. to withdraw this support in the late 1950s. An increasingly potent anti-Batista movement moved closer to toppling the dictator.[33]

With Batista weakened by the loss of U.S. support, a guerilla movement led by a young lawyer, Fidel Castro, moved quickly and drove the dictator into exile on January 1, 1959. At this point, Castro kept his distance from Cuban communists. But his revolutionary government moved decisively, and violently, to establish itself in power. Many of Batista's supporters were executed and others driven out of the country. Castro ended American corporations' domination of the Cuban economy and shut down the Mafia's gambling institutions.

Analysts still debate the inevitability of Castro's turn toward an alliance with the Soviet Union. Some argue that his main concerns were with Cuban independence and that his government's actions sought mainly to eliminate any chance of a Batista return or subversion by American corporate interests. In this view, Castro hoped for a relationship of peaceful coexistence with the American government. Had the U.S. been willing to allow for this, the argument goes, Castro would not have felt the need to turn to the Soviets for support.[34]

As it turned out, from the beginning the U.S. government viewed Castro's revolution with hostility. Four months after taking power, Castro visited the U.S., hoping for an audience with Eisenhower and a chance to establish

---

33. Jones, *Bay of Pigs*, 10.
34. Blum, *Killing Hope*, 184–93.

a relationship. Eisenhower left town rather than meet with Castro.[35] Some in the administration urged patience. America's Cuban ambassador, Philip Bonsal, worked for positive relationships following Castro's rise to power early in 1959. Bonsal asserted that at this time, Castro was free from communist domination. In contrast, CIA director Allen Dulles argued from early on that Castro was a threat to the U.S. He saw Cuba "drifting toward communism." Vice President Richard Nixon echoed this sentiment: Cuba is "being driven toward communism more and more."[36]

The American government ultimately accepted the worst-case scenario, and the CIA began to make plans to overthrow the Castro government. The CIA expected the Cuban people to rise up against Castro—in ignorance of the hostility the population had felt toward Batista and its consequent affirmation of the revolution. These plans did not remain hidden. The CIA began to work with Cuban exiles in the U.S., a community Castro had infiltrated. Learning of American violent intentions, Castro turned toward the Soviet Union for aid to enhance Cuban security, a turn Castro had initially resisted in hopes of retaining Cuba's independence and developing a positive relationship with the U.S.[37]

A group of anti-Castro Cuban exiles with CIA-supplied training, weapons, and leadership undertook an invasion of Cuba in April 1961—the so-called Bay of Pigs action. Unlike with Iran and Guatemala, in this case the luck ran bad instead of good. The invasion failed.

At first, the recently installed Kennedy administration denied that it had been involved—lying even to its own secretary of state and its United Nations ambassador.[38] In time, Kennedy could not hide the evidence that indeed the U.S. had been directly involved, and he publicly accepted responsibility for the disastrous action. This public disgrace did not, however, deter Kennedy from supporting continued (unsuccessful) efforts to assassinate Castro.

Within months of the failed invasion, and with Castro being all too aware of the American government's efforts to take his life, Cuba made arrangements with the Soviet Union to have Soviet nuclear weapons stationed in Cuba. The Soviets hoped both to protect Cuba and to gain the ability to deter an American nuclear attack on the Soviet Union. The Soviets could not at this point come close to matching American delivery capabilities.

35. Jones, *Bay of Pigs*, 11.
36. Quotes from ibid., 11–12.
37. Prados, *Safe for Democracy*, 204–35. "Actual exchanges of Cuban and Soviet diplomats occurred only during the summer of 1960, when the CIA already had its project [to overthrow Castro] in motion" (234).
38. Wills, *Bomb Power*, 155–56.

Only the Americans had intercontinental missiles. In the Soviets' view, having the ability to bomb the U.S. from bases in Cuba was a provocation no greater than the Americans having nuclear weapons based in Turkey and aimed at the neighboring Soviet Union. The Soviets, that is, sought no more than a rough balance of power. Castro agreed to the nuclear weapon deployment in order to deter a U.S. invasion—which, of course, had already been covertly attempted. He feared the next attempt would be made with more overwhelming American military force.[39]

In October 1962 the United States moved again to the brink of using nuclear weapons. As with Truman and his advisors a decade earlier, Kennedy's closest advisors advocated attacking the Cuban missile bases, an act that everyone knew would almost surely lead to nuclear war.[40] And, as Truman a decade earlier, Kennedy managed to withstand strong pressure and step back from the brink. He negotiated with Khrushchev to have the Soviets take their nuclear weapons back, while the Americans would (secretly) withdraw a number of their nuclear missiles stationed in Turkey that targeted the Soviet Union.

Though Kennedy did refuse to initiate a nuclear conflagration, the person who truly blinked in this confrontation was Khrushchev. He agreed to withdraw all Soviet nuclear weapons from the western hemisphere. Hundreds of American nuclear weapons remained in the eastern hemisphere—plus the U.S. retained an enormous lead in intercontinental weapons delivery capability. The U.S. came through this conflict with a heightened position of superiority (for the time being); the Soviets came through the conflict having lost significant face.

The Cuban missile crisis led directly to Khrushchev's removal from leadership in the Soviet Union within two years.[41] The Soviets learned that they had to seek strategic parity with the United States. Clearly, the Americans were ready to use their weapons on the Soviet Union. If there could be no deterrent in Cuba, something else would have to be done. So the Soviets ratcheted up even more intensely their nuclear weapons development. They created a large collection of intercontinental missiles that could directly target the United States. That is, the American response to the Cuban missile crisis led directly to a tremendously *weakened* level of security for the American people.

39. Ibid., 158–59.
40. Carroll, *House of War*, 279.
41. Morris, *Iron Destinies, Lost Opportunities*, 236.

VIETNAM

Probably the greatest foreign policy disaster in American history came as a direct consequence of U.S. policymakers' disregard for the values expressed in the Atlantic Charter. Of particular significance is point three: "They [Roosevelt and Churchill] respect the right of all peoples to choose the form of government under which they will live; and they wish to see sovereign rights and self-government restored to those who have been forcibly deprived of them."[42]

Given the Atlantic Charter's wide visibility over the next several years, people throughout the world who sought an end to colonial domination took this point about political self-determination quite seriously.[43] Certainly, political leaders in the French colony of Vietnam in Southeast Asia noticed the promise of support for self-determination. French domination of Vietnam dated back to the mid-1800s and had always met with strong resistance. Ho Chi Minh became the most important leader of the Vietnamese anticolonial movement in the twentieth century. Ho first sought to get American support for Vietnam's self-determination when he tried to gain an audience with President Woodrow Wilson during Wilson's participation in the formulation of the Versailles Treaty following World War I. Wilson refused to see Ho.

During World War II, Vietnamese nationalists actively resisted Japan's occupation, but the Japanese, even so, managed to extract many resources from Vietnam and to devastate the economy. Japan's policies led to a famine that in 1944–45 resulted in as many as two million Vietnamese deaths. During World War II, Vietnamese nationalists worked closely with the American spying agency, the OSS, to rescue American pilots who had been shot down. Ho Chi Minh was even formally recognized as an OSS operative.[44]

After being rebuffed by Wilson in 1919, Ho had turned to Leninism because it seemed to take seriously the aspirations of colonized people for self-determination. From that point on, Ho identified with the Communist International. However, his priority was always Vietnamese independence; communism for him served his nationalist aspirations.[45]

In 1944, the Japanese took over direct control of the colony for the final months of the War. During the time of chaos, the Vietnamese nationalists (the Viet Minh) greatly increased their role in public life and managed to

---

42. The Atlantic Charter. See the U.S. National Archives website: http://www.archives.gov/education/lessons/fdr-churchill/images/atlantic-charter.gif.

43. Bills, *Empire and the Cold War*, 8.

44. Young, *Vietnam Wars*, 10.

45. Anderson, "Vietnam War," 15–17.

gain de facto control of six provinces in northern Vietnam. They instituted numerous reforms, including the recruitment of self-defense forces, abolition of colonial taxes, reduction of rents, and redistribution of land owned by French landlords. The Viet Minh also worked to overcome the famine by distributing rice reserves.[46] They hoped when the War ended to continue their work, free from colonial domination.

These efforts at social change in Vietnam gained the sympathy of many Americans stationed in Vietnam—but not with the government back in Washington. An American in Hanoi reported to the State Department that the Vietnamese "seemed to feel that every American contained within himself all the virtues and accomplishments of the nation they wanted most to emulate." Those Vietnamese working for independence understood that the U.S. promised the Philippines full independence at war's end and expected similar support for themselves.[47]

The Viet Minh sought to cooperate with the Allies to effect a peaceful transition to a self-governed Vietnam. They dissolved the Communist Party prior to the January 1946 elections to elect Vietnam's new government. However, in the French stronghold in the South, participation in the election was banned. The northern two-thirds elected a government dominated by pro-independence forces that over the next six months achieved much.

Historian Marilyn Young summarizes thus:

> Careful rationing and a mass campaign for planting food crops brought the famine to an end by March 1946. It was a stunning achievement, and it joined a growing list of reforms in other areas (literacy, taxation, labor legislation) that were not merely decreed but acted upon. Within six months of taking power, under their own government and without assistance from any foreign country, the people of North and Central Vietnam were free of famine and colonial taxation, and on the way to universal literacy.[48]

The French, however, retained a strong foothold in southern Vietnam. After negotiations in 1946, the French government and the new Vietnamese government agreed on a plan that would allow the French to send fifteen thousand troops to Vietnam where they would be joined by ten thousand Vietnamese troops under French command to oversee a time of transition. Over the next six years, these troops would gradually be withdrawn, so by

46. Young, *Vietnam Wars*, 9.
47. Quotes from ibid., 13.
48. Ibid., 13.

1952 a Vietnam free of all foreign troops would be recognized as a "free state" within an "Indochinese federation of the French Union."[49]

Their plan was scuttled by the French military leader in southern Vietnam, who announced the establishment of a separate Republic of Cochinchina in June 1946. Colonial authorities believed that recognizing the Viet Minh in any way would inevitably lead to the French being driven out of Indochina altogether. They concluded that the only way to preserve their new "republic" was to go to war with the North, which they commenced to do in November 1946.[50]

Ho Chi Minh and his colleagues had had high hopes that U.S. policy might actually be shaped by the stated values of supporting self-determination for the world's peoples. In the immediate aftermath of World War II, even in the stronghold of the Viet Minh in northern Vietnam, the U.S. was held up in the popular consciousness as the model their nation wanted to emulate. When Ho declared Vietnamese independence, he self-consciously alluded to the American Declaration of Independence.[51]

However, because of the Viet Minh's links with communism, the U.S. entered this conflict with a strong bias against the independence movement. Also, the U.S. felt strong pressure from their interests in Europe to keep France in the anti-Soviet bloc of nations.[52] These dynamics led to an American disposition to support French colonial interests.

The U.S. gave France a grant of $160 million to use in Vietnam and allowed the French to divert millions in economic and military aid intended for French domestic reconstruction. Nonetheless, it was not certain in 1946 that the U.S. would wholeheartedly join with the French in their struggle against Vietnam's self-determination. The State Department sought to discern "how communist" Ho truly was.

According to Young, "over and over, the answer came back that [Ho] was certainly a Communist, but that he put nationalism first, had no known direct ties to the Soviet Union, but was relentless in his pursuit of direct ties to the United States. Almost every American who met with Vietnamese officials in these early years reported back constant appeals for aid, capital, technology—and no signs of a Soviet presence." In September 1948, the State Department released an analysis of the situation that reiterated the failure to find any evidence of close ties between the Soviets and Vietnamese. A report one month later "was chagrined to find Soviet influence

49. Ibid., 14.
50. Ibid., 18.
51. Patti, *Why Viet Nam?*, 250.
52. Prados, *Vietnam*, 19–25.

throughout Southeast Asia, but not in Vietnam. 'If there is a Moscow-directed conspiracy in Southeast Asia, Indochina is an anomaly so far,' the report concluded."[53]

However, by this time, Truman had issued his "doctrine" and the U.S. was fully committed to fighting Soviet communism throughout the world. The U.S. would view any and all inclinations toward communism as part of the one communist movement taking its marching orders from the Kremlin. So, despite a lack of evidence, Secretary of State Dean Acheson asserted that when independence movements succeed, "their objective necessarily becomes subordination [of the] state to Commie purposes."[54]

For the next several years, America offered massive amounts of aid to France in the French quest to hold on to their colony. The widespread popular support throughout Vietnam for independence (support much wider than direct support for the Viet Minh themselves) and the resourcefulness of the Vietnamese military doomed the French struggle.

By 1950, two separate governments claiming sovereignty over all of Vietnam were in place. The government in the South was recognized by the United States and Great Britain, the government in the North by the Soviet bloc. By this time, the Viet Minh had turned to the Soviets for assistance in their independence quest; yet Soviet assistance to the Vietnamese was much smaller than U.S. assistance to the French.[55] Finally, in the spring of 1954, even with all the American support for the French, the Vietnamese won the decisive Battle of Dien Bien Phu. Despite American pressure to stay, the French decided to leave Vietnam.

Between May and July 1954, a major conference in Geneva, Switzerland, sought to establish political peace in Vietnam. The conference concluded with a cease-fire signed by the Viet Minh and the French. An agreement was reached that "free general elections by secret ballot" would be held in July 1956. There was to be no increase in troop levels, armaments, foreign military aid, or alliance. Also, the 17th parallel boundary between the North and South was "not to be construed in any way as a political or territorial boundary" but a temporary division meant to be ended after the elections. This agreement was signed by all the participants in the conference (French, Chinese, Soviets, and Vietnamese) except one—the United States.[56]

---

53. Young, *Vietnam Wars*, 23.
54. Quoted in ibid., 23.
55. Kolko, *Anatomy of a War*, 37–39.
56. Young, *Vietnam Wars*, 38–40.

PART TWO: Aftermath					The Cold War 143

In fact, the Americans had no intention of allowing an independent Vietnam under the leadership of the Viet Minh to come into existence. They set up a puppet government in southern Vietnam, subverted the promised elections, and fostered a low-intensity conflict that echoed the French colonialists' a decade earlier—understanding that the only way the southern "republic" could survive would be to defeat the North militarily.

CIA-led covert activities that subverted the Geneva Agreements were underway even prior to the signing of the accord on July 21, 1954. These activities, supposedly based on learning from French failures, sought to beat the Vietnamese at their own "military-political-economic" game.[57] As it turned out, this initial action taken by the CIA evolved into a two-decade exercise in continual repetition of the doomed strategies of the French.

At several key moments, the destruction that the Western powers visited upon Vietnam could have been avoided. The first came in 1946.[58] If the French had willingly stuck with their commitment to allow an independent Vietnam, the pre-Truman Doctrine Americans likely would have supported such a move. But the French, having been humiliated by their capitulation to the Nazis in 1940, sought to restore some sense of their great power status and retain control of their empire. Hence, they reneged on their agreements with the Viet Minh.

Then, after the Vietnamese defeated the French in 1954, the great powers met in Geneva and created a road map that may well have, even at that point, led to a united, independent Vietnam and to the end of the bloodshed. This time, the *Americans* were captive to great power illusions—and refused to cooperate with the agreements the other nations had reached.[59]

Over the next eight years, American intervention did not go well, even as the level of involvement gradually increased. Early in 1963, the Americans faced a crossroads where, had they accurately read the evidence, they could have recognized the futility of their efforts to prop up puppet governments in the South that had little popular support. The Americans could have accepted the will of the majority of Vietnamese people for genuine independence. Even at that point, though the Viet Minh had forged strong links with the Soviets, it may well be that an independent Vietnam would have sought mutual relationships with Western nations.

Instead, the Americans decided to take the opposite path, and they greatly heightened their level of intervention.[60] Over the next several

57. Ibid., 45.
58. Prados, *Vietnam*, 45.
59. Ibid., 31.
60. Ibid., 67–74.

years, Vietnam became the largest military engagement for the U.S. in the post-World War II era. From start to finish, this expanded war by the Americans was a disastrous failure. Government officials soon realized they were fighting a losing battle. For the last several years of his presidency, Lyndon Johnson's main motivation in expanding the war effort was to avoid being "the first American president to lose a war." By the end of his term, Johnson had decided that the war could not be won and tried to ratchet down the war effort.[61] Even so, it took from 1968 to 1975 for the U.S. actually to withdraw.

Johnson's successor, Richard Nixon, recognized that domestic opposition to the war required him to continue the reduction of troop levels. So he borrowed from the philosophy that governed the British and American area bombing campaigns during World War II and sought a better settlement from the Viet Minh through intensive bombing.

Remarkably, in the few years after 1968, the United States bombed Indochina several times more heavily than the British and U.S. combined had bombed Germany and Japan during the entire Second World War (apart from the atomic bombs dropped on Hiroshima and Nagasaki). The bombs dropped on Southeast Asia failed to achieve American war aims. However, they did devastate Vietnam, Cambodia, and Laos.[62]

The American war on Southeast Asia led to the premature end of the presidencies of both Lyndon Johnson and Richard Nixon, caused the deaths of millions of Indochinese, destroyed the civil society of Cambodia and created the conditions for the Khmer Rouge genocide, led to fifty thousand American war dead, and resulted in lifelong trauma for countless other American soldiers. The war finally ended in 1975.

In reflecting on the moral legacy of World War II, we must recognize the connection between the impact of the War on America's pursuit of this later war. The key connection lies with the militarization of the American federal government. Consequent ideological blind spots prevented American leaders from recognizing the true nature of the conflict in Vietnam and pushed the U.S. into a self-defeating quicksand pit of military intervention.

LATIN AMERICA

One key element of America's post-World War II national security regime was the willingness to project American military force throughout the world. The Truman Doctrine spurred worldwide projections of force, but this larger focus did not diminish the use of violence closer to home—all

---

61. McMahon, "Turning Point."
62. Young, "Bombing Civilians," 162–67, and Turse, *Kill Anything That Moves*.

PART TWO: Aftermath   *The Cold War*   145

in the name of resisting "communism." Two paradigmatic expressions of American resistance to Latin American people's attempts to exert more self-determination resulted in enormous long-term suffering. These were the overthrow of the democratically elected Chilean government in the early 1970s and the U.S. sponsorship of the Contra War in Nicaragua in the 1980s.

During the 1950s, nations in the southern cone of South America—Brazil, Uruguay, Argentina, and Chile—developed democratic traditions. They pursued policies that utilized a strong government sector to encourage wide public participation in economic and political life. Then, in the 1960s and 1970s, these countries became military dictatorships that served corporate interests and disenfranchised large segments of their population.[63]

"By Chile's historic 1970 elections, the country had moved so far left that all three major political parties were in favor of nationalizing the country's largest source of revenue: the copper mines then controlled by U.S. mining giants."[64] The victor in that 1970 election was the major party candidate the farthest to the left, Salvador Allende, who led a coalition of leftist parties under the umbrella of the Chilean Socialist Party. It was the Socialists' first presidential victory in Chilean history.

The Nixon administration opposed Chile's move to nationalize its copper industry and drive out the American corporations.[65] Allende was a radical but also a believer in the democratic process. He rejected the Cuban path to socialism through violent revolution. However, the Americans painted him as simply another communist and hence a puppet for the Soviets. According to the Truman Doctrine, then, Chile required American intervention.

For political reasons, the intervention remained covert. Nixon gave the CIA directives "to make the economy scream" following Allende's election.[66] Over the next three years the U.S. disrupted Chile's economy and undermined Allende's attempts to implement his policies—and strengthened forces within Chile hostile toward Allende's administration.[67]

By September 1971, some Chilean business leaders began to plot a regime-change strategy. Led by the CIA-funded National Association of Manufacturers, they decreed that "Allende's government was incompatible with freedom in Chile and the existence of private enterprise, and that the

---

63. Klein, *Shock Doctrine*, 57–71.
64. Ibid., 63.
65. Herring, *From Colony to Superpower*, 786–88.
66. Weiner, *Legacy of Ashes*, 357.
67. Blum, *Killing Hope*, 206–15.

only way to avoid the end was to overthrow the government." A "war structure" was to work with the military to create a plan for a new regime.[68]

The coup happened on September 11, 1973. Allende committed suicide rather than allow himself to be executed by the new military dictatorship led by General Augusto Pinochet. As a historian of the CIA, Tim Weiner, summarizes, "The CIA immediately forged a liaison with the general's junta. Pinochet reigned with cruelty, murdering more than 3,200 people, jailing and torturing tens of thousands in the repression called the Caravan of Death."[69]

Many years later in congressional testimony, a CIA representative confessed, "There is no doubt that some CIA contacts were actively engaged in committing and covering up serious human rights abuses." One such "contact" was Colonel Manuel Contreras, the head of the Chilean intelligence service under Pinochet. Contreras worked with the CIA even as he was known to be complicit in the murder and torture of thousands of Chileans. He also masterminded the assassination in 1976 of Allende's American ambassador Orlando Letelier and Letelier's American associate Ronni Moffitt with a car bomb just a few blocks from the White House. "Contreras then blackmailed the United States by threatening to tell the world about his relationship with the CIA, and blocked his extradition and trial for murder."[70]

Nicaragua did not have the democratic traditions of Chile. American corporations were even more dominant there; they had sponsored the Somoza dictatorship since the 1930s. Franklin Roosevelt had famously said of Somoza that he was a son of a bitch, "but he's *our* son of a bitch."[71] Somoza's son and successor was overthrown by the revolutionary Sandinistas in 1979.

Again, we have a leftist group, certainly inspired by Cuba's example, but first of all a nationalist movement. James Carroll summarizes: "The Nicaraguan revolution was inspired by a mix of Socialist and Catholic ideology, and the makeup of the *commandantes* of the Nicaraguan 'Directorate' reflected that. Three of the eight members of the ruling junta were Catholic priests, one was a hardcore Marxist, and the others were left-wing nationalists."[72]

The Sandinistas redistributed land, turned large estates into cooperatives and encouraged peasants to become landowners. In general, though, the economy remained in private hands. The Sandinistas did not censor the

---

68. Quotes from Klein, *Shock Doctrine*, 70.
69. Weiner, *Legacy of Ashes*, 366.
70. Ibid., 366–67.
71. Quoted in Carroll, *House of War*, 399.
72. Ibid.

PART TWO: Aftermath   The Cold War   147

media. Due to the profound influence of Catholics who had been shaped by liberation theology, the Sandinistas sought to follow a "third way" between Marxism and corporate-centered capitalism.[73]

President Carter viewed the Sandinistas with suspicion. Yet, his administration did not actively work against the Sandinistas when they won the revolution. Shortly afterward, Ronald Reagan came into power surrounded by advisors hostile toward the Sandinistas—labeling them communists and warning of Soviet incursions in America's "backyard."[74] Immediately after coming into power, Reagan accelerated the military aid sent to authoritarian dictatorships in Guatemala, Honduras, and El Salvador. These countries served as bases for an American-led effort to wage war on Nicaragua through Nicaraguan "Contras," trained by American "advisors."

With massive aid from the U.S., the Contras effectively scuttled the Sandinistas' efforts to revitalize the Nicaraguan economy. The Reagan administration greatly expanded military aid to Nicaragua's neighbors, "three of the most repressive regimes in the world, just as their police-state methods reached new levels of savagery, all in the name of staving off the [communists]. It was the Truman Doctrine carried to its extreme."[75]

The Sandinista revolution had encouraged anti-dictatorship forces in other Central American nations, as well. With American aid, the governments of these countries "set death squads loose, killing people by the thousands."[76] Many of the military actors in this government terrorism had been trained in the United States, at the infamous School of the Americas at Ft. Benning, Georgia.

Unlike with the other covert interventions I have mentioned above (and the many I didn't mention), this time the involvement of the U.S. in sponsoring great violence became a matter of public debate. Congress actually took action to limit American intervention. As it turned out, the Reagan administration defied the legal restraints, rendering congressional restraint ineffective. The U.S. successfully undermined Sandinista power, culminating in an election in which Nicaraguan voters defeated the Sandinistas in hopes of ending the violence that had devastated their country. The new government returned the Nicaraguan economy to its pre-Sandinista footing, as Nicaragua became one of the most poverty-stricken countries in the world.

73. Ibid.
74. Blum, *Killing Hope*, 290–305; Herring, *From Colony to Superpower*, 884–93.
75. Carroll, *House of War*, 399–400.
76. Ibid., 400.

Besides showing how limited Congress had become in its ability to restrain presidential-initiated military action, the American involvement in violent resistance to the Nicaraguan government also revealed the impotence of international law in restraining the violence of the United States. Against international law, the U.S. planted explosives in Nicaraguan harbors. Though the Nicaraguans took the U.S. to the International Court and won the case, with the result that in 1986 the Court condemned the U.S. for "unlawful use of force," the violence continued.[77]

The International Court's ruling, in a clear sense, drew directly on the spirit of the Atlantic Charter of 1941 that outlined the philosophy of international order that the American and British war effort was intended to serve, for the sake of "a better future for the world." The Atlantic Charter played an important role in the foundation of the United Nations and the related efforts to build a tradition of international law. However, the United States openly defied the Court's ruling concerning its violation of international law in its efforts to undermine Nicaragua's government. Such defiance symbolically reflects disregard for the values explicitly emphasized in gaining support for World War II.

At the end of the Cold War in the early 1990s, the first era following the end of World War II, we are given a sense of how the U.S. itself measured up in relation to the moral criteria used to justify World War II. According to these criteria, established by the U.S. government itself, the moral legacy of the War ended up being one actually of the U.S. *rejecting* the core moral values for which the War was said to have been fought.

James Carroll argues that activists' efforts to oppose the war in Nicaragua pushed Reagan to his surprising level of openness toward Mikhail Gorbachev's remarkable initiatives to bring an end to the Cold War.[78] Regardless of how the complicated dynamics might be understood, it is the case that by 1990, the generation of deep enmity that defined American-Soviet relations came to a close—at which point the U.S. faced another opportunity to show its true colors and to make clear the moral legacy of World War II. The main stated justification for American militarism and engagement in international conflicts came to an end. The Truman Doctrine no longer was necessary. Its enemy, Soviet communism, no longer existed. How would the Americans respond to the removal of what they had claimed to be the world's main threat to peace? Would they tear down their enormous military regime and utilize the opportunity to move the world toward authentic peaceableness?

77. Chomsky, *Hegemony or Survival*, 99.
78. Carroll, *House of War*, 345–417.

7

Full Spectrum Dominance

THE COLD WAR ENDS

On a sunny spring day in April 1990, I biked to work as usual. Along the bike path in west Eugene, Oregon, I stopped and paid attention to my feelings. I realized that a weighty anxiety I had lived with going back to the civil defense drills of my early childhood was gone. At times I had been quite self-conscious about this anxiety, but mostly it was simply a part of life, something always there but usually in the background.

My sense of relief almost overwhelmed me. I stopped and simply reveled in it. I never expected this day to come. All through the 1980s, with the arms buildup and talk of the Soviet Union as the evil empire, the Contra War, talk of an impending bloodbath in South Africa that could turn nuclear, the squashing of the Solidarity Movement in Poland—to imagine that in the early months of 1990 we would see the beginning of the end of the Cold War and apartheid—both essentially achieved nonviolently—seemed pure fantasy. For that brief moment in 1990 the basic story I have recounted that began with American entry into World War II, an extraordinarily discouraging story, came to an unexpected point of possibility, where the ideals of the Atlantic Charter actually seemed achievable.

During the presidency of Ronald Reagan (1981–89), forces advocating a dramatic expansion of the already enormous American reliance on military violence gained prominence. Reagan's policies included expansions in nuclear weaponry and a militarized reaction to the Sandinista revolution. Both of these efforts galvanized large-scale peace movements. In time, these peace movements played a major role in pressuring Reagan to a surprising openness to initiatives from the Soviet Union that contributed to the end of the Cold War.[1]

Reagan surrounded himself with militant Cold Warriors, and he clearly supported the reactionary policies his administration implemented.[2] He was always a bit of an outsider, however, in relation to the Washington military-industrial elite. He affirmed the quest for American world domination, but he also had a strong desire for approval from the American people. So, Reagan was shaken when opposition to his acceleration of the arms race expanded greatly with the emergence of the nuclear freeze movement early in his presidency. Then, the war in Central America that drove hundreds of thousands of refugees into the United States triggered a widespread antiwar movement in the U.S. The opposition to Reagan's Central American policies led to legislation to limit American support of the Contras—laws the Reagan administration violated. The so-called Iran-Contra scandal led to several Reagan administration members being indicted and convicted for illegal activities.

Reagan finessed the freeze movement by advocating a new program, the Strategic Defense Initiative (SDI, or "Star Wars").[3] SDI promised to render nuclear weapons obsolete through the capability of destroying incoming warheads. No matter that SDI was a fantasy that was never practicable, that it was mainly fueled by the weapons industry (which made billions from it), and that even if effective it would have destabilized the Cold War by empowering American first-strike capability. Significant numbers of those who had supported the freeze movement accepted Reagan's claims. Support for a freeze dwindled. However, the Iran-Contra scandal renewed public anger against Reagan.

As Reagan sought to restore his popularity, the Soviet Union found itself with a new leader, Mikhail Gorbachev—a leader different than any the Soviets (or Americans, for that matter) had had in power throughout the modern era.[4] At the same time Reagan faced the fallout from the Iran-Contra scandal, Gorbachev made several serious moves to break the momentum of the arms race. Surprisingly, Reagan attempted to respond creatively rather than simply toe the party line espoused by his militarist advisors.

According to James Carroll, "Reagan realized just in time that what the new Soviet leader was holding out to him was a lifeline, a way to rescue his

1. Carroll, *House of War*, 397–417.
2. Wilentz, *Age of Reagan*, 151–68.
3. Fitzgerald, *Way Out There*.
4. Sebestyen, *1989*, 109–20.

reputation, his very presidency—and he took it."[5] Gorbachev understood, in ways probably no other major leader in the U.S or U.S.S.R. in the years following World War II had, that the arms race was a race to destruction. He resolved to do something about it.[6] Almost immediately after gaining power, Gorbachev took several steps to diminish Cold War tensions. The Soviets unilaterally ended deployment of their missiles in Europe, and followed that step with calls to end nuclear weapons tests and to cut nuclear weaponry. Gorbachev replaced longtime foreign minister Andrei Gromyko (an unreconstructed Cold Warrior) with Eduard Shevardnadze, a leader much more compatible with Gorbachev's "new thinking."

Reagan's advisors responded to Gorbachev's initiatives with suspicion. Reagan himself continued his strident anti-Soviet rhetoric in the early days of Gorbachev's rule. However, he did agree to a summit meeting in November 1985—the first American-Soviet summit in Reagan's presidency. This meeting, while not resulting in major agreements, did help Gorbachev recognize in Reagan a sincerity about ridding the world of nuclear weapons—a recognition crucial for encouraging Gorbachev to continue his peace initiatives.[7]

American suspicions that Gorbachev was merely engaging in propaganda rather than making fundamental changes in the Soviet Cold War stance stemmed from ignorance of the changes occurring within the Soviet Union. Gorbachev raised key issues in February 1986 at the Communist Party Congress. He called for an elimination of nuclear weaponry by the end of the century, and backed that goal up by announcing significant changes in his nation's military philosophy: "instead of superiority, he was aiming at 'reasonable sufficiency'; instead of class conflict, he called for an 'interdependent and in many ways integral world'; instead of threatened mutual destruction, he proposed that the United States and the Soviet Union seek 'comprehensive mutual security.'" Gorbachev asserted that the Soviets, in a break from past practice, would accept intrusive verification measures for arms reduction agreements. Despite American insistence on retaining SDI, the Soviets would still work to eliminate intermediate-range nuclear weapons. Finally, Gorbachev announced an end to the war in Afghanistan with an admission of Soviet defeat.[8]

Gorbachev and Reagan met again in October 1986, in Reykjavik, Iceland. The two leaders came close to an agreement to dismantle their nuclear

---

5. Carroll, *House of War*, 404.
6. Rhodes, *Arsenals of Folly*, 187–93.
7. Carroll, *House of War*, 405.
8. Ibid., 407.

weapons systems. Only Reagan's refusal to give up SDI (a refusal supported by his advisors) prevented this agreement.

This is how Carroll summarizes the kind of thinking that would have led Reagan's secretary of state, George Schultz, to reject Gorbachev's proposal:

> Such a drastic dismantling of nuclear arsenals, while not necessarily destroying at a stroke the Cold War structure on which the American economy depended, would have set off tremors whose short- and long-term effects were impossible to calculate. The nuclear arsenal was the ground on which the national security system stood, and that system defined the politics, economy and culture of the United States, indeed of the West. A stock market crash, economic dislocation, mass unemployment, loss of Washington's dominance over its allies, European outrage, the Pentagon deprived of its central place in government, the service branches demanding huge allocations for a conventional buildup—such consequences would have followed, immediately or over time, from a Gorbachev-Reagan nuclear abolition deal.[9]

Paranoia continued to determine American policies—even when it became clear that the Soviet threat itself was ending.[10]

Gorbachev announced in February 1987 that the Soviets were going to separate the issue of intermediate-range nuclear missiles from other issues: "He proposed that the United States and the Soviet Union sign an agreement 'without delay' to remove all such missiles from Europe within five years. This was Moscow's acceptance without conditions of the 'zero option' that Reagan's doctrinaire arms controllers had put forward five years earlier, an offer they made assuming a Soviet rejection."[11]

American arms control officials registered numerous objections to Gorbachev's proposal concerning the intermediate missiles.[12] These included absolute insistence on on-site inspections, a step the Soviets had never before been willing to accept. This time, though, Gorbachev said yes, shocking the Americans and exposing their bluff. The *Americans* became the ones unwilling to accept arms control measures if they involved inspections: "The fifty-year myth of American openness to inspections was punctured in an instant."[13] However, despite his advisors, Reagan said yes to Gorbachev's

9. Ibid., 409.
10. Fitzgerald, *Way Out There*, 364–65.
11. Carroll, *House of War*, 411.
12. Leffler, *For the Soul of Mankind*, 420.
13. Carroll, *House of War*, 411–12.

proposal concerning intermediate missiles. This time, an American president did take steps toward genuine disarmament. The treaty was signed on December 8, 1987.

Gorbachev continued to work toward an end to the Cold War. In 1988, he spoke before the United Nations.

> Necessity of the principle of freedom of choice is clear. Denying that right of peoples, no matter what the pretext for doing so, no matter what words are used to conceal it, means infringing even that unstable balance that it has been possible to achieve. Freedom of choice is a universal principle, and there should be no exceptions.

He renounced the reliance on violence that had been required for the Soviet empire to remain intact. This would involve, he declared, reducing by five hundred thousand the number of soldiers in the Soviet military—a move linked with Soviet withdrawal from Eastern Europe.[14] Self-determination. Disarmament. Core values of the Atlantic Charter. The values marginalized by American foreign policy for more than a generation. They were back on the table.

Gorbachev offered his reforms in order to save the Soviet Union. As it turned out, he was too late. The momentum of his turn toward self-determination kept increasing, and the Soviet satellite states sought separation. Gorbachev showed how committed he was to his words spoken at the United Nations. Rather than use force to stop the exodus out of the empire, he let them go. The Cold War ended—and by the end of 1991, the Soviet Union was no more.

Going back to the 1947 Truman Doctrine, the U.S. had always justified military preparedness, nuclear weapons expansion, CIA practices, willingness to go to war in places such as Korea and Vietnam, and the need to resist Soviet "expansionism." Even the change in terminology from "War Department" to "Department of Defense" reflected this rationale—against whom is defense needed? The Soviet quest for world dominance. Now, the Soviet Union was no more. Without this enemy, would the priorities that shaped American foreign policy change? This was what World War II was for, right? A time of genuine peace characterized by self-determination everywhere on earth, a time of enhancing key human freedoms.

---

14. Quotes from ibid., 414–15.

THE GULF WAR

The Soviet withdrawal from the Cold War helped move the world closer to peace than it had been at any time since Hitler gained power. One symbol of the move toward peace was the clock of the *Bulletin of the Atomic Scientists* that since 1947 measured international tensions, especially as related to the possibility of nuclear war.[15]

In 1947, the first clock read seven minutes to midnight. When the Soviets successfully tested their first nuclear weapons in 1949, the clock moved to three minutes to midnight. Four years later, after the United States decided to produce hydrogen bombs, the clock moved to two minutes to midnight, the latest it has ever been. With the Nuclear Test Ban Treaty of 1963, the clock moved back to twelve minutes before midnight. Reagan's acceleration of the arms race in the 1980s moved the clock forward to three minutes before midnight.

Then the world, it seems, was pulled back again from the brink. In 1991, the Soviet Union disbanded, allowing a peaceful move toward independence by Warsaw Pact nations and even parts of the U.S.S.R. itself. The nuclear arsenals of both the Soviets and the Americans were reduced and taken off hair-trigger alert. At this time the clock moved all the way back to seventeen minutes before midnight.

The movement toward world peace brings us to a crucial moment in our story. Through the presidency of Ronald Reagan, American militarism was consistently justified as necessary in order to counter the threat of the totalitarian Soviet "evil empire" bent on world conquest. Then in 1991, the U.S. faced the big test. The threat is over; was it time for a "peace dividend"? Was it time finally to implement the ideals for which America supposedly fought World War II?

In January 1992, Ronald Reagan's successor as president, George H.W. Bush, asserted in his State of the Union speech that the United States indeed had "won the Cold War."[16] The underlying question remained—what did this "victory" signify? The victory could have meant that now that our enemy is no more we will, as we did after every war prior to World War II, demobilize, draw the military down, and invest instead in social welfare. Certainly in 1992, the broader world and the United States itself could have used such investment. Or, the victory could have meant, if commitment to the values of the Atlantic Charter truly had been forgotten, a chance for the world's one remaining "superpower" to expand its domination.

15. See the *Bulletin*'s website for a history of when the clock's hands have moved: http://www.thebulletin.org/content/doomsday-clock/timeline.
16. Carroll, *House of War*, 421.

As it turned out, the U.S. experienced no "peace dividend" with the end of the Cold War. In fact, one of the main artifacts of the Cold War, the North Atlantic Treaty Organization, did not follow the Warsaw Pact in disbanding but, to the contrary, expanded.[17] Whereas former Soviet republics such as Belarus, Kazakhstan, and Ukraine immediately got rid of their nuclear weapons at the point of their independence and affirmed the Nuclear Non-Proliferation Treaty, the United States continued to defy that treaty by developing more nuclear weapons.[18] But now, who were those weapons to be aimed at? And why?

The failure of the U.S. to take the opportunity to turn away from its militarism provides a perspective for looking at the entire history of the Cold War. Time after time, when it appeared that relations might improve, new threats emerged to nip peace in the bud.

> *Sputnik*, the so-called missile gap, the Cuban Missile Crisis, the Vietnam War, the Soviet invasion of Afghanistan, the Sandinista revolution, the Iranian hostage crisis, the downing of KAL 007, the Socialist takeover of the Caribbean Island of Grenada, even the attempted assassination of a pope. Each incident "rescued" Cold War rigidities, reinforced the profitable insecurities of the military-industrial complex, and kept the Niagara current of the arms race flowing. This dynamic always assumed the permanent malevolence of a Kremlin-centered enemy.[19]

As American policymakers watched the transformation of the Soviet Union, they may well have realized that this time the threat that justified American militarism actually was dissipating—and with it, perhaps their own power as tenders of that militarism would diminish. American leaders recognized that what they needed to protect most was "the enormous machine set in motion in the 1950s, a perpetual motion machine that was built for war and that advances its interests in making war."[20]

The Bush administration faced significant pressure to reduce its militarism. Our enemy is gone; let us ourselves change our priorities toward peaceful public investments. Reluctantly, the Defense Department agreed to the largest cuts in the size of the military since right after the War. Top military leaders opposed these cuts, mostly because they feared they would only be the first step in a series of deeper cuts that would solidify the end of the Cold War. But then, at the last minute before beginning the cuts, things

---

17. Gardner, *Long Road to Baghdad*, 104.
18. Gerson, *Empire and the Bomb*, 207–25.
19. Carroll, *House of War*, 423–24.
20. Cumings, "Wicked Witch," 91.

changed. "The date of the announcement [to cut the military] was August 1, 1990. The next day, against almost all expectations—and against CIA intelligence estimates—Saddam Hussein's [Iraqi] army crossed the border into Kuwait."[21]

We may note how history repeated itself with these events. Forty years earlier, North Korea crossed the border into South Korea and began the Korean War just as President Truman appeared ready to succumb to budgetary pressures and to solidify substantial military cuts. Historian Bruce Cumings wrote of the Korean conflict, "Just in time, it snatched defense and military production lines from the jaws of oblivion."[22] What followed Saddam's invasion of Kuwait echoed the events of 1950. At that time, the opportunity to go to war in Korea had likewise enabled the militarists to resist pressure greatly to reduce military spending.

Saddam Hussein had been a key leader in Iraq since 1968 and had ruled ruthlessly as president since 1979—largely with American support. As Carroll puts it, "Saddam Hussein, truly a son of a bitch, had been, in Franklin Roosevelt's words about Somoza, '*our* son of a bitch.' He had taken power by force and been supported by the United States in its power plays against Moscow and Tehran. His worst crimes, including his genocidal gassing of Kurds and Shiites in the early 1980s, had never drawn protests from Washington, but now those crimes were run up the flagpole of American indignation as if committed yesterday. Suddenly Saddam Hussein was Adolf Hitler reincarnate."[23]

Saddam had the misfortune of making his move against Kuwait at a time when it served the interests of American leaders to pursue a military confrontation over what would have, at most other times, been an occasion for diplomatic resolution.[24] As the U.S.-imposed deadline of January 15, 1991, for the removal of Iraqi forces from Kuwait approached, Saddam offered to withdraw with certain conditions. Rather than continue the discussion, Bush ordered the bombing to commence on January 16. What followed was a decisive American military victory called Operation Desert Storm. After driving back the Iraqi military and causing immense casualties, the Americans stopped short of overthrowing Saddam altogether, instead beginning a decade of economic sanctions that helped transform Iraq from one of the most prosperous Middle Eastern nations into one of the most impoverished.

21. Carroll, *House of War*, 434.
22. Cumings, "Wicked Witch," 90.
23. Carroll, *House of War*, 435.
24. Gardner, *Long Road to Baghdad*, 85–89.

PART TWO: Aftermath   *Full Spectrum Dominance*   157

The Americans at that point established a permanent and massive direct military presence in the Middle East—in contrast to the earlier post-World War II era in which the Americans relied on surrogates such as the Shah of Iran and the leaders of Saudi Arabia. The decisive American victory over Iraq actually only problematized the American role in the region, triggering an uprising of anti-American sentiment that has yet to peak two decades later.[25]

The Gulf War succeeded in turning the tide away from the "peace dividend." The U.S. now found an effective replacement for the Soviet Union as the enemy that justifies the national security system.[26] The clock of the *Bulletin of the Atomic Scientists* began a gradual move back toward midnight. The tremendous opportunity the United States was given to turn from the abyss was squandered.

Ironically, although Bush's decision to go to war in January 1991 triggered record-high presidential approval ratings, less than two years later Americans voted him out of office. Bill Clinton's successful campaign focused on domestic issues—he had little experience with or even interest in foreign affairs. When Clinton began his presidency, he appointed as his key foreign affairs policymakers people who generally shared his interest in scaling back on militarism. From the very start, however, Clinton put little energy into challenging the Pentagon and his appointees generally distinguished themselves by their ineffectiveness.[27]

As a consequence, during Clinton's eight years in office, military spending actually increased and the Pentagon's favorite power projection programs met with little opposition. Little was done to stem the conflictual momentum started in the Arab world by the Gulf War and expanded American military presence.

Clinton's inability to exercise authority in relation to the Pentagon meant that the militarism reignited by the Gulf War continued to grow, despite Clinton's intentions. The military budget, following the end of the Cold War, actually increased from $260 billion in 1992 to $300 billion in 2000. The U.S. also stepped away from commitments Reagan and Bush had made to move toward disarmament, most notably reneging on the agreement not to expand NATO. Gorbachev had been willing to accept a unified Germany with the understanding that NATO would not expand to the east. He believed that Bush's secretary of state, James Baker, had promised "not one inch eastward." However, U.S. military leaders successfully pushed for just

25. Bacevich, *New American Militarism*, 175–204.
26. Johnson, *Sorrows of Empire*, 283–309.
27. Herring, *From Colony to Superpower*, 925–38.

that type of expansion. They supported this growth not for security reasons (given Russia's decline) but in order to make major arms sales to the former Warsaw Pact nations. "Instead of dismantling NATO, as the disappearance of its Cold War rationale might have suggested, an unfettered Pentagon, trumping traditional State Department concerns, was free to turn it into an enriching new source of power."[28]

SEPTEMBER 11, 2001

After suicide bombers hijacked and flew airplanes into the Pentagon and World Trade Center on September 11, 2001, many commentators drew comparisons with the Japanese attack on Pearl Harbor of December 7, 1941.[29] Certainly these two dates are etched into the consciousness of many Americans and will be for a long time. These were said to be the two successful foreign strikes against the United States (though most people making this point don't seem to remember that in 1941, Hawaii was a colonial outpost that had been annexed by the U.S. less than half a century earlier, not yet a state[30]), both resulting in roughly three thousand deaths.

The most striking parallel between Pearl Harbor and 9/11 surely has to be similar outcomes following the original incidents. In both cases, the U.S. president took the opportunity to push the country into major military conflicts. The actual development of the conflict was quite different, but the use of the attacks to galvanize public opinion for war and for greatly expanded military empowerment was a similar ploy.

One could say, though, that the consequences of these two events could not be more different. It may even turn out that Pearl Harbor and 9/11 will be seen as bookends, one event marking the beginning and the other the end (or at least the beginning of the end) of the Pax Americana. In the case of Pearl Harbor, the Japanese made a terrible miscalculation; their attack did deal a severe blow to the American navy, but in the longer run triggered the destruction of the Japanese empire that had launched the attack. In the case of the September 11 suicide attacks, the perpetrators likely succeeded far beyond their expectations. They provoked the United States to initiate two wars that severely damaged American interests in numerous ways.

Bill Clinton's administration had strengthened the establishment of America's long-term military presence in the Middle East. When he turned the presidency over to George W. Bush in January 2001, the global issue

28. Carroll, *House of War*, 454–55.
29. Dower, *Cultures of War*, 3–41.
30. Kinzer, *Overthrow*, 9–30.

that the outgoing administration emphasized to the newcomers was conflict arising from resistance by these relatively powerless peoples' to the projection of American power. The term that became central for the Americans to describe the resistance was *terrorism*.

The widespread use of the term *terrorism* goes back to the early days of the Reagan administration when the opposition to "terrorism" became a central part of American foreign policy. Ironically, the opposition to "terrorism" justified many acts of terror-enhancing violence by the United States. The term tends not to have a stable meaning but generally seems to have a more ideological use, signifying those who resist the Pax Americana. A stable meaning for *terrorism* could look something like this:

> A US Army manual defined *terrorism* as "the calculated use of violence or threat of violence to attain goals that are political, religious, or ideological in nature . . . through intimidation, coercion, or instilling fear" . . . The British government's definition is similar: "Terrorism is the use, or threat, of action which is violent, damaging or disrupting, and is intended to influence the government or intimidate the public and is for the purpose of advancing a political, religious, or ideological cause."[31]

According to these definitions, American behavior (and that of America's allies) has also often been "terrorism." The area bombings of Germany by the British and of Japan by the Americans clearly had as their main purpose "using violent action to intimidate the public of those countries for the purpose of advancing a political cause." Likewise, the massive bombings the U.S. perpetrated in the war on Vietnam and the actions the U.S. supported in Nicaragua during the Contra War (remember above the mention of America's guilty conviction by the World Court for terrorist acts) fall within the stable definition.[32]

When George W. Bush and his advisors came into power in 2001, they heard from their predecessors that "terrorism" should be their main concern and that storm clouds were gathering. However, Bush and his people had other priorities. So they did not pay much attention as warnings about some impending "terrorist" act within the U.S. grew sharper.

Tim Weiner, in his history of the CIA, writes about how American intelligence agents were unable to focus the warnings and unable to get the president to pay attention:

---

31. Chomsky, *Hegemony or Survival*, 188.
32. Coady, "Bombing and the Morality of War."

> Bush and [CIA director George] Tenet met at the White House almost every morning at eight. But nothing Tenet said about [Osama] bin Laden fully captured the president's attention. . . . Tenet told the president, [Vice President Richard] Cheney, and national security adviser Condoleeza Rice about the portents of al Qaeda's plot to strike America. But Bush was interested in other things—missile defense, Mexico, the Middle East. He was struck by no sense of emergency. . . . Tenet could not convey a coherent signal to the president. . . .Warnings were pouring in from Saudi Arabia and the Gulf states, Jordan and Israel, all over Europe. The CIA's frayed circuits were dangerously overloaded. Tips kept coming in. . . . "When these attacks occur, as they likely will," [White House counterterrorism czar Richard] Clarke e-mailed Rice on May 29, "we will wonder what more we could have done to stop them."[33]

On the morning of September 11, 2001, in a brilliant tactical operation, a handful of men commandeered four commercial airliners in the eastern United States. One airplane flew directly into the Pentagon, two into the World Trade Center, and the fourth seemed to be heading toward another Washington DC target, perhaps the White House, before a passenger counterattack crashed the plane in the southwestern Pennsylvania countryside.

By the time the second plane hit the World Trade Center, the world was watching in horror. Despite the concerns raised by many intelligence officers, the U.S. was unprepared for these attacks. One notable failure was that of the North American Aerospace Defense Command (NORAD), a program begun in 1958 to protect the U.S. from airborne attacks; 9/11 was NORAD's first real-life test. "Despite the billions of dollars spent on 'ready alert,' it failed miserably, a shocking lesson in the foolishness of both America's generation-old illusion of air defense and its ludicrous hopes for a future National Missile Defense. NORAD failed on September 11 because, never imagining that enemy aircraft could attack from within, it responded to threats as defined by the Cold War, which had ended a full decade earlier."[34]

Ironically, the action that prevented the fourth plane from finding its target was not a high-tech response of the expensive military program but a very low-tech reaction by the passengers on that plane, who overpowered the hijackers and crashed the plane themselves.

Right after 9/11, the U.S. again came to a war-or-peace crossroad. Or, perhaps by now, a better image is that of a large semitruck driving ever faster down a steep mountain highway and continually ignoring emergency

33. Weiner, *Legacy of Ashes*, 552–53.
34. Carroll, *House of War*, 486.

turnoffs that would allow the truck to pull safely off the road and avoid its destruction. American leaders could have treated this incident as a terrible, murderous crime. They could have drawn on resources from the global community to apprehend and bring to justice the perpetrators of the attacks. As it seemed likely that the perpetrators were linked with al-Qaeda, even the militantly Islamic government of Afghanistan evinced a willingness to cooperate with a police action.

Such an approach would have had enormous potential to legitimize and strengthen the newly expanded regime of international law. Here was a kind of ideal situation with a strong consensus that what had happened was a terrible crime that required swift and decisive action. And the main player was the world's most powerful nation. Had the United States used this as an opportunity to give its support to the international justice processes, it could have established strong precedents for the use of such processes to help the world respond to wrongdoing in nonmilitaristic, peace-enhancing ways.[35]

The U.S. could also have taken the 9/11 attacks as an opportunity for serious self-examination—certainly on the level of a critical look at the breakdowns across the board in intelligence gathering and analysis, the failure of NORAD, the general dynamic of having constructed a national security system that proved to be helpless in the face of a genuine challenge to America's security. What went wrong? How could it be remedied? On a deeper level, the 9/11 attacks could have provided an opportunity for the U.S. to ask, why do we have these enemies? What elements of our foreign policies of the past generation have given rise to hostilites from others that clearly make us more insecure? How could we have so foolishly squandered the opportunities that the end of the Cold War gave us to move toward world peace?

As it turned out, the Bush administration had no interest in taking either the opportunity to enhance the capabilities of the emerging international justice system or to undergo a serious process to analyze the problems that had led to these attacks. On the contrary, as with various past "crossroads" since World War II, American leaders approached 9/11 as a marvelous opportunity to expand the militarization of American society and to move faster into the spiral of responding to threats with violence. Rather than try to find ways to slow the mad rush down the mountain highway, Bush and his advisors only pressed harder on the accelerator.[36]

---

35. Ibid., 497–98.
36. Pfaff, *Irony of Manifest Destiny*, 108–10.

We should note one point before we proceed to look more closely at the specifics of the American response to 9/11. One main lesson of the story we have considered so far is that the mad rush down the mountain began long, long before George W. Bush's disastrous presidency. The present book makes the case that the rush to the abyss took its most important turn with America's all-out engagement in World War II. The move to speed the descent into the abyss came under Democratic presidents at least as much as under Republican presidents.[37]

With Bush Jr. we hear echoes of American leaders' decisions to make their early monopoly on nuclear weapons an opportunity for greater dominance rather than international cooperation. We hear echoes of the decision to reject the Geneva agreements concerning Vietnam and instead seek to defeat the Viet Minh rather than acknowledge their status as the country's chosen leaders. We hear echoes of the decision to take the end of the Cold War as another opportunity to push for domination rather than dismantle the costly mass destruction project.

AMERICA AT WAR AGAIN

September 11, 2001, may stand as one of the defining dates of the twenty-first century for the United States—though not for the reasons many Americans seem to think. It's not that this was the opening date in a newly clarified "war on terror" or "World War IV," as some call it ("World War III" being the Cold War). Nor will it be seen as a date that marked a new expression of unassailable American power.

Rather, 9/11 may well signify for generations to come the last gasp of the national security system created by America's militaristic way of dealing with international affairs during World War II, fully institutionalized by the early 1950s.[38] The Bush administration's response to the attacks of 9/11 merely carried out the script prepared by "one presidential administration after another since 1943."[39]

We see how thoroughly the militarization of American national security has been accepted by the American people in the popular support for Bush's decision for intensely violent acts of revenge within weeks of 9/11.

---

37. This is a central argument in Scahill, *Dirty Wars*.

38. See Garry Wills' sketch of the pieces of America's national security system put into place in the years between 1945 and 1952: Wills, *Bomb Power*, "Part II: The National Security State," 57–102.

39. Carroll, *House of War*, 496.

Support for the bombing of Afghanistan spread across the political spectrum in the U.S. as Bush's approval ratings reached toward the stratosphere.

No matter that in attacking Afghanistan the U.S. brought death to people who had no role in the 9/11 attacks. No matter that the U.S. didn't actually have a carefully prepared plan to exact vengeance on those who had planned the attacks. No matter that in launching directly into a war response, the U.S. disregarded the emerging structures the world community sought to establish in order to deal with criminal acts such as the 9/11 attacks.

As it turned out, Bush's attempt to avoid accountability to international law may have been prescient. The U.S. since 9/11 has followed a course that has surely many times violated international law—most egregiously with the initiation of a war of aggression against Iraq without the approval of the United Nations Security Council.

The initial military action against Afghanistan did drive the militant Islamic government of the Taliban out of power. The Taliban had direct links to forces within Afghanistan who had received major CIA funding and training in the conflict with the Soviets. By the early twenty-first century, they had moved from friend to enemy due to their friendliness toward al-Qaeda. However, the Taliban was not so much defeated as pushed into a strategic retreat. After a few years, the Bush administration turned its focus toward Iraq, and the Taliban returned in force.

Ever since the early 1990s when Saddam Hussein invaded Kuwait and his relationship with the U.S. changed from semi-client to archenemy, important members of the American policymaking elite had hoped to remove Saddam from power. The devastating sanctions regime during the Clinton years was justified as a means to undermine Saddam's standing within Iraq—though the actual impact seemed to strengthen his position. Iraq, of course, is the home of some of the world's richest oil deposits. Since the Carter administration, the U.S. had named access to Middle East oil a central element of its set of national security interests. Many of Bush's main advisors, as well as Bush himself, had close ties to the oil industry.

To the surprise of many who focused their concerns on al-Qaeda, the Bush administration began talking up the need to look to Iraq as part of the problem—naming Iraq along with Iran and North Korea as the triumvirate that made up "the axis of evil."[40] The administration gave several contestable reasons for turning the focus toward Iraq as a major concern in the "war on terror." Some advocates for military action against Iraq implied that there

---

40. Gardner, *Long Road to Baghdad*, 116–48.

was a link between Iraq and al-Qaeda—counting on their listeners' ignorance about the mutual hostility between Saddam and Osama bin Laden.

The main claim that drove the pro-intervention campaign was Saddam's alleged quest for weapons of mass destruction (WMD). Because of Iraq's high levels of secretiveness, this claim was difficult to disprove (or to substantiate). However, with the war clouds gathering, Iraq did submit to UN inspections. The inspections did indicate that in fact, as Saddam claimed, Iraq did not have any WMDs. The Bush administration did not wait for the conclusion of the inspections, however, but instead—insisting that its intelligence provided strong evidence for the existence of WMDs somewhere in Iraq—prepared to take military action.[41]

The U.S. took its case to the U.N. Security Council, hoping to get approval in the same way it had for the Gulf War in 1991 and for the attacks on Afghanistan in 2001. This time, however, the U.N. refused to grant such approval before the inspection process could be completed. If the rationale for the attack was to be Iraq's illegal possession of WMDs, such possession would have to be verified before military action could be taken.

The Americans were in a hurry, though, and with the support of a handful of other countries (most notably Great Britain), in March 2003 they launched an invasion. Lacking the approval of the U.N., this invasion violated international law.[42] However, unmatched American power and unwillingness to submit to international law made that violation moot.

As with the military action against Afghanistan, the invasion of Iraq quickly drove the existing government out of power. But also, as with the earlier action, the toppling of the Iraqi government did not resolve the conflict. Even though Bush declared victory in his "mission accomplished" speech of May 1, 2003, just six weeks after the initial invasion, the Iraq War became a quagmire in which many more lives were lost following Bush's declaration of "victory" than were lost prior to it.

A third rationale for the invasion became more prominent with the failure after the invasion to uncover WMDs and with the failure to establish a link between Iraq and 9/11. The U.S., it was claimed, went into Iraq to overthrow a terrible tyrant and help the Iraqis transform their society into a Western-style democracy.

In the event, the American invaders proved themselves unprepared to transform Iraq into a genuine democracy. Their presence, rather than being celebrated as was promised by pro-invasion advocates, became the occasion for extraordinary levels of resistance, widespread violence, and in

---

41. Herring, *From Colony to Superpower*, 938–51.
42. Swanson, *War Is a Lie*, 304–5.

time a whole new level of devastation in a society already devastated by its 1980s war with Iran, the earlier American war, and the ongoing economic sanctions. A country that had had the highest levels of education, the best medical system, the broadest distribution of wealth in the entire Middle East was pauperized by the American invasion and occupation.[43]

Actual American actions (rather than the rationales given by policymakers) point toward four likely objectives for the American invasion: (1) to establish permanent military bases in the region, partly to make up for the insecurity of bases in Saudi Arabia;[44] (2) to weaken a significant anti-Israeli center of power in the region; (3) to provide large amounts of money to major military contractors; and, probably most important, (4) to insure access to Iraqi oil for major corporate allies of the Bush administration.[45]

Huge, seemingly permanent military bases were constructed in Iraq. However, the ongoing instability of the political situation there made the future of these bases somewhat less than certain. Also, given the deepening economic crisis in the United States itself, it is questionable whether the bases will be economically sustainable over the long term.

The devastation visited upon Iraq and the execution of Saddam have lessened the regional threat to Israel from that quarter. It remains to be seen, though, what kind of government will eventually hold power in Iraq. It could be that down the line, the Israelis will remember Saddam as a much more predictable and manageable "enemy" (especially given Saddam's longtime pre-1991 dependence on American support) than his ultimate successors.

The corporate profits that emerged from the invasion and occupation have been immense. This one objective seems to have been fulfilled without qualification.[46]

The ultimate control of Iraq's oil resources remains up in the air. It does not seem that American companies will necessarily be major players. The war itself led to severe damage to the infrastructure of Iraq's oil industry and the output of Iraqi oil dropped severely. This objective may end up mostly unachieved. In fact, in a terrible irony aligned with many other terrible ironies in the longer story of this book, it seems that the overall impact of America's war on Iraq will be quite harmful to many of the economic interests that drove the push for this war.

As the economically driven overthrow of Iran's democratic government in 1953 in the long run made things worse for American economic

43. Klein, *Shock Doctrine*, 325–82.
44. Johnson, *Dismantling the Empire*, 109–32.
45. Klare, *Blood and Oil*, 94–105.
46. Klein, *Shock Doctrine*, 341–59.

interests after the Shah was deposed in 1979, we may see similarities with Iraq. With the recognition by Bush Jr. during his second term that victory in Iraq had become impossible, it then became a matter of time before a government decidedly hostile to the United States would come to power in Iraq. Such a government may be more likely to turn to China, India, and Europe for markets for its oil than to the United States.

By the middle of Bush's second term, growing disillusionment with his presidency and his Republican Party led to major gains in Congress for Democratic candidates. Then in the 2008 presidential campaign, the presumptive heavy favorite for the Democratic Party's nomination, Hillary Clinton, lost to a relative political newcomer, Barack Obama. One of Obama's main points of difference with Clinton, which he exploited to the fullest, was that while Clinton had voted in favor of the U.S. war on Iraq, Obama (before he was elected to the U.S. Senate) had spoken out against it. Quite likely, the issue was decisive in Obama's victory over Clinton—a statement from the electorate that reinforced the 2006 midterm elections' statement against these wars.

Though Obama's race against Republican John McCain (who supported Bush's military actions) ended up being fairly close, the young Democrat, with a base of activists who took seriously Obama's promise of "change we can believe in," prevailed. And, as in 2006, congressional races went to the Democrats—partly, at least, as a statement against Bush's wars.

So, the year 2008 brought the United States to another crossroads. This time, the public seemed to make a strong statement about turning from the mad rush down the mountain of wars and preparation for wars. As we consider the consequences of the 2008 presidential election, our question once again will be, What happened when our latest president came to this crossroads (or at least, what happened as he approached another emergency turn-off on the steep downhill grade of the mountain highway)?

BUSINESS AS USUAL

People throughout the world who had been increasingly alarmed by the global policies of the Bush administration responded with hope to the election of Barack Obama. A sense of this hopefulness was seen in the surprise awarding to Obama the Nobel Peace Prize in 2009. The Nobel award clearly had more to do with hopes for Obama than with any concrete achievements in his short political career.

As Steven Erlanger and Sheryl Gay Stalberg reported in the *New York Times*,

PART TWO: Aftermath   Full Spectrum Dominance   167

This prize, to a 48-year-old freshman president for "extraordinary efforts to strengthen international diplomacy and cooperation between peoples" seemed a kind of prayer and encouragement by the Nobel committee for future endeavors and more consensual American leadership.[47]

The oppositional energy that Bush had created found a focus in Obama's campaign. With Obama's victory, hopes were high, as the Nobel Peace Prize indicated. However, attentive people expressed caution even during the campaign that actual change might be minimal. Obama stated consistently that he had supported the military action against Afghanistan right after 9/11. He criticized Bush for diverting attention from the effort in Afghanistan to focus on Iraq. He actually proposed *expanding* the presence of the American military in Afghanistan. Also, Obama proposed expanding America's on-the-ground military forces, the army and marines.[48]

That Obama managed to present himself as a peace candidate spoke more to the antipathy many felt toward Bush's policies (almost anybody could seem like a peace candidate compared to Republican candidate John McCain, who if anything came across as more militaristic than Bush) than to anything genuinely peaceable in Obama's positions. Retired Army Colonel Andrew Bacevich summarizes the election thus:

> The contestants portrayed their differences as fundamental, notably so with regard to national security. Yet what actually ensued was a contest between different species of hawks. In one camp were those like . . . McCain who insisted that the Iraq War, having always been necessary and justified, was now—thanks to the surge—successful as well. In the other camp were those like . . . Obama who derided the Iraq War as disastrous, but pointed to Afghanistan as a war that needed to be won. No prominent figure in either party came within ten feet of questioning the logic of configuring U.S. forces for global power projection or the wisdom of maintaining a global military presence.[49]

Shortly after Obama won the election, he placed in positions of power people known to be militarists: retired marine James Jones as National Security Council head, Bush's secretary of defense Robert Gates (also a former CIA director) to continue in that role, and Hillary Clinton (who, Obama claimed during the campaign, had been too pro-war) as secretary of state. Pakistani pundit Tariq Ali stated it this way: Obama's "first act was

47. Erlanger and Stolberg, "Surprise Nobel for Obama."
48. Engelhardt, *American Way of War*, 135–61.
49. Bacevich, *Washington Rules*, 210.

to keep on Bush's defense secretary Robert Gates, longtime CIA functionary and veteran of the Iran-Contra affair, in the Pentagon. A cruder and more demonstrative signal of political continuity could hardly have been conceived."[50]

In the face of a financial crisis beginning in 2008 that plunged the United States into a severe recession, Obama nonetheless refused to consider serious reductions in military spending. In fact, remarkably, given the militaristic excesses of the Bush years, Obama actually oversaw an *increase* in military spending.

At the end of his first year in office, Obama's staff conducted a three-month review of the war in Afghanistan. Perhaps he faced at that time his one opportunity to distance his administration from his predecessor. Instead, the U.S. committed itself to accelerating an already failing military campaign. This decision to invest even more extensively in such a certain policy failure emphasizes just how powerful the hold militarism has on the United States government.

George W. Bush had concluded his second term as an extraordinarily unpopular president. Obama's promise of change fueled his successful campaign.

> It was clear where change was needed. Illegal acts should cease—torture and indefinite detention, denial of habeas corpus and legal representation, unilateral canceling of treaties, defiance of Congress and the Constitution, nullification of law by signing statement. Powers given the President under the unitary executive theory should not be exercised. Judges should not be confirmed who are willing to give the President any power he asks for.[51]

Promising change is quite different than delivering it, however—especially in the face of the seemingly inexorable momentum toward expanded presidential powers. As we have seen, since the War, the president has gained increasing power in foreign affairs. The control of the nuclear button, expansion of military bases that insure nuclear supremacy, ever-growing secrecy, the permanent sustenance of a war footing from World War II through the Cold War and then the "war on terrorism"—all make the possibility of dismantling the national security state seem dim indeed. "Sixty-eight straight years of war emergency powers (1941–2009) have made the abnormal normal, and constitutional diminishment the settled order."[52]

50. Ali, *Obama Syndrome*, 44.
51. Wills, *Bomb Power*, 237.
52. Ibid., 237–38.

PART TWO: Aftermath   *Full Spectrum Dominance*   169

Obama's presidency only exacerbated the dynamics of militarism.[53] Right away he signaled his unwillingness to challenge those dynamics when he reappointed Bush's militaristic secretary of defense. Also, Obama and his appointees made it clear that they would not hold members of the Bush administration accountable for circumventing the Constitution and approving of torture.[54]

Barack Obama's Nobel Peace Prize speech in December 2009 brings us near to the end of our story of the moral legacy of World War II. It is sadly fitting that Obama drew directly on that legacy. At several points in his speech Obama echoed the ideals stated by Roosevelt and Churchill back in 1941 that we have been tracking throughout this book. In doing so, he reinforced the ongoing role of those ideals both in providing the stated aspirations of American leaders and in giving us criteria for evaluating the actual practices of those leaders.

It is in relation to this second role that Obama's speech becomes most interesting. He implies that indeed the ideals have determined America's actual practices over the past seventy years—an implication the above pages refute. And he uses these ideals as a basis to affirm the need to continue America's war on Afghanistan, even being brazen enough to assert that this "is a conflict that America did not seek; one in which we are joined by 43 other countries—including Norway—in an effort to defend ourselves and all nations from further attacks."[55]

Of course, everyone knows that this is indeed a war that the U.S. *did* seek in September 2001 as an act of revenge for 9/11. It is a war that has brought death to thousands of Afghanis, people who had nothing to do with the 9/11 attacks and who have no interest in "further attacks." And everyone also knows that from the beginning this has been America's war and America's war alone, even with the very thin veneer of support from various allies who have had and continue to have virtually no say in the events of the war.

In his speech, Obama does pay lip service to the witness of Gandhi and Martin Luther King Jr., but mainly in order to assert the limits of that witness, even alluding to Hitler: "As a head of state sworn to protect and defend my nation, I cannot be guided by their examples alone. I face the world as it is, and cannot stand idle in the face of threats to the American people. For make no mistake: Evil does exist in the world. A nonviolent movement could not have halted Hitler's armies. . . . The United States of America has

---

53. Scahill, *Dirty Wars*.
54. Wills, *Bomb Power*, 237–38.
55. This quote and subsequent quotes come from the White House website: www/whitehouse.gov/the-press-office/remarks-president-acceptance-nobel-peace-prize.

helped underwrite global security for more than six decades with the blood of our citizens and the strength of our arms."

Actually, contrary to Obama's assertion, if there is a lesson in the story we have been tracing, it is that the United States has underwritten global *insecurity*. The presidents of the United States, including apparently Barack Obama, have shown a striking inability to understand and respond creatively to "the world as it is." Obama directly touches on one of the main reasons for this inability to understand when he speaks of "evil . . . in the world" with the clear sense that this "evil" resides out there with the enemies of the United States alone.

Until leaders in the United States recognize the evils of *American* policies and practices—the insistence on using its early nuclear weapons monopoly as a basis for seeking world domination, not international cooperation; the direct action taken to overthrow democratic governments such as that of Iran (contradicting Obama's pious assertion that "America has never fought a war against a democracy"); the refusal to abide by the agreements that ended the French conflict with Vietnam and instead subjecting that nation to twenty years of the most devastating brutality imaginable; the subsidization and training of untold agents of torture and death in Latin America; the refusal to accept the Soviet Union's gift in the late 1980s as an opportunity to achieve genuine disarmament; the rejection of the emerging international justice structures in order to seek a military conflict in Afghanistan and Iraq—we have no hope that the United States will indeed be a force to help the world embody the ideals of the Atlantic Charter. The main moral legacy of World War II for the United States has been a disastrous one, a legacy of the fruitless and destructive quest for militarized global domination.

So, the story of the moral legacy of World War II is the story of the American nation-state's inability and unwillingness truly to seek to make real the ideals of the Atlantic Charter—most notably the ideals of self-determination and disarmament, the ideals of genuine peace.

We must not end the story with this ongoing failure. The American nation-state, the entity that set the American people on the path of militarization under the guise of seeking long-term genuine peace, did not actually pursue peace. The American state left the world with a legacy of moral failure—and by so doing placed the moral legitimacy of World War II itself in severe doubt. However, the state's failure does not mean that the ideals of the Atlantic Charter have not been effectively sought and embodied in the light of World War II.

Below, in part three of this book, "Alternatives," I will tell the stories of many who did pursue self-determination and disarmament—and found

PART TWO: Aftermath

at least some success. These stories have roots that go back further than the 1940s; however, in important ways the War served as a catalyst for many of them. The lesson to be learned from these stories, I will suggest, is that *in spite* of war, genuine peace is possible to embody. This part of the story of the moral legacy of World War II will reinforce the parts we have already considered. That World War II was a moral disaster for America is borne out in the story we have considered. That moral good also emerged out of these same events actually emphasizes all the more the problematic reality of the War. That some good emerged from the immorality underscores the true nature of the immorality, and shows us as well that the immorality need not have the final say.

PART THREE: Alternatives

8

No to the War

World War II was the ultimate test for American pacifists. Their members had grown to unprecedented levels during the 1920s and 1930s following disillusionment with the Great War. Many thousands swore that they would never take up arms.

However, prowar propaganda from the Roosevelt administration exploited legitimate fears stirred by German, Italian, and Japanese aggression in central Europe, northern Africa, and eastern Asia. Many erstwhile pacifists changed their views. Then, with the Japanese attack on Pearl Harbor and the German war declaration, the U.S. hurtled full tilt into the War—with almost unanimous public support.

A tiny pacifist[1] remnant (made up of diverse elements) remained resolute, even in the face of the desertion of most who had promised during the 1930s never to go to war. This remnant was virtually without influence during the war years, but did prevent the ideals of war refusal from dying out altogether. From the ranks of World War II pacifists came important visionaries and on-the-ground leaders who energized efforts to overcome the curse of violence. Their various counter-witnesses to the emergence and terrible evolution of the Pax Americana and its national security state, if not powerful enough to halt movement toward a militaristic abyss, nonetheless offer elements for a blueprint for social healing.

---

1. The meaning of the term *pacifism* is often debated. I use it here in the simplest sense, to mean "principled opposition to participation in all war." For discussions of the debate over the meaning of *pacifism*, see my "Christian Pacifism in Brief" and "Core Convictions for Engaged Pacifism."

This final section of *The Good War That Wasn't—and Why It Matters* will look at various ways alternatives to militarism have found expression. My treatment will be impressionistic and fragmentary. The general lack of success of these efforts at stemming the tide toward the ever-widening influence of violent forces testifies more to the power of those violent forces than to mistakes by peace advocates. Each failed effort to break the spiral of violence nonetheless remains instructive. Even if it is not clear yet precisely how the spiral will ultimately be broken, the fact remains that such a breaking *must* happen. Surely the only way to achieve a peaceful world will be through an accumulation of wisdom gained from all these various resistance efforts.

THE ROOTS OF WAR RESISTANCE

Pacifism gained a foothold in North America when the British government granted William Penn, a member of the Religious Society of Friends (Quakers), a charter to establish the colony of Pennsylvania in 1682.[2] The Friends had emerged as a distinct movement in Britain in the mid-1650s under the leadership of George Fox. Fox combined a close adherence to the teaching of Jesus in the Sermon on the Mount with a mystical sense of the presence of God's Spirit in the believer's heart, in the hearts of all other human beings, and in the broader creation.

As they combined priority on the message of Jesus with belief in the active work of the Spirit throughout the world, Friends affirmed at the core of their faith the belief that *all* human relationships should be characterized by compassion, respect, and mutuality. Their belief led them to repudiate warfare as a legitimate way for human beings to settle their differences.

In its early years, Pennsylvania operated under the leadership of members of the Society of Friends. The colony sought to establish peaceable relationships with the Native Americans who were living within its borders. The colony also saw itself as a haven for other religious dissenters who shared values similar to those of the Friends, thereby becoming a pioneering political community that practiced genuine religious freedom and did not center its policies around the sword.

From the start, the colony of Pennsylvania lived with significant tensions between the ideals of its Quaker leadership and the realities of the broader colonial enterprise in North America. In time, the number of colony residents who were not Quakers (or those with similar convictions)

---

2. Brock, *Quaker Peace Testimony*, and Anderson and Cayton, *Dominion of War*, 54–103.

grew to be larger than the population of Friends. In the face of growing conflicts between non-Quakers and Native Americans in the western part of the colony, the Friends had fully withdrawn from leadership by 1756.

During these seventy-five years, though, Pennsylvania became not only a home for Quakers but also a haven for a few other sizeable pacifist groups, most notably Mennonites and Brethren. The Mennonite tradition actually predated the Quakers by about 130 years. Its origins lay in the Anabaptist movement that split off from the Swiss Reformation in the 1520s.

Presaging key Quaker convictions, the early Anabaptists took Jesus' direct teachings as the focus for their beliefs and practices, especially as expressed in the Sermon on the Mount. From very early, for most of the Anabaptists, the teaching of Jesus concerning love of enemies and turning from the sword led to a principled pacifism.[3] Over the next several decades following the first Anabaptist baptisms in 1525, the beliefs about nonparticipation in war became one of their convictional pillars. As the movement gained a strong foothold in Holland, a former Catholic priest named Menno Simons became an important leader, and ultimately most of the various Anabaptist groups took his name—"Mennonites."

The Mennonites faced generations of harsh persecution in Switzerland, Germany, and Holland. Though Mennonite groups remain in those countries, many communities and individuals migrated to locales that offered them safety—including the Pennsylvania colony, beginning in 1683. The state of Pennsylvania remains today the home of the largest concentration of Mennonite communities in the U.S.

Early in the eighteenth century, a new movement arose in Germany, deeply influenced by Anabaptist convictions but remaining a distinct fellowship. Members of this emerging movement, numbering only in the dozens, migrated en masse to Pennsylvania not long after their emergence and in North American took the name Church of the Brethren. The Brethren, like the Mennonites and Quakers, had as one of their defining characteristics belief in nonparticipation in war.[4] During the last few decades of Quaker rule in Pennsylvania, the Brethren and Mennonites offered what support they could—and welcomed the freedom to practice their faith (including open commitment to pacifism).

Members of all three groups (sometimes called the historic peace churches) in time moved to the west and south from Pennsylvania, establishing communities in other colonies. The war that marked the American colonies' effort to break free from British control (the Revolutionary War)

3. Mast and Weaver, *Defenseless Christianity*.
4. Bowman, *Church of the Brethren and War*.

proved difficult for peace church members, and a number migrated to Canada to avoid the conflict. By and large, though, the pacifism of peace church members was respected by government and they were allowed to avoid military involvement.

In the early nineteenth century, the United States, the world's pioneering democracy, became the home of numerous citizens' groups, established for numerous reasons—some having to do with social justice, some with education, some with various other civic issues. In this ferment of activity, the world's first nondenominational peace societies were formed.[5]

The early peace societies signaled the spread of explicit convictions about rejection of warfare beyond the peace churches. These may be the first organizations in the world with the specific purpose of political opposition to war as an instrument of state policy. Some elements of the small peace movement connected with some elements of the much larger antislavery movement. Prominent abolitionist William Lloyd Garrison was an outspoken pacifist as well and sought to hold the two movements together.

During the Civil War, both the Union and the Confederacy imitated practices Napoleon had initiated half a century earlier and formally conscripted young males into their militaries. In the Union, the prominence of the Quakers, particularly, led Congress to make provisions for conscientious objection. These provisions were somewhat ad hoc; the process did not altogether satisfy either the peace church communities or those who opposed conscientious objection. However, those whose convictions led them to reject participation in warfare in principle were generally able to avoid fighting.[6] And precedents were set that would inform later confrontations between principled pacifists and warring American governments.

More than half a century after the Civil War, the U.S. once again geared up for a major conflict and reinstated the draft. President Woodrow Wilson, elected in 1912, had strong connections with Britain, and in 1914, after Britain entered what became known as World War I, Wilson moved ever closer to a commitment to that conflict. Finally, in 1917, the Americans took the big step and for the first time entered into a war in Europe as a formal belligerent.

The immensity of the war led to the formation of several important pacifist organizations. Four in particular would play major roles in the story of war resistance during the century to follow. Two of these groups were linked with specific peace church denominations—the American Friends Service Committee and the Mennonite Central Committee. The other

5. Brock, *Radical Pacifists*.
6. Schlissel, *Conscience in America*, 87–126.

PART THREE: Alternatives   No to the War   179

two—the Fellowship of Reconciliation and the War Resisters League—sought a wider membership.

The American Friends Service Committee (AFSC) was formed when the U.S. entered the war in 1917.[7] Quakers sought to find service that pacifists could perform in place of going to war. By that time, the devastation in Europe was clear and so there was no lack of need for food distribution and medical care. The AFSC sought to find potential COs to inform them of the possibilities for alternative service and to gain the military's acceptance of these alternatives. As the war ended fairly soon after the Americans entered it, the AFSC programs barely got started. The most successful program was service in war zones as medics and ambulance drivers.

Many Mennonites wanted to help people who suffered the most from the war's consequences. North American Mennonites created a new organization to bring together Mennonites from their various branches into one Mennonite Central Committee (MCC) for the purpose of offering aid to the severely traumatized Mennonites in eastern Europe, especially Mennonites suffering famine in the Ukraine. After a burst of activity offering such aid to the Russian Mennonites, MCC remained relatively dormant for a number of years.[8]

The Fellowship of Reconciliation (FOR) began among British pacifists opposed to World War I in December 1914. An American FOR originated in November 1915, and the International FOR in 1919.[9] The FOR drew its membership from Quakers, others influenced by the Social Gospel movement that had emerged at the turn of the century, participants in the Young Men's Christian Association, and participants in the women's movement.[10] It grew rapidly following World War I, becoming a gathering place for many people who were disillusioned with war because of the less-than-satisfactory outcome of the Great War. Many leaders in American Protestant denominations (especially Methodist, Congregational, Episcopalian, and Presbyterian) affiliated with the FOR, giving it a prominent place in ecumenical interactions.[11]

Other pacifists desired an organization that would be more open to non-Christians than was FOR in its early years. With the FOR's blessing, FOR member Jessie Wallace Hughan established a new organization in 1921 initially called the Committee for Enrollment Against War. Over the next

7. Weisbrod, *Some Form of Peace*.
8. Bush, *Two Kingdoms, Two Loyalties*, 26–128.
9. Dekar, *Creating the Beloved Community*.
10. Ibid., 34.
11. Kosek, *Acts of Conscience*.

few years, the term "War Resisters League" (WRL) came increasingly to be used and, by 1923, became the group's official name. The WRL provided moral support and guidance for people who rejected warfare in principle and did not have connections with religious communities. The WRL's declaration stated, briefly, its core conviction: "War is a crime against humanity. I, therefore, am determined not to support any kind of war, international or civil, and to strive for the removal of all the causes of war."[12]

A fifth pacifist group that will play a major role in our story also began during the interwar period. The Catholic Worker Movement got its start with Dorothy Day and Peter Maurin; Day was a young adult convert to Catholicism and Maurin a French immigrant. The two met in the early 1930s in New York City and found they were kindred spirits with a deep concern for people suffering in the depths of the Great Depression.

They began publishing a newspaper called *The Catholic Worker*, and they established houses of hospitality modeled after rescue missions but without coercive religiosity. Day became the main leader of the movement. She wanted the Catholic Church to be involved in caring ministries that would provide a basis for a nonviolent kind of revolution. So she sought to work closely with the church and to remain in positive relationships with the Catholic hierarchy.

Day's theology remained fairly simple. She drew more on the gospels than on Catholic natural law–based moral philosophy. From the beginning, she advocated pacifism. She insisted that the Worker as a whole be pacifist—especially as represented in the newspaper. Because of the obvious fruitfulness of the Worker's service-oriented ministry, many Catholics, including bishops and cardinals, provided support, and the Worker expanded greatly during the 1930s.[13]

INTERWAR PACIFIST INTERNATIONALISTS

These five organizations—American Friends Service Committee (AFSC), Catholic Worker, Fellowship of Reconciliation (FOR), Mennonite Central Committee (MCC), and War Resisters League (WRL)—represent distinct streams of philosophy and practice. They do not exhaust the varieties of pacifism[14] but do reflect a representative sampling. Each one has remained active down to the present. Even with their diversity, these five pacifist

12. Bennett, *Radical Pacifism*, 21.
13. Piehl, *Breaking Bread*.
14. John Howard Yoder discusses some twenty-nine "varieties of religious pacifism" in his *Nevertheless*.

streams share important characteristics. Each of them rejected the assumption of American policymakers that military force has to be central for dealing with international conflicts, and each supported those who refused military service.

Stated ideals in favor of democracy and civilization and self-determination have provided motivational bases for going to war—linked with an assumption that military force is necessary to achieve those ideals. Pacifists challenge those assumptions on several levels. While they affirm Atlantic Charter ideals such as political self-determination and disarmament, pacifists reject the necessity of using war to achieve them. In fact, pacifists argue that war is incompatible with democracy. They believe that democracy has been established in places in the past several centuries in spite of warfare, not because of it. All five groups share the conviction that constructive work in the world is possible, that ideals such as self-determination and disarmament are worth pursuing and may be pursued fruitfully—and that this work may be (indeed must be, to be truly fruitful over the long run) nonviolent.

The "peace story" of the work of these five groups may be juxtaposed with the war story we have considered up to now. Certainly these two stories involve quite different arenas of life. I want to suggest, though, that significant areas overlap. Both stories, at their heart, address the issue of "democracy" (not necessarily as a style of running a nation-state so much as a means of achieving self-determination, freedom, and disarmament).

Most importantly, our two stories provide clear alternative options for ordinary citizens. When the state (appropriately) challenges citizens to take up the moral task of helping further democracy, options remain about how best to do that. We have seen so far in this book that the option of seeking to fulfill this moral task through warfare has in fact proved to be problematic. Instead of being an agent for the spread of genuine democracy "everywhere on earth" as promised to those who accepted the necessity to join in World War II, the American nation-state has instead often been an agent for massive violence and injustice. It has thereby actually undermined possibilities for the peoples of the earth to achieve self-determination and disarmament.

The twentieth century, the "century of total war," nevertheless (and not coincidentally) has also been the century in which the principled rejection of warfare expanded beyond what the world had ever before seen.[15] For the first time, in the 1930s, large numbers of people stated publicly that should their nation go to war they would not participate. As it turned out, when war did actually come, most of these professed pacifists supported and even participated in the War—but not all. And toward the end of the

---

15. Schell, *Unconquerable World*.

century, American young men's opposition to participation in the Vietnam War pushed the government to end conscription, with the strong likelihood that it will not return.

Along with the rejection of warfare, and the willingness of increasing numbers to embody that rejection by suffering, the twentieth century also saw the expansion of two powerful types of nonviolent action: (1) nonviolent activism for social change inspired by the philosophy of Mahatma Gandhi, and (2) widespread investment in relief and development work undertaken out of pacifist convictions by organizations such as AFSC and MCC.

In the United States, the catalyst for these expanding expressions of nonviolence was when President Woodrow Wilson led America into Europe's Great War. The formation of the International FOR and WRL International shortly after the war's end provided an organizational focus for international ties of fellowship as a counter to the tendency to treat national boundaries as reasons for mistrust and conflict.

The American Friend Service Committee also forged strong international connections in the years following the Great War. In the immediate aftermath of the war, Europe faced devastating shortages of food and other essential materials. At first, the AFSC worked with displaced persons in France, providing emergency relief. In time, their work expanded to Poland, Serbia, Russia, Germany, and elsewhere. They performed an extraordinary service and saved millions of lives.

The Quakers established centers in numerous European cities. They paid close attention to the rise of Nazism in Germany during the late 1920s and early 1930s and raised early alarms about the treatment of Jews following Hitler's rise to power in 1933. In May 1934, the AFSC executive secretary, Clarence Pickett, traveled to Germany to meet with Jewish leaders, including Rabbi Leo Baeck, the head of Berlin's largest synagogue. Pickett said he was going to Europe "to explore whether we could do anything to help prevent the barbaric treatment of Jews and to assist the immigration of those who were so fortunate to be able to get to the United States or elsewhere."[16]

As the violence against Jews in Germany increased, in 1938 AFSC representatives, including AFSC founder Rufus Jones, directly approached Nazi leaders. They drew on their credibility that stemmed from Quaker relief work in Germany during the years immediately following World War I. They did find a somewhat receptive audience. After a meeting with Gestapo officials, the delegation was given permission to "investigate the sufferings of Jews and to bring such relief as they see necessary." In his report on the visit,

---

16. Pickett, *For More than Bread*, 93.

PART THREE: Alternatives	No to the War

Jones stated, "it is the settled purpose of the German government to drive out Jews.... Until a plan of rapid emigration, especially for young, effective persons is established, the authorities consider the problem unsolved, and further outrages are likely to occur, bringing greater suffering and injustice." Jones stated that the message they received from Jews they saw underscored the need for Jews to get out of the country. "They said, 'Don't put food and hunger first. We can stand hunger. We can stand anything, but get us out before something more awful happens.'"[17]

So the Quakers redoubled their already frantic efforts to aid Jewish refugees in finding sanctuary in the United States and elsewhere, especially from their various Quaker houses scattered throughout Germany and Austria. They met with constant reluctance, however, on the part of American embassies and the federal government. At this point, the Nazis welcomed Jewish emigration, and acting almost alone, the Quakers sought to use the opportunity. The lack of responsiveness of the American and British governments greatly limited the numbers who were able to leave and thereby exacerbated the tragedy that unfolded.

By the late 1930s, the likelihood of war increased by the day. Along with the Quakers, many other pacifist Americans spoke against American participation in such a war. These pacifists rejected the arguments of the isolationist strand of American neutralism because they did not accept the notion of "America First." But they also rejected the idea that warfare could solve the problem of international conflict.[18] They did recognize the evils of Hitler's philosophy and practice. They challenged the American economic interests that were linked closely with German Nazism. However, the pacifists also feared that efforts to meet Nazi militarism with a military response would lead to the victory of militarism, not of democracy.

John Haynes Holmes, a Unitarian pastor in New York City and FOR founding member, published an article in the *Christian Century* in December 1940 that warned that going to war with the Nazis would not eradicate the spirit of Nazism. Holmes asserted that Hitler's admitted injustices were not new. Christians have long persecuted Jews, Holmes wrote, and whites in America accepted "the myth of race superiority" over blacks long before Hitler stated such a myth. Hitler's were not the first concentration camps— the Spanish had imposed them on the Cubans, the British on the Boers, the Americans on the Filipinos. "He did not initiate the totalitarian state, which is only an extremity of tyranny as transmitted in our time by the Hapsburgs and Romanovs. He did not invent the idea of the subjection of helpless

17. Quotes from Baker, *Human Smoke*, 109.
18. Kosek, *Acts of Conscience*, 154.

people, as witness the British in India, France in Morocco, and Belgium in the Congo."

Holmes argued that Hitler did not create Germany's powerful military machine on his own. Various nations provided the Nazi military with its hardware: Britain the tanks, America and France the bombers, America the machine guns and submarines. "This man, so cruel, so ruthless, so revengeful, is not alien to ourselves. He is the perversion of our lusts, the poisoned distillation of our crimes. We would not be so aghast at his appearance did we not see in him, as in a glass darkly, the image of the world that we have made. Our sins have found us, that's all."

Our big danger in face of Hitler is that we would meet him "with the weapon which he has so terribly turned against us." Should we do so, we would confirm Augustine's fifth-century statement in *The City of God*: "the conquerors are ever more like to the conquered than otherwise." The Nazis will triumph should they transform their enemies "into their own likeness by the sheer necessity of adopting Nazi weapons, and Nazi methods in the use of these weapons, as a means of victory." We must find another way of dealing with their tyrannies, Holmes concluded.[19]

NEGOTIATING WITH THE STATE

It has been estimated that in 1938 the peace movement in the United States had twelve million adherents and an income of over one million dollars per year.[20] However, with the advent of World War II, the vast majority of those twelve million came to support the War as at worst a necessary evil.[21] This switch was clear, for example, in the sudden change of heart among the leaders of the Methodist Church. In May 1939, they proclaimed that the church "would never officially support, endorse, or participate in war." A mere nineteen months later, they affirmed that "the Methodists of America will loyally support our President and our nation" as it enters World War II.[22]

Once it became clear that the U.S. would go to war, pacifist leaders increasingly turned toward working to secure adequate provision for conscientious objectors (COs). This especially characterized peace church leaders, including the previously politically withdrawn Mennonites. Representatives

19. Holmes, "Same Old War," 74–75.
20. Wittner, *Rebels Against War*, 1.
21. For example, see Sevareid, *Not So Wild a Dream*, a memoir of the war years by one who changed from a pacifist to a pro-war perspective, first published in 1946.
22. Quoted in Wittner, *Rebels Against War*, 37.

PART THREE: Alternatives   No to the War   185

from the peace churches began meeting together in the mid-1930s to plan for what seemed to them to be the high likelihood of government conscription.[23]

Starting in 1935, peace church leaders along with a few other pacifists testified to House and Senate Committees on Military Affairs. This interaction revealed that Congress had little sympathy for their position. The initial version of the draft legislation, introduced to Congress in June 1940 and known as the Burke-Wadsworth bill, treated conscientious objection in almost exactly the same way as World War I legislation. This meant, among other things, that only men from recognized peace churches could claim deferment and that all COs would be under direct military control.

Pacifist leaders hoped for more liberal provisions. They argued for legislation modeled after that in Great Britain. The British legislation allowed complete exemption for absolutists who could show that it would violate their conscience to participate in conscription in any way, made allowance for acceptance of all objectors regardless of religious affiliation or lack thereof, and provided for completely civilian-based alternative service. This system worked (in 1940) even as Britain fought for its life against Germany.

When the Burke-Wadsworth bill passed on August 28, 1940, it included none of the progressive British provisions. Unlike British COs, American absolutists whose convictions forbade that they cooperate in any way with conscription would not be exempted. Alternative service work would not be independent of the ultimate supervision of Selective Service, though it was not to be under direct military control. Also, prospective COs would be required to have convictions based on "religious training and belief."

The pacifists did manage to effect some changes in the draft vis-à-vis World War I. (1) CO status, still tied to religion, no longer required affiliation with a recognized peace church. This meant that any religious pacifist could be a CO. (2) COs could now appeal local boards' classification to the national Selective Service. (3) The law explicitly made provision for alternative service to include work "of national importance" that would be under *civilian* control. (4) Prosecution for draft law violation would be handled by the federal court system and not military courts.[24]

The law allowed for alternative service of a civilian nature, but it included nothing regarding the nature of that service, leaving resolution of that issue to the "discretion of the President." The law said nothing about how the work would be financed or whether (and if so, how) the COs would be compensated for their work. The establishment of the Selective Service

23. Wachs, "Conscription," 50.
24. Wherry, *Conscientious Objection*, 89–90.

as the ultimate supervisor of Civilian Public Service (CPS) placed a serious contradiction at the heart of the program. On the one hand, idealistic COs and the Service Committees of the three peace churches saw CPS as a means for witnessing against war, growing in their pacifist beliefs and practices, and performing meaningful humanitarian service of "national importance."[25]

On the other hand, the Selective Service pragmatically sought to avoid any compromise in national unity in support of the War. Selective Service "tolerated" COs because it perceived that not to do so would hinder its primary mission—to draft soldiers to fight in the War. So, though Selective Service willingly allowed for COs, it did so with the basic attitude of keeping COs out of sight and out of mind. To allow the COs freedom of action and a public role (as, for example, might have happened through foreign relief service) had the potential, in Selective Service's eyes, to alienate the vast majority of American citizens who "willingly made sacrifices."[26]

When Selective Service was created, Roosevelt named Clarence Dykstra as director. Dykstra, chancellor of the University of Wisconsin, showed a high level of respect in conversations with pacifist lobbyists. However, shortly after the U.S. entered the War, Dykstra stepped down and was replaced by Colonel Lewis Hershey, who was immediately promoted to general. For the pacifists, this seemed an ominous change, threatening the policy that the classification of COs and their alternative service would be under civilian direction.

The government's lack of sympathy for the ideals of the peace churches soon became clear. Roosevelt signed the draft law in September 1940. Shortly thereafter he surprised Dykstra and the peace churches with his hostile response to their proposals regarding alternative service. He insisted that no government funds be used to finance CPS. Dykstra informed the peace churches that they faced a choice—either take on full responsibility to finance and administer the camps (though Selective Service would still have ultimate supervisory authority, as events came to show) or cede all control to the government and thereby give up any possibility of supervision even over young men from their own churches. These developments distressed

---

25. Great diversity existed among COs and the Service Committees themselves over the shape this idealism took and the relative potential of the work that they actually did to meet those ideals. But even those happiest about the realities of CPS and most grateful for government "tolerance" had idealistic views about the purpose of CPS. Naively, it now seems, these "optimists" failed to perceive that Selective Service did not share those ideals. Though those who saw through more "rose-colored glasses" kept the contradictions between Selective Service's and the Service Committees' basic perceptions regarding the purpose further from the surface, those contradictions nevertheless existed in all cases.

26. Wherry, *Conscientious Objection*, 1–2.

PART THREE: Alternatives

the pacifists a great deal. After intense debate, the National Service Board for Religious Objectors (NSBRO) decided to go ahead with full responsibility for CPS.[27]

In the beginning, Selective Service mandated that all camps be church-run and that all legally recognized COs, regardless of religious affiliation, go to church-run camps. Also, CPS would receive no government funds for the maintenance of the camps or camper expenses (however, the government did fund the actual work projects by paying for equipment and supervisory personnel). This placed a heavy financial burden on the peace churches, especially when they had to subsidize all comers into their camps.[28]

The actual CPS program also failed to meet the condition of full NSBRO control over the camps. Selective Service gave NSBRO and the peace church Service Committees no binding assurance that the camps under their administration would actually be under their control. This vagueness later haunted the Service Committees and NSBRO as a whole when Selective Service increasingly interfered with the internal operations and policies of the camps.

As the program progressed, Selective Service exercised its supervisory function in several ways.[29] It regulated the hours of work in the base camps, the establishment of overhead quotas, and the conditions of absence from camp, including furlough, liberty, and leave regulations. It imposed restrictions on assignees living outside officially designated quarters. In these and other ways, Selective Service restricted the Service Committees' control over the campers' situation in spite of the fact that the Service Committees had to fund the CPS program.

The first CPS camps opened in May 1941. The initial months saw morale at its highest level. The campers, administrators, and their supporters viewed CPS as an opportunity for COs to make a significant witness against war and at the same time to render a service of peace to society.[30] They saw the hardships that it engendered as bearable since the commitment at this time was only for twelve months. An atmosphere of congeniality prevailed among the campers and administrators along with a sense of gratitude for the chance to serve in this way.[31]

The entire dynamic changed in early December 1941, with the entry of the U.S. into World War II. Public opinion strongly favored fighting the

27. Sibley and Jacob, *Conscription of Conscience*, 120.
28. Keim and Stoltzfus, *Politics of Conscience*, 104–26.
29. Eisan, *Pathways of Peace*, 376–77.
30. Ibid., 182.
31. Sibley and Jacob, *Conscription of Conscience*, 121.

war—a poll on December 10 showed only 2 percent opposed to entry.[32] By implication, public opinion appeared unlikely to have much sympathy for those whose convictions forbade them to fight. American churches, even those most influenced by the interwar peace movement, rallied to the flag.

Though most COs surely desired an Allied victory once the War started, they still did not find the War morally justifiable, truly necessary, or something morally acceptable for them to fight. The strong sense of isolation they felt from mainstream American society troubled many COs. The realization that they now faced enrollment in the program for the duration of the War, likely several years at least, had a powerful effect on CPSer morale. Joining the military or going to prison offered the only ways out of CPS. In the months to come several took one of those routes, especially those CPSers who did not come from communities strongly supportive (both emotionally and materially) of their CO stand.

CIVILIAN PUBLIC SERVICE

General Lewis Hershey, who replaced Clarence Dykstra as director of Selective Service in early 1942, believed that he could not allow accommodating COs to hamper the overriding task of Selective Service to recruit manpower for the military. He saw alternative service as a "privilege" granted to those who would tend to undercut military efficiency and discipline if inducted, and he saw COs' privileges as contingent upon their cooperating fully with Selective Service regulations.[33]

Hershey did occasionally allow changes in response to NSBRO requests. He got along well with those within CPS (especially the Mennonites) who supported the program as established. He had little patience with, little respect for, and little understanding of those who resisted what they saw to be overly strong government control of CPS. Following Pearl Harbor, the government required CPSers, same as soldiers, to render service for the duration of the War plus six months. But unlike those in the military, CPSers received no pay or benefits. Hershey's ascendancy signaled the beginning of an ever-increasing tightening of Selective Service control over CPS.[34]

During 1942, along with rapid growth in numbers in CPS, came an increasing dissatisfaction with the CPS program. COs who had entered CPS with hopes of doing "meaningful" work unhappily found themselves relegated to farm and forestry projects. By March 1942, CPS began to create

---

32. Wittner, *Rebels Against War*, 34.
33. Sibley and Jacob, *Conscription of Conscience*, 308.
34. Wachs, "Conscription," 114.

PART THREE: Alternatives   No to the War   189

"detached service" projects. By the end of the War the majority of CPSers served in these projects rather than remaining in the "base camps."

Selective Service limited the options available for detached service due to perceived public opinion constraints. Hershey continually expressed his view that it would be best to keep COs out of sight and out of mind.[35] Working as attendants in mental hospitals became by far the COs' most popular option.[36] With the establishment of a unit in the Eastern State Mental Hospital in Williamsburg, Virginia, in June, CPSers began serving as attendants.[37] By March 1947, when the CPS program ended, 1.7 million workdays had been spent by COs in mental hospitals.[38]

Over the course of the War, the founders of NSBRO (as a rule, representatives of the peace churches) who had a more service-oriented approach to pacifism came into conflict with the more politically oriented objectors. The issue of church cooperation with the government in carrying out the draft emerged as a major one. Eventually, those opposing such cooperation—representatives of the Federal Council of Churches, Fellowship of Reconciliation, and War Resisters League—all withdrew from NSBRO.

This controversy moved NSBRO director Paul C. French, a Quaker, to defend church cooperation with the state in the CPS program. He asserted that NSBRO's perspective was the most realistic. The evils of the loss of civil liberties are inevitable during war. The first duty of the pacifist is to refuse to fight rather than to spend one's main energies protesting the conditions that accompany war. Imperfect as it is, the CPS program is the best possible arrangement for facilitating that refusal. French also supported church funding given CPS's purpose to display the *religious* orientation of the COs' pacifism. In his view, this "second-mile" approach displays this orientation quite effectively. To insist upon government funding might be a just stance, but such would be a "purely political" approach that would not be adequate for Christians.[39]

In March 1942, five CPSers in the AFSC-run Big Flats, New York, camp went on a work strike to protest the Selective Service–mandated increase in the CPS workweek from forty to forty-eight hours. The strike, though short-lived, presaged an ongoing battle between COs who resisted cooperating

---

35. Wherry, *Conscientious Objection*, 168–69.
36. Taylor, *Acts of Conscience*, 73–102.
37. Wherry, *Conscientious Objection*, 169.
38. Zahn, "Descriptive Study," 30.
39. French, *Civilian*, 3–4.

with the war system in any way and the authoritarian and often arbitrary Selective Service, with the Service Committees often caught in the middle.[40]

In testimony before Congress, Hershey explained why he supported CPS. To attempt to force COs to fight would compromise the efficiency of the military. "If you arouse opposition [from COs], you develop a martyr complex and they would do anything rather than fight. I would like to deprive the Army of having that problem to deal with." But he did hope to convince CPSers *voluntarily* to join the military. "We have salvaged about 700 out of [the] 7,000 [total CPSers] already. I think, in time, more will be salvaged."[41]

Ongoing dissatisfaction from non-church-affiliated CPSers eventually forced Selective Service to open a few government-administered camps. The first one opened at Mancos, Colorado, in July 1943, followed by Lapine, Oregon, in January 1944 and Germfask, Michigan, in May 1944. The experience in the government camps proved unsatisfactory for many involved. The work projects continued to be of the forestry/agricultural type, and many campers especially considered the dam-building projects at Mancos and Lapine to be of dubious value. CPSers saw the government camps as disciplinary camps in which Selective Service could collect those who caused problems in other camps.[42]

The Service Committees continued to find themselves in the middle between the inflexible Selective Service on the one side and the strong resisters on the other side. In the view of historians Mulford Sibley and Philip Jacob, the Service Committees became more strict in their discipline of assignees in order to retain responsibility for CPS and secure "leverage" to win Selective Service concessions. For the Friends, especially, this meant a deliberate and painful decision to abandon their initial commitment to a high level of democracy in the camps.[43]

With the conclusion of the European war in May 1945 and the Asian war in August, CPSers could now see the end in sight. But morale went down, if anything.[44] On the one hand, Selective Service only very slowly began to demobilize CPS. Despite early hopes that CPSers would be demobilized at the same rate as the military, they were not, partly because Congress insisted that soldiers get priority. On the other hand, many CPSers feared life after release. Unlike those in the military, they would receive

40. Grimsrud, "Ethical Analysis of Conscientious Objection," 65–66.
41. Quoted in ibid., 67.
42. Ibid., 58–59.
43. Sibley and Jacob, *Conscription of Conscience*, 283.
44. Kovac, *Refusing War, Affirming Peace*, 138–49.

no governmental assistance whatsoever. They received no financial benefits such as the separation allowance, aid for college, assistance to buy a house or start a trade or business, or help in securing employment. They feared discrimination even in attempting on their own to find employment and in returning to regular life in general.[45]

On March 29, 1947, the CPS program formally ended.

Roughly one hundred thousand draftable young men expressed a CO commitment during World War II. This included the fifty thousand who were drafted or sent to prison (twelve thousand CPSers, six thousand convicted of draft evasion, and more than thirty thousand legally recognized noncombatants in the military) and an estimated fifty thousand deferred for various reasons (e.g., occupational deferments for doing "essential" work such as farming and civil service work, dependency needs, physical problems).[46]

The twelve thousand CPSers gave almost six million project workdays. CPSers constructed and maintained 2,000 miles of fence, 475 miles of telephone and electric power lines, 814 miles of truck trails, and 7,640 miles of stock and foot trails. They planted around forty million trees, did 1,800 miles of work on fire trails and roads, and for 48,000 workdays fought forest fires. CPSers built several irrigation dams and spent 1.5 million workdays in mental hospitals, 120,000 in veterans hospitals, 105,000 in public health work, and 150,000 in research projects on effects of starvation, diet, and disease control. If the government had paid for the work of CPSers at the same rate it paid for its military, it would have spent over $18 million. As it was, this work—which presumably would not have been done otherwise—cost the government next to nothing.[47]

Not only did the CPS program meet with less governmental tolerance than envisioned by its founders, it also cost the peace churches and other supporting groups much more money. They expected the government to pay for administering the camps, especially for those CPSers not members of a peace church. As events proved, except for the few government camps, the peace churches and other church groups provided all the administrative funds for CPS, an amount that totaled over $7 million for the three peace churches. Small donations from generally rural people with limited financial resources provided most of this money.

That so many of their young men joined the military disappointed pacifist leaders; even among the Mennonites about one-half of those drafted

45. Sibley and Jacob, *Conscription of Conscience*, 303.
46. Ibid., 464.
47. Ibid., 125–26; Wherry, *Conscientious Objection*, 209–10.

became soldiers. But those who did join CPS remained committed to their pacifist ideals. Only 7.6 percent of the CPSers left for military service—quite a small number considering the hardships imposed upon CPSers due to the restrictive government policies.[48]

THOROUGHGOING RESISTANCE

Only a few World War II COs resisted the draft to the point of going to prison. Of the six thousand men imprisoned for their draft resistance due to principled opposition to participation in the military, about forty-five hundred were Jehovah's Witnesses, whose opposition was based on a strong sense of separation from the "secular world."[49] Hence, imprisoned politically oriented war resisters totaled about fifteen hundred.

These thoroughgoing resisters saw war as intrinsically evil and so refused to compromise their principled stance. They saw conscription as inextricably tied to war itself. Donald Wetzel is an example of a pacifist who initially accepted alternative service but quickly discovered that it required too much of a compromise. So he walked out of his CPS camp and spent the rest of the War in federal prison as a draft law violator. Wetzel concluded that war would not be possible without conscription; thus conscription itself must be resisted.[50]

Igal Roodenko, who became a longtime leader in the War Resisters League, summarized two basic reasons for resisters to refuse to compromise with Selective Service and the direction of the draft and CPS program. He first reasoned that the absolute evil of war depends upon conscription, hence conscription itself must be resisted. He also reasoned that since the individual is the basic unit in society and not to be violated, the way in which conscription sacrifices the individual to the altar of the state must be resisted. Conscription, he believed, led to totalitarianism.[51]

For many, resistance to compromise on conscription meant refusing to be drafted at all, since they saw accepting alternative service as too much of a compromise. Lowell Naeve, Arle Brooks, and Frederick H. Richards are three examples of men who did this and went to prison.

Draft officials persuaded Naeve to register, but he refused to report. He intended from the beginning to go to prison. "By registration for the draft I felt I had, as a 'responsible individual,' given the government the 'go-sign'

48. Zahn, "Descriptive Study," 89.
49. Grimsrud, "Ethical Analysis of Conscientious Objection," 205–30.
50. Wetzel, *Pacifist*, 198–99.
51. Grimsrud, "Ethical Analysis of Conscientious Objection," 85.

for a war," an action he then repudiated. His sense of responsibility dictated to him total noncooperation.[52]

Brooks emphasized the connection between conscription and warfare and asserted that he simply could not cooperate, even though he himself could have received a ministerial exemption. He wrote during the War, "Registration is the first and necessary step for conscription. My conscience will not permit me to take that first step. As a minister I could have received complete exemption. I felt it my moral duty to do all within my power to protect against conscription which will eventually weaken and destroy democracy. I am not evading the draft. I am defending democracy."[53]

Richards also emphasized the voluntary nature of his submission to arrest out of principled opposition to the draft, as he had chosen to return from humanitarian service in Mexico openly to resist the draft. He wrote, "Conscription is the denial of the personal responsibility of a man to live up to the right as he sees it; the right to obey a Higher Law than that of the state—the law of God as revealed to his conscience—the Inner Light of the Quakers." Though deeply devoted to helping others, Richards had to resist conscription because it denied freedom of conscience. "Conscription is the legal enforcement of the proposition that human beings exist only for the purpose of doing what the government wills."[54]

Jim Peck, who spent the war years in prison as a draft resister, emphasized opposing the evils of warfare. "The most effective way for an individual to start outlawing war," he asserted, "is simply to refuse to take part in it."[55] He would not fight against Hitler, not due to a lack of a sense of responsibility to stop Hitler, but rather due to a stronger sense of responsibility to stop war.[56]

A group of resisters meeting in Chicago in April 1943 issued a collective statement that asserted that their refusal to fight needed to be a positive act as well as a way to say "No." They characterized pacifism as a "courageous, non-violent opposition to injustice" undertaken out of a strong sense of calling to overcome injustice in this world. Part of this responsibility is to make the message of active nonviolence known to the world. Their statement asserted,

> Instead of clamoring for personal privilege and exemption, pacifists who see pacifism as active resistance feel they should

52. Naeve, *Field of Broken Stones*, 3.
53. Quoted in Pickett, *For More than Bread*, 334.
54. Quoted in Grimsrud, "Ethical Analysis of Conscientious Objection," 86.
55. Peck, *Underdogs vs. Upperdogs*, 100.
56. Ibid., 18.

take the offensive by placing their message before the people of the world. This at times would seem to lead to negative action—refusing to register, refusing to take a physical exam, refusing to go to camp, walking out of camp. But it also demands what is easily recognized as positive action—becoming involved in the non-violent fight for racial justice, participating in all kinds of symbolic acts such as publicly demanding a people's peace, uncompromsingly opposing conscription of labor, and campaigning for a democratic world by opposing imperialism in India and elsewhere.[57]

Resisters experienced widespread uncertainty over the most responsible direction to take in their opposition to the War. FOR leader A. J. Muste initially supported CPS but then led the FOR out of involvement with CPS. He himself refused to register when Selective Service extended registration to men between the ages of forty and sixty-five. His commitment to pacifism meant noncooperation with "evil,"[58] including by the end of the War noncooperation with CPS.

Many resisters went back and forth between CPS and prison in their search for the most responsible action to take. Agard Bailey, for example, went to prison as a draft resister before accepting parole into CPS at the Mancos, Colorado, government camp. He then decided that CPS did not offer a useful alternative. He wrote,

> In prison I felt I should be doing work of national importance. Having done this so-called work for more than a year while on parole, I now see that the work in this camp is merely boondoggling. I can do my country infinitely more good by opposing conscription, the right hand of war, than by engaging in the frenzied inefficiency which characterizes this project. To me, opposing those things which lead to war is work of highest national importance. I am guilty and responsible for war when I fail to oppose what makes for war.[59]

Notions of nonviolent social action greatly influenced many resisters, especially as formulated and practiced by Gandhi. For others, simply their own sense of unwillingness to cooperate in any way with the war-making state and its instruments influenced them most. Indirectly at least, such earlier champions of individual conscience as Henry David Thoreau and Leo Tolstoy influenced all resisters.

57. Quoted in Grimsrud, "Ethical Analysis of Conscientious Objection," 89.
58. Muste, *World Task of Pacifism*, 39.
59. Quoted in Grimsrud, "Ethical Analysis of Conscientious Objection," 91.

Some of the COs in prison would have denied that their resistance in prison was ineffective, pointing to an action that led to racial integration of the dining hall at Danbury Federal Prison as an important example of successful nonviolent resistance and as training for postwar work. They also would have pointed to the publicity surrounding the abusive treatment that COs Stanley Murphy and Louis Taylor received from federal prison personnel as a widely known reminder to people of the continuing possibility of resistance.[60]

The COs who ended up in prison took various paths in getting there. For some, such as Jim Peck, prison loomed as their likely fate from the time of the passage of the draft law. Peck believed right away that to compromise with the warring state in any way would fundamentally violate his conscience. Others, such as Donald Wetzel, felt more ambivalence and went into CPS initially before quickly realizing that CPS involved too much compromise. And others went into CPS with few doubts and only gradually came to realize that they could no longer cooperate. In these latter two instances, going to prison resulted from walking out of CPS camps and being arrested for noncompliance with the provisions of the draft law.

A central characteristic of the resister prison population was its refusal to accept CPS as a legitimate option. Most chose to reject that possibility when offered. In some cases (e.g., Agard Bailey, mentioned above), COs in prison accepted the CPS option before being disillusioned by their CPS experience and deciding that they could not stay in CPS. In other cases (e.g., Lowell Naeve), COs served their initial sentence, gained release, then faced rearrest and reimprisonment for failure to register with Selective Service. Resisters who started out in CPS often found prison to be a psychologically more satisfying situation than CPS, since it was much more "involuntary" and hence freed them from constant doubt about their level of compromise.[61]

Resisters who went to prison, in following their strong convictions and rejecting any kind of compromise with the claims of the state, ironically found themselves placed under the control of an even more thorough system of institutionalized coercion than they would have found in CPS or the military. However, many accepted prison because they believed they could maintain their integrity and know that their convictions could not be diluted by promises of comfort or social approval. And they did see their resistance bear some fruit—if nothing else, the knowledge that they maintained individual values in the face of authoritarian dehumanization and hence

60. Sibley and Jacob, *Conscription of Conscience*, 374, 412–16.
61. Ibid., 360; Wetzel, *Pacifist*, 50.

kept some kind of spark alive in the darkest of times.[62] Further, the training in nonviolent action that many resisters received both in prison and in CPS camps paid dividends after the War. In several significant cases, resisters put this training to use in postwar civil rights and antinuclear activism.[63]

In 1942, A. J. Muste echoed the assertion African-American church leader Howard Thurman made after a 1935 visit to India that Gandhian nonviolence might have a major role to play in gaining civil rights for blacks in the United States. In line with that assertion, Muste supported the Fellowship of Reconciliation when it hired James Farmer and Bayard Rustin to begin efforts to make that application.[64] Rustin, a Quaker, spent time in prison during the War as a draft resister.

Many resisters in prison suffered from their separation from society, and many violated their convictions due to the unrelenting pressure of the coercive prison system. On the other hand, many worked hard (somewhat successfully) at resisting the prison Leviathan and effected a small measure of reform. The coordinated work strike that successfully ended racial segregation in the dining hall at Danbury Federal Prison serves as one example.[65]

Several COs gained experience in prison that served them in postwar activism. One was Dave Dellinger, who became an important social justice leader. A second was civil rights movement leader Bayard Rustin. Danbury veteran Jim Peck also became active in the civil rights movement. "These demonstrations constituted our attempts to apply effectively on the outside the nonviolent methods of protest which we had used in prison," he later explained. "Somehow it seemed a continuation of the same struggle." Peck "felt certain that nonviolence would prove as effective in combating racial discrimination on the outside as it had been in Danbury."[66] Two pacifists, Holley Cantine and Dachine Rainer, looking back upon the prison rebellions, concluded that COs "salvaged from their years of captivity ideas of immeasurable value to all of us who contemplate in the coming totalitarian days a continual warfare with the state—both in and out of its prisons."[67]

These activists received some immediate encouragement. As Peck wrote,

> During [the prison] strikes we had been under constant scrutiny and control of uniformed screws mostly hostile to our

62. Wittner, *Rebels Against War*, 85–86.
63. Tracy, *Direct Action*.
64. Wittner, *Rebels Against War*, 64.
65. Tracy, *Direct Action*, 12–20; Bennett, *Radical Pacifism*, 98–133.
66. Quoted in Wittner, *Rebels Against War*, 92.
67. Ibid.

aims and therefore to us. During the demonstrations on the outside, we were similarly scrutinized by uniformed cops, who often expressed their hostility through violence or illegal arrest. The issues involved on the outside—amnesty, opposition to conscription—were of course broader. The methods, such as picketing and leaflet distribution, were different. Yet, somehow it seemed a continuation of the same struggle, a struggle against what we believed to be an injustice. We discovered that a small number of COs—not more than 30—could get national and even international publicity for pacifism by means of well-timed public demonstrations of such an unusual nature that the press could not ignore them. We were anxious, primarily, to get our fellow-COs freed and to win a general amnesty, and secondly to carry on an effective campaign against war and against the threat of permanent conscription in the US.[68]

We have seen earlier in this book that the U.S. turn toward total war has become a mad, downhill rush toward destruction that seemingly cannot be derailed. And yet, this handful of naysayers, who even in the face of the "Good War" retained their convictions that war simply cannot achieve genuine social well-being, did keep a small candle of alternative possibilities burning.

When we take a second look at the aftermath of World War II, we see along societal margins genuine possibilities of something different. The few who rejected warfare as an appropriate response to evildoing in the first half of the 1940s sustained various forms of a vision for an alternative story for the human project.

We will look now at some of the expressions of that vision that may in the long run turn out to be the most important moral legacy of World War II. That this view of an alternative, antimilitaristic approach to achieving the ideals of social wholeness did find at least some embodiment in the postwar years also underscores the moral bankruptcy of the War itself.

---

68. Peck, *Underdogs vs. Upperdogs*, 61. See also Bennett, *Radical Pacifism*, 134–203.

9

Social Transformation

To capture the moral impact of World War II, we could say this: as never before, the War simply obliterated the basic human belief in the preciousness of life.[1] It boggles the mind to list the countries where at least *one million people* died due to the War: Japan, China, the Philippines, Indonesia, the Soviet Union, India, Vietnam, Poland, Yugoslavia, and Germany. One of the pillars of authentic human civilization is the organization of society in light of the belief in the preciousness of life. That is why we put so many resources into, for example, health care, education, sanitation, and agriculture. We seek to protect human life.

Powerfully countering all this momentum toward enhancement of life, the War treated human life as shockingly expendable. The best and most creative resources of Western civilization focused on killing, not on enhancing life. In the United States, the moral legacy of World War II may be seen in how, all these years later, changing the nation's priorities (as seen in, say, Defense Department budgets) from death toward life seems impossible.

Some who recognized this problem have tried to overcome it. For such people, in the words of historian Joseph Kip Kosek, "the problem of the twentieth century . . . was the problem of violence. It was not, as such, Fascism, Communism, economic inequality, or the color line, though all of these were deeply implicated. It was, above all, the fact of human beings killing one another with extraordinary ferocity and effectiveness."[2]

---

1. The notion of the preciousness of life as a crucial moral category and its violation by World War II is developed in Hallie, *Lest Innocent Blood Be Shed*.
2. Kosek, *Acts of Conscience*, 5.

The resources the United States devoted to resisting fascism and communism did not in fact result in enhanced human well-being. Those efforts did not recognize as fundamental the profound problem of violence. By using violence to counter the twin ideologies of communism and fascism over the past seventy years, the U.S. has found itself on a rapid descent toward militaristic self-destruction. At the margins, though, some people have resisted this descent. Their efforts provide a counternarrative to the spiral of violence.

THE CIVIL RIGHTS MOVEMENT

The American civil rights movement, in important respects, reflects an attempt to keep the problem of violence at the forefront and to challenge a devastating social problem in light of the centrality of violence. By refusing to subordinate the problem of violence to some other problem, for a brief but extraordinarily fruitful moment the American civil rights movement actually made enormous progress in genuine social transformation.

This progress had roots in the peace movement that arose in the United States during the 1920s and 1930s and that found itself reduced to a tiny remnant by the end of World War II. Those few who retained their strong opposition to warfare and other types of inter-human violence did not disappear, however. For one thing, the War had left much of the world in tatters. The opportunities for service work to meet the survival and self-determination needs of countless people were endless. These opportunities provided the context for the expansion of peace church agencies such as the American Friends Service Committee and Mennonite Central Committee. Also, the conclusion of the War with the attacks on Hiroshima and Nagasaki, those demonstrations of a previously unimagined destructive power, shocked many who had doubts about the moral validity of warfare. The great powers then responded to the development of nuclear weaponry by moving into a competitive arms race instead of developing structures that would enhance possibilities for peaceful coexistence. This development galvanized antiwar sentiment into various antinuclear disarmament movements.

The American entry into World War II, justified as it was by appeal to ideals such as the Four Freedoms, contained a powerful irony. The American moral basis for committing to this total war existed alongside virulent racism that shaped life throughout the United States. An earlier American exercise in total war allegedly for the sake of social justice (the Civil War) had failed to bring genuine freedom and self-determination to

African-American people. The injustices that remained after the Civil War fueled social movements devoted to overcoming American racism.

These movements made only halting progress through the early decades of the twentieth century, with minimal impact on the broader society. The creative practice of Mohandas Gandhi in resisting the British in India raised new possibilities of effective nonviolent resistance. Several leaders in the American civil rights movement, most notably Howard Thurman of Howard University and Benjamin Mays of Morehouse College, recognized the potential in Gandhi's approach. Thurman visited Gandhi in the 1930s and began to advocate for nonviolent activism in America, though not yet with widespread support.[3]

During the War, African-Americans in the U.S. received mixed messages. Many were drafted into the military and were expected to fight. Arms industries also called upon African-Americans for factory work. In both cases, racism minimized opportunities for advancement and also led to many incidents of discriminatory violence.[4] Not a few African-Americans noted the contradictions as they devoted time and energy and risked their lives for the sake of a country that continued to treat them as second-class citizens. In general, returning soldiers found themselves once again bitterly mistreated, especially in the segregationist South.

Bayard Rustin was a different kind of World War II veteran.[5] As a Quaker, he philosophically opposed war and spent several of the war years imprisoned as a draft resister. In 1941, the Fellowship of Reconciliation (FOR) hired him as a staff person along with a fellow African-American pacifist, James Farmer. Farmer helped found the Congress of Racial Equality (CORE) in 1942, a ministry of the FOR, and Rustin joined with him shortly thereafter.

Farmer published an important essay in 1942 that connected nonviolence with work for racial justice. He discussed two themes essential to ending racism while avoiding a bloodbath in the U.S.: universalism and a commitment to nonviolent methods. Christian pacifists, in Farmer's words, affirmed "the Judeo-Christian faith in the universal community, the world fellowship, the unity of the human family." War violates this fellowship, acting as a kind of fratricide—in a parallel way, racism also violates human fellowship.

Conscientious objection to war, not service in the military, provided Farmer's model for winning the struggle versus racism. He linked

---

3. Ibid., 108.
4. Rose, *Myth of the Greatest Generation*, 134–58.
5. Anderson, *Bayard Rustin*; D'Emilio, *Lost Prophet*.

opposition to war with a positive appropriation of Gandhian approaches to exercising power. Farmer wrote, "What we must not fail to see is that conscience should imply not only refusal to participate in war, but also, so far as is humanly possible, refusal to participate in, and cooperate with, all those social practices which wreak havoc with personality and despoil the human community." Farmer insisted on an inextricable link between active opposition to war and opposition to racism. He believed that COs' opposition to the War would prepare them for ongoing civil rights activism.[6]

CORE and other groups, such as the National Association for the Advancement of Colored People (NAACP), emphasized training in nonviolent techniques. In 1955, a longtime civil rights activist in Montgomery, Alabama, Rosa Parks, became a catalyst for a major step forward in the movement's nonviolent activism. On December 1, 1955, after a tiring workday, Parks refused to give up her seat to a white person on a segregated city bus. She was arrested, an event that triggered a boycott of the Montgomery bus system.[7]

A young Baptist pastor newly arrived in Montgomery, Martin Luther King Jr., became a boycott leader and then a national spokesperson for the movement and, with several colleagues, founded the Southern Christian Leadership Conference (SCLC) to further the work for desegregation. In 1955, though, King had not yet fully embraced nonviolence as a principled commitment; he well understood that a civil rights movement, to be effective in the United States, must not resort to violence. Nonviolence thus became a central part of his message and the broader message of the SCLC. In a November 1956 speech that announced the successful end of the bus boycott, King asserted the need for the movement to remain nonviolent: "Now I'm not asking you to be a coward. If cowardice was the [only] alternative to violence, I'd say to you tonight, use violence. Cowardice is as evil as violence. . . . What I'm saying to you this evening is that you can be courageous and yet nonviolent."[8]

As it turned out, many African-American church leaders were not ready to embrace King's movement.[9] In fact, some bitterly opposed him. While both the centrality of his Christian convictions and his social location led King for the rest of his life to work within the church, he in time realized

---

6. Quotes from Kosek, *Acts of Conscience*, 182–83. The original article was James Farmer, "The Race Logic of Pacifism," *Fellowship*, February 1942.

7. Morris, *Origins of the Civil Rights Movement*, 51–63.

8. Quoted in Kosek, *Acts of Conscience*, 216.

9. Branch, *Parting the Waters*.

that his hopes for a unified and galvanized church working for racial justice were not going to be fulfilled.

By the late 1950s, King knew that the movement needed more concrete strategies to move the work ahead. He wasn't sure how to make this happen, however. The answer to the civil rights movement's dilemma—how to find concrete ways to expand the movement and bring about direct change—came almost as an accident. Leaders and activists such as Bayard Rustin and James Farmer had deep roots in the antiwar community that had opposed World War II. Older educators such as Howard Thurman and Benjamin Mays had strong Gandhian tendencies. And King himself, along with some of his close colleagues,[10] increasingly found himself moving toward a principled pacifism. However, the movement as a whole had yet to find a broadly effective way to move ahead on a Gandhian path.

Then, in 1957, King met a young Methodist pastor, James Lawson, who provided needed leadership to help the movement take crucial steps forward. Lawson brought some distinctive perspectives to his work.[11] He had grown up in the North in the largely white Methodist Church, the son of a minister. From an early age, he had committed himself to pacifism and to civil rights work. While he was in college, Lawson became convinced of a moral link between segregationist laws and the laws that enforced the military draft.

His convictions led Lawson to refuse to cooperate with the draft, even though he was eligible to receive a ministerial exemption. He spent a year in federal prison during the Korean War as a draft resister. He became friends with several FOR leaders active in civil rights work such as A. J. Muste, Bayard Rustin, and Glenn Smiley. He also became deeply attracted to Gandhian philosophy, and upon his release from prison spent a couple of years in India with a Methodist mission program, where he studied the Gandhian movement firsthand.

Martin Luther King was intrigued by Lawson's training and commitment and convinced Lawson to move to Nashville. The FOR hired Lawson as a fieldworker. He also enrolled as one of the first African-American students at Vanderbilt Divinity School. He recruited college students to come together for a campaign to integrate Nashville.[12] Under Lawson's guidance, the Nashville campaign proceeded carefully and meticulously. A period of

10. King's closest colleague, Ralph Abernathy, served in the military during World War II. Abernathy came to nonviolence more as an effective tactic than as a principled commitment. His views evolved on this topic. Saxe, *Settling Down*, 180–90.

11. Halberstam, *Children*, 27–50.

12. For the Nashville campaign, see Ackerman and Duvall, *Force More Powerful*, 305–33; Hogan, *Many Minds, One Heart*, 13–34; and Halberstam, *Children*.

thorough training prepared dozens of activists to initiate a series of sit-ins intended to integrate lunch counters in downtown Nashville.

The desegregation campaign met with great success. It followed the rules of a Gandhian *satyagraha* campaign to the letter. The campaign gained national attention and, because of the self-discipline of the activists, gathered wide support. The downtown businesses accepted integration at the lunch counters, and the willingness to integrate spread across most of the city.

Several of the college students who joined in this campaign became significant leaders in the broader civil rights movement, taking with them deep commitments to nonviolence. James Bevel became an important colleague of Martin Luther King and played a major role in several of the crucial events in which King's impact fostered key advances. Diane Nash, John Lewis, and Bernard Lafayette also had influential roles.[13]

About the same time as the Nashville campaign's successes, a number of activists linked with CORE decided to push the confrontations further into the South—further into the heart of segregationism. They organized a mixed-race group that would travel into the Deep South via the interstate bus system; they called this action a "freedom ride."[14] They began in Washington DC. When they got to Alabama, strong resistance to their action led to overt violence. The bus they rode on was stopped and burnt and several of the activists (including a World War II draft resister we met earlier, Jim Peck) were severely beaten. The level of violence surpassed the expectations of the activists, and they abandoned their action.

Rather than let the momentum die, however, a number of the activists who had served in the Nashville campaign led an attempt at a second freedom ride in May 1961. Again, the bus drove into a maelstrom of hostility and violence. This time, though, with greater numbers, a clearer sense of what to expect, and a stronger support structure, the freedom riders sustained their action. John Lewis nearly lost his life due to a beating, and several others also suffered severe injuries, but the ride continued into Mississippi, where the activists were arrested and sent to the notorious Parchman Penitentiary. By this time, the riders had gained national attention.

Challenged by the sit-in movement, which also had a strong presence in Greensboro, North Carolina, and elsewhere, the SCLC provided funding in 1960 to begin a new organization that would center its efforts on providing support to younger activists. This organization, the Student Nonviolent

---

13. Halberstam, *Children*, follows the careers of each of these activists. See also Lewis, *Walking With the Wind*.

14. Arsenault, *Freedom Riders*.

Coordinating Committee (SNCC), in its early years proved extraordinarily effective in embodying Gandhian nonviolence in ways that brought genuine change.[15]

SNCC activists drew heavily on the teaching of James Lawson and other advocates of nonviolent direct action. Several of the Nashville activists, most notably John Lewis, provided leadership for the SNCC actions. Along with public actions such as the freedom rides and mass demonstrations in cities such as Montgomery and Selma, Alabama, SNCC also undertook significant (and highly dangerous) education and voting registration campaigns in rural areas in Mississippi, Alabama, and other Southern states.

The American civil rights movement in the decade between Rosa Parks' 1955 Montgomery action that initiated the bus boycott and passage of the Voting Rights Act of 1965 had a practical (if not always principled) commitment to nonviolence. This nonviolence had important roots in the anti-World War II communities (as seen in the influence of A. J. Muste, Bayard Rustin, and James Farmer, as well as the inspiration James Lawson received from his draft-resisting predecessors). Martin Luther King Jr. provided a public articulation of the practical and (increasingly, as his own convictions deepened) philosophical bases for nonviolence.[16]

The reaction to the civil rights movement by supporters of segregation was breathtaking in its violence, reaching its apex in the murder of King himself in 1968. The civil rights campaigns retained their nonviolent, nonretaliatory practices in face of the extreme violence of the defenders of the racist status quo.[17] Such steadfastness pushed legislators and public opinion in general toward a growing willingness to include racial minorities as full participants in the nation's common life. This phase of the civil rights movement culminated in new federal legislation and government enforcement of the legislation.

As it turned out, though, the country could only partly accept the gifts offered it by the civil rights movement. When, under King's leadership, the movement extended its activism to the North, it met with shocking resistance. President Lyndon Johnson's commitment to social justice in the United States, unprecedented in comparison to any other American president before or since, ran aground in face of his simultaneous commitment to the disastrous war in Southeast Asia. The civil rights movement itself could not sustain its commitment to nonviolence.[18]

15. Carson, *In Struggle*; Hogan, *Many Minds, One Heart*.
16. Branch, *Pillar of Fire*, 24–26; Branch, *At Canaan's Edge*, 770–71.
17. Moses, *Revolution of Conscience*; Nojeim, *Gandhi and King*.
18. Branch, *At Canaan's Edge*.

King himself grew ever more committed to principled nonviolence, leading eventually to his costly critique of the American war on Vietnam. However, other committed pacifists such as James Lawson and John Lewis were pushed to the margins of the movement by those who did not share this commitment.[19] The ongoing violent intransigence of those opposed to the civil rights agenda—certainly in the South but also in the North—strengthened the arguments of those within the movement who opposed nonviolence.

By the time of King's murder in 1968, the civil rights movement as an expression of transformative nonviolence had lost its momentum. Its agenda has remained unfulfilled to a large extent—witness the disparity in the United States today in wealth between whites and blacks; witness also the evolution of the American criminal justice system into a powerful means of disenfranchising wide swaths of the African-American community.[20] The achievements of the movement remain of utmost importance, however, and those achievements may be seen as a product of nonviolent activism embodied by an enormously creative and dedicated generation of activists.

ANTINUCLEAR WEAPONS

Except for the small handful of people involved in its creation, the advent of nuclear weaponry came as a shock to everyone. Overall, the American public strongly affirmed the use of these bombs, especially when, within days of the attack, Japan surrendered and World War II came to an end. Those few who had opposed the War itself responded to Hiroshima and Nagasaki with unqualified horror. Selling out to warfare, they argued, has led to the possibility of bringing an end to human life itself. At first, however, the pacifists offered a somewhat muted outcry in that they tended to see the nuclear bombs, terrible as they were, mainly as the logical outworking of the war spirit, just one more step toward the abyss, but not necessarily something qualitatively new.

For a number of others, still a small minority in society, the use of nuclear weapons led to some uncertainty about the war they had supported. Historian Joseph Kip Kosek labels those with such uncertainty "prowar liberals." Prominent thinkers such as Reinhold Niebuhr supported "limited" war—though they used use the notion of "limited" in a very loose sense. In this view, once the War was undertaken, it required sufficient force to bring

19. Halberstam, *Children*; Lewis, *Walking With the Wind*.
20. Western, *Punishment and Inequality in America*; Logan, *Good Punishment?*; Alexander, *New Jim Crow*.

the conflict to a successful outcome. However, nuclear weapons seemed to go beyond what was necessary. The clear moral accomplishment of the Allies' military victory, in the view of these prowar liberals, may well have been decisively undermined by the degree of destruction caused by the nuclear bombs.

Kosek points out that before long, the emergence of the consensus in support of the American side in the Cold War would mute the negative views of the use of nuclear weapons. For a brief time, however, "regret flowed freely." He cites Lewis Mumford, a leading liberal prowar advocate, who stated, "our methods of fighting have become totalitarian; that is, we have placed no limits upon our capacity to exterminate or destroy. [The result was] moral nihilism, the social counterpart of the atomic bomb." A report called "Atomic Warfare and the Christian Faith," prepared by liberal Protestant leaders, including Reinhold Niebuhr, came out in 1946 and expressed opposition to the use of nuclear bombs on Japan.[21]

The other main expression of dissent over the morality of bombing Hiroshima and Nagasaki came from within the very community that had created these terrible weapons. Several of the nuclear physicists who initially participated in the Manhattan Project did so out of fear that the Nazis might create their own nuclear weapons. At least some of these scientists hoped to contribute to a kind of counterweight to the Germans that would never actually be used. Hence, once it became clear that the Nazis lacked the potential to create nuclear weapons after all, these scientists advocated that the Manhattan Project be scrapped.

Two key physicists, the Hungarian Leo Szilard and the Dane Niels Bohr, spoke forcefully against the negative possibilities of continued development of nuclear weapons and a postwar arms race.[22] Their efforts failed. During the summer of 1945, as the work to create the bomb neared its successful conclusion, Szilard initiated a petition signed by many nuclear scientists that urged President Truman not to use the bomb on Japan: "A nation which sets the precedent of using these newly liberated forces of nature for purposes of destruction may have to bear responsibility of opening the door to an era of devastation on an unimaginable scale."[23]

As it turned out, the director of the Manhattan Project, Brigadier General Leslie Groves, kept this petition from President Truman until after the bombing of Hiroshima and Nagasaki. Groves had been strongly committed

---

21. Quotes in Kosek, *Acts of Conscience*, 193–94.
22. Wittner, *One World or None*, 22–23.
23. Quoted in Carroll, *House of War*, 60.

PART THREE: Alternatives   *Social Transformation*

to using the bomb at the soonest possible moment and made sure Truman was not deterred from that action.[24]

Though many of the scientists who joined the Manhattan Project were motivated by concerns that the Germans might create atomic bombs, only one actually left the project once it became clear that the Germans would not have nuclear weaponry. This lone defector was Joseph Rotblat, one of the original scientists who worked in the crucial Los Alamos, New Mexico, laboratory. "When it became evident, toward the end of 1944, that the Germans had abandoned their bomb project," Rotblat wrote, "the whole purpose of my being in Los Alamos ceased to be, and I asked for permission to leave and return to Britain." Rotblat, who had fled Poland for Great Britain several years earlier, sustained his antinuclear weapons convictions; with Bertrand Russell he cofounded the Pugwash Conferences on Science and World Affairs, and in 1995, Rotblat and the Pugwash Conferences jointly won the Nobel Peace Prize.[25]

A second influential scientific organization that brought scientists critical of nuclear weapons together was the Federation of American Scientists (FAS). It was formed in November 1945. Its mission from the beginning was to free "humanity from the threat of nuclear war."[26] The FAS published the *Bulletin of the Atomic Scientists*, a major voice in the scientific community and beyond for disarmament. This movement among American scientists played an important role in providing at least a small counterweight to the momentum for always expanding the quantity and quality of the American nuclear arsenal. However, though many scientists supported the FAS, the government never lacked scientists willing to devote their energies to creating ever more powerful weapons of mass destruction.

The antinuclear scientists joined with many others who were concerned about the spread of nuclear weapons in placing great hope in the possibilities of world government. The establishment of the United Nations fueled those hopes. In time, however, it became clear that the leaders of the United States and the other great powers were not interested in ceding power to international agencies that would limit their nuclear weapons capabilities.

Because of the overwhelming forces in the United States that were committed to pursuing dominance over the Soviet Union, a widespread public movement opposing nuclear weaponry failed to gain much traction

---

24. Alperovitz, *Decision to Use the Atomic Bomb*, 603–8.
25. Carroll, *House of War*, 58–59.
26. Wittner, *One World or None*, 60.

in the decade following Hiroshima and Nagasaki.[27] By 1954, though, the number of people around the world who were uneasy about the growth of nuclear weaponry began to reach a critical mass that would lead to more significant expressions of resistance. Their urgency was intensified as the hydrogen bomb was developed—a weapon one thousand times more powerful than the bomb dropped on Hiroshima. "Deeply disturbed by this turn of events, many of the early critics of the Bomb renewed their calls for nuclear arms control and disarmament—measures which appealed to ever larger sections of the public."[28]

Through the rest of the 1950s, the movement grew steadily. In many places around the world, antinuclear activists created some of the largest protests their countries had seen for years, if ever. The movement found its greatest support in the "West" (North America, Western Europe, Japan, and Australasia) where earlier peace movements had been established.

Lawrence Wittner, a historian of the antinuclear movement, reports that "the nuclear disarmament movement became genuinely international, mobilizing as many as half a million people simultaneously for street demonstrations and other popular manifestations against the Bomb in dozens of nations." Mass movements independent of government control were impossible in Eastern Bloc countries, but the movement did win "converts in high places, particularly among Soviet scientists and other intellectuals, who pressed the Soviet government to halt key aspects of the nuclear arms race."[29]

As the movement gained wide participation, it drew strength especially from young people. The movement also attracted many participants from the ranks of intellectuals and the broader educated middle class, while receiving continued support from many scientists. Plus, many women felt a strong pull to work for disarmament.[30]

For all its accomplishments, the antinuclear movement of the 1950s and 1960s certainly fell far short of its aspirations. Activists galvanized support around a simple demand: Ban the Bomb. Decision-making elites in the nuclear-armed nations well understood that to pursue this straightforward path would require major changes in national security policies. These elites were somewhat responsive to the popular sentiment in favor of disarmament, but also worked strenuously, and by and large successfully, to minimize genuine change. "Under great popular pressure, policymakers might

---

27. Brock and Young, *Pacifism in the Twentieth Century*, 245–50.
28. Wittner, *Resisting the Bomb*, 1.
29. Ibid., 463.
30. Ibid., 464.

limit nuclear testing, regulate the arms race, or draw back from nuclear war. But, for the most part, they were not about to give up their nuclear weapons or, for that matter, reform the international system." The movement thus centered its concerns on the weapons themselves rather than on the underlying dynamics of international relations. And as a consequence, the potential for genuine change was limited.[31]

Even so, the movement did have an impact. As Wittner summarizes,

> In the face of bitter opposition from many government leaders, it had helped to end atmospheric testing, secure the world's first nuclear arms control agreements, and lessen the possibilities of nuclear war.... It unleashed a new wave of dynamic social forces—most notably movements among students, women, and intellectuals—as agencies of social change. Even as they put aside nuclear concerns, they took up other issues of great moment, including the Vietnam War, environmental protection, women's liberation, and assorted campaigns for social justice. Often they drew on the movement's innovative techniques, including mass marches and nonviolent resistance.[32]

The movement reached its peak around 1960. Various factors, including the ban on atmospheric testing as well as the emergence of a more immediate concern in the growing war in Vietnam, led to an eclipse of widespread antinuclear activism. Nonetheless, several pro-disarmament organizations that emerged in the 1950s survived, ready to be revived when the times allowed for it.

Wittner argues at the end of the second of his three-volume account of these movements that, though it fell far short of its goals, the antinuclear movement of the 1950s and early 1960s nonetheless had a positive impact. It curbed the arms race in significant ways, preventing what could have been disastrous outcomes. To a remarkable degree "our survival, physical and moral, has resulted from the activities of those men and women who worked to free humanity from the menace of nuclear annihilation."[33]

The actual impact of the positive moves that resulted from the 1954–64 peace movement was more than matched by major moves in the other direction. As has been typical for American militarists ever since World War II, acceptance of modest limitations masked efforts to expand the arsenal in general. Along with the effort by the American militarists to avoid letting this new arms control regime actually challenge their core agenda, in the

31. Ibid., 472.
32. Ibid.
33. Ibid., 473.

1960s the Soviets actually took major strides to challenge U.S. dominance—likely the only time they gained significant ground during the Cold War.

The humiliation the Soviets faced in the Cuban missile crisis led to the removal of Nikita Khrushchev from leadership and a renewed effort greatly to expand the Soviet arsenal in order to approach something like parity with the United States. As a consequence, the global threat of nuclear destruction significantly *increased* following the arms control measures Khrushchev and John Kennedy achieved.[34] Yet, the antinuclear movement was greatly diminished by the end of the 1960s and remained so throughout most of the 1970s. The reduction of energy resulted in part from complacency due to the positive gains the movement did achieve and in part from having its focus turned to the more immediate problem of America's greatly expanded war on Vietnam.[35]

After the end of the Vietnam War in 1975, many activists renewed their opposition to the arms race. They gained hope from the election of Jimmy Carter as president in 1976, a victory at least in part based on Carter's campaign as a peace candidate. He entered office with what seemed to be sincere hopes to help stem the momentum of the arms race. Early in his administration, Carter challenged the Pentagon's joint chiefs of staff to reduce America's nuclear arsenal significantly. That is, rather than being satisfied with "arms control," Carter actually had hopes to achieve "disarmament."

According to James Carroll, when Carter began his presidency, he actually sought to challenge the dynamic of the Cold War itself:

> [He] grasped . . . that the initiative in the arms race had more or less consistently belonged to the United States: the Soviet build-ups in the late 1940s, the early 1950s, the early to mid-1960s, and the 1970s had followed [in each case America's initiative to enhance its arsenal]. America deployed its atomic bomb in 1945; Moscow did it in 1949. America's intercontinental bomber came in 1948, Moscow's in 1955. America's hydrogen bomb in 1952, Moscow's in 1955. America's submarine-launched ballistic missile in 1960, Moscow's in 1968. America's multiple-warhead missile in 1964, Moscow's in 1973. . . . And now America was ahead on the long-range cruise missile. If America could take the lead on the way up the arms ladder, why not on the way down?[36]

---

34. Morris, *Iron Destinies, Lost Opportunities*, 235–68.
35. Wittner, *Toward Nuclear Abolition*, 1–20.
36. Carroll, *House of War*, 364.

PART THREE: Alternatives   *Social Transformation*

As it turned out, Carter was not up to the challenge. During his time in office, the U.S. did not lead the way "down the arms ladder." Carter did not find a way to exercise his authority effectively in face of the intransigence of the American war system, both inside the Pentagon and outside the official government, among the promilitary lobby. Also, Carter's focus on human rights, in many ways a laudatory emphasis that has had a positive impact even to the present day, ended up being twisted into a tactic in the Cold War. He tended to scold the Soviet Union more than he sought to bring about changes within the American sphere of influence. This one-sided focus led to the alienation of the Soviets, significantly reducing Carter's potential to negotiate reductions in nuclear weaponry.

On the contrary, by the end of his one term in office, Carter had initiated major increases in military spending. He announced the disastrous Carter Doctrine in his 1980 State of the Union speech, laying claim to permanent access to Persian Gulf oil. The U.S. would sustain this access by "any means necessary, including military force." Carter thus signaled a change in emphasis. Before this time, American initiative in the Middle East generally was channeled through surrogates; now the U.S. would more quickly and directly intervene and greatly expand its military presence in the area. At the beginning of his tenure, Carter had advocated reducing U.S. dependence on Persian Gulf oil; in the end, he advocated using the American military to support this dependence. "The consequences of this shift ordered by Carter would be played out in 1991, with the Gulf War, and in 2003, with the war against Iraq. By then, oil imports (still mainly from the Persian Gulf) had risen to more than half of the U.S. supply."[37]

Already during Carter's tenure, however, other forces in the United States and elsewhere were stirring—forces that within a few years would lead to the greatest public outcry against governmental militaristic policies the world had ever seen.

At the urging of the American government in 1979 (with Carter in office), the nations that were part of the North Atlantic Treaty Organization (NATO) announced a major intensificaton of the nuclear danger to Europe, a decision that led to a significant expansion of nuclear weaponry stationed in western and southern Europe. In response, antinuclear activists in Europe issued a widely endorsed statement in opposition to the deployment of NATO's new nuclear weapons and to the presence of all nuclear weapons in Western Europe. Their statement, the European Nuclear Disarmament

---

37. Ibid., 371–72.

Appeal (END), was issued hoping that it would stimulate a widespread disarmament movement. That hope was fulfilled over the next several years.[38]

The END movement organized massive demonstrations throughout Western Europe, as well as yearly conventions that met in various European cities, the final one meeting in Moscow in 1991. END worked to form ties with dissident groups in Eastern Europe, groups that played major roles in the peaceful end of communist rule in Warsaw Pact countries by the early 1990s. The emergence of the END movement helped stimulate a major revival of the work of the Campaign for Nuclear Disarmament (CND), a British organization that had been active during the 1950s and 1960s but had become mostly moribund by the mid-1970s. The membership of CND grew rapidly, jumping from four thousand to one hundred thousand between 1979 and 1984. The success of the European antinuclear movement was seen in NATO's decision in 1987 to withdraw the nuclear weapons whose deployment in 1980 had triggered the rebirth of the movement.

Parallel to the emergence of this mass movement in Europe, in the U.S. antinuclear activism also was re-energized. Two key expressions of the U.S. activism were the freeze movement that gained great traction and the Plowshares movement, a much smaller, intense effort to raise public awareness of the problems with nuclear weaponry.[39]

A key figure in the freeze movement was Randall Forsberg, a political science graduate student at Massachusetts Institute of Technology, who formulated the original call for a nuclear weapons freeze and became one of the major public spokespersons for the movement once it gained a mass audience. The call for a freeze intensified as the depth of Reagan's antipathy toward the Soviet Union became clear early in his presidency. The Reagan administration almost immediately gave up even pretending to seek arms control agreements.

Forsberg's freeze proposal sought for simplicity. In its two brief paragraphs, it called upon the two great powers, first, to "decide when and how to achieve a mutual and verifiable freeze on the testing, production, and future deployment of nuclear warheads, missiles, and other delivery systems." Second, the proposal asked the powers "to pursue major mutual and verifiable reductions in nuclear warheads, missiles, and other delivery systems, through annual percentages or other effective means, in a manner that enhances stability."[40]

---

38. Wittner, *Toward Nuclear Abolition*, 63–89.
39. Ibid., 169–201.
40. Quote from Carroll, *House of War*, 385.

The formal nuclear freeze campaign began with a conference in Washington DC, only two months after Reagan's 1981 inauguration. The campaign did not fully achieve its goals; however, its challenge to Reagan's militarism from the very beginning of his presidency prevented the arms race from causing even more damage. The freeze campaign gained wide support from its inception, quickly becoming what James Carroll characterizes as "the most successful American grassroots movement of the twentieth century." Within a couple of months of the initial conference, hundreds of city councils and state legislatures around the country passed versions of the freeze resolution. "Official bodies in 43 states passed the resolution. More than a million people signed freeze petitions in barely more than a few weeks. Two out of three congressional districts across the country had freeze chapters."[41]

In 1982, a freeze resolution came within one vote of passage in the House. This campaign put Reagan on the defensive. Even though Reagan's policies in general were not popular, his own standing had been given a strong boost when he was wounded in an assassination attempt in March 1981. By the end of 1982, though, that boost was history and the freeze campaign (among other factors) had contributed to a major loss of support for Reagan. He "and his advisers realized that the strategic-nuclear-weapons policies the administration had been pursuing could no longer be sustained."[42]

In a somewhat desperate but masterful and ultimately successful shift of rhetoric, Reagan came out in 1983 as a seeming advocate of disarmament. This followed the victory of the freeze resolution in the House of Representatives in March 1983. "After the resolution passed in Congress, [Reagan] ingeniously denounced the freeze because it did not go far enough."[43] He started talking about doing away with nuclear weapons altogether. This idea of the abolition of nuclear weapons became something Reagan could suggest, however, because of the emergence of the Strategic Defense Initiative (SDI)—a fanciful program that allegedly could obliterate incoming nuclear weapons.[44] The SDI was never viable, mostly serving as an immense boondoggle that funneled billions of dollars to the arms industry. But it worked rhetorically for Reagan. His new talk of abolishing nuclear weapons helped defuse the freeze movement just as it moved to the brink of actual legislative accomplishment.

41. Ibid., 386.
42. Ibid., 388.
43. Ibid., 390.
44. Wittner, *Toward Nuclear Abolition*, 325–29; Fitzgerald, *Way Out There*.

Simultaneously with the popular and widely embraced freeze movement, another group of peace activists took a more radical stance. Daniel and Philip Berrigan, two Roman Catholic priests, had been leaders of the anti-Vietnam War movement in the 1960s. The Berrigan brothers and their close colleagues practiced the public symbolic act, gaining wide exposure for the first time when, in 1968, they used homemade napalm to detroy draft files in a Selective Service office in Catonsville, Maryland (their subsequent trial became known as the case of the Catonsville Nine). They eventually served several prison terms for their activism, and Philip left the priesthood while continuing to devote his life to antiwar activism.[45]

Between 1980 and the end of the millennium, Plowshares activists performed roughly one hundred public actions.[46] Their acts, "in the military's view, [were] sabotage, gravely threatening, yet no one was ever injured—not the demonstrators, workers, guards, or arresting officers."[47] The Plowshares movement was more about witness than social transformation. The freeze movement, working in the mainstream of American society, did seek social transformation but ended up in many ways being outflanked by Ronald Reagan's devious use of the SDI—in actuality, a program to escalate the arms race—to underwrite his rhetoric of nuclear abolition.[48]

Ironically, though, while the Reagan administration never truly believed in disarmament, a new government came into power in the Soviet Union that did. With the emergence of Mikhail Gorbachev, the pieces were in place for the first time since the arms race began for actual disarmament.[49]

Gorbachev moved mountains to hold Reagan accountable to the latter's rhetoric about disarmament. And he came amazingly close to succeeding. The big achievement of the nuclear freeze movement was to challenge Reagan to change his rhetoric. As it turned out, Reagan, in his own internally contradictory way, did believe in getting rid of nuclear weapons and he was responsive enough to Gorbachev's initiatives to encourage the Soviet leader to continue on his path toward disarmament.[50]

Important achievements followed—such as the withdrawal of nuclear weapons from Europe and the shockingly peaceful transition away from communism as the Soviets allowed their empire to be dismantled and accepted self-determination for Eastern and Central European peoples. As

---

45. Polnar and O'Grady, *Disarmed and Dangerous*.
46. Laffin, "Chronology of Plowshares Disarmament Actions."
47. Carroll, *House of War*, 419–20.
48. Fitzgerald, *Way Out There*, 210–64.
49. Rhodes, *Arsenals of Folly*, 212–26.
50. Carroll, *House of War*, 404–6.

PART THREE: Alternatives Social Transformation   215

with the earlier nuclear disarmament movement in the 1960s, the movement in the 1980s only partly achieved its goals. But, also as before, its efforts did help the world take a step back from the abyss.

The work of the freeze movement, joined with Gorbachev's remarkable initiatives, set the stage for a move away from the abyss (the *Bulletin of the Atomic Scientists* moved its doomsday clock to an unprecedented seventeen minutes till midnight). Tragically, the failure of the American national security system to fulfill the ideals for which Americans had been sent to war in 1941 soon negated, in many ways, the move from the abyss.

At the end of his authoritative three volumes on the antinuclear movements from 1945 to 2003, Lawrence Wittner concludes that the leaders of the great powers, with a few exceptions, never intended to achieve disarmament. These important exceptions (Olof Palme of Sweden, Andreas Papandreou of Greece, Rajiv Gandhi of India, and Mikhail Gorbachev) were happy with the emergence of the antinuclear movement. Wittner writes,

> But most officials had a more negative view of the nuclear disarmament campaign, for it challenged their reliance upon nuclear weapons to foster national security. And yet they could not ignore the movement, either, particularly when it reached high tide. Confronted by a vast wave of popular resistance, they concluded, reluctantly, that compromise had become the price of political survival. Consequently, they began to adapt their rhetoric and policies to the movement's program. Within a relatively short time, they replaced ambitious plans to build, deploy, and use nuclear weapons with policies of nuclear disarmament and nuclear restraint. Most of this was accomplished, it should be noted, *before* the disappearance of the Soviet Union. Thereafter, when the antinuclear movement waned, the nuclear arms race resumed.[51]

THE UNCONQUERABLE WORLD

Efforts to resist racism and nuclearism show how deeply entrenched these problems are in the U.S. Powerful efforts that mobilized thousands upon thousands of people who sought change brought only grudging and fragile improvements. In the case of both sets of issues, the gains sadly were followed by losses, and our situation today remains one of peril and injustice.

World War II marked a bit of progress in racial justice. Yet many African-American soldiers left the military frustrated by racism even as

---

51. Wittner, *Toward Nuclear Abolition*, 486.

they answered their country's call to serve. More so, they encountered oppression as they returned to a profoundly racist country that continued to treat these veterans as second-class citizens. Not only did they return to the same old same old in terms of ongoing discrimination, but they also found themselves deprived of many of the benefits white veterans received.

Out of these experiences, many African-Americans deepened their resolve to work for change. So the civil rights movement that emerged in force in the second half of the 1950s owed some of its energy to the common experience of the contradictions in America where the demand for military service for the sake of "freedom" was accompanied by the denial of basic freedoms to those who served.[52]

The nuclear threat arose directly from World War II. The development of usable nuclear weapons could not have happened without the willingness of the American government to devote immense resources to the effort. Almost certainly, no peacetime government would have undertaken this kind of an effort, especially one that had such a highly uncertain outcome.

The U.S. was not capable of turning away from the use of nuclear weapons or from the attempt to develop them and to seek a monopoly on their possession. As Garry Wills shows in his book *Bomb Power*, the resources devoted by American policymakers to the weapons of death drastically undermined American democracy and placed the entire world in enormous peril.[53] Then, after the American "victory" in the arms race in the early 1990s, the country proved unable to put an end to its years of pouring its treasure into these systems of destruction.

Nonetheless, despite the seeming intractability of these problems, movements to overcome them offer important lessons for the future of humanity. The violent legacy of World War II has been challenged, effectively. And the challenges to this legacy have created momentum toward change—even if this momentum may not always be discernible. Rosa Parks' initiating the sit-in in December 1955, and the emergence of an international mass movement against nuclear weapons when American policymakers pursued the hydrogen bomb, marked key moments of resistance to the trajectory toward more and more violence.

The various social movements that resisted the spiral of violence have shared a couple of crucial characteristics. A key start is simply to step out of the pro-violence consensus. Certainly one of the most powerful moral legacies of World War II from the beginning was the basic assumption that violence worked well to defeat the enemies of our country. With this

---

52. Saxe, *Settling Down*, 156–90.
53. Wills, *Bomb Power*.

assumption came the belief that the institutions that emerged as the managers of the violence should be trusted as necessary and appropriate at the heart of our federal government. However, the movements for social change we have looked at have had at their core a rejection of that "necessary violence" narrative.

To jettison the narrative of necessary violence is the basis for genuine security and reflects a central tenet in Gandhian political philosophy. Gandhi argued that the ability of governing elites to manage their societies depends upon the consent of the people being governed. To recognize this law of social reality provides those who seek social change with a crucial strategic principle. To bring about social change, the change agents must focus on consent. If enough people withhold their consent, the ability of the governing elites to work their will is certain to be profoundly undermined.[54]

The key moments of genuine change—the integration of the American South, the creation of the first arms limitation treaties, the withdrawal of forward-based nuclear weapons from Western Europe, the disintegration of the Iron Curtain (we could also include the remarkably nonviolent dismantling of the apartheid regime in South Africa)—all had at their core the fact that consent to the status quo was being withheld.

As people step out of the pro-violence consensus created and sustained by the power elites in Western societies, significant numbers, at times with powerful effectiveness, take the next step and band together in communities devoted to creating change. The "beloved community" of the American civil rights movement, the mass movement of protest against the U.S.-Soviet nuclear madness, and others have found ways (rarely sustainable, sadly) to create sufficient critical mass to move society in more peaceable directions.

Bringing people together reinforces the moves many make to disbelieve the power elites' narrative concerning necessary violence. Many people may have doubts about the "necessary violence" narrative, but finding others of like mind will reinforce their questions and provide possibilities for effective dissent. One key element in the end of the Soviet empire was the gradual emergence of various communities that provided confirmation and support for the increasing numbers who sought a different kind of world. We see parallel dynamics in the American civil rights movement.

An important step in going beyond simple protest is the construction of alternative narratives to the standard violence-is-necessary-for-security story. The movements of protest and the emergence of communities of resistance challenge the standard story. Often, however, they have not been

---

54. Sharp, *Power and Struggle*, 7–48; Ackerman and Duvall, *Force More Powerful*.

accompanied by thoroughgoing articulations of different views of how society might be structured based on peaceable values.

The pioneering work of Gandhi has played an important role in the gradual development of alternative social narratives. Martin Luther King brought together Gandhian influences and insights drawn from biblical sources, and he reframed the American struggle for democracy as the story of a quest for genuine freedom rather than as a quest for world domination. The antinuclear movement included elements of thought and advocacy that have worked at imagining the actual parameters of a nonnuclear world.

While these movements did achieve advances, perhaps their most important contribution was simply to stimulate the gradual emergence of social developments that have moved humanity closer to what social thinker Jonathan Schell has called the "unconquerable world."[55] Schell traces the emergence in the twentieth century of the inexorable drive that human societies have for self-determination. The collapse of the great empires of the early twentieth century (and the collapse of the German, Japanese, and Soviet empires that emerged later in the twentieth century) make the possibility of greater political self-determination more realistic—a hope fueled by the stated purposes of World War II.

The disastrous insistence by several "democracies" after World War II to resist the ending of their empires (for example, France in Vietnam and Algeria, the Netherlands in Indonesia, and Great Britain in Kenya) led to several "peoples wars" that brought untold numbers of casualties. Numerous of these "peoples wars" did end external domination, but even the successful ones often resulted in the imposition of authoritarian postrevolutionary governments.

Schell argues, however, that in most cases the key factors leading to the defeat of the external forces were not their military firepower so much as the revolutionaries' ability to undermine the consent of the governed. It was not military might but the political success of the movements that drove the occupation forces out.

Gandhi's work in India and then the late twentieth-century movements in Central and Eastern Europe and in South Africa made it clear that the revolutionary task may actually be achieved largely through nonviolent means—as did the nonviolent transition in Latin America from a region of dictatorships toward democracies.[56] Such a possibility rose again in northern Africa in 2010–11. Schell sees growing clarity about how movements for

---

55. Schell, *Unconquerable World*. For a parallel analysis, see Kaldor, *Global Civil Society*.

56. See Nepstad, *Nonviolent Revolutions*.

self-determination might be based on nonviolence along with a sense of the actual impotence of nuclear weaponry and all-out warfare. These dynamics, even in the face of the continued militarization of American foreign policy, make peace a greater possibility in the world.

Schell helps show that people in the U.S. could bury the myth that World War II was a "good war" that has a positive moral legacy. The long shadow of World War II plays a key role in the death-enhancing dynamics that the U.S. still embraces in its out-of-control militarism. To see the War as problematic would be a major step toward a shift in trust: from trust in the myth of redemptive violence as a necessity for security toward trust in what Schell calls "cooperative power." Schell summarizes thus:

> The power that flows upward from the consent, support, and nonviolent activity of the people is not the same as the power that flows downward from the state by virtue of its command of the instruments of force, and yet the two kinds of power contend in the same world for the upper hand, and the seemingly weaker one can, it turns out, defeat the seemingly stronger.... It is indeed a frequent mistake of the powers that be to imagine that they can accomplish or prevent by force what a Luther, Gandhi, a Martin Luther King, or a [Vaclav] Havel can inspire by example. The prosperous and mighty of our day still live at a dizzying height above the wretched of the earth, yet the latter have made their will felt in ways that have already changed history, and can change it more.[57]

In the present, the instruments of self-determination that make up what is called "civil society"[58] and the global forums that give a voice to those outside the power elite offer genuine hope for a more peaceful world. These instruments stand directly on the shoulders of the civil rights and the antinuclear movements that emerged in the 1950s as direct responses (ad hoc and fragmented as they were) to the failure of World War II to live up to its promise as an agent for self-determination and disarmament.

In the final chapter of Part Three, I will focus on another type of response to the failures of the war system to facilitate human well-being. We will look at several examples of movements that have sought alternative models for achieving humane social dynamics as a direct expression of pacifist convictions. In each case (we will look at the American Friends Service Committee, the Mennonite Central Committee, and the Catholic Worker), the pacifist communities faced adversity during World War II due

---

57. Schell, *Unconquerable World*, 230–31.
58. Kaldor, *Global Civil Society*.

to their principled unwillingness to support that war. Yet by emerging from the War with those principles largely intact—and in fact, deepened—these communities were well situated to devote immense energies immediately after the War to the survival needs of many devastated by the War. They were then able to move on to work at longer-term peacemaking and service efforts.

One fruit of the expanding work of these pacifist communities is how each in their own way made major contributions to an unprecedented mass movement in the United States during the 1960s and 1970s—the unprecedented, widespread opposition to a war while that war was happening that in important ways contributed to its end: the anti-Vietnam War movement.

10

Servanthood

The civil rights and nuclear disarmament movements sought directly to transform American culture through social activism. They were ad hoc uprisings comprised of a variety of citizens whose energies ebbed and flowed over the time of the movements' activities. Their significance lies in their quest, at times remarkably successful, for genuine democracy from the bottom up, based not on coercive force but on the exercise of self-determination.

Alongside these transformation-seeking movements, we should also be attentive to several long-term efforts, largely motivated by pacifist sensibilities, to work for self-determination and disarmament through acts of service. The first of these "service committees" was the American Friends Service Committee. I will also discuss two other quite different but parallel service-oriented groups: the Mennonite Central Committee and the Catholic Worker.

AMERICAN FRIENDS SERVICE COMMITTEE

The origins of the American Friends Service Committee (AFSC) go back to the First World War. Some members of the Religious Society of Friends (Quakers) sought to find ways actively to serve human well-being that could also provide alternatives to participation in the war. The organizers of the AFSC included representatives from several heretofore somewhat alienated branches of Quakerism who recognized the need to cooperate in this kind of venture. The AFSC was formed in 1917 under the directorship of Haverford

College professor and well-known author Rufus Jones.[1] "We wanted," Jones wrote, "to show our faith in action and to show it in a way that would both bring healing to the awful wounds of war and carry us into the furnace where others were suffering."[2]

To this end, AFSC created the "Haverford Emergency Unit" to provide war relief to people in France. They negotiated to get Selective Service to authorize this war relief work as alternative service for conscientious objectors who had been drafted into the military. After some months, approval was gained, and during the final days of the war conscientious objectors were active in relief work.

In the aftermath of World War I, AFSC expanded its efforts and distributed food and other essentials to desperately suffering war victims. Over the next few years, the work of AFSC saved millions of lives. From the start, AFSC's identity was centered both on its close link with the Quaker tradition (though it was not formally affiliated with any specific Quaker denomination) and its openness to the participation of any person who shared its basic convictions.

AFSC established a presence in numerous international locations during the interwar years, but also invested significant time and money in working inside the U.S. in relief and development work during the Great Depression. AFSC leaders worked skillfully with government officials—even to the point that longtime AFSC director Clarence Pickett developed a strong working relationship with Eleanor Roosevelt, and through her had significant contact with President Roosevelt himself.

Three different kinds of activities in the late 1930s indicate the breadth of AFSC's concerns. In face of widespread poverty among mineworkers in southwestern Pennsylvania, AFSC helped create a self-supporting community of former mineworkers that provided possibilities for economic self-determination. This community faced numerous barriers but did manage to succeed in many ways and provide a model for others.

AFSC had links with numerous Quaker centers throughout western Europe that had begun with the post-World War I relief work. With the rise of Nazism, these Quakers, with support from AFSC, sought to facilitate the emigration of beleaguered Jews. They met with resistance from the American and British governments and so were unable to help nearly as many people as they wanted to. But they helped some, they sounded the alarm (too seldom heeded) about the increasing danger faced by Jews, and they

---

1. Brock and Young, *Pacifism in the Twentieth Century*.
2. Quoted in Weisbord, *Some Form of Peace*, xvii–xviii.

challenged (though not successfully enough) the political structures in the U.S. to respond to this crisis.

The third example of AFSC efforts was its work to provide draftees with alternatives to military service. With their years of work with government, Quaker leaders were uniquely situated to lead peace church efforts to shape government policy toward conscientious objectors. They worked with government officials to create and operate what became the Civilian Public Service (CPS) program in collaboration with Mennonite Central Committee and the newly created Brethren Service Committee.

As it turned out, the Friends CPS camps attracted a wide range of COs from various traditions (the Mennonite camps were populated mostly by Mennonites, and the Brethren camps had a strong Brethren identity), partly due to a disappointingly small number of Quakers who chose to be COs. Throughout the war years, AFSC leaders debated whether the agency should cooperate so closely with the war-making government. In the end, when the government insisted that the CPS camps continue for nearly two years even after the War ended, AFSC opted out of its involvement with CPS.[3]

As with World War I, so also in the devastating aftermath of World War II, AFSC effectively devoted extraordinary resources to relief work. This work was recognized when AFSC and its British counterpart, the Friends Service Council, were awarded the Nobel Peace Prize for their relief work.

During the Cold War years, AFSC continued with its relief and development work, giving special focus to offering aid to victims of warfare. As had been the case since its founding in 1917, AFSC gained wide respect from various sides in these conflicts as an organization genuinely oriented toward humanitarian aid and not political partisanship.

At the same time, within the United States, AFSC did take strong stands critical of the American national security system. One influential AFSC publication, *Speak Truth to Power: A Quaker Search for an Alternative to Violence*, issued in 1956, gained wide attention for its critique of American (and Soviet) nuclearism and its articulation of an alternative vision for the international order based on "the effectiveness of love in human relations."[4]

AFSC provided important support and leadership in the early development of the civil rights and nuclear disarmament movements. When American participation in the Vietnam War escalated during the mid-1960s, AFSC joined with various other long-term peace organizations (such as Fellowship of Reconciliation, Women's International League for

---

3. Sibley and Jacob, *Conscription of Conscience*.
4. DeBenedetti, *American Ordeal*, 16.

Peace and Freedom, and War Resisters League) to provide organizational resources for the antiwar movement.

Throughout the Vietnam War years, AFSC worked hard at antiwar activities, provided widespread draft counseling to aid prospective inductees who sought CO classification, worked with members of the military who sought help in dealing with their traumatic experiences, and engaged in extensive aid and development work in Southeast Asia.

During a time of intense debate, agitation, turmoil, aggressive protest, and polarizing conflicts, AFSC provided a distinctive presence. On the one hand, operating from a consistently pacifist perspective, AFSC offered a rigorous critique of American involvement in this war. This critique also included skepticism toward the various public relations efforts by American governmental officials. Yet, also drawing on its pacifist convictions, AFSC rejected the more militant and at times even violent reactions by some in the antiwar movement against American policies and policymakers.[5]

Its rootedness in a centuries-long tradition of pacifist commitments and respect for other perspectives (the belief in the presence of God in each person) sustained AFSC in its consistent witness against the war in the midst of the great turmoil in the U.S. during the decade from 1965 to 1975. Their consistency allowed AFSC to continue their antiwar witness even after President Nixon pursued his "Vietnamization" policy of reducing American presence on the ground while heightening the American aerial devastation of Vietnam.

The Vietnam War finally drew to a close in 1975 following Nixon's fall from power and Congress's belated willingness to end funding for the conflict. The same mainly pacifist groups that had initiated opposition to the war remained the main voices of continued opposition after the antiwar movement shrank. As with FOR, WILPF, and WRL, for AFSC this was witness to core convictions that centered on an opposition to all war as inherently immoral.

After 1975, AFSC worked hard at reconciliation efforts with the Vietnamese, actively but futilely seeking the normalization of relationships between the United States and Vietnam. AFSC also actively participated in efforts to resist American intervention in Nicaragua and elsewhere in Central America during the Sandinista years. Probably most controversially, AFSC has supported the Palestinian resistance to Israel.

Prominent Quaker sociologist and peace educator Elise Boulding offered this evaluation of the efforts of the AFSC:

5. Ibid.

> The AFSC had gone far in acknowledging kinship with and staying in relationship with groups whose lifeways differ sharply from those of middle-class pacifists, groups that sometimes seek more far-reaching changes than the average pacifist feels called upon to support. This has led the AFSC into uncomfortable situations that many of us have never had to confront. Keeping a steady and loving spirit in those situations, and upholding the commitment to nonviolence requires great inner strength. Certainly the AFSC has made mistakes. But they have been the mistakes of love and concern. We can choose to stay in risk-free spaces where the purity of our pacifism is never questioned, or we can choose to move into those spaces where humanity's growing pains are more acutely on display.[6]

In spite of, or perhaps in some sense because of, the messiness of its direct engagement in peacework in the midst of intense conflicts—an engagement that has certainly included remarkable and exemplary relief work but also has gone beyond relief work to attempt to address the causes of conflicts and advocate on behalf of the victims of warfare (hot and cold)—the AFSC has embodied a powerfully transformative ethic of servanthood.

Part of the power of the AFSC surely has followed from its rootedness in a particular Christian tradition. It has certainly practiced an impressive inclusiveness both in welcoming as its workers people from a variety of religious and nonreligious traditions, and in offering its services to all in need regardless of ethnicity or creed. Yet it has also remained firmly anchored within the Quaker tradition and drawn most of its support from Quaker sources.

MENNONITE CENTRAL COMMITTEE

In 1920, Ukranian Mennonite representatives approached North American Mennonites with an urgent request for assistance. They faced extreme suffering due to the civil war in the Soviet Union and a resultant famine. Various Mennonite groups responded positively. Due to concerns of possible chaos should each group's efforts remain separate, a single agency to coordinate the assistance was needed. Thus, Mennonite Central Committee (MCC) was born.[7]

MCC has served as the main expression of common Mennonite values and convictions. The work of MCC started out with a focus on famine relief.

---

6. Quoted in Brock and Young, *Pacifism in the Twentieth Century*, 343–44.
7. Juhnke, *Vision, Doctrine, War*, 249.

By the time of World War II, the work expanded to include MCC's role as the coordinating agency representing Mennonites to the U.S. government in the formation and operation of the Civilian Public Service (CPS) program for conscientious objectors.

American Mennonites' experience during World War II shaped their pacifist convictions in several important ways. The generosity Mennonites expressed through MCC's relief work was also expressed in the churches' financial support of the CPS program. Mennonites supported their own CPSers, but their contributions also underwrote the expenses of other COs who lived in the Mennonite-operated CPS camps.

For many, CPS participation led to greatly expanded horizons. If, prior to World War II, Mennonites had tended to think of their pacifist convictions primarily in terms of living faithfully as "the quiet in the land" who practiced their nonresistant faith in neighborly ways in their isolated communities, as a consequence of their exposure to the wider world, many accepted the challenge to apply their convictions much more broadly after the War ended.[8]

This urge to apply Mennonite peace convictions more broadly led to an expanded ministry for Mennonite Central Committee. It also led to the establishment of several new agencies that sought to address human needs. Three were formed by the early 1950s: Mennonite Mental Health Services (MMHS), Mennonite Economic Development Associates (MEDA), and Mennonite Disaster Service (MDS).

The work of MMHS emerged from CPSers' work in various mental health hospitals throughout the U.S. These COs witnessed horrendous conditions and emerged from that experience with a strong desire to see some alternatives. MCC developed a program that would lead to the establishment of several new mental health facilities staffed by professionally trained Mennonite caregivers (a big challenge, since as of 1945 there was not a single trained Mennonite psychiatrist[9]).

Mennonites formed MEDA in 1953 to complement MCC's relief work with an explicit focus on development assistance. As with MCC itself, MEDA began by focusing on needy Mennonites, in this case Russian and Prussian refugees who had settled in South America following the War. Supported mostly by North American Mennonite businesspeople, MEDA focused on "offering grants and loans for long-term economic development

---

8. For accounts of the evolution of North American Mennonite pacifism, see Bush, *Two Kingdoms, Two Loyalties*, and Driedger and Kraybill, *Mennonite Peacemaking*.

9. Toews, *Mennonites in American Society*, 210.

instead of charity for immediate needs,"[10] and in time expanded its reach far beyond Mennonite communities.

MDS originated with former CPSers who saw a need for organized assistance to victims of natural disasters. By its twenty-fifth anniversary in 1976, MDS had grown to involve nearly two thousand congregations. Except for a single paid executive director, MDS's work has been done by volunteers. "Yet the record of this vast, decentralized organization, as its historian Katie Funk Wiebe has written, 'reads like a roll call of national disasters. Name the disaster and you'll find MDS was there.'"[11]

The biggest consequence of World War II for Mennonite peace concerns was the greatly expanded international ministry of MCC. In 1940, MCC's work was mainly to aid impoverished Mennonites in the Soviet Union and those who had migrated from the Soviet Union to South America. Over the next several years, MCC began to work in England, France, Poland, India, China, Egypt, and Puerto Rico. Immediately following the War, MCC entered seventeen more countries in Europe, Asia, Africa, and South America.[12] MCC sought to be uninvolved in partisan politics. However, in a broader sense, MCC's work was deeply political. MCC did seek to further self-determination everywhere—echoing the ideals of Roosevelt's Four Freedoms and the Atlantic Charter—without the use of coercive methods.

When the United States reinstated the military draft in the late 1940s, the policies concerning alternative service changed. Instead of requiring COs to take assignments in government-operated Civilian Public Service camps, nongovernmental agencies could provide assignments for COs. Also, the service was no longer restricted to North America. Consequently, during the 1950s and 1960s, MCC accepted thousands of COs performing alternative service and placed them throughout the world.[13]

The emergence of MCC and growing Mennonite acculturation led to a "gradual metamorphosis" in the application of their pacifist convictions.[14] According to historians Peter Brock and Nigel Young, "Three issues, successively, dominated church discussions of peace and war and led in turn

10. Ibid., 209.

11. Ibid., 212. I can personally attest to Wiebe's statement. In December 1964, my hometown of Elkton, Oregon, suffered a "hundred year flood" that devastated the surrounding area. At that time, I had never heard of Mennonites. About fifteen years later, after I had become acquainted with Mennonites, I met a Mennonite pastor who had been living in Oregon at the time. It turned out that he had been part of an MDS team that had spent time in my community offering much-needed assistance.

12. Ibid., 201.

13. Redekop, *Pax Story*.

14. Driedger and Kraybill, *Mennonite Peacemaking*.

to a radical restructuring of the North American Mennonite peace witness: the question of political responsibility, the draft, especially during the Vietnam War, and the liberation of the socially oppressed, particularly in Latin America where missionary activity had led to the emergence of indigenous Mennonite churches in virtually every country there."[15]

One major impact of World War II on Mennonite young adults was an exposure to the wider society through their CPS work. For many, this exposure led to an interest in applying their pacifist convictions to problems of the day. They also tended as a consequence to have a more positive attitude both toward other peacemakers outside their Mennonite communities than had been the case in earlier generations and toward society and the state in general. The long-term, deep-seated Mennonite suspicion toward "political involvement" began to dissipate.

Numerous Mennonites responded positively to Martin Luther King's active nonviolence. For example, Guy Hershberger, the prominent author of the standard book on Mennonite peace convictions, *War, Peace, and Nonresistance* (1944), made an effort in the 1950s to understand King's work and ended up as a supporter, even arranging for King to visit Goshen College, the Mennonite school where Hershberger taught.[16]

The civil rights movement of the 1960s, led by King and inspired by Gandhi's practice of nonviolent resistance, made a strong impact on many Mennonites. An African-American Mennonite pastor, Vincent Harding, worked closely with King and thus also helped acquaint Mennonites with nonviolent resistance. Harding also played a major role as King's own peace witness became more radical. He wrote the initial draft of King's widely noted speech, given on April 4, 1967, that sharply critiqued the Vietnam War.[17]

Mennonites responded much differently to the Vietnam War than they had to World War II. A Kansas Mennonite, James Juhnke, won the Democratic nomination and ran (unsuccessfully) for Congress as a peace candidate. A number of Mennonites practiced tax resistance and joined in public antiwar demonstrations (including civil disobedience). Also, for the first time in the U.S., some Mennonite young men refused to cooperate with the draft, choosing prison or exile in Canada over alternative service.[18]

During the entirety of World War II, not one American Mennonite went to prison as a draft resister. With Vietnam, several dozen Mennonites

---

15. Brock and Young, *Pacifism in the Twentieth Century*, 347.
16. Schlabach, *War, Peace, and Social Conscience*, 447–70.
17. Branch, *At Canaan's Edge*, 603.
18. Brock and Young, *Pacifism in the Twentieth Century*, 348–50.

did go to prison and numerous others exiled themselves to Canada.[19] Their resistance reflected a growing acceptance of non-Mennonite exemplars for war resistance such as Thoreau, Gandhi, and King. Many Mennonite resisters had contact with the wider antiwar movement. They also felt unease with what they saw as Mennonite privilege in relation to Selective Service that tended to result in favored treatment. They "thought Mennonite draftees should take their stand on an equality with others who opposed war and refused to fight; and they tended to see their own stance, though it brought them into conflict with the law, as a 'prophetic witness' to the excessive demands of the state."[20]

Though the actual number of Mennonite draft resisters was quite small, their stance did gain the official approval of the two largest Mennonite denominations. Later, when President Carter reinstated draft registration in the late 1970s as a means to "show resolve" toward the Soviets, a number of Mennonite young men refused to register. The denominations supported these resisters (while not recommending the same course of action for all registrants). The main governmental sanction for non-registrants has been the refusal to allow non-registrants to receive government financial assistance for college. So the Mennonite Church USA offers grants for non-registrants to offset that loss in part.

With the end of the Vietnam War in 1975, the focus of Mennonite peacemakers changed to several new initiatives with links to MCC, as well as continued relief and development work. MCC had earlier established a "Peace Section" to further reflection on peace issues in light of Mennonite theology and a "Washington Office" to aid in listening to federal political issues and to provide a base for witnessing to legislators. Early in the history of the Washington Office, MCC facilitated the testimony to Congress of various MCC workers who had served in Vietnam during the war years.

In the late 1970s and early 1980s, MCC established new staff positions for people working in the emerging areas of restorative justice and conflict resolution. Mennonites provided important pioneering work in both of these areas and established a widely respected graduate program at Eastern Mennonite University that focused on both arenas. Also in the 1980s, Mennonites initiated a direct action–oriented ministry called Christian Peacemaker Teams that sent workers to various conflict areas around the world to seek to establish a peaceable presence.[21]

19. Miller and Shenk, *Path of Most Resistance*.
20. Brock and Young, *Pacifism in the Twentieth Century*, 349.
21. For an account focusing on both the conflict resolution work and peacemaker teams, see Sampson and Lederach, *From the Ground Up*. On restorative justice, see Zehr, *Changing Lenses*. On Christian Peacemaker Teams, see Kern, *In Harm's Way*.

THE CATHOLIC WORKER

At the beginning of the twentieth century, the Roman Catholic Church in the United States would scarcely have been considered a peace church. Educated Catholics likely knew of the just war doctrine's call for limitations to warfare, but the general Catholic view of warfare would have reflected Augustine's fourth-century expectation: Christian citizens leave the determination of the justification for war to their governments; their task is to obey the call to go to war when it comes.

By the time of the Vietnam War, however, Catholics made up the largest group of COs of any religious group in America. Catholic activists, including numerous priests and nuns, gained wide visibility in their active opposition to that war. During the massive movement against nuclear weapons during the late 1970s and 1980s, the American Catholic bishops issued a widely noted pastoral letter that spoke sharply against the arms race and explicitly presented Christian pacifism as one legitimate response to war.

Many factors contributed to this evolution among Catholics—and it should be noted that the vast majority of American Catholics still support American militarism. If we had to pick just one American Catholic who exercised the most influence in her increased opposition to warfare, it would be a remarkable Catholic convert and layperson, Dorothy Day, cofounder with French immigrant Peter Maurin of the Catholic Worker Movement.[22]

Day, who was born in 1897, became a Catholic in her late twenties. In 1933, at the height of the Great Depression, Day and Maurin established the first of their "houses of hospitality" to provide food and shelter for needy people. Day, who had a background in radical journalism, decided also to start a newspaper that would speak to the crises of the American system, but from an explicitly Christian personalist perspective. She chose the name Catholic Worker to convey both a sense of connection with the concerns of those engaging these crises from a Marxist perspective (whose paper was called the *Daily Worker*) and a sense of distinctiveness. This was a *Catholic*, not a communist, movement.

From the start, Day affirmed a gospel-centered ethic. The message of Jesus provided the Catholic Worker's direction, most obviously in the call to offer acceptance and general sustenance to those in need. Also, though, Day saw as part of this gospel message an uncompromising commitment to nonviolence. The newspaper expressed strong affinity with the other pacifist currents prominent in the U.S. during the 1930s.

From the start the Worker relied upon donations from church sources—though the Worker houses and publications always retained their

22. Miller, *Dorothy Day*.

formal independence. During the 1930s, the houses of hospitality clearly met a significant need. They generally were popular with church officials because they provided a Catholic presence amidst the struggles of the needy.

However, the onset of World War II changed everything for the movement. Day and her closest colleagues remained resolute in their opposition to all warfare, even in the face of strong support for the War among their main constituency. As a whole, Catholics supported the War at least as strongly as the wider American population. During the war years, support for the Catholic Worker shrank drastically. Numerous houses had to close due to lack of support, and the paper's circulation dropped to a fraction of its prewar number.[23]

About one hundred Catholics chose to enter Civilian Public Service, most of them (though not all) linked with the Catholic Worker. These numbers were high enough to warrant the creation of a CPS camp specifically for Catholics that would be supported financially by the Catholic Worker. This camp was established in Massachusetts but did not receive enough support to remain viable; it lasted only about a year.[24] The Catholic Worker's costly pacifist stance became a foundation for the expansion of Catholic peace activism in the following generation.

Two Catholic converts helped shape the Catholic Worker peace witness in the Cold War years. Robert Ludlow, a World War II CO, wrote about Gandhian nonviolence in the *Catholic Worker*, presenting it "as a potential substitute for war and as 'a new Christian way of social change.'" Ammon Hennacy, a World War I socialist CO and a lifelong political radical, joined with the Worker and pushed the group to more direct engagement in peace activism.[25]

Dorothy Day herself made the news beginning in 1954 for being arrested for her refusal to participate in legally mandated civil defense drills—participation that she believed implied an acceptance of American nuclear weapons policies. This was the first step in what has since become a long tradition of Catholic pacifist civil disobedience.

With impetus from the Catholic Worker, Pax Christi, an international Catholic peace group founded by French and German Catholics in 1945, established an American branch in 1962—notable for bringing together pacifists and nonpacifists. Two years later, a new group with an overt pacifist

---

23. Piehl, *Breaking Bread*, 191–98.

24. Zahn, *Another Part of the War*. Zahn himself was a CO who served at Camp Simon. Unusually for a World War II Catholic CO, he came to his convictions totally apart from the Catholic Worker. After the War, though, Zahn became closely linked with the Worker during his career as a prominent sociologist, author, and peace activist.

25. Brock and Young, *Pacifism in the Twentieth Century*, 369.

commitment also got underway—with the intent of complementing the work of Pax Christi. The Catholic Peace Fellowship, with strong Catholic Worker connections, affiliated with the Fellowship of Reconciliation. The FOR connection signaled a new—and permanent—bridge between Catholic pacifists and organized Protestant pacifism.[26]

Another inspiration for American Catholic peace activism was the brief, transformative papacy of John XXIII. John convened Vatican II to move Catholics into the twentieth century. Shortly before he died, John issued the encyclical *Pacem in Terris*, a call for peace that made it possible for "good Catholics" to begin to consider pacifism as a valid option. "Among those lobbying at the Council in favor of pacifism and conscientious objection were two Americans, the Trappist monk and mystic Thomas Merton and the lay theologian James Douglass. Both men helped to shape the further development of American Catholic pacifism."[27]

Merton, a prolific writer read far beyond Catholic circles, advocated for Gandhian nonviolence and sharply critiqued America's war in Vietnam. While Merton's understanding of peacemaking continued to develop, his conviction about "the essentially nonviolent character of the Christian message" remained firm. He believed that nonviolent tactics were always best in responding to evil and oppression. "Merton made his mark on American Catholic thinking on war . . . by the skillful manner in which he blended Gandhian *satyagraha* with the Sermon on the Mount and made the former an acceptable component of Catholic peacemaking."[28]

James Douglass, also a prolific writer, had a major impact as a creative antiwar activist—most notably with the Ground Zero Center for Nonviolent Action near Seattle in the 1970s and 1980s. Douglass's writings, beginning with *The Non-Violent Cross* in 1968, broke important ground in Catholic theology by presenting Jesus as a nonviolent revolutionary.[29]

The names most commonly associated with Catholic resisters to the Vietnam War are Daniel Berrigan and his younger brother Phil. Both were priests, and they collaborated with close colleagues to perform a series of acts of civil disobedience beginning in 1968 that stretched Catholic peace concern to new extremes.[30]

The Berrigans had close connections with the Catholic Worker, FOR, and Catholic Peace Fellowship. They valued Merton's writings highly and

26. Ibid.
27. Ibid., 370.
28. Ibid., 370–71.
29. See, most notably, Douglass, *Nonviolent Coming of God*.
30. Polnar and O'Grady, *Disarmed and Dangerous*.

drew deeply on Jesus' teachings (more than on the Catholic natural law tradition). Their additional step was to perceive a calling to go so far in their protests as to destroy government property. They believed, though, that such protests remained consistent with nonviolence—even as they burned draft board files or despoiled them with demonstrators' blood. In face of the horrendous war they were ready to become "criminals for peace."[31]

The Catholic resistance sustained its activities—moving after the end of the Vietnam War to antinuclear activism and involvement in the sanctuary movement that resisted American intervention in Central America. Philip Berrigan especially received prison sentences on many occasions. He worked closely with Catholic Worker communities, which had retained a thoroughly pacifist witness even after Dorothy Day's death in 1980.[32]

The influence of Catholic pacifists became so extensive by the early 1980s that they played a major role in the writing and discussion of the American Catholic Bishops' pastoral letter on nuclear war, *The Challenge of Peace*. This letter was issued in 1983 in the midst of the freeze movement that challenged the Reagan administration's acceleration of the arms race. It gained much attention in Catholic circles and far beyond.[33] The bishops were seen as making an extraordinary statement in opposition to the American role in the arms race, even if that opposition was expressed in nuanced terms.

The letter did not fully embrace pacifism. However, to an unprecedented degree it affirmed pacifism as a fully legitimate option for Catholic Christians. Notably, at this time several American bishops did publicly express thoroughgoing pacifist convictions—including the influential bishop of Seattle, Raymond Hunthausen, who worked closely with James Douglass and the Ground Zero Community. Hunthausen and the other pacifist bishops also cited Dorothy Day and the Catholic Worker as an important influence along with the writings and witness of Thomas Merton.

ANTIWAR ACTIVISM

After the U.S. and the Soviet Union signed their treaty in 1963 that banned atmospheric testing of nuclear weapons, the widespread citizen's movement that had helped make the treaty possible rapidly dissipated. It would be well over a decade before this movement rekindled and pushed the nuclear powers again toward disarmament.

31. Brock and Young, *Pacifism in the Twentieth Century*, 372.
32. Laffin and Montgomery, *Swords into Plowshares*.
33. Murnion, *Catholics and Nuclear War*.

However, another crisis arose in the U.S. that drew many of the same activists into creating another movement. The expansion of the American war effort in Southeast Asia gradually met with resistance. As with the antinuclear movement, the antiwar effort never coalesced into a large, unified force—and, as with the antinuclear movement, the antiwar effort did not succeed in gaining its core goals. Yet, also as with the antinuclear movement, the antiwar effort did accomplish a gargantuan task in the face of an intransigent state committed to expanded militarism: it helped prevent the worst case scenario from occurring.

Organized opposition to the Vietnam War began in the early 1960s with the witness of many of the pacifist organizations we have met already—the Fellowship of Reconciliation, the Catholic Worker, the War Resisters League, and the American Friends Service Committee (with its allied organization, the Friends Committee on National Legislation). In time, war opposition expanded greatly and in many ways departed from its pacifist roots.

The American war effort ultimately became untenable when President Nixon's successor Gerald Ford could not overcome Congress's willingness to defund the war. At this point, in 1975, the main antiwar activists who remained were representatives of the original antiwar movement. Peace historian Charles DeBenedetti says this about the final phase of antiwar activism:

> [In January, 1975], the Assembly to Save the Peace Agreement was the last gathering of the movement. Here . . . were the organizations that antedated the nation's involvement in Vietnam: the FOR, the AFSC, the Women's International League for Peace and Freedom, the WRL, and FCNL. They had provided much of the initiative for the reconstruction of the modern peace movement in the late 1950s and had been the core of antiwar activism.[34]

The basic stance of most of these pacifist organizations in the early 1960s was one of principled opposition to Cold War militarism and to an American foreign policy that tended to respond with military interventions to the efforts of formerly colonized peoples to gain self-determination.[35] The antinuclear weapons movement provided the foundation for the emergence of the anti-Vietnam War movement that succeeded it in the mid-1960s. The core pacifist groups provided one stream and the other came from the more politically centrist elements that had opposed nuclear weapons, such as the Committee for a Sane Nuclear Policy (SANE).

34. DeBenedetti, *American Ordeal*, 373.
35. Ibid., 22.

When American military involvement in Vietnam first gained the attention of peace activists in the early 1960s, the critique that emerged focused on four concerns. First, critics argued that the American military intervention was immoral. By this time, Americans were beginning to implement "scorched earth" policies such as the use of napalm, highly toxic chemical defoliants, and the forced relocation of peasants. Second, critics strongly doubted whether it would ever be possible, especially through the method of massive military violence, for the US to cultivate a genuinely independent, anti-communist South Vietnam (the stated goal of the intervention). Third, this intervention quite likely would endanger rather than enhance regional and global political stability. Finally, expanding this war in the face of domestic dissent would lead to repression of this dissent with disastrous consequences for American democracy.[36]

These four points remained at the heart of the antiwar argument for the next decade. The pacifist elements of the movement especially focused on the moral critique. They articulated persuasive arguments—but the broader antiwar movement tended to focus on the pragmatic parts of the critique. As the war's lack of success became more apparent, even in the face of the Johnson administration's dramatic expansion, opposition widened. But with the widening of the movement, many pacifist concerns were marginalized.

A particularly important fruit of the activists' antiwar work was the development of an alternative narrative to the government's pro-war propaganda. For example, the journal *Liberation*, largely founded and sustained by the War Resisters League, provided an outlet for thorough and sophisticated examinations of American policies and their consequences. The Friends and Mennonites, among others, provided an important resource by sending young people, often conscientious objectors performing alternative service, to Vietnam to engage in relief and development service. These on-the-ground participants supplied first person witness to the devastating consequences of the American intervention.[37]

The Catholic Worker peace witness among Catholics provided a powerful catalyst for what came to be some of the most widespread and influential expressions of Christian antiwar activity. Several young Catholic pacifists, including James Douglass, who as a graduate student in Rome had consulted with several bishops on peace issues during Vatican II, and Tom Cornell, who first burned his draft card in 1960, joined with the prominent Catholic writer-monk Thomas Merton to form the Catholic Peace Fellowship (CFP) in 1964. CFP members Daniel Berrigan and his fellow

36. Ibid., 88–90.
37. Miller, *Wise as Serpents*, 124–60.

priest brother Phil, became prominent antiwar activists during the Vietnam years. Both brothers sustained their radical pacifist witness in the decades following.[38]

A major innovation that strengthened activists' ability to get their message out emerged in March 1965 with the teach-in movement. The first teach-in was organized at the University of Michigan. It triggered a rapidly expanding movement. In the next week, more than thirty-five other colleges hosted teach-ins on Vietnam, and the number expanded to well over one hundred by the end of the school year. The expertise of peace groups such as FCNL and MCC as well as academics in various disciplines provided a solid core of content for these gatherings and the ongoing bases for persuasive alternative analyses of the war.[39]

Martin Luther King strongly opposed the war. He believed it posed a terrible danger to the effort to deepen racial and economic justice in the US as he presciently perceived that the government would be much more likely to cut back on its "war on poverty" should it feel the need to pour more resources into the war. Probably even more fundamentally, King rejected the war because of its inherent immorality. In the summer of 1965, King's tentative public war opposition drew strong fire from his pro-Johnson allies. By April 1967, though, King felt that he had no choice but to speak out unequivocally against the war. His speech, delivered at New York City's Riverside Church (and drafted in its first version by King's Mennonite associate Vincent Harding), provided a sophisticated critique both on pragmatic and principled grounds—and irrevocably deepened the gulf between King and Johnson.[40]

Though Richard Nixon defeated Johnson's vice-president Hubert Humphrey in the closely contested 1968 presidential election by claiming to have a "secret plan" for peace, he came into office with the intention to squash the antiwar movement. "For Nixon, antiwar activists were not communists. They were worse. They were Americans whose attack on the creed of global toughness represented an irresolution which Nixon saw as the Achilles' heal of democracy."[41] Nixon followed Johnson and tried to discredit war opponents as anti-American with the help of often illegal activities by the CIA and FBI.

In the fall of 1969, the antiwar movement organized its largest protests, the October Moratorium. At this point, a clear majority of American people polled identified themselves as "doves" (55 percent) rather than "hawks" (31

38. Polnar and O'Grady, *Disarmed and Dangerous*.
39. DeBenedetti, *American Ordeal*, 107–9.
40. Branch, *At Canaan's Edge*, 581–97.
41. DeBenedetti, *American Ordeal*, 240.

percent) and about 80 percent were "fed up and tired of the war." Yet, fewer than half of those polled supported the Moratorium action and about 60 percent agreed with Nixon's contention that "antiwar demonstrations aided the enemy."[42]

Over the next several years Nixon transformed the U.S. war effort—the numbers of American soldiers on the ground in Southeast Asia decreased while the air war accelerated. Nixon's popularity fluctuated wildly, as did the support for the opposition effort. At the time of the 1972 election, though Nixon managed to gain one of the largest landslide victories in American history, the antiwar forces in Congress also gained ground.

Nixon's hostility toward war opponents led to an increase in his administration's illegal actions, culminating in the Watergate scandal and his resignation. Even then, the new president, Gerald Ford, sought to continue American investment in the military victory of South Vietnam in the war. Finally, war opponents in Congress asserted themselves forcefully enough to make Ford end this support and pull American forces out altogether.[43] The South Vietnamese government very quickly collapsed and the successors to Ho Chi Minh (who had died in 1969) claimed victory and unified Vietnam under their communist government.

The antiwar movement gained strength by 1971 from an influx of veterans who, with great credibility, spoke against the war.[44] Another element that increased its influence was the draft resistance movement, and the willingness of potential draftees to seek conscientious objector status. By 1971, the Selective Service System had become overwhelmed with protests and appeals for reclassification and reached the point of collapse, leading the Nixon Administration to end the draft in 1972.[45]

For almost certainly the first time in world history, a massive protest movement opposing a nation's war arose *in the midst of* the war being fought. The antiwar movement clearly restrained the war-making proclivities of the American government—during the Vietnam War and in the years since. In the end, even after Nixon's resignation in disgrace as a result of his illegal efforts to undermine the antiwar movement, the American government's support for the war could well have continued indefinitely had not Congress finally pulled the plug on funding—due largely to the impact of the antiwar movement. After thirty years of continuously conscripting young Americans into the military, widespread resistance to the draft brought it to an end.

42. Ibid., 264.
43. Young, *Vietnam Wars*, 281–99.
44. DeBenedetti, *American Ordeal*, 306.
45. Ibid., 308–9.

And yet, the antiwar movement did not turn the tide against American militarism. Those responsible for the U.S. entering and prosecuting this terrible and self-destructive war suffered few repercussions. American militarism survived this period more or less intact, ready for reinvigoration in the 1980s with Ronald Reagan's contra war in Central America and expansion of nuclear weapons programs. In the years after 9/11, with the "war on terror," militarism expanded yet more. This sustenance of militarist dynamics even in the face of such a major failure as Vietnam stands as witness to the transformation wrought by the creation and maintenance of the American national security state directly as a consequence of the nation's investment in total war during World War II.[46]

The Vietnam War experience was a major contest between American democracy and American militarism. The military project experienced extraordinary on-the-ground failures and a strong consensus against the war effort that finally solidified by the early 1970s. Yet still, the momentum we may trace from Franklin Roosevelt's gearing up for military intervention in 1940 to Barack Obama's expanding of the American war effort in Central Asia seventy years later barely slowed.

The key element of the story of the opposition to the Vietnam War indeed may not be the movement's ineffectiveness nearly so much as the intransigence of the American federal government. Key policy makers realized after Lyndon Johnson's decision to expand the American military intervention that the war was unwinnable already in the mid-1960s.[47] The realization eventually spread to the highest levels (e.g., Johnson's defense secretary Robert McNamera and eventually Johnson himself). Yet the U.S. continued to visit tremendous destruction upon this small corner of the world for nearly a decade more—mainly for the purpose of international appearances. Sustaining this war profoundly damaged American democracy despite the extraordinary efforts of the antiwar movement.

CIVIL SOCIETY AND PEACEBUILDING

If the twentieth century saw unprecedented levels of destructive war-making, it also saw the emergence of numerous strategies to overcome the curse of warfare. The mass movements inspired by Gandhi, civil rights activism, resistance to nuclear weaponry and the Vietnam War, and the emergence of widespread development and relief work by organizations such as AFSC and MCC all witnessed to unprecedented levels of creative peacemaking.

46. Scahill, *Dirty Wars*.
47. Ellsberg, *Secrets*, 126–42.

PART THREE: Alternatives   *Servanthood*   239

In the latter part of the century, promising alternatives to ever-spiraling militarism and violent responses to conflicts emerged, often linked under the rubric "civil society." Mary Kaldor, one of the field's more prominent thinkers, defines civil society as "the process through which individuals negotiate, argue, struggle against, or agree with each other and with the centers of political and economic authority." These "individuals" address their concerns "through voluntary associations, movements, parties, [and] unions."[48]

Widespread use of the term *civil society* arose in the 1970s and 1980s in resistance movements that brought change—mostly without violence—in central and eastern Europe and in Latin America. Both regions were dominated by militarized governments, and in both cases dictatorships ended and political cultures changed due to the success of largely nonviolent resistance.[49] People from these two regions, although they faced similar problems and approached them in similar ways at roughly the same time, had little if any direct interaction. Kaldor suggests that they failed to collaborate because the Latin American movement gained impetus from the political left and included numerous Marxists while the European movement was self-consciously anti-Marxist.[50]

Despite the lack of synergy between the two efforts, civil society became a global movement. Latin Americans during the 1970s and 1980s forged important ties with North American human rights activists, and the central and eastern Europeans linked closely with those in western Europe who worked for peace and human rights. The various movements all sought to utilize their respective countries' formal acceptance of international human rights legislation.[51]

We may understand "civil society," in a broad sense, as efforts to construct and cultivate alternatives to military-centered concepts of social order. Certainly these well-known efforts at social change in Europe and Latin America are important examples, as is the work in South Africa to end apartheid.[52] On a much smaller scale, illuminating a "servanthood approach," we may consider Mennonite contributions to civil society.

For Mennonites, World War II and the Vietnam War both became times of creativity. In the run up to World War II, Mennonites played a major role in negotiations with the government, leading to the establishment

48. Kaldor, *Human Security*, 136.
49. See Ackerman and Duvall, *Force More Powerful*, especially chs. 3 ("Poland: Power from Solidarity") and 7 ("Argentina and Chile: Resisting Repression").
50. Kaldor, *Human Security*, 137–38.
51. Ibid., 139–40.
52. See Ackerman and Duvall, *Force More Powerful*, ch. 9 ("South Africa: Campaigning against Apartheid").

of Civilian Public Service. To a lesser extent than other groups of conscientious objectors, Mennonites did not find CPS to be an unacceptable case of government control over dissent. Mennonites, by and large, were happy with their experience in finding freedom to express their unwillingness to participate in the War and with their opportunity to find outlets for their service concerns.[53] Mennonites were ready when the War ended to devote creative efforts to war relief and international development, mostly under the auspices of the Mennonite Central Committee.

With Vietnam, Mennonite responses reflected increased acculturation. Unlike World War II, when no Mennonite COs refused to cooperate with the draft, during Vietnam numerous Mennonites were non-cooperators. Some went to prison and others moved to Canada.[54] A number of other Mennonites who did cooperate with Selective Service, actually performed their alternative service in Southeast Asia and ended up playing a role in educating legislators and the broader American public about the actual events on the ground in the war areas.[55]

In part to facilitate the witness in the U.S. of their personnel who served in Southeast Asia, MCC established a formal presence in Washington DC. MCC's Washington Office also sought to speak to governmental officials on other issues and to report to Mennonite congregations of events in the nation's capital. This presence in Washington signaled important shifts in Mennonite understandings of the shape of their tradition's convictions about peace.[56]

Increasing numbers of Mennonites sought to exert a more direct influence on their wider political culture. Mennonites were no longer as content with a separatist pacifism.[57] Although the new development did involve Mennonites in political advocacy centered on trying to influence governmental leaders, Mennonites also sought to find other avenues as well for their social concerns. Interest in these other avenues led Mennonites to seek alternatives to warfare and violence that linked with the civil society movement. The most common term by the beginning of the twenty-first century for these efforts was "peacebuilding."

The roots of the Mennonite involvement in peacebuilding go back at least to the years shortly after World War II. As soon as possible after the

---

53. Grimsrud, "Ethical, Analysis of Conscientious Objection," 163–204.
54. Miller and Shenk, *Path of Most Resistance*.
55. See Martin, *Reaching the Other Side*.
56. Miller, *Wise as Serpents*.
57. Driedger and Kraybill, *Mennonite Peacemaking*; Stutzman, *From Nonresistance to Justice*.

War, American Mennonites spread around the world as personnel with MCC. They encountered first hand the devastation of the War, offering the help they could (help that indeed meant the difference between life and death for many people). While glad for the opportunity to serve in these ways, numerous MCCers came to the conviction that more than relief was needed. One of these relief workers told how she was challenged in a way typical to many others: "What you're doing here is fine," she was told. "But it's Band-Aid work. You came after the war, after the damage was done. Why don't you go home and work for peace and get at the root causes of evil and war?"[58]

Many Mennonites took this challenge to heart and came to believe they should try to address the dynamics that lead to international violence. "Mennonite relief workers were taught by their hosts that it was not enough for relief workers to distribute food and clothing to the starving and homeless. The starving and homeless articulated the need for more than material assistance. Mennonites were asked also to be peacemakers, to work at changing systems and institutions that caused suffering."[59]

Even with this catalyst to stimulate Mennonite efforts to broaden their practice of peacemaking,[60] it took another couple of decades after the War and the trauma of the Vietnam War for clear and distinct efforts to coalesce. Specifically, I will mention conflict resolution, restorative justice, and direct intervention in places of conflict around the world.[61]

Peace studies professor Robert Kreider (himself a World War II CO) accurately sketched in a June 9, 1975, memo developments to come:

> We sense there may be need and receptivity for the services of a panel of persons on tap to intervene, mediate, and provide consultative services in crisis situations—including a variety of conflict skills such as assessment, strategizing, organizing,

---

58. This quote concerns MCC relief worker Hedy Sawatsky. Quoted in Miller, "History of the Mennonite Conciliation Service," 7.

59. Ibid.

60. For one account of responses to the military draft during the 1950s and 1960s, see Redekop, *Pax Story*.

61. We may also note a different kind of peacemaking fruit that emerged from the experience of Mennonite Central Committee workers in post-World War II relief work. John Howard Yoder was a North American Mennonite relief worker who began serving in Europe in 1949. Over the next decade, responding to his immersion in helping bring life back after the War's devastation, Yoder began to develop a distinctive theological program that is now recognized as the most profound effort to ground pacifism in Christian convictions. This effort gained its most notable expression in his *Politics of Jesus*. The story of the direct link between Yoder's European experience and his influential books is told in Zimmerman, *Practicing the Politics of Jesus*, 70–100.

coalition-formation, negotiation, empowerment, etc. . . . [This] could open avenues for peacemaking that go beyond the traditional roles of making statements on issues of war and peace.[62]

A few years later, MCC hired a full-time staff person to begin Mennonite Conciliation Services (MCS). Mennonites found conciliation and mediation attractive options that provided a possibility for peacemaking activity that would stand in the "middle ground between protest and civil disobedience, on the one hand, and traditional quietism, on the other." This kind of peacemaking activity "was considered more socially engaging and less radical."[63]

As conciliation work evolved among Mennonites, it naturally spread to include taking peacebuilding expertise to various conflicts around the world where Mennonite conciliators make important contributions—for example, Northern Ireland, Somalia, and Nicaragua. MCC began a new effort, the International Conciliation Services. A graduate program in peacebuilding was established at Eastern Mennonite University in the mid-1990s, and the program's founding professor, John Paul Lederach, became an international authority.[64] One of the most influential efforts of this peacebuilding program is its Summer Peacebuilding Institute that every year attracts hundreds of students from dozens of countries, many of whom return home to play leadership roles in their nation's social life, especially in conflict resolution work on all levels.[65]

About the same time Mennonites established MCS, an independent effort also emerged that drew on many of the same cultural and convictional resources from Mennonite communities. This work in the pioneering arena of restorative justice—efforts in the criminal justice field to reduce violence and increase possibilities for reconciliation between victims and offenders—also gained MCC support.

Mennonites established some of the first Victim-Offender Reconciliation Programs in the 1970s and MCC established a Criminal Justice Office in 1977. This office was staffed by Howard Zehr who became an international leader in the restorative justice movement. Zehr's book *Changing Lenses*[66] provided philosophical and theological bases for approaching

62. Quoted in Miller, "History of the Mennonite Conciliation Service," 9–10.
63. Ibid., 11.
64. One of Lederach's particularly important books was published by the United States Institute of Peace: *Building Peace*.
65. Probably the most famous alum of this program is Liberian Leymah Gbowee, winner of the Nobel Peace Prize in 2011.
66. Zehr, *Changing Lenses*.

criminal justice with a focus more on bringing healing to victims, offenders, and their communities than on retributive and punitive policies that tend only to heighten the spiral of violence.

Restorative justice has gained quite a bit of traction in various segments of the criminal justice system. It has also, especially as presented by Zehr, other Mennonites,[67] and allies,[68] provided perspectives for a broader philosophy of dealing with conflict and wrongdoing.

Along with these recent developments in peacebuilding, Mennonites have remained committed to resisting war itself. Militancy in war resistance that grew in segments of the broader society during the Vietnam War had parallels in Mennonite communities. In the years following the end of that war, Mennonites and likeminded pacifists worked to establish a nonviolent peacekeeping force that began in 1986 called Christian Peacemaker Teams (CPT).[69] CPT activists visit various hot spots around the world (e.g., Israel/Palestine, Colombia, Iraq, the Chiapas region in Mexico) seeking both to "get in the way of war" and to observe and provide first-hand reports on these various conflicts.

These examples (conflict mediation, restorative justice, and peacemaker teams) reflect the fruitfulness of Mennonite "servanthood" that sought to find concrete ways both to address the roots of war and to aid in actual conflict situations. All are examples of "civil society" work as defined by those in the 1980s who reinvigorated that concept in face of intractable authoritarian and totalitarian governments. As such, their efforts stand in contradistinction with the spiral toward ever-dominant militarism traced in the first two sections of this book. Their weight is tiny, but they point to what is likely the only way out of the "iron cage" of the national security state.

---

67. See Redekop, *Changing Paradigms*, and Sawatsky, *Justpeace Ethics*.

68. See Christopher Marshall's two books: *Beyond Retribution* and *Compassionate Justice*.

69. The definitive history, from a participant, is Kern, *In Harm's Way*.

11

Conclusion: World War II's Moral Legacy

In uncountable discussions I have had over the years about the ethics of war and peace, whenever pacifism comes up, so too does World War II. At least for Americans, this war stands not as the "war that ended other wars" nearly so much as the "war that justified other wars." World War II shows, in the American "good war" mythology, that sometimes going to war is the best option when it comes to dealing with the "bad guys."

Unfortunately, seeing war as sometimes the best option leads to empowering the societal structures that are needed to *prepare* for war—and such empowerment has loosed on American society transformative forces. In the past the nation inclined toward an attitude that you go to war as a last resort. Now, the nation sees many conflicts throughout the world that require a militarized first response. Hence, the extraordinary American military presence around the world, the way the United States spends about as much on its military as the rest of the world combined, and the situation that has faced American voters where their choice has been limited to two versions of militarism.

Borrowing from social critic Naomi Klein's analysis of recent American history, *The Shock Doctrine: The Rise of Disaster Capitalism*, we could say that the "shock" of total war in the early 1940s led directly to the takeover of the United States by advocates of the American national security ideology. That point of vulnerability led to the creation of permanent structures such as the Pentagon, the Central Intelligence Agency, and the nuclear weapons program. As a consequence of the transformative influence of these entities, in the United States "all politics is a politics of war" (Walter Wink).[1]

It is also the case that seriously to doubt the justness of World War II is almost entirely unheard of. Even historians who raise questions about the War's justness almost invariably conclude that indeed the War ultimately was just.[2] And for many others, likely the large majority of American historians, simply to raise moral questions about the War is unacceptable. As Eric Bergerud wrote: "I find it almost incomprehensible that anyone would claim to discover moral ambiguity in World War II.... If World War II was not necessary, no war has been."[3]

Certainty such as that expressed by Bergerud, though, does not free us from critical moral reflection on World War II. The need for moral reflection is actually heightened given the impact of beliefs such as his on attitudes about militarism in the generations since that war. Though we do not see much evidence of it actually working this way, the just war tradition has at its core claims that should lead to a rejection of Bergerud's assertion that a war stands as a just war simply because it is deemed "necessary."

This book has presented a case for the way just war analysis—and moral reflection in general—*should* work. Such reflection establishes stable criteria for moral evaluation and then applies those objectively to the actions of both one's enemies and of oneself and one's friends and allies. Norman Davies, a rare historian who does apply this approach to his account of World War II, expresses it this way: "All sound moral judgments operate on the basis that the standards applied to one side of the relationship must be applied to all sides."[4]

NOT A JUST WAR

As I have argued, when we use the two basic categories of just war analysis—cause and conduct—we may find a great deal of evidence (decisive, in my view) that this was not a just war for the United States.

It is true that the official entry of the United States into the War as a full-fledged protagonist came about due to two events that few would question provided just cause: (1) the Japanese attack on the American naval base

---

1. Wink, *Engaging the Powers*.
2. See, for example, Bess, *Choices Under Fire*, 338–45; Rose, *Myth of the Greatest Generation*, 251–54.
3. Bergerud, "Critique of *Choices Under Fire*," 41.
4. Davies, *No Simple Victory*, 63.

at Pearl Harbor, December 7, 1941, and (2) the German declaration of war on the United States a few days later.

However, neither of these events initiated the U.S. involvement in the War—involvement that was anything but an expression of genuine neutrality (the official status of the U.S. in relation to the conflicts prior to Pearl Harbor). The U.S. was strongly on the side of Great Britain in the conflict with the Germans and on the side of China in the conflict with the Japanese. The events in early December 1941, thus, were actually steps of acceleration in an ever-growing conflict between the U.S. and the Axis powers rather than the beginning of the conflict.

So, we should ask if the American entry into the conflict prior to the overt declarations of war had just causes. But when we do, things get more ambiguous. The "good war mythology" tends to cite three main reasons why U.S. involvement in the War meets the criterion of just cause: (1) the need to protect the U.S. from a direct invasion by Germany and/or Japan; (2) the moral imperative to stop the domination of the tyrannies of Nazi Germany and imperial Japan in the cause of furthering democracy; and (3) the need to do everything possible to rescue the Jews who were being annihilated by the Nazis.

In the actual event, though, it appears that none of these three reasons actually played a major role in American involvement. We have no evidence that either the Japanese or the Germans had in mind a serious attempt to conquer and occupy the United States. And no one who understood military possibilities could have imagined a successful invasion of the United States that would have to cross either the Pacific or Atlantic Oceans.

Surely, many Americans opposed the tyrannical dynamics in Japan and, especially, Germany. However, the United States and Britain joined in alliance with a regime equally tyrannical as Hitler's Germany—the Soviet Union under the dominance of Stalin. Insofar as this alliance actually helped sustain and even advance Soviet tyranny, we can scarcely say that the cause for the U.S. engaging in the conflict was to defeat tyranny.

The question of "saving Jews" is perhaps even more clear-cut than the other two. Many American and British leaders looked positively upon the Nazis in 1933 as a bulwark against communist influences. When the Nazis came into power they immediately began implementing anti-Jewish policies. As the violence toward Jews increased, humanitarian voices were raised to offer aid for the beleaguered Jews. Mostly the humanitarian efforts were thwarted by U.S. and British political leaders. When the War actually began and the genocidal violence increased, these leaders continued to *resist* efforts to offer help. The western Allies simply were not motivated by a desire directly to save Jewish lives. In fact, the War's expansion likely had the impact of making the lot of Europe's Jews even worse.

Why, then, did the U.S. engage in policies that made war inevitable and then engage in a total war to defeat the Axis powers? Partly, the U.S. had been involved in a clash of imperialisms with Japan dating back at least to the 1920s and accelerating with competing desires for dominance in China. The war with Japan happened because of a series of escalating moves taken by both sides in the conflict.

As well, the U.S. developed close ties with Great Britain, and so offered ever-increasing aid to the British after September 1939 and the outbreak of war in Europe. This aid took an ever-more overtly militaristic cast and involved the U.S. in the conflict as a partisan ally of the British. The British war with the Germans initially most overtly stemmed from the British war-alliance with the Polish dictatorship, an alliance entered into largely due to British imperial concerns (not due to noble motives such as self-determination and disarmament as later claimed).

In time, it became clear that the United States would benefit greatly from this war and that the forces within the United States who would benefit the most were the military and business elites. The War was an opportunity for the military to move into an unprecedented place of power and influence within the federal government, and it was an opportunity for American corporations to profit immensely from the U.S. becoming the one global economic superpower.

None of these dynamics satisfy the traditional criteria for just cause for going to war (e.g., self-preservation, defending innocent victims, serving the interests of the entire country, leading to a better peace than existed before the war).

Many who write about World War II seem to assume that the causes were just—and then act as if that ends the process of moral discernment. Even if the causes were clearly just (and I believe that they were not), the just war tradition—based on its stated values—*should* insist that the moral discernment is only beginning. The second area of concern for just war thought, after reflection on whether the cause is just, is to reflect morally on how the war is conducted. In brief, the two main criteria used to judge conduct are proportionality (that the damage caused by the fighting not outweigh the good the war accomplished) and noncombatant immunity (that those not engaged as soldiers in the conflict not be the direct object of military actions).

In relation to both of these criteria, the conduct of the United States military clearly crossed the line into forbidden behavior. Most obviously, the U.S. provided support when the British attacked the inner city of

Hamburg and intentionally created a firestorm that killed tens of thousands of noncombatants. Later, the Americans cooperated fully with the attack February 1945 on the defenseless German city of Dresden, a city with no military significance—an attack that likely killed well over fifty thousand noncombatants.

As the U.S. turned its focus on Japan, the first of a series of attacks on defenseless Japanese cities, March 9, 1945 on Tokyo, created another firestorm, surpassing the deaths caused in the bombing of Dresden. The climax of the American attacks on Japanese civilian populations came in August 1945 with the first use of atomic bombs—first on Hiroshima, then on Nagasaki. With these attacks, any pretense of adhering to standards of proportionality and noncombatant immunity was abandoned.

We might also add the practices of America and Britain's key ally in the War, the Soviet Union. The Soviets' conduct was extraordinarily brutal. In allying with the Soviets the U.S. actually empowered a spirit at least as vicious as the spirit of Nazism—the spirit of Stalinism. As the Soviets turned back the German invasion and moved toward Berlin, their tactics were some of the most brutal violations of just conduct criteria that had ever been perpetrated upon enemy noncombatant populations—murder, rape, destruction of civilian infrastructure, and more.

When I apply the just war criteria to the American involvement to World War II, I conclude that it was not a just war. I do acknowledge that the Axis powers were guilty of aggression and many atrocities and, thus, that those who tried to stop them did so with justice on their side. However, it does not actually appear that the main focus of the aggression of the Axis was aimed toward the U.S., certainly not until after the Americans had devoted much effort to opposing the Axis. And it also does not actually appear that the Allies were motivated by the need to stop the atrocities—and in fact one of the three main Allies (the Soviet Union) had itself engaged in extraordinary atrocities in the years prior to the War.

And even if the Axis powers did egregiously violate just conduct standards from the start of the conflict, that does not justify violations by the Allies. The U.S. did not enter World War II for just cause or prosecute it with just means. As well, the moral legacy of the War does not only have to do with what had happened through August 1945. We also need to consider the impact of prosecuting the War on American society and the aftermath of the War in relation to American foreign policy as explored in Part Two above.

What if World War II was an unjust war? Obviously that judgment cannot change the past (I will reflect below on how we can imagine different policies, though, and the limited relevance of such imagining). The main issue related to how we now think about World War II is how this might impact our *current* disposition toward American military policies and toward warfare in general.

If we conclude that World War II was unjust, and if we join with that conclusion a conviction that we should never act unjustly or support unjust actions (which *should* be part of the set of assumptions just war philosophy affirms), then we will no longer use that war as a basis for arguing for the necessity of warfare. If we can't use the War as such a basis, we will have a much more difficult time making such an argument in general. Certainly the wars the U.S. has engaged in since World War II have even less chance of meeting the criteria for just wars.

WHY THIS UNJUST WAR WAS A MORAL DISASTER FOR THE UNITED STATES

At the end of World War II, the U.S. stood with unprecedented economic power and unmatched international prestige as the bearer of the ideals portrayed to great effect in statements such as the Atlantic Charter and the initial declaration of the "United Nations." These statements rallied people to defeat forces in the world that stood implacably against ideals such as self-determination and disarmament.

The generations that have followed have shown that the U.S. was not a good steward of the power it possessed in 1945. What the War actually did for the United States was push the country in deeply problematic directions. The impact of the War was to: (1) decisively corrupt the American democratic polity, (2) decisively empower the forces of militarism in the country that have since 1945 led the U.S. into foreign policy disaster after foreign policy disaster and visited so much violence and destruction on major sections of the world that the term "American holocaust"[5] may not be much of a hyperbole, and (3) decisively shift the economic center of gravity in the country toward the corporate sector, setting the country on a path of long-term corruption, exploitation, and—in a genuine sense—economic self-immolation.

The basic moral lesson we should learn from World War II is that we must find ways to *resist* the lure of trust in military action. Certainly the rise of the Axis powers created the need for decisive resistance to their politics of extraordinarily destructive nationalistic brute power and nihilism. But the path of resistance that American society took, while in a superficial and short-term sense victorious, actually itself led to the long-term victory of

5. Blum, *Killing Hope*.

"nationalistic brute power and nihilism." If even this "good war" led to such a moral disaster, then Americans (for their own sake and for the sake of the wider world) must find ways to resist the evils of aggressive militarism that do not rely on the use of aggressive militarism.

Pursuing an unjust war, as you would expect, had numerous long-term morally devastating consequences. When a democracy pursues a war that does not clearly have a just cause, it is inevitable that the democratic processes will be corrupted. In theory, a just war approach should enhance democracy because if the benefit of doubt is against going to war, it will take clear and persuasive evidence to justify the war. This evidence should be publicly presented, with open debate, and if the case is *not* made, then the nation should not go to war. And just causes should be factors that are consistent with genuine national security and the best interests of the nation.

In the lead up to World War II, though, we do not see from the democratically elected government led by Franklin Roosevelt an honest setting out of the factors for and against intervention and an illumination of the democratic values at stake. Rather, we see a propaganda campaign that was an exercise in pro-war advocacy that distorted the facts and, perhaps most tellingly, fanned unwarranted fears of American national security being breached through the dangers of invasion.

When the War did come, the stage was set for *ongoing* policymaking that paid little heed to democratic practices and would long outlast the "emergency" that initially justified it. The most notable examples are the creation of the atomic weapons program and the insistence upon unconditional surrender as a nonnegotiable war goal.

The prosecution of World War II permanently transformed the American way of fighting. A main example would be the reluctance to target civilians that characterized the philosophy of the emerging American air warfare prior to 1941. This reluctance was completely gone by the end of the War; witness the firebombing of Tokyo and the use of atomic bombs on Hiroshima and Nagasaki. The ensuing wars—Korea and Vietnam most notably—saw unrestrained air warfare that completely disregarded the just war criteria of proportionality and noncombatant immunity.

And, of course, the continued development and willingness to deploy ever-more destructive nuclear weapons witnesses to such a disregard for just war constraints. Numerous times (e.g., Korea, Cuba, Vietnam, even Central America in the 1980s) major policy makers in the U.S. actively advocated the use of nuclear bombs. That they were in the end not used does not change the reality that they easily could have been.

In 1937, the U.S. military was small and peripheral to the society as a whole. It ranked in size sixteenth in the world, between Portugal and

Romania. Today, we cannot imagine the U.S. as such a *non-militarized* society. In the late 1930s, important people in the country did not approve of what they called military "unpreparedness." They were ready to take advantage of the deteriorating international order. They moved the country toward what proved to be an extraordinary reorientation of the nation's priorities that shifted the American military from the periphery to the center of the society—permanently.

At first, public opinion and congressional policies remained reluctant to move from the official neutrality and nonintervention of American foreign policy. After Germany invaded Poland in September 1939 and America's close British ally declared war, the pro-intervention campaign increased its intensity, and Roosevelt moved the country closer toward engagement. Even two years later, though, while the U.S. was actively supporting the British war effort—as well as the Chinese struggle against Japanese aggression—the votes still were not present for Roosevelt to move the country the final step into open warfare.

Three months before the U.S. formally entered the War, ground was broken for the Pentagon on September 11, 1941—at a location, both symbolically and geographically, some distance from the center of the federal government across the Potomac River. The huge physical structure was completed with remarkable speed. The stage was set for the American military to gain a large measure of freedom from the constraints of the democratic checks and balances of Washington politics and governmental oversight. Then, the next month, Roosevelt approved the establishment of a program to create atomic weapons. The Manhattan Project remained top secret but soon absorbed tremendous resources and inexorably moved the country into a future of tremendous peril.

The War itself saw an irreversible transformation. Never again would it be thinkable that the American military would rank with second- and third-rate militaries such as Portugal and Romania. By the end of the War, the U.S. military was the world's most powerful. World War II provided the "shock" that empowered those supportive of the armed forces to establish and empower these key engines for ongoing militarization. The Pentagon and the nuclear weapons program gained their sense of legitimacy from the "needs" of total war—and then, when the War was over—devoted their energies to retaining and actually expanding their domination of the American body politic.

Then, the National Security Act of 1947 established the Central Intelligence Agency and consolidated the various branches of the military. It also created the National Security Council as a top leadership group to guide the nation's policies. Around this same time, President Truman delivered his famous speech that delineated the Truman Doctrine that asserted, in effect, that any resistance to American hegemony anywhere in the world would be seen as a communist threat and a basis for military intervention. The die was cast.

So, World War II was a test of whether war in fact can ever serve the moral good. In effect, it was an effort to test the hypothesis that war might occasionally be necessary and can even be good. After all, we may point to many reasons why this war was necessary. We probably cannot overstate the moral corruption of Nazi Germany and its aggressive efforts to spread that corruption. Imperial Japan was almost as bad. And, for the United States, at least, the war was won at relatively low cost and led to unprecedented prosperity and power in its aftermath—that is, the world's pioneering democracy was in position to further its ideals of freedom and self-determination.

Yet, look what happened. The very effort of prosecuting this greatest of all wars led directly to a transformation of the United States—from a nonmilitarized, relatively free and democratic nation to a global power that became seemingly unable to turn away from a devastatingly self-destructive pursuit of empire.

What do we learn? That war does not work. War resembles the "one ring of power" of J. R. R. Tolkien's *Lord of the Rings*. The One is a product of evil and ultimately can only serve evil. Many "good" people tried or imagined trying to wrest the One ring for life-enhancing purposes. But the ring always would win out and the wielder would be transformed. The story of World War II as a moral disaster confirms that Tolkien's insights apply to the "one ring" of warfare.

THE DISASTER THAT WAS WORLD WAR II: HOW COULD THINGS HAVE BEEN DIFFERENT?

I have tried in this book to focus on the actual events that happened in the lead up to World War II, in the War itself, and in its aftermath. I have argued that what did happen was a moral disaster for the United States—both the War itself and its aftermath. Here I want to spend a bit of time on a thought experiment. I will imagine various events that could have been handled differently and possibly led to a morally better result.

I suggest that nothing was inevitable. The disastrous events need not have happened like they did. More than make a case concerning the moral failures of decision makers, though, I emphasize that we need not continue on the same spiral toward disaster that the U.S. seems stuck in. If those decisions could have been different, so too could current and future decisions.

As well, I argue in this book against the mythology that valorizes World War II as a necessary war, a good war, that was fought in the most just way possible. To suggest a number of ways things could have been different might lead us even more to question the necessity, goodness, and justness of the War. And that could lead us to reject the logic that links the "goodness" of World War II to the need today to prepare for future "necessary" wars.

I have chosen nine examples of how things could have been different—with less disastrous results. I avoid a series of hypotheticals where one is dependent upon one or more earlier hypothetical. Generally, each example accepts that earlier alternative scenarios did not happen. I focus mainly on decisions Americans made (or did not). Almost all of these follow from just war criteria and ideals. None assumes pacifism. I believe that all would have been pragmatically preferable for American interests (that is, the interests of the American people, if not the American business and political elite).

Don't Enter World War I

Many people now say that what we call World War I and World War II were not actually two distinct conflicts but more one extended struggle. At the least, it seems certain that the devastation wrought by World War I set the stage for World War II. Had the first war not happened surely the second would not have either.

The Great War was well underway before the United States entered it in 1917. However, the U.S. entry did tip the balance toward Great Britain and France and led to their victory. Had the U.S. not entered this war, we can easily imagine a less definite outcome. While we can't say what the long-term consequences would have been had this war ended in something closer to a draw, it does seem likely that the seeds for World War II that were sown in the uneasy peace established following the Great War might well have not been sown. Germany might not have faced the bitterness-enhancing punitive damages. It is possible to imagine an outcome that might have been less problematic for future peace. So, the U.S. choice to enter the Great War had negative consequences—and it certainly was not inevitable.

If the U.S. had truly played a neutral role, focusing its energies on obtaining a peaceful outcome rather the victory of one side over the other, it is also quite likely that the U.S. would have been positioned to play a major role in the post-Great War world. Plus, the possibility of playing such a role likely would not have aroused the hostility within the U.S. toward international engagement that the actual fighting in the war did. So the U.S. would have been situated to play a more significant role in international affairs than it did, and likely as a peacemaker rather than as a partisan.

Work for Better Postwar Relationships

The U.S. could have worked harder and more effectively for a more just and peace-fostering arrangement after the war ended—by insisting, for example, that the British and French not treat Germany so punitively. At the least, the Americans could have done more to aid Germany in postwar reconstruction and to support democratic forces in the Weimer Republic.

As well, the U.S. could have done more to seek a positive relationship with the ultimate victors in the Russian Revolution. A more positive relationship with the Bolsheviks may have helped strengthen more moderate forces in what became the Soviet Union and prevented the disastrous takeover by Stalin and his supporters. And even after Stalin gained power, the U.S. could have done more to reduce the fears the Soviet government justifiably had that the Western powers sought their overthrow—fears that surely made life much worse for people in the Soviet Union and strengthened the position of its most militaristic and tyrannical forces.

Cultivate a Positive Relationship with Japan

This point may be the most obvious one on this list. Not many Americans today realize that Japan had been an ally of the Allies during World War I. Japan had an especially strong relationship with the British. Japan's desire to sustain this relationship may be seen in its willingness to sign treaties that limited the size of its navy in relation to the U.S. and Britain shortly after World War I.

However, the U.S., with its ambitions to heighten its economic presence in the Far East tended to see Japan as a rival. In the 1920s, the Americans exerted strong pressure on the British to distance themselves from the Japanese, despite the recent history of close alliance between the British and Japanese. This was a fateful move by the Americans, as it understandably distressed the Japanese to be pushed away.

Japan during the 1920s and 1930s endured intense internal political struggles between those more inclined toward cooperative relationships with the West and those who sought a militarized style of Japanese independence and dominance of the Far East. The latter forces tended to have the upper hand, partly due to a series of assassinations of more moderate political leaders. The Japanese military grew in power, its ability to do so

PART THREE: Alternatives   Conclusion: World War II's Moral Legacy   255

greatly enhanced by the Americans' efforts to prevent the sustenance of the Japanese/British alliance and in other ways to exacerbate tensions between the two nations.

Overtly Work to Aid Threatened Jews in Germany after the Nazis Came to Power

We have seen that the plight of Europe's Jews actually had little effect on the American entry into the conflict nor on the way that the War was prosecuted once the U.S. became a full participant. So earlier efforts to help threatened Jews would not have themselves provided an alternative to going to war in the actual event.

However, to the extent that the War is at least after the fact justified as necessary for the sake of the Jews, we could say that earlier intervention would have made the war *less* necessary. One of the great ironies of the events in the lead-up to the War is that it was in fact principled pacifists who worked the hardest to address the emerging crises for Europe's Jews. Some Quakers even intervened directly, drawing on their positive reputation in Germany due to post-World War I relief efforts to lobby with Nazi leaders for openness for Jewish emigration. The hold up came not from the Nazis but from the American and British leaders who refused to make allowance for more than a tiny number of Jewish immigrants and, later, refugees.

It would seem that hundreds of thousands of Jews who perished in the Holocaust could have escaped that fate had the nations of the world been willing to allow them refuge. The tone-setters for the refusal to do so were the Americans and British. Concrete support for Jews may also have reduced the impunity with which the Nazis prosecuted their genocidal work.

Even more ironic, then, is that the main response America had to German tyranny was military-centered, ultimately total war. This response pushed the Nazis toward genocide rather than deportation as their means of dealing with the "Jewish problem." Even after it became known on the outside that the genocide was happening, America's war leaders insisted on ignoring that set of atrocities in favor of focusing on simply winning the war and achieving "unconditional surrender"—making it possible for the Nazis to come much closer to their goal of total eradication of Europe's Jews.

Don't Move the Pacific Fleet to Pearl Harbor

The U.S. took what was surely an intentionally provocative step in moving the core of its Pacific naval force to the base at the American colony of

Hawaii in the late 1930s. This occurred in the midst of growing tensions with Japan and only added to the Japanese sense that the Americans sought militarily to dominate the Pacific region.

Now, certainly the Japanese aggression on China and expansionistic policies in general heightened the sense of conflict between the Japanese and U.S. The move to Pearl Harbor could reasonably be justified as an effort simply to enhance American preparedness in face of the growing problems. However, a different strategy that took steps diplomatically to reduce the tensions rather than act directly to exacerbate them would have been possible.

When the Japanese attacked Pearl Harbor, they took a step that made the ensuing war inevitable. However, if the U.S. had not so greatly expanded their Hawaiian presence, it is almost certain the Japanese would not (nor could not) have undertaken such an attack. Many U.S. military leaders had opposed the move to Hawaii partly because they believed it would make the American forces more vulnerable to such an attack—and partly because they believed that that move would not actually noticeably enhance American military readiness.

Don't Begin the Manhattan Project, and Don't Build the Pentagon in Virginia

The two steps that most decidedly moved the U.S. toward its permanent war footing both were taken *before* the U.S. entered World War II. These were the initiation of the effort to construct nuclear weapons—the Manhattan Project—and the decision to build the Pentagon. Neither of these steps were necessary at the time, but once taken proved to be irreversible.

When the initial proposal to create nuclear weapons came to President Roosevelt, no one knew whether such a weapon would work. But it was clear that the effort to make nuclear weapons would require an extraordinary expenditure of finances and scientific creativity. Roosevelt could have decided not to pursue this path—maybe on pragmatic grounds that the success was not assured, that it was difficult to imagine any other nation being able to create such a weapon, and that the resources could be better spent elsewhere. Not to mention, Roosevelt could have decided that the nation's best energies should be spent in creating peace and preventing the expansion of the War. Roosevelt could also have decided on moral grounds that such a weapon must not be built. He could have recognized that a bomb of such a magnitude would by definition wreak unjustifiable destruction on civilian populations and the natural world.

With the Pentagon, American political leaders could have insisted that the tradition of keeping the military under civilian control meant that moving military headquarters away from the center of the federal government in Washington would not be acceptable. Surely, if it truly was necessary for the military leadership to expand its footprint in face of the emerging "emergency," space could have been found for new construction in the District of Columbia nearer the civilian centers of government.

Roosevelt could have recognized and shaped his actions by the concern that once the military was allowed the kind of autonomy the construction of the Pentagon would provide, it would be impossible to reign the armed forces back in. At the least, he could have insisted more firmly on his initial command (that was ignored by Pentagon builders) greatly to reduce the size of the facility and made more sure that the military headquarters would move back to DC once the War ended.

Respond Positively to Japanese Initiative Just Prior to Pearl Harbor

We seemingly have no way of knowing how seriously to take the peace initiatives taken by Japanese prime minister, Fuminaro Konoe, in the summer and early fall of 1941. However, it is difficult to excuse the Roosevelt administration for not at least meeting with Konoe and seeing what possibilities for avoiding a military confrontation he might have offered.

Konoe was scarcely a peace advocate, and he likely had only limited control over the dynamics within Japan. He may not actually have been in a position to resist the movement toward war that characterized the military leaders. However, it does appear that Konoe recognized the likelihood of a major conflict and sensed that this would be disastrous for Japan. He did have the role as the official leader of the Japanese government and may have had the ability to shape the direction policies would go.

The tragedy here lies in Roosevelt's unwillingness even to try to find a path around the impending conflict. What we do know is that finally, following one American rebuff after another, Konoe resigned as prime minister and was replaced by one of Japan's most extreme militarists, General Hideki Tojo. Within a couple of months, under Tojo's leadership, the Japanese attacked Pearl Harbor.

Don't Insist on Unconditional Surrender

One central element of the criteria for waging a just war is the expectation that when one goes to war, one seeks to resolve the conflict as soon as possible and that one does as little damage as necessary. The American commitment to making unconditional surrender a non-negotiable commitment in how the War would be prosecuted violated this just war expectation.

Had the Americans not insisted on the centrality of unconditional surrender (and it is important to note that neither Churchill nor Stalin agreed with Roosevelt's decision), the War more likely could have been fought in ways that satisfied just conduct criteria. It would have been more possible to remain committed to noncombatant immunity and refrain from joining in the British saturation bombing of German cities and, especially, to refrain from the fire-bombing of Tokyo. These excesses not only did not succeed in directly leading to surrender, they also set terrible precedents for the practice of air war in future conflicts such as Korea and Vietnam.

Being open to "conditional surrender" would also have empowered more moderate forces within the German and Japanese governments. The unwavering pursuit of unconditional surrender meant that the most extreme factions in those countries were justified in insisting on fighting to the death, since they would have to be totally at the Allies' mercy no matter what.

The Allied insistence on unconditional surrender had its worst consequences in the European war in the scorched earth practices the Soviet military pursued in driving the Germans clear back to Berlin. Besides the enormous death toll, these events also led to even more devastation of the nations located between the Soviet Union and Germany.

Being open to "conditional surrender" would also have freed the Allies to be more positive in their response to the peace feelers the Japanese government sent out in the spring and early summer of 1945. Had the Allies been open to making peace with Japan earlier (and by this time the main condition sought by the Japanese seemingly was simply the continuation of Emperor Hirohito in office—ironically, a request that was honored after the unconditional surrender was achieved), they would have saved hundreds of thousands of lives and pre-empted the use of the atomic bomb. In other words, they would have come closer to meeting the just war criteria.

REVERSING WORLD WAR II'S MORAL LEGACY

We have seen that World War II and its long shadow, at least in the United States, have played a central role in the expansion and hegemony of the national security state. The domination of the institutions of militarism and the ideology of necessary violence seem nearly irresistible. The strength of the current moving the American nation state toward the abyss of self-destruction seems overwhelmingly powerful.

Until we actually reach the abyss, people who hope for self-determination and disarmament everywhere on earth will (must!) always hope that the current may be slowed enough that it may be redirected. Such people will (must!) devote their best energies to such a redirection. Part three of the present book surveyed ways peacemakers have spent their energies, implying possible agendas for the present and future.

However, I want to conclude this book with a word of honest appraisal. I see very little hope that the strong current toward the abyss will be redirected. This is our paradoxical, almost unbearable, situation: We *must* redirect our culture (American culture, for sure, but truly all other dominant cultures throughout the world) away from the abyss toward which institutionalized redemptive violence pushes us. But we actually have very little hope of doing so—at least on a large scale.

The movement in Central Europe that in the 1970s and 1980s resisted Soviet totalitarianism gives us a crucial image. Activists recognized that large-scale, top-down reform seemed impossible. Violent resistance against the systemic violence of the communist regimes tended actually to empower the sword-wielding state. So thoughtful resisters, recognizing that acquiescing to the System was intolerable while overthrowing it through direct resistance was impossible, articulated their hopes is exceedingly modest terms.

They spoke simply of creating spaces to be human.[6] In doing so, they self-consciously rejected the story of reality told by the System, but they did not devote their energies to reform it or to overthrow it through direct action. More so, they focused on creating relatively small spaces where they could build communities, where they could express creativity, where they could patiently chip away at the portrayal of reality that filled the official media.

As it turned out, these small acts of resistance and counter-culture formation coincided with large-scale crises of legitimacy at the top of the Soviet empire. The System crumbled and major changes happened—though sadly the changes did not go as far as hoped for in enabling self-determination

---

6. Havel, *Open Letters*; Konrad, *Anti-Politics*; Michnik, *Letters from Prison*.

and disarmament (for example, the U.S.-led militarization of Western alliances through the North Atlantic Treaty Organization absorbed several of the former Soviet-bloc nations who provided wonderful markets for military hardware).

However, this emphasis on creating spaces to be human remains instructive and inspirational. If it is the case that a top-down transformation for peace is impossible in our current militarized national milieu, the possibilities for small-scale spaces for "being human" in peaceable ways do exist. And we never know what impact cultivating those spaces might have on the bigger picture.

We should also notice that the ways of creating spaces to be human practiced in the Central European freedom movement were not separated from an awareness of issues on national, social policy levels. The activists did not require "seats at the table of power" to embark on their transformative practices—but they were ready and willing to participate in the larger arena when opportunities arose. And in many instances, at least, they participated in ways that remained faithful to their core convictions.[7]

Likewise for peace workers today. Our ways of making peace, our practices of resistance, and our creating of alternatives do not depend upon getting "seats at the table." To be effective over the long term we likely need self-consciously to resist extensive compromises that would gain approval of political and corporate elites. And yet, what the world needs are large solutions and alternatives. So peacemakers need to be thinking in ways that allow for exercise of effective influence on as wide a scale as possible (while remaining faithful to their core values).

We saw above in part three ("Alternatives") three broad elements of peacemaking that play essential roles for imaging a healthy future: *resistance*, *transformation*, and *service*.

With regard to *resistance*, activists recognized, for example, the evils of the nuclear arms race and the U.S. war on Vietnam. In both cases, mass movements arose that sought to turn the nation back from those misguided and terribly destructive policies. And in both cases, they fell far short of their goals. The arms race continued until finally one side (the Soviet Union) surrendered leaving the U.S. the unchallenged victor—a victor that nonetheless continues the race. The Vietnam War did finally grind to a close, with the American withdrawal and the victory of the anti-imperialist forces. But it was in many ways a pyrrhic victory given the extraordinary level of destruction the American forces visited on that small nation.

---

7. For example, see the story of the Polish Solidarity movement in Ackerman and Duval, *Force More Powerful*, 113–74.

However, these movements of resistance did create restraints that slowed the policies of death down a bit. They also energized masses of activists and stimulated peacemaking activities that ripple down to the present. Other resistance movements (e.g., opposition to wars on Central American and Iraq and the current effort to resist policies that exacerbate climate change) have arisen in the years since Vietnam, inspired and guided by the experiences of that pioneering effort, through mass resistance, to slow down and even stop a war in progress.

In all of these resistance movements, education played a major role. Partly, to learn more about the various archaeologies of the social ills strengthens the attraction to and the ability to act in resistance. Partly, the process of education has unveiled many of the undemocratic, authoritarian ways that the American power elite has pursued destructive policies. So resistance remains essential—even if one of the main lessons from these past mass efforts to resist has been just how intransigent the System has been.

The most instructive movement to effect *social transformation* in the U.S. since World War II surely has been the civil rights movement. We have a great deal to learn from the effectiveness and limitations of that movement. One of our main lessons, which we still need to grapple with, is the power of coherent, organized, self-consciously *nonviolent* mass action.

The accomplishments of the civil rights movement were enormous. It is unlikely that someone who lived in the American South during the early part of the 1950s could have imagined how widespread the changes that were about to come would be—and how little violence would be required to effect these changes. However, the U.S. still falls terribly short of what is needed to eradicate dehumanizing racism and discrimination. Perhaps, partly, the transformation sought by the civil rights movement did not fully happen due to its turn from nonviolence.

Regardless, strategies and organized movements to effect social transformation remain a necessary part of peacemaking work, along with widespread resistance. Peacemakers learn about the systemic violence of the status quo and about strategies and policies that the power elite follow to prevent that systemic violence being rooted out. This learning leads to saying no, to awareness, to acts of resistance. *And*, peacemakers come together to organize movements that seek positive transformation away from the systems of violence toward what Martin Luther King Jr. called the "beloved community."

We have also seen a third component in the needed work of social healing—*service*. This aspect is often left out of discussions of social change. However, the efforts directly to care for the needy, to provide food and water to the hungry and thirsty, and to enhance the power of vulnerable people around the world are part of the work of peacemaking along with resistance to the national security state and direct action for social transformation.

Works of service help meet immediate human needs and thereby provide possibilities for better futures. They also provide options for constructive work in face of severe limitations and even hostile reactions that hinder efforts of resistance and transformation. The work of American conscientious objectors who served in Civilian Public Service during the War illustrates this possibility. The state stifled and even crushed dissent. It also repressed efforts at constructive intervention to provide alternatives to warmaking in addressing international problems.

The one avenue that remained open for peacemakers was doing works of service, such as caring for America's forests and farmlands and providing much-needed assistance for people institutionalized with mental illnesses. These acts were of value in themselves, but in addition, in performing alternative service peacemakers gained experiences that made possible more healing work. Examples are leadership in civil rights and antinuclear efforts and a great expansion of humanitarian aid offered throughout the world after the War by organizations such as the American Friends Service Committee and Mennonite Central Committee.

To conclude, I believe that the critical reflection on the story of World War II I have offered in this book might help in the needed (if "impossible") work of redirecting the overwhelming trajectory toward militarism I have sketched. That is, this story might help us reverse World War II's moral legacy. Reversing this moral legacy would help us create space to be human—work that is not dependent upon the state, an institution in our current setting that seems unalterably wed to the dynamics of national security.

Speak Accurately about the War

We may start by naming World War II for what it actually was. It was not a necessary war, certainly not a good war, for the United States. It did not serve to protect America from invasion, to save Jews in the midst of genocide, or to resist tyranny and further democracy around the world. It was an exercise in extraordinary and largely out of control violence that transformed the United States into a militarized global hegemon and severely undermined American democracy.

PART THREE: Alternatives   Conclusion: World War II's Moral Legacy   263

Rigorously Apply Just War Principles

As we name World War II for what it was—an exercise in mass killing and unleashed militarism—we might also resolve to use the just war philosophy that many people claim to honor in a way that has teeth. One of the assumptions of this philosophy has commonly been that we apply the philosophy in order to identify and reject unjust wars. In this book, I have attempted to apply criteria such as just cause, non-combatant immunity, and proportionality to the events of America's involvement in World War II. I have concluded that the American war effort did not satisfactorily meet those criteria and hence that World War II was an unjust war.

Refuse to Support Unjust Wars

I suggest in this conclusion that if indeed the War was unjust, we should name it as such and resolve never again to participate in such a war. To take this point a step further, many people agree that World War II was the most "just" or "necessary" war the United States has ever fought. Part of the power of this myth of a necessary war has been to make it much, much easier to justify preparing for future wars. However, if we recognize that World War II was an *unjust* war and that adherence to the just war philosophy requires us to say no to unjust wars, we quite likely will be led to conclude that the U.S. is almost certainly never going to participate in a just war. Hence, we will refuse to support the preparation for what would almost certainly be unjust wars.

Reject the National Security State

As we have seen, one of the main outcomes of the War for the U.S. was the permanent expansion and entrenchment of what we may call the U.S. as national security state. Key elements that directly emerged from the War were the nuclear weapons program, the Pentagon and greatly enlarged military establishment, and the CIA. Application of just war philosophy would lead to a repudiation of this arrangement. If we understand that human needs–oriented states should be founded on and have the responsibility to seek "justice for all," we will recognize that these institutions that emerged from the War are antithetical to the appropriate structure and purposes of the U.S. government.

Hold Government Accountable to Its Stated Democratic Ideals

The purpose statements that emerged to explain to the public the reasons why the U.S. entered and fought World War II actually cohere pretty well with the values of authentic democracy and the just war philosophy—especially the quest for self-determination and disarmament everywhere on earth. What was lacking during the War and in the generations since has been a steadfast effort to hold the democratically elected government of the U.S. to those stated ideals. One way to reverse the moral legacy of World War II is to insist on holding states to such ideals—and withholding consent when those ideals are ignored or violated.

Be Skeptical of People in Power

Like many others, I believe that Franklin D. Roosevelt was one of the best presidents the United States has ever had. Perhaps the title of H. W. Brands' fine biography of FDR is a bit hyperbolic: *A Traitor to His Class: The Privileged Life and Radical Presidency of Franklin Delano Roosevelt*, especially the use of the word *radical*. Still, Roosevelt's New Deal, with all its limitations, moved the American state in a humane direction more than just about any other presidency before and since. Nonetheless, as we have seen, Roosevelt probably more than any other person set in motion the dynamics that led to total war leading to Cold War leading to war on terrorism leading to the abyss. The lesson for peacemakers should be one of intense skepticism towards people in power. We should always assume the worst about what those in office say and do—things are almost always worse than they seem. We should never give people in power the benefit of the doubt, but treat what they say critically and require strong evidence of actual peaceable *action* before offering strong support.

Build Communities of Resistance

The flip side of skepticism toward people in power and the refusal to give consent to the national security state is the need to cultivate communities of resistance. The work of creating space to be human generally is work that requires a critical mass of people to sustain the work in face of hostility from the System. Back in World War II, the people in the U.S. who most consistently said no to the War and most steadfastly refused to support the war effort were communities of Mennonites.[8] Though these communities had

---

8. This story is told in Grimsrud, "Ethical Analysis of Conscientious Objection."

little political awareness and did not see themselves as directly challenging the policies of their government, they did sustain their resistance to participation in the War through consistent education of community members concerning their core convictions, through material support for those who performed alternative service at great financial cost to themselves, and through clear communication to the government and outside world that they would not compromise on their priorities regardless of the cost.

Prevent Tyranny rather than War Against It

The best answer to the standard "what about Hitler" question that is commonly thrown at peacemakers is surely to say that what is needed is work to *prevent* a Hitler from coming into power again. The idea that the best response to the Hitler question is to prepare militarily is to ignore the past seven decades where we have seen a gradual expansion of the spirit of militarism (one of the main elements of Nazism) in the name of stopping the next Hitler. This gives Hitler a posthumous victory. Instead, the best lesson to learn from World War II is that the conditions that made Hitler possible must be prevented through self-determination and disarmament. Perhaps the Atlantic Charter was mainly a cynical exercise in wartime propaganda and self-righteousness, but the ideals it expressed nonetheless provide one of our best blueprints for preventing the need for such exercises in cynical propaganda—that is, for preventing the quest for "peace" through total war.

Treat All Life as Precious

Resolve never to minimize the conviction that all of life is precious. Perhaps the greatest moral legacy of World War II was the practical repudiation of that conviction. The biggest cost of such a war was the loss of the sense of human solidarity, that we are all together precious beings who should be treated with respect and care. As a direct consequence of this War, as we have seen, the U.S. has embarked on a still accelerating process of diminishing the value of human beings by creating and deploying weapons of unimaginable mass destruction and seeking domination around the world as the cost of millions upon millions of direct deaths as a result of America's wars—all fought for unjust causes using unjust means. An unwavering commitment to the preciousness of all life provides a powerful interpretive key for understanding and responding to America's national security state with clarity, conviction, and resolve.

Bibliography

Ackerman, Peter, and Jack Duvall. *A Force More Powerful: A Century of Nonviolent Conflict*. New York: Palgrave, 2000.

Alexander, Michelle. *The New Jim Crow: Mass Incarceration in the Age of Colorblindness*. New York: New Press, 2010.

Ali, Tariq. *The Obama Syndrome: Surrender at Home, War Abroad*. New York: Verso, 2010.

Alperovitz, Gar. *The Decision to Use the Atomic Bomb and the Architecture of an American Myth*. New York: Knopf, 1995.

Alterman, Eric. *When Presidents Lie: A History of Official Deception and Its Consequences*. New York: Viking, 2004.

Anderson, David L. "The Vietnam War and Its Enduring Historical Relevance." In *The Columbia History of the Vietnam War*, edited by David L. Anderson, 1–89. New York: Columbia University Press, 2011.

Anderson, Fred, and Andrew Cayton. *The Dominion of War: Empire and Liberty in North America, 1500–2000*. New York: Viking, 2005.

Anderson, Jervis. *Bayard Rustin: Troubles I've Seen, A Biography*. New York: HarperCollins, 1997.

Arsenault, Raymond. *Freedom Riders: 1961 and the Struggle for Racial Justice*. New York: Oxford University Press, 2006.

Austin, Jay E., and Carl E. Bruch. *The Environmental Consequences of War: Legal, Economic, and Scientific Perspectives*. New York: Cambridge University Press, 2000.

Bacevich, Andrew J. *The New American Militarism: How Americans Are Seduced by War*. New York: Oxford University Press, 2005.

———. *Washington Rules: America's Path to Permanent War*. New York: Metropolitan, 2010.

Baker, Nicholson. *Human Smoke: The Beginnings of World War II, the End of Civilization*. New York: Simon and Schuster, 2008.

Beevor, Antony. *The Second World War*. New York: Little, Brown, 2012.

Bell, Daniel M., Jr. *Just War as Christian Discipleship*. Grand Rapids: Brazos, 2009.

Bennett, Scott H. *Radical Pacifism: The War Resisters League and Gandhian Nonviolence in America, 1915–1963*. Syracuse: Syracuse University Press, 2003.

Bergen, Doris L. *War and Genocide: A Concise History of the Holocaust*. 2nd ed. Lanham, MD: Rowman and Littlefield, 2009.

Bergerud, Eric. "Critique of *Choices Under Fire*." *Historically Speaking: The Bulletin of the Historical Society* 9 (2008) 38–41.

Bess, Michael. *Choices Under Fire: Moral Dimensions of World War II*. New York: Knopf, 2006.

Bills, Scott L. *Empire and Cold War: The Roots of US-Third World Antagonism, 1945–47*. New York: St. Martin's, 1990.

Blum, William. *Killing Hope: U.S. Military and C.I.A. Interventions since World War II*. Monroe, ME: Common Courage, 2004.

Bowman, Rufus D. *The Church of the Brethren and War*. Elgin, IL: Brethren Press, 1944.

Bradley, James. *The Imperial Cruise: A Secret History of Empire and War*. Boston: Back Bay, 2009.

Branch, Taylor. *At Canaan's Edge: America in the King Years, 1965–68*. New York: Simon and Schuster, 2006.

———. *Parting the Waters: America in the King Years, 1954–63*. New York: Simon and Schuster, 1988.

———. *Pillar of Fire: America in the King Years, 1963–65*. New York: Simon and Schuster, 1998.

Brands, H. W. *Traitor to His Class: The Privileged Life and Radical Presidency of Franklin Delano Roosevelt*. New York: Doubleday, 2008.

Brock, Peter. *Radical Pacifists in Antebellum America*. Princeton: Princeton University Press, 1968.

———. *The Quaker Peace Testimony, 1660–1914*. Syracuse: Syracuse University Press, 1991.

Brock, Peter, and Nigel Young. *Pacifism in the Twentieth Century*. Syracuse: Syracuse University Press, 1999.

Brock, Rita Nakashima, and Gabriella Lettini. *Soul Repair: Recovering from Moral Injury after War*. Boston: Beacon, 2012.

Brokaw, Tom. *The Greatest Generation*. New York: Random House, 1998.

Buchanan, Patrick J. *Churchill, Hitler, and the Unnecessary War: How Britain Lost Its Empire and the West Lost the World*. New York: Crown, 2008.

Burleigh, Michael. *Moral Combat: A History of World War II*. London: HarperCollins, 2010.

Bush, Perry. *Two Kingdoms, Two Loyalties: Mennonite Pacifism in Modern America*. Baltimore: Johns Hopkins University Press, 1998.

Carroll, James. *House of War: The Pentagon and the Disastrous Rise of American Power*. Boston: Houghton Mifflin, 2006.

Carson, Clayborne. *In Struggle: SNCC and the Black Awakening of the 1960s*. Cambridge: Harvard University Press, 1995.

Childers, Thomas. *Soldier from the War Returning: The Greatest Generation's Troubled Homecoming from World War II*. Boston: Houghton Mifflin Harcourt, 2009.

Chomsky, Noam. *American Power and the New Mandarins*. 2nd ed. New York: New Press, 2002.

———. *Hegemony or Survival: America's Quest for Global Dominance*. New York: Metropolitan, 2003.

———. "The Revolutionary Pacifism of A. J. Muste: On the Background of the Pacific War." In *American Power and the New Mandarins*, 159–220. 2nd ed. New York: New Press, 2002.

Clarke, Peter. *The Last Thousand Days of the British Empire: Churchill, Roosevelt, and the Birth of the Pax Americana*. New York: Bloomsbury, 2008.

Coady, C. A. J. "Bombing and the Morality of War." In *Bombing Civilians: A Twentieth-Century History*, edited by Yuki Tanaka and Marilyn B. Young, 191–214. New York: New Press, 2009.
Cumings, Bruce. *The Korean War: A History*. New York: Modern Library, 2010.
———. "The Wicked Witch of the West Is Dead. Long Live the Wicked Witch of the East." In *The End of the Cold War: Its Meaning and Implications*, edited by Michael J. Hogan, 87–101. New York: Cambridge University Press, 1992.
Dallek, Robert. *The Lost Peace: Leadership in a Time of Horror and Hope, 1945–1954*. New York: Harper, 2010.
Davies, Norman. *No Simple Victory: World War II in Europe, 1939–1945*. New York: Penguin, 2006.
Dawidowicz, Lucy. *The War Against the Jews*. New York: Bantam, 1986.
DeBenedetti, Charles. *An American Ordeal: The Antiwar Movement of the Vietnam Era*. Syracuse: Syracuse University Press, 1990.
DeGroot, Gerard J. *The Bomb: A Life*. Cambridge: Harvard University Press, 2004.
Dekar, Paul R. *Creating the Beloved Community: A Journey with the Fellowship of Reconciliation*. Telford, PA: Cascadia, 2005.
D'Emilio, John. *Lost Prophet: The Life and Times of Bayard Rustin*. New York: Free Press, 2003.
Douglass, James W. *The Nonviolent Coming of God*. Maryknoll, NY: Orbis, 1991.
Dower, John W. *Cultures of War: Pearl Harbor, Hiroshima, 9-11, Iraq*. New York: Norton/New Press, 2010.
———. *Embracing Defeat: Japan in the Wake of World War II*. New York: Norton, 1999.
Driedger, Leo, and Donald B. Kraybill. *Mennonite Peacemaking: From Quietism to Activism*. Scottdale, PA: Herald, 1994.
Eisan, Leslie. *Pathways of Peace: A History of the Civilian Service Program*. Elgin, IL: Brethren Press, 1948.
Ellsberg, Daniel. *Secrets: A Memoir of Vietnam and the Pentagon Papers*. New York: Penguin, 2002.
Engelhardt, Tom. *The American Way of War: How Bush's Wars Became Obama's*. Chicago: Haymarket, 2010.
Erlanger, Steven, and Sheryl Gay Stolberg. "Surprise Nobel for Obama Stirs Praise and Doubts." *New York Times*, October 9, 2009, http:www.nytimes.com/2009/10/10/world/10nobel.html.
Fiala, Andrew. *The Just War Myth: The Moral Illusion of War*. Lanham, MD: Rowman and Littlefield, 2008.
Fitzgerald, Frances. *Way Out There in the Blue: Reagan, Star Wars, and the End of the Cold War*. New York: Touchstone, 2000.
Fox, Richard Wightman. *Reinhold Niebuhr: A Biography*. New York: Harper and Row, 1987.
Freeman, Joshua B. *American Empire: The Rise of a Global Power, the Democratic Revolution at Home, 1945–2000*. New York: Viking, 2012.
French, Paul Comly. *Civilian Public Service*. Washington, DC: NSBRO, 1943.
Gardner, Lloyd C. *The Long Road to Baghdad: A History of U.S. Foreign Policy from the 1970s to the Present*. New York: New Press, 2008.
Gerson, Joseph. *Empire and the Bomb: How the U.S. Uses Nuclear Weapons to Dominate the World*. London: Pluto, 2007.

Glantz, David M., and Jonathan House. *When Titans Clashed: How the Red Army Stopped Hitler*. Lawrence: University Press of Kansas, 1995.

Goodman, Melvin A. *Failure of Intelligence: The Decline and Fall of the CIA*. Lanham, MD: Rowman and Littlefield, 2008.

Grayling, A. J. *Among the Dead Cities: The History and Moral Legacy of the WWII Bombing of Civilians in Germany and Japan*. New York: Walker, 2006.

Grimsrud, Ted. "Anabaptist Faith and American Democracy." *Mennonite Quarterly Review* 78 (2004) 341–62.

———. "An Ethical Analysis of Conscientious Objection to World War II." PhD diss., Graduate Theological Union, 1988.

———. "Christian Pacifism in Brief." In *A Pacifist Way of Knowing: John Howard Yoder's Pacifist Epistemology*, edited by Christian Early and Ted Grimsrud, 1–21. Eugene, OR: Cascade, 2010.

———. "Core Convictions for Engaged Pacifism." *Conrad Grebel Review* 28 (2010) 22–38.

Halberstam, David. *The Children*. New York: Random House, 1998.

———. *The Coldest Winter: America and the Korean War*. New York: Hyperion, 2007.

Hallie, Philip. *Lest Innocent Blood Be Shed: The Story of the Village of Le Chambon, and How Goodness Happened There*. New York: Harper and Row, 1978.

Hamerow, Theodore S. *Why We Watched: Europe, America, and the Holocaust*. New York: Norton, 2008.

Harbutt, Fraser J. *Yalta 1945: Europe and America at the Crossroads*. New York: Cambridge University Press, 2010.

Hasegawa, Tsuyoshi. "Were the Atomic Bombings of Hiroshima and Nagasaki Justified?" In *Bombing Civilians: A Twentieth-Century History*, edited by Yuki Tanoka and Marilyn B. Young, 97–134. New York: New Press, 2009.

Hastings, Max. *Inferno: The World at War, 1939–1945*. New York: Knopf, 2011.

Havel, Václav. *Open Letters: Selected Writings, 1965–1990*. New York: Knopf, 1991.

Herman, Arthur. *Gandhi and Churchill: The Epic Rivalry That Destroyed an Empire and Forged Our Age*. New York: Bantam, 2008.

Herring, George C. *From Colony to Superpower: United States Foreign Relations since 1776*. New York: Oxford University Press, 2008.

Hitchcock, William I. *The Bitter Road to Freedom: A New History of the Liberation of Europe*. New York: Free Press, 2008.

Hogan, Wesley. *Many Minds, One Heart: SNCC's Dream for a New America*. Chapel Hill: University of North Carolina Press, 2007.

Holmes, John Haynes. "The Same Old War." *The Christian Century*, December 11, 1940. Reprinted in *The End of Illusions: Religious Leaders Confront Hitler's Gathering Storm*, edited by Joseph Loconte, 71–77. Lanham, MD: Rowman and Littlefield, 2004.

Hough, Lynn Harold. "Defending Justice despite Our Own Injustice." *Christianity and Crisis*, April 21, 1941. Reprinted in *The End of Illusions: Religious Leaders Confront Hitler's Gathering Storm*, edited by Joseph Loconte, 215–20. Lanham, MD: Rowman and Littlefield, 2004.

Inboden, William. *Religion and American Foreign Policy, 1945–1960: The Soul of Containment*. New York: Cambridge University Press, 2008.

Johnson, Chalmers. *Dismantling the Empire: America's Last Best Hope*. New York: Metropolitan, 2010.

———. *The Sorrows of Empire: Militarism, Secrecy, and the End of the Republic.* New York: Owl, 2005.
Jones, Howard. *The Bay of Pigs.* New York: Oxford University Press, 2008.
Judt, Tony. *Postwar: A History of Europe since 1945.* New York: Penguin, 2005.
Juhnke, James. *Vision, Doctrine, War: Mennonite Identity and Organization in America, 1890–1930.* Scottdale, PA: Herald, 1989.
Kaldor, Mary. *Global Civil Society: An Answer to War.* Malden, MA: Polity, 2003.
———. *Human Security: Reflections on Globalization and Intervention.* Malden, MA: Polity, 2007.
Karp, Walter. *The Politics of War: The Story of Two Wars which Altered Forever the Political Life of the American Republic (1890–1920).* New York: Franklin Square, 2003.
Keegan, John. *The Second World War.* New York: Penguin, 1989.
Keim, Albert, and Grant Stoltzfus. *The Politics of Conscience: The Historic Peace Churches and America at War, 1917–1955.* Scottdale, PA: Herald, 1988.
Kennedy, David. *Freedom from Fear: The American People in Freedom and War, 1929–1945.* New York: Oxford University Press, 1999.
Kern, Kathleen. *In Harm's Way: A History of Christian Peacemaker Teams.* Eugene, OR: Cascade, 2009.
Kershaw, Ian. *Fateful Choices: Ten Decisions That Changed the World, 1940–1941.* New York: Penguin, 2007.
———. *Hitler: 1889–1936; Hubris.* New York: Norton, 1998.
———. *Hitler: 1936–1945; Nemesis.* New York: Norton, 2000.
Kinzer, Stephen. *Overthrow: America's Century of Regime Change from Hawaii to Iraq.* New York: Times Books, 2006.
Klare, Michael. *Blood and Oil: The Dangers and Consequences of America's Growing Dependency on Imported Petroleum.* New York: Owl, 2004.
Klein, Naomi. *The Shock Doctrine: The Rise of Disaster Capitalism.* New York: Metropolitan, 2007.
Kolko, Gabriel. *Anatomy of a War: Vietnam, the United States, and the Modern Historical Experience.* New York: Pantheon, 1985.
Konrad, George. *Anti-Politics: An Essay.* New York: Harcourt Brace Jovanovich, 1984.
Kosek, Joseph Kip. *Acts of Conscience: Christian Nonviolence and Modern American Democracy.* New York: Columbia University Press, 2009.
Kovac, Jeffrey. *Refusing War, Affirming Peace: A History of Civilian Public Service Camp No. 21 at Cascade Locks.* Corvallis: Oregon State University Press, 2009.
Kristof, Nicolas. "The Big (Military) Taboo." *New York Times*, December 25, 2010, http://www.nytimes.com/2010/12/26/opinion/26kristof.html.
Laffin, Arthur J. "A Chronology of Plowshares Disarmament Actions, September 1980–January 1996." In *Swords into Plowshares: Nonviolent Direct Action for Disarmament, Peace, Social Justice*, edited by Arthur J. Laffin and Ann Montgomery, 48–85. Marion, SD: Fortkamp/Rose Hill, 1996.
Laffin, Arthur J., and Anne Montgomery, eds. *Swords into Plowshares: Direct Action for Disarmament, Peace, Social Justice.* Marion, SD: Fortkamp/Rose Hill, 1996.
Lederach, John Paul. *Building Peace: Sustainable Reconciliation in Divided Societies.* Washington, DC: United States Institute of Peace Press, 1997.
Leffler, Melvyn P. *For the Soul of Mankind: The United States, the Soviet Union, and the Cold War.* New York: Hill and Wang, 2007.

Lepore, Jill. *The Name of War: King Philip's War and the Origins of American Identity*. New York: Vintage, 1998.

Lewis, John. *Walking With the Wind: A Memoir of the Movement*. New York: Simon and Schuster, 1998.

Lindqvist, Sven. *A History of Bombing*. Translated by Linda Haverty Rugg. New York: New Press, 2001.

Linenthal, Edward T., and Tom Englehardt, eds. *History Wars: The Enola Gay and Other Battles for America's Past*. New York: Henry Holt, 1996.

Loconte, Joseph, ed. *The End of Illusions: Religious Leaders Confront Hitler's Gathering Storm*. Lanham, MD: Rowman and Littlefield, 2004.

Logan, James. *Good Punishment? Christian Moral Practice and U.S. Imprisonment*. Grand Rapids: Eerdmans, 2008.

Logevall, Frederik. *Embers of War: The Fall of an Empire and the Making of America's Vietnam*. New York: Random House, 2012.

Maialo, Joseph. *Cry Havoc: How the Arms Race Drove the World to War, 1931–1941*. New York: Basic Books, 2010.

Markusen, Eric, and David Kopf. *The Holocaust and Strategic Bombing: Genocide and Total War in the Twentieth Century*. Boulder, CO: Westview, 1995.

Marshall, Christopher. *Beyond Retribution: A New Testament Vision for Crime, Justice, and Punishment*. Grand Rapids: Eerdmans, 2001.

———. *Compassionate Justice: An Interdisciplinary Dialogue with Two Gospel Parables on Law, Crime, and Restorative Justice*. Eugene, OR: Cascade, 2012.

Martin, Earl S. *Reaching the Other Side: The Journal of an American Who Stayed to Witness Vietnam's Transition*. New York: Crown, 1978.

Mast, Gerald J., and J. Denny Weaver. *Defenseless Christianity: Anabaptism for a Nonviolent Church*. Telford, PA: Cascadia, 2009.

McMahon, Robert J. *The Cold War: A Very Short Introduction*. New York: Oxford University Press, 2003.

———. "Turning Point: The Vietnam War's Pivotal Year, November 1967–November 1968." In *The Columbia History of the Vietnam War*, edited by David L. Anderson, 191–216. New York: Columbia University Press, 2011.

Michnik, Adam. *Letters from Prison and Other Essays*. Berkeley: University of California Press, 1985.

Miller, Joseph S. "A History of the Mennonite Conciliation Service, International Conciliation Service, and Christian Peacemaker Teams." In *From the Ground Up: Mennonite Contributions to International Peacebuilding*, edited by Cynthia Sampson and John Paul Lederach, 3–29. New York: Oxford University Press, 2000.

Miller, Keith Graber. *Wise as Serpents, Innocent as Doves: American Mennonites Engage Washington*. Knoxville: University of Tennessee Press, 1996.

Miller, Lawrence McK. *Witness for Humanity: A Biography of Clarence E. Pickett*. Wallingford, PA: Pendle Hill, 1999.

Miller, Melissa, and Phil Shenk, eds. *The Path of Most Resistance: Stories of Mennonite Conscientious Objectors Who Did Not Cooperate with the Vietnam War Draft*. Scottdale, PA: Herald, 1982.

Miller, William D. *Dorothy Day: A Biography*. New York: Harper and Row, 1982.

Morris, Aldon D. *The Origins of the Civil Rights Movement: Black Communities Organizing for Change*. New York: Free Press, 1984.

Morris, Charles R. *Iron Destinies, Lost Opportunities: The Arms Race between the U.S.A. and the U.S.S.R., 1945–1987*. New York: Harper and Row, 1988.

Moses, Greg. *Revolution of Conscience: Martin Luther King, Jr., and the Philosophy of Nonviolence*. New York: Guilford, 1997.

Moss, Norman. *Picking Up the Reins: America, Britain, and the Postwar World*. New York: Overlook, 2008.

Murnion, Philip J., ed. *Catholics and Nuclear War: A Commentary on* The Challenge to Peace, the U.S. Catholic Bishops' Letter on War and Peace. New York: Crossroad, 1984.

Muste, A. J. *The World Task of Pacifism*. Pendle Hill Pamphlet 13. Wallingford, PA: Pendle Hill, 1941.

Naeve, Lowell. *A Field of Broken Stones*. Glen Gardner, NJ: Libertarian Press, 1950.

Nepstad, Sharon Erickson. *Nonviolent Revolutions*. New York: Oxford University Press, 2011.

Nichols, John, ed. *Against the Beast: A Documentary History of American Opposition to Empire*. New York: Nation Books, 2004.

Niebuhr, Reinhold. "An End to Illusions." *The Nation*, June 29, 1940. Reprinted in *The End of Illusions: Religious Leaders Confront Hitler's Gathering Storm*, edited by Joseph Loconte, 128–31. Lanham, MD: Rowman and Littlefield, 2004.

Nojeim, Michael J. *Gandhi and King: The Power of Nonviolent Resistance*. Westport, CT: Praeger, 2004.

Novick, Peter. *The Holocaust in American Life*. Boston: Mariner, 2000.

Patti, Archimedes L. A. *Why Viet Nam? Prelude to America's Albatross*. Berkeley: University of California Press, 1980.

Peck, Jim. *Underdogs vs. Upperdogs*. Canterbury, NH: Greenleaf, 1969.

Pfaff, William. *The Irony of Manifest Destiny: The Tragedy of America's Foreign Policy*. New York: Walker, 2010.

Pickett, Clarence E. *For More than Bread: An Autobiographical Account of Twenty-Two Years' Work with the American Friends Service Committee*. Boston: Little, Brown, 1953.

Piehl, Mel. *Breaking Bread: The Catholic Worker and the Origin of Catholic Radicalism in America*. Philadelphia: Temple University Press, 1982.

Plokhy, S. M. *Yalta: The Price of Peace*. New York: Viking, 2010.

Pollitt, Katha. "Blowing Smoke." *The Nation*, April 21, 2008, 9.

Polnar, Murray, and Jim O'Grady. *Disarmed and Dangerous: The Radical Life and Times of Daniel and Philip Berrigan, Brothers in Religious Faith and Civil Disobedience*. Boulder, CO: Westview, 1997.

Powers, Thomas. *Intelligence Wars: American Secret History from Hitler to Al-Queda*. New York: New York Review Books, 2002.

Prados, John. *Safe for Democracy: The Secret Wars of the CIA*. Chicago: Dee, 2006.

———. *Vietnam: The History of an Unwinnable War, 1945–1975*. Lawrence: University Press of Kansas, 2009.

Redekop, Calvin W. *The Pax Story: Service in the Name of Christ, 1951–1976*. Telford, PA: Cascadia, 2001.

Redekop, Paul. *Changing Paradigms: Punishment and Restorative Discipline*. Scottdale, PA: Herald, 2007.

Rhodes, Richard. *Arsenals of Folly: The Making of the Nuclear Arms Race*. New York: Knopf, 2007.

———. *Dark Sun: The Making of the Hydrogen Bomb.* New York: Simon and Schuster, 1995.

———. *The Making of the Atomic Bomb.* New York: Simon and Schuster, 1986.

Ricoeur, Paul. *The Symbolism of Evil.* New York: Harper and Row, 1967.

Rose, Kenneth D. *Myth of the Greatest Generation: A Social History of Americans in World War II.* New York: Routledge, 2008.

Sampson, Cynthia, and John Paul Lederach, eds. *From the Ground Up: Mennonite Contributions to International Peacebuilding.* New York: Oxford University Press, 2000.

Sawatsky, Jarem. *Justpeace Ethics: A Guide to Restorative Justice and Peacebuilding.* Eugene, OR: Cascade, 2009.

Saxe, Robert Francis. *Settling Down: World War II Veterans' Challenge to the Postwar Consensus.* New York: Palgrave Macmillan, 2007.

Scahill, Jeremy. *Dirty Wars: The World Is a Battlefield.* New York: Nation Books, 2013.

Schell, Jonathan. *The Unconquerable World: Power, Nonviolence, and the Will of the People.* New York: Metropolitan, 2003.

Schlabach, Theron F. *War, Peace, and Social Conscience: Guy Hershberger and Mennonite Ethics.* Scottdale, PA: Herald, 2009.

Schlissel, Lillian, ed. *Conscience in America: A Documentary History of Conscientious Objection in America, 1757–1967.* New York: Dutton, 1968.

Sebestyen, Victor. *1989: The Fall of the Soviet Empire.* New York: Pantheon, 2009.

Seldon, Mark. "A Forgotten Holocaust: U.S. Bombing Strategy, the Destruction of Japanese Cities, and the American Way of War from the Pacific War to Iraq." In *Bombing Civilians: A Twentieth-Century History,* edited by Yuki Tanaka and Marilyn B. Young, 77–96. New York: New Press, 2009.

Sevareid, Eric. *Not So Wild a Dream.* New York: Atheneum, 1976.

Sharp, Gene. *Power and Struggle.* Boston: P. Sargent, 1973.

Sheehan, James J. *Where Have All the Soldiers Gone? The Transformation of Modern Europe.* Boston: Houghton Mifflin, 2008.

Sherry, Michael. *In the Shadow of War: The United States since the 1930s.* New Haven: Yale University Press, 1995.

Sibley, Mulford Q., and Philip E. Jacob. *Conscription of Conscience: The American State and the Conscientious Objector, 1940–1947.* Ithaca: Cornell University Press, 1952.

Snyder, Timothy. *Bloodlands: Europe between Hitler and Stalin.* New York: Basic Books, 2010.

———. "A New Approach to the Holocaust." *New York Review of Books,* June 23, 2011, 54–56, http://www.nybooks.com/articles/archives/2011/jun/23/new-approach-holocaust/.

Spanos, William V. *In the Neighborhood of Zero: A World War II Memoir.* Lincoln: University of Nebraska Press, 2010.

Stout, Harry S. *Upon the Altar of the Nation: A Moral History of the American Civil War.* New York: Viking, 2006.

Stutzman, Ervin R. *From Nonresistance to Justice: The Transformation of Mennonite Church Peace Rhetoric, 1908–2008.* Scottdale, PA: Herald, 2011.

Swanson, David. *War Is a Lie.* Charlottesville, VA: David Swanson, 2010.

Takaki, Ronald. *Hiroshima: Why America Dropped the Bomb.* Boston: Little, Brown, 1995.

Tanaka, Yuki. "British 'Humane Bombing' in Iraq during the Interwar Era." In *Bombing Civilians: A Twentieth-Century History*, edited by Yuki Tanaka and Marilyn B. Young, 8–29. New York: New Press, 2009.

Tanaka, Yuki, and Marilyn B. Young, eds. *Bombing Civilians: A Twentieth-Century History*. New York: New Press, 2009.

Taylor, Alan. *American Colonies*. New York: Viking, 2001.

Taylor, Steven J. *Acts of Conscience: World War II, Mental Institutions, and Religious Objectors*. Syracuse: Syracuse University Press, 2009.

Thompson, Nicholas. *The Hawk and the Dove: Paul Nitze, George Kennan, and the History of the Cold War*. New York: Henry Holt, 2009.

Toews, Paul. *Mennonites in American Society, 1930–1970: Modernity and the Persistence of Religious Community*. Scottdale, PA: Herald, 1996.

Tracy, James. *Direct Action: Radical Pacifism from the Union Eight to the Chicago Seven*. Chicago: University of Chicago Press, 1996.

Turse, Nick. *Kill Anything That Moves: The Real American War in Vietnam*. New York: Metropolitan, 2013.

Wachs, Theodore. "Conscription, Conscientious Objection, and the Context of American Pacifism, 1940–1945." PhD diss., University of Illinois, 1976.

Walzer, Michael. *Arguing About War*. New Haven: Yale University Press, 2005.

———. *Just and Unjust Wars: A Moral Argument with Historical Illustrations*. New York: Basic Books, 1977.

———. "World War II: Why Was This War Different?" *Philosophy and Public Affairs* 1 (1971) 3–21.

Weiner, Tim. *Legacy of Ashes: A History of the CIA*. New York: Anchor, 2008.

Weisbord, Marvin R. *Some Form of Peace: True Stories of the American Friends Service Committee at Home and Abroad*. New York: Viking, 1968.

Westbrook, Robert B. *Why We Fought: Forging American Obligations in World War II*. Washington, DC: Smithsonian, 2004.

Western, Bruce. *Punishment and Inequality in America*. New York: Sage, 2007.

Wetzel, Donald. *Pacifist, or, My War and Louis Lepke*. Sag Harbor, NY: Permanent Press, 1986.

Wherry, Neal W. *Conscientious Objection*. U.S. Selective Service System Special Monograph 11. Washington, DC: Selective Service System, 1950.

Wilentz, Sean. *The Age of Reagan: A History, 1974–2008*. New York: Harper, 2008.

Williams, William Appleman. *Empire as a Way of Life: An Essay on the Causes and Character of America's Present Predicament along with a Few Thoughts about an Alternative*. New York: Oxford University Press, 1980.

Wills, Garry. *Bomb Power: The Modern Presidency and the National Security State*. New York Penguin, 2010.

Wink, Walter. *Engaging the Powers: Discernment and Resistance in a World of Domination*. Minneapolis: Fortress, 1992.

Wittner, Lawrence S. *One World or None: A History of the World Nuclear Disarmament Movement through 1953*. Stanford: Stanford University Press, 1993.

———. *Rebels Against War: The American Peace Movement, 1941–1960*. New York: Columbia University, 1969.

———. *Resisting the Bomb: A History of the World Nuclear Disarmament Movement, 1954–1970*. Stanford: Stanford University Press, 1997.

———. *Toward Nuclear Abolition: A History of the World Nuclear Disarmament Movement, 1971 to the Present.* Stanford: Stanford University Press, 2003.

Wyman, David. *The Abandonment of the Jews: America and the Holocaust.* 2nd ed. New York: New Press, 1998.

Yoder, John Howard. *Nevertheless: The Varieties and Shortcomings of Religious Pacifism.* 2nd ed. Scottdale, PA: Herald, 1992.

———. *The Politics of Jesus.* 2nd ed. Grand Rapids: Eerdmans, 1994.

———. *When War Is Unjust: Being Honest in Just-War Thinking.* 2nd ed. 1996. Reprint, Eugene, OR: Wipf and Stock, 2001.

Young, Marilyn B. "Bombing Civilians from the Twentieth to the Twenty-First Centuries." In *Bombing Civilians: A Twentieth-Century History*, edited by Yuki Tanaka and Marilyn B. Young, 162–67. New York: New Press, 2009.

———. *The Vietnam Wars, 1945–1990.* New York: Harper Perennial, 1991.

Zahn, Gordon. *Another Part of the War: The Camp Simon Story.* Amherst: University of Massachusetts Press, 1979.

———. "A Descriptive Study of the Social Backgrounds of Conscientious Objectors in Civilian Public Service during World War II." PhD diss., Catholic University of America, 1953.

Zehr, Howard. *Changing Lenses: A New Focus for Crime and Justice.* 3rd ed. Scottdale, PA: Herald, 2005.

Zelizer, Julian E. *Arsenal of Democracy: The Politics of National Security—from World War II to the War on Terrorism.* New York: Basic Books, 2010.

Zimmerman, Earl. *Practicing the Politics of Jesus: The Origin and Significance of John Howard Yoder's Social Ethics.* Telford, PA: Cascadia, 2007.

Name Index

Abernathy, Ralph, 202
Acheson, Dean, 115, 127, 142
Ackerman, Peter, 202n12, 217n54, 239n49, 239n52, 260n7
Alexander, Michelle, 205n20
Ali, Tariq, 167, 168n50
Allende, Salvador, 145–46
Alperovitz, Gar, 113n20, 207n24
Alterman, Eric, 91n29
Anderson, David, 139n45
Anderson, Fred, 21n28, 176n2
Anderson, Jervis, 200n5
árbenz, Jacobo Guzmán, 133–34
Arévalo, Juan Jose, 133
Arsenault, Raymond, 203n14
Augustine, 184, 230
Austin, Jay E., 79n2
Bacevich, Andrew, 157n25, 167, 167n49
Baeck, Leo, 182
Bailey, Agard, 194, 195
Baker, James, 157
Baker, Nicholson, 4, 31n7, 35n17, 37n21, 41n29, 61n15, 84n13, 183n17
Batista, Fulgencio, 136–37
Beevor, Antony, 35n17
Bell, Daniel, 69n36
Bennett, Scott H., 180n12, 196n65, 197n68
Bergen, Doris, 84, 85n16
Bergerud, Eric, 11n18, 55, 55n3, 56, 56n5, 245, 245n3
Berrigan, Daniel, 214, 232, 235
Berrigan, Philip, 214, 232–33, 236

Bess, Michael, 10–11, 11n16, 11n18, 55–56, 64, 64n25, 65, 65n26, 65n27, 66n29, 67, 112n16, 245n2
Bevel, James, 203
Bills, Scott L., 51n52, 139n43
Bin Laden, Osama, 160, 164
Blum, William, 110n12, 120n39, 132n25, 135n32, 136n34, 145n67, 147n74, 249n5
Bohr, Niels, 206
Bonsal, Philip, 137
Boulding, Elise, 224
Bowman, Rufus, 177n4
Bradley, James, 43n36
Branch, Taylor, 201n9, 204n16, 204n18, 228n17, 236n40
Brands, H. W., 32n8, 36n20, 38n23, 39, 39n27, 44n38, 45, 46, 46n39, 47, 47n42, 47n44, 50n50, 68n35, 70n37, 71n39, 71n41, 85n18, 91n28, 95n43, 264
Brittain, Vera, 74–75
Brock, Peter, 176n2, 178n5, 208n27, 222n1, 225n6, 227, 228n15, 228n18, 229n20, 231n25, 233n31
Brock, Rita Nakashima, 8n11
Brokaw, Tom, 1n2, 81
Brooks, Arle, 192–93
Bruch, Carl E., 79n2
Buchanan, Patrick J., 41n32, 58n8, 97n48
Burleigh, Michael, 11, 11n17, 56n5

277

Name Index

Burns, Ken, 1n2, 64n25
Bush, George H. W., 96, 154–57
Bush, George W., 4, 158–69
Bush, Perry, 226n8
Byrnes, James, 113, 115
Cantine, Holley, 196
Carroll, James, 57n6, 71n40, 72n42, 86, 86n20, 93, 93n33, 98n50, 99n53, 105n2, 106n6, 108, 108n8, 112n16, 114n21, 115, 115n24, 122n45, 127n2, 127n7, 128n8, 130, 130n15, 130n17, 131n20, 138n40, 146, 146n71, 147n75, 148, 148n78, 150, 150n1, 151n5, 151n7, 152, 152n11, 152n13, 154n16, 155n19, 156, 156n21, 156n23, 158n28, 160n34, 162n39, 206n23, 207n25, 210, 210n36, 212n40, 213, 214n47, 214n50
Carson, Clayborne, 204n15
Carter, Jimmy, 147, 163, 210–11, 229
Castro, Fidel, 136–38
Cayton, Andrew, 21n28, 176n2
Chamberlain, Neville, 35–36, 41, 59
Cheney, Richard, 160
Chiang Kai-shek, 29, 32, 44, 89, 117
Childers, Thomas, 81, 81n4, 82n7
Chomsky, Noam, 44n37, 49n47, 96n47, 98n49, 148n77, 159n31
Churchill, Winston, 4, 7, 17, 35–37, 39, 41, 50, 58–59, 63, 70–72, 80, 88, 95, 97, 124, 139, 169, 258
Clarke, Peter, 95n42, 103n1, 123n50
Clarke, Richard, 160
Clinton, Bill, 157–58, 163
Clinton, Hillary, 166–67
Coady, C. A., 159n32
Contreras, Manuel, 146
Coolidge, Calvin, 28
Cumings, Bruce, 128, 129n11, 130n19, 155n20, 156, 156n22

D'Emilio, John, 200n5
Dallek, Robert, 106n5, 121n41, 123n47
Davies, Norman, 10, 10n14, 11, 43, 43n34, 56n5, 64n25, 245, 245n4
Dawidowicz, Lucy, 83n10
Day, Dorothy, 180, 230–31, 233
DeBenedetti, Charles, 223n4, 234, 234n34, 236n39, 236n41, 237n44
DeGroot, Gerard J., 105n3, 114n23, 130n16
Dekar, Paul R., 179n9
Dellinger, Dave, 196
Donovan, William J., 117–18
Douglass, James W., 232, 232n29, 233, 235
Dower, John, 49n48, 76n52, 82n9, 95n45, 99n52, 158n29
Driedger, Leo, 226n8, 227n14, 240n57
Dulles, Allen, 119–20, 137
Dulles, John Foster, 119, 132, 134
Duvall, Jack, 202n12, 217n54, 239n49, 239n52, 260n7
Dykstra, Clarence, 186, 188
Einstein, Albert, 111
Eisan, Leslie, 187n29
Eisenhower, Dwight, 119, 127, 132, 134–37
Eisenhower, Edgar, 132
Ellsberg, Daniel, 238n47
Engelhardt, Tom, 49n49, 112n15, 167n48
Erlanger, Steven, 166, 167n47
Farmer, James, 196, 200, 201–2, 204
Federspiel, Howard, 135
Fiala, Andrew, 57n7
Fitzgerald, Francis, 150n3, 152n10, 213n44, 214n48
Ford, Gerald, 234, 237
Forrestal, James, 115
Forsberg, Randall, 212
Fox, George, 176
Fox, Richard Wightman, 28n4
Franco, Francisco, 30
Freeman, Joshua B., 93n33

Name Index 279

French, Paul C., 189, 189n39
Gandhi, Mohandas, 169, 182, 194, 196, 200–204, 217–19, 228–29, 231–32, 238
Gandhi, Rajiv, 215
Gardner, Lloyd C., 155n17, 156n24, 163n40
Garrison, William Lloyd, 178
Gates, Robert, 167–68
Gbowee, Leymah, 242
Gerson, Joseph, 116, 116n26, 155n18
Glantz, David M., 64n25, 89n24
Goebbels, Joseph, 71, 83
Goodman, Melvin, 93n35, 120n36
Gorbachev, Mikhail, 150–53, 157, 214–15
Grant, Ulysses S., 22, 70
Grayling, A. J., 57n6, 59n9, 59n11, 60, 60n12, 60n14, 62n18, 63n22, 63n24, 70n38, 74n48, 98n51
Grimsrud, Carl, 1–2, 27–28
Grimsrud, Ted, 16n23, 175n1, 190n40, 192n49, 192n51, 193n54, 194n57, 194n59, 240n53, 264n8
Gromyko, Andrei, 151
Groves, Leslie, 93–94, 108, 111, 113, 206
Halberstam, David, 129n13, 202n11, 202n12, 203n13, 205n19
Halifax, Lord (E. L. F. Wood), 35–36
Hallie, Philip, 198n1
Hamerow, Theodore S., 43n35, 52n53, 83n12, 85, 85n17
Harbutt, Fraser J., 88n23
Harding, Vincent, 228, 236
Harding, Warren, 28, 109
Harris, Arthur, 60, 63
Hasegawa, Tsuyoshi, 99n52
Hastings, Max, 41n31
Havel, Václav, 219, 259n6
Hennacy, Ammon, 231
Herman, Arthur, 36n19
Herring, George C., 28n3, 90n26, 95n45, 105n4, 145n65, 147n74, 157n27, 164n41

Hershberger, Guy F., 228
Hershey, Lewis, 186, 188–90
Hirohito, Emperor, 75, 112, 258
Hitchcock, William I., 66n30, 86n22
Hitler, Adolf, 2, 12, 28, 30–31, 34–35, 40–43, 47, 61, 64, 66, 72, 83, 111, 121, 154, 156, 169, 182–84, 193, 246, 265
Ho Chi Minh, 139, 141, 237
Hogan, Wesley, 202n12, 204n15
Holmes, John Haynes, 183–84, 184n19
Hoover, Herbert, 28, 61
Hough, Lynn Harold, 34n16
House, Jonathan, 64n25, 89n24
Hughan, Jessie Wallace, 179
Hughes, Richard D., 98n50
Humphrey, Hubert, 236
Hunthausen, Raymond, 233
Hussein, Saddam, 156, 163–65
Inboden, William, 16n24
Jacob, Philip E., 187n27, 188n33, 190, 190n43, 191n45, 195n60, 223n3
Johnson, Chalmers, 95n44, 157n26, 165n44
Johnson, Louis, 127
Johnson, Lyndon, 144, 204, 235–36, 238
Jones, Howard, 136n33, 137n35
Jones, James, 167
Jones, Rufus, 84, 182–83, 222
Judt, Tony, 55n4, 65n26, 67n32, 82n9
Juhnke, James, 225n7, 228
Kaldor, Mary, 218n55, 219n58, 239, 239n48, 239n50
Karp, Walter, 22–23, 23n31
Keegan, John, 90n25
Keim, Albert, 187n28
Kennedy, David, 32n10, 38, 38n22, 38n24, 73n46, 91n27
Kennedy, John F., 137–38, 210
Kern, Kathleen, 229n21, 243n69
Kershaw, Ian, 34n15, 35n18, 40n28, 42n33, 46n41, 47n42, 47n43, 51n51, 61n16
Khrushchev, Nikita, 138, 210

Name Index

Kim Il-Sung, 129
King, Martin Luther, Jr., 169, 201–5, 218–19, 228–29, 236, 261
Kinzer, Stephen, 131n21, 133n26, 134, 158n30
Klare, Michael, 165n45
Klein, Naomi, 15n22, 145n63, 146n68, 165n43, 165n46, 244
Kolko, Gabriel, 142n5
Konoe, Fumimaro, 44, 46, 257
Konrad, George, 259n6
Kopf, David, 57n6, 63n21
Kosek, Joseph Kip, 179n11, 183n18, 198, 198n2, 201n6, 201n8, 205, 206, 206n21
Kovac, Jeffrey, 190n44
Kraybill, Donald B., 226n8, 227n14, 240n57
Kreider, Robert, 241
Kristof, Nicolas, 3n4
Lafayette, Bernard, 203
Laffin, Arthur J., 214n46, 233n32
Lawson, James, 202, 204–5
Lederach, John Paul, 229n21, 242, 242n64
Leffler, Melvyn, 53n55, 122n44, 132n24, 152n12
Lepore, Jill, 21, 21n29
Letelier, Orlando, 146
Lettini, Gabriella, 8n11
Lewis, John, 203–5, 205n19
Lilienthal, David, 127
Lincoln, Abraham, 22
Lindbergh, Charles, 50
Lindqvist, Sven, 59n10, 60n13, 75n51
Linenthal, Edward T., 49n49, 112n15
Loconte, Joseph, 33n11, 33n14, 92n30, 95n46
Logan, James, 205n20
Logevall, Frederik, 120n38
Ludlow, Robert, 231
MacArthur, Douglas, 73, 119, 129–30
Maialo, Joseph, 28n2
Mao Zedong, 89

Markusen, Eric, 57n6, 63n21
Marshall, Christopher, 243n68
Marshall, George, 92, 129
Martens, Robert, 135
Martin, Earl S., 240n55
Mast, Gerald, 177n3
Maurin, Peter, 180, 230
Mays, Benjamin, 200, 202
McCain, John, 166–67
McCloy, John, 118
McKinley, William, 23
McMahon, Robert J., 124, 124n52, 127n4, 144n61
McNamera, Robert, 238
Merton, Thomas, 232–33, 235
Michnik, Adam, 259n6
Miller, Joseph, 241n58, 242n62
Miller, Keith Graber, 235n37, 240n56
Miller, Lawrence McK., 83n11
Miller, Melissa, 229n19, 240n54
Miller, William D., 230n22
Moffitt, Ronni, 146
Montgomery, Anne, 233n32
Morris, Aldon D., 201n7
Morris, Charles R., 138n41, 210n34
Moses, Greg, 204n17
Moss, Norman, 68n33, 95n42, 121n43, 124n51
Mossadegh, Mohammad, 131, 132, 133
Mumford, Lewis, 206
Murnion, Philip J., 233n33
Murphy, Stanley, 195
Mussolini, Benito, 29, 31
Muste, A. J., 98n49, 194, 194n58, 196, 202, 204
Naeve, Lowell, 192, 193n52, 195
Nash, Diane, 203
Nepstad, Sharon Erickson, 218n56
Nichols, John, 23n33
Niebuhr, Reinhold, 11, 28n4, 29, 33n13, 205, 206
Nitze, Paul, 127
Nixon, Richard, 19, 137, 144–45, 224, 234, 236–37
Nojeim, Michael J., 204n17
Novick, Lynn, 1n2

Name Index

Novick, Peter, 86n21
Nye, Gerald, 45
O'Grady, Jim, 214n45, 232n30, 236n38
Obama, Barack, 166-70, 238
Palme, Olof, 215
Papendreou, Andreas, 215
Park, Richard, 117
Parks, Rosa, 201, 204, 216
Patterson, Robert, 74
Patti, Archimedes L., 141n51
Peck, Jim, 193, 193n55, 195-96, 197n68, 203
Penn, William, 176
Pétain, Phillipe, 41
Pfaff, William, 161n36
Pickett, Clarence, 182, 182n16, 193n53, 222
Piehl, Mel, 180n13, 231n23
Pinochet, Augusto, 146
Plokhy, S. M., 88n23
Pollitt, Katha, 4, 4n6
Polnar, Murray, 214n45, 232n30, 236n38
Pope John XXIII, 232
Powers, Thomas, 93n35
Prados, John, 93n35, 110n12, 118n31, 120n37, 134n30, 137n37, 141n52, 143n58
Prine, John, 19n25
Rainer, Dachine, 196
Rankin, Jeanett,e 47
Reagan, Ronald, 96, 147-52, 154, 157, 159, 212-14, 233, 238
Redekop, Calvin, 227n13, 241n60
Redekop, Paul, 243n67
Reza, Mohammad (Shah of Iran), 132, 157
Rhodes, Richard, 76n53, 94n37, 94n38, 105n3, 111n14, 126n1, 151n6, 214n49
Rice, Condoleeza, 160
Richards, Frederick H., 192-93
Ricoeur, Paul, 13n20
Rockwell, Norman, 38, 97
Rogers, Edith, 84
Roodenko, Igal, 192
Roosevelt, Eleanor, 75, 222
Roosevelt, Franklin D., 4, 7, 11, 15, 17, 24, 28, 32-33, 36-39, 43-51, 54, 59, 65, 68-76, 80, 87-88, 91-95, 97-99, 104, 108-9, 111-12, 117, 139, 146, 156, 169, 175, 186, 222, 227, 238, 250-51, 256-58, 264
Roosevelt, Theodore, 23
Rose, Kenneth D., 80n3, 200n4, 245n2
Rotblat, Joseph, 207
Russell, Bertrand, 207
Rustin, Bayard, 196, 200, 202, 204
Sampson, Cynthia, 229n21
Sawatsky, Hedy, 241n58
Sawatsky, Jarem, 243n67
Saxe, Robert Francis, 81n6, 202n10, 216n52
Scahill, Jeremy, 162n37, 169n53, 238n46
Schell, Jonathan, 181n15, 218, 218n55, 219, 219n57
Schlabach, Theron F., 228n16
Schlissel, Lillian, 178n6
Schultz, George, 152
Sebestyen, Victor, 150n4
Seldon, Mark, 74n47
Sevareid, Eric, 184n21
Sharp, Gene, 217n54
Sheehan, James J., 3n3
Shenk, Phil, 229n19, 240n54
Sheridan, Philip, 22
Sherman, William Tecumseh, 22
Sherry, Michael, 92n31, 93n33
Shevardnadze, Eduard, 151
Sibley, Mulford Q., 187n27, 187n31, 188n33, 190, 190n43, 191n45, 195n60, 223n3
Simons, Menno, 177
Smiley, Glenn, 202
Snyder, Timothy, 65n26, 84n15
Somoza, Anastasio Garcia, 146, 156
Spaatz, Carl, 122
Spanos, William, 63n23
Stalin, Joseph, 28, 65-66, 71-72, 88, 106, 111, 114-15, 121-22, 124, 129-30, 246, 248, 254, 258

Stimson, Henry, 112–15, 118, 122, 127
Stolberg, Sheryl Gay, 166, 167n47
Stoltzfus, Grant, 187n28
Stout, Harry, 10, 10n13, 21, 22n30
Stutzman, Ervin R., 240n57
Suharto, 135
Sukarno, 134–35
Swanson, David, 164n42
Syngman Rhee, 129
Szilard, Leo, 111, 111n13, 206
Taft, Robert, 45
Tanaka, Yuki, 57n6, 60n13
Taylor, Alan, 20, 20n26
Taylor, Louis, 195
Taylor, Steven J., 189n36
Temple, Kathleen, 19
Tenet, George, 160
Thompson, Nicholas, 127n3, 127n5
Thoreau, Henry David, 194, 229
Thurman, Howard, 196, 200, 202
Toews, Paul, 226n9
Tojo, Hideki, 44, 46, 49, 257
Tolkien, J. R. R., 252
Tolstoy, Leo, 194
Tracy, James, 196n63, 196n65
Trenchard, Hugh, 59, 60
Truman, Harry, 16, 48, 76, 93–94, 113–15, 117–19, 121–25, 127–32, 138, 142–45, 147–48, 153, 156, 207, 251–52
Turse, Nick, 144n62
Vandenberg, Arthur, 122
Wachs, Theodore, 185n23, 188n34
Wagner, Betty, 2
Wagner, Robert, 84
Walzer, Michael, 9n12, 27, 27n1, 52, 52n54, 55n2
Weaver, J. Denny, 177n3
Weiner, Tim, 68n34, 93n35, 110n12, 117n28, 118n32, 119n34, 120, 120n40, 129n14, 135n31, 145n66, 146, 146n69, 159, 160n33
Weisbord, Marvin R., 179n7, 222n2

Westbrook, Robert B., 38n25
Western, Bruce, 205n20
Wetzel, Donald, 192, 195, 195n61
Wherry, Neal W., 185n24, 186n26, 189n35, 189n37, 191n47
Wiebe, Katie Funk, 227
Wilentz, Sean, 150n2
Williams, William Appleman, 23n32, 123n48
Willkie, Wendell, 36, 37
Wills, Garry, 15n21, 93, 93n32, 94, 94n39, 107n7, 109n11, 113n19, 116, 116n27, 119n33, 121n42, 127n6, 137n38, 162n38, 168n51, 169n54, 216, 216n53
Wilson, Woodrow, 23, 28–29, 32, 47, 90, 110, 139, 178, 182
Wink, Walter, 13, 13n19, 13n20, 14–16, 245, 245n1
Wittner, Lawrence S., 76n54, 184n20, 184n22, 188n32, 196n62, 196n64, 196n66, 206n22, 207n26, 208, 208n28, 209, 210n35, 212n38, 213n44, 215, 215n51
Wyman, David, 43n35, 52n53, 85n19
Yoder, John Howard, 5n7, 54n1, 69n36, 180n14, 241n61
Young, Marilyn B., 57n6, 120n38, 139n44, 140, 140n46, 141, 142n53, 142n56, 144n62
Young, Nigel, 208n27, 222n1, 225n6, 227, 228n15, 228n18, 229n20, 231n25, 233n31
Zahn, Gordon, 189n38, 192n192, 231n24
Zehr, Howard, 229n21, 242, 242n66, 243
Zelizer, Julian E., 23n34, 29n6, 93n33
Zimmerman, Earl, 241n61

Subject Index

Afghanistan, 3, 4, 60, 151, 155, 161, 163–64, 167–70
Allied powers, 5–6, 10–12, 17, 28, 43, 52, 56–59, 61, 64–68, 70–72, 76–77, 79–80, 83–88, 90–91, 96, 99, 103–4, 106, 111–12, 123, 134, 140, 248, 254, 258
American Friends Service Committee (AFSC), 83, 178–80, 182, 199, 219, 221–25, 234, 238, 262
Anti-interventionists, isolationists, 28, 33, 37, 45–46, 49–50, 92, 95, 183
Antinuclear movement, 205–15, 218, 233–34
Antiwar movement (Vietnam), 214, 224, 228–29, 232–38
Atlantic Charter, 7, 17, 37, 39–40, 49, 58, 65, 67, 87, 97, 104–5, 110, 124, 139, 148–49, 153–54, 170, 181, 227, 249, 265
Atomic Energy Commission (AEC), 126–27
Axis powers, 7, 9, 33, 39, 45, 47, 68, 70–71, 79–80, 99, 103–04, 112, 246–49
Brethren, Church of, 177, 223
Bulletin of the Atomic Scientists, 154, 207, 215
Catholic Worker, 180, 219, 230–35
Central Intelligence Agency (CIA), 15, 93–94, 100, 110, 117–21, 132–35, 137, 143, 145–46, 153, 156, 159–60, 163, 167–68, 244, 263
Chile, 51, 145–46, 239
China, 28–29, 32, 37, 41, 44, 46, 51–52, 55, 65, 79, 87–90, 99, 114, 117, 119, 129–30, 141–42, 144, 166, 198, 227, 246–47, 251, 256
Civil Rights Movement, 196, 199–205, 216–17, 219, 221, 223, 228, 238–39, 261–62
Civil society, 238–43
Civil War (United States), 10, 21–22, 24, 90, 107, 188, 199–200,
Civilian Public Service (CPS), 186–92, 194–96, 223, 226–28, 231, 240, 262
Cold War, 16, 68, 89, 95, 105, 115, 121, 124, 126–55, 157–58, 160–62, 168, 206, 210–11, 223, 231, 234, 264
Communists, Communism, 16, 30–31, 34–36, 40–43, 66, 78, 87–90, 99, 114, 121, 123–25, 127–29, 132, 134–37, 139–42, 145, 147–48, 151, 198–09, 212, 214, 230, 235, 237, 246, 252, 259
Conscientious objectors (COs), 178–79, 184–90, 192, 195–97, 201, 222–24, 226–27, 230, 235, 240
Cuba, 124, 136–38, 146, 155, 183, 210, 250
Czechoslovakia, 36, 41–42, 88

"Day of Infamy" speech, 47–48, 54, 68, 98
Demobilization of military, 2, 16, 23, 90, 92, 107–09, 122, 154
Department of Defense, 109–10, 127, 140, 153, 155, 198
Disarmament, 7, 9, 52, 58, 67, 78, 87–89, 100, 104–5, 107, 110, 120, 124, 153, 157, 170, 181, 199, 207–15, 219, 221, 223, 233, 247, 249, 259–60, 264–65
Draft resistance, 192–97, 200, 203–4, 233, 237
Dresden, 63, 248
Fellowship of Reconciliation (FOR), 179–80, 182, 189, 194, 196, 200–201, 223, 232, 234
Foreign policy, 6, 12, 24, 28, 51, 94, 110–11, 115–16, 118, 120, 123–28, 136, 139, 153, 157, 159, 219, 234, 248–49
Four Freedoms, 11, 17, 37–38, 40, 49, 58, 65, 69, 87, 97, 199, 227
France, 30, 33, 35–36, 41–43, 61, 67, 79, 84, 91, 97, 117, 139–43, 170, 180, 182, 184, 218, 222, 227, 230–31, 253–54
Friends, Quakers, 83, 176–80, 182–83, 190, 193, 199, 219, 221–23, 234–35, 255, 262
Genocide, 43, 72, 85–87, 144, 255
Germany, 5–7, 9, 15, 28–36, 40–47, 50–52, 54, 58–74, 76, 78–80, 83–88, 91–92, 95, 97–98, 105, 111–12, 115, 117, 144, 157, 159, 175, 177, 182–85, 198, 206–7, 218, 231, 246–48, 251–55, 258
"Good war", ix, 1–6, 9, 12, 17–18, 40, 43, 54–55, 57, 67, 197, 244, 246, 250, 252–53, 262
Great Britain, 32–39, 41–45, 50, 52–53, 57, 59–68, 70, 78–80, 83, 85, 91, 94–95, 97–98, 103, 106, 124, 131–32, 142, 164, 176, 178, 184–85, 207, 218, 246–48, 253–54
Great Depression, 23, 27–28, 40, 79, 82, 180, 222, 230
Greece, 114, 121–25, 225
Guatemala, 106, 120, 133–35, 137, 147
Gulf War, 154–58, 164, 211
Hamburg, 63, 248
Hawaii, 33, 44, 46, 73, 158, 256
Hiroshima, 48–49, 57, 76, 99, 106, 112–15, 126, 144, 199, 205–6, 208, 248, 250
Holocaust, 43, 82–86, 255
Hydrogen bomb, 126–27, 154, 208, 210, 216
Incendiary bombs, 63, 75–76
India, 35, 79–80, 108, 116, 134, 166, 184, 194, 196, 198, 200, 202, 215, 218, 227
Indonesia, 79–80, 120, 134–35, 198, 218
International law, 56, 104, 148, 161, 163–64
Interventionists, 11, 15, 24, 31–37, 40, 45, 92, 251–52
Iran, 106, 120, 127, 131–35, 137, 150, 155, 157, 163, 165, 168, 170
Iraq, 60, 114, 156–57, 163–67, 170, 211, 243, 261
Isolationists, 33, 45, 49–50, 90, 95, 183
Italy, 7, 29, 31, 46–47, 70, 79, 114
Japan, 1, 5–7, 9, 15, 28–29, 31–34, 37, 43–52, 54–55, 57–58, 64, 68–76, 78–80, 82, 87, 89–92, 94–95, 98–99, 103, 105, 112–14, 117, 126, 134–35, 139, 144, 158–59, 175, 198, 205–6, 208, 218, 245–48, 251–52, 254–58
Jesus, 19, 176–77, 230, 232–33, 241
Jews in Europe, 42–43, 51–52, 54, 65, 67, 72, 82–86, 182–83, 222, 246–47, 255, 262

Just cause for war, 4, 8, 10–11, 27, 51, 53–54, 56–58, 66, 77, 99, 245–48, 250, 263, 265
Just conduct of war, 5, 10, 12, 21, 27, 54–58, 64, 66, 69, 77, 96, 98–99, 245, 247–48, 258
Just war, 4–5, 9, 10–12, 18–19, 21, 27, 54–77, 85, 97, 98–99, 148, 230, 244–50, 253, 258, 263–65
Korean war, 77, 119, 125, 129–31, 153, 156, 202, 250, 258
League of Nations, 28–30, 104
Manchuria, 29, 44, 46, 90, 113
Manhattan project, 76, 94, 106–7, 111–12, 116, 206–7, 251, 256
Mennonite Central Committee (MCC), 178–80, 182, 199, 219, 221, 223, 225–29, 236, 238, 240–42, 26
Mennonites, 19, 20, 177–80, 184, 188, 191, 199, 219, 221, 223, 225–29, 235–36, 239–40, 242–43, 262, 264
Militarism, 3–4, 15, 20, 24, 40–41, 45, 50, 55, 58, 105, 148, 154–55, 157, 168–69, 176, 183, 213, 219, 230, 234, 238–39, 243–45, 249–250, 259, 262–63
Military draft, conscription, 19, 107, 168, 178, 185–86, 189, 191–97, 200, 202–04, 214, 222–24, 227–30, 233, 235–37, 240–41
Morality, 1, 4–12, 17–19, 21, 24, 27, 31, 33, 37, 40, 43, 49–50, 54–61, 64–67, 69, 77, 82, 86–87, 90, 97, 99–100, 104, 111, 121, 144, 148, 169–71, 180–81, 188, 193, 197–99, 202, 206, 209, 216, 219, 235, 246–50, 252, 256, 262, 265
Moscow, 120, 142, 152, 156, 210, 212

Myth of redemptive violence, 2–4, 12–16, 20–24, 31, 46, 219, 259
Nagasaki, 48–49, 76, 99, 106, 112–14, 116, 119, 144, 205, 208, 248, 250
National Security Act, 15, 109–10, 118–19, 251
National Security Council, 15, 110, 131, 163–64, 167, 223, 251
National security state, 15–16, 93, 107, 116, 144, 161–62, 168, 175, 238, 243, 259, 262–65
National Service Board for Religious Objectors (NSBRO), 187–89
Nazis, Nazism, 3–4, 9, 10, 30, 33–36, 39–43, 52, 54–55, 58–59, 62–69, 71–72, 78, 83–87, 89, 106, 118, 122–23, 143, 182–84, 206, 222, 246, 248, 252, 255, 265
Nicaragua, 145–48, 159, 224, 242
Noncombatant immunity, 57–59, 69, 77, 98, 247–48, 250, 258, 263
Nonviolence, 3, 182, 193, 196, 200–205, 209, 217–19, 225, 228, 230–33, 243, 261
North Atlantic Treaty Organization (NATO), 125, 155, 157–58, 211–12, 260
NSC-68, 127–28, 131
Nuclear freeze, 150, 212–15, 233
Nuclear weapons, atomic weapons, 12, 15, 48–49, 53, 57–58, 76–77, 88, 94, 96, 99–100, 103, 105–7, 111–16, 119–20, 122, 126–27, 129–30, 137–38, 144, 149–55, 162, 168, 170, 196, 199, 205–19, 221, 233, 230–31, 233–34, 238, 244, 248, 250–51, 256, 258, 260, 262–63
Pacifism, 3–5, 18–19, 33, 175–78, 180, 189, 193, 197, 201–02, 225–26, 230, 232–33, 240–41, 244, 253
Patriotism, 10, 19

Pax Americana, 95, 107, 121, 124, 131, 158–59, 175
Peacebuilding, 240–43
Pearl Harbor, 1, 24, 33, 37, 43–46, 48–51, 55, 68, 73–74, 91–92, 98, 104, 111, 117, 158, 175, 188, 246, 255–57
Pentagon, 15, 93–94, 99–100, 105, 107–11, 127, 131, 152, 157–58, 160, 168, 210–11, 244, 251, 256–57, 263
Philippines, 52, 73, 79, 140, 198
Poland, 30, 31, 35, 41–42, 44, 52, 59, 65–67, 79, 87–88, 91, 97, 149, 182, 198, 207, 239, 247, 251, 260
Proportionality, 12, 57–58, 69, 77, 98, 247–248, 250
Restorative justice, 242–43
Royal Air Force (RAF), 59–63, 70, 74, 76, 85
Self-determination, 7, 9, 33, 42, 51–52, 58, 67, 78, 87–88, 97, 100, 104–5, 107, 120, 124, 133–36, 139, 141, 145, 153, 170, 181, 199, 214, 218–19, 221–22, 227, 234, 247, 249, 252, 259, 264–65
September 11, 2001, 4, 158–64, 167, 169, 238
Six Pillars of Peace, 7, 11, 17
Soviet Union, Russia, 16, 28–31, 33–35, 39–40, 42–43, 47, 51, 53, 61, 64–68, 73, 78–79, 87–89, 94–95, 103–4, 106, 111–15, 118–24, 126–31, 135–38, 141–43, 147–55, 157–58, 163, 170, 182, 198, 207–8, 210–12, 214–15, 217–18, 223, 225–27, 229, 233, 246, 248, 254, 258–60
Spanish-American War, 22–24, 136
State Department, 96, 110, 117, 127, 131, 140–41, 158

Strategic Defense Initiative (SDI), 150–52, 213–14
Terrorism, 16, 59, 95, 134, 147, 159–60, 162–63, 168, 264
Tokyo, ix, 75, 77, 80, 98, 112, 248, 250, 258
Truman Doctrine, 121, 124,25, 127–28, 131–32, 142–45, 147–48, 153, 252
Turkey, 91, 121, 125, 138
Unconditional surrender, 49, 68–72, 74–76, 86, 99, 112–13, 255, 258
United Nations (UN), 7, 39, 95, 104, 137, 148, 153, 163, 207, 249
Viet Minh, 139–44, 162
Vietnam war, x, 3, 8, 19, 77, 79, 90, 108, 120, 124, 139–44, 153, 155, 159, 162, 170, 182, 198, 205, 209–10, 214, 218, 220, 223–24, 228–30, 232–41, 243, 250, 258, 260–61
Violence, 4, 12–14, 16, 18, 20–21, 23–24, 30–31, 33, 48, 54–56, 84, 90, 94, 117, 120, 124, 134, 144, 147–49, 153, 159, 161, 164, 175–76, 181–82, 197–201, 203–4, 216–17, 219, 223, 235, 239–43, 246, 249, 259, 261–62
War Resisters League, 179–80, 182, 189, 192, 224, 234–35
Warsaw Pact, 88–89, 154–55, 158, 212
West Point Code, 21–22
World War I (The "Great War"), 15, 22–23, 28–32, 40, 43, 59, 84, 92, 104, 109–10, 175, 178–79, 182, 185, 222–23, 253–55
Yalta, 88, 123–24
Yugoslavia, 79, 134, 198